SPEAK·TRUTH·TO·POWER

COMMANDER
STEVEN HAINES
ROYAL NAVY

Power, Law and the End of Privateering

Power, Law and the End of Privateering

Jan Martin Lemnitzer
Lecturer in History, Pembroke College, Oxford University, UK

First published 2014 by
PALGRAVE MACMILLAN

Palgrave Macmillan in the UK is an imprint of Macmillan Publishers Limited, registered in England, company number 785998, of Houndmills, Basingstoke, Hampshire RG21 6XS.

Palgrave Macmillan in the US is a division of St Martin's Press LLC, 175 Fifth Avenue, New York, NY 10010.

Palgrave Macmillan is the global academic imprint of the above companies and has companies and representatives throughout the world.

Palgrave® and Macmillan® are registered trademarks in the United States, the United Kingdom, Europe and other countries.

ISBN 978–0–230–30185–6

This book is printed on paper suitable for recycling and made from fully managed and sustained forest sources. Logging, pulping and manufacturing processes are expected to conform to the environmental regulations of the country of origin.

A catalogue record for this book is available from the British Library.

A catalog record for this book is available from the Library of Congress.

For Ella and Karin

Contents

List of Tables	ix
Acknowledgements	x
List of Abbreviations	xii

Introduction: Power, Law and the Declaration of Paris	1
1 'More Serious than the Eastern Question Itself' – The Crimean War Compromise	17
2 The Crimean War and Maritime Law	26
'The dawn of a better day in warfare': The new rules in practice	26
'The total suppression of privateering': Britain and letters of marque	36
'Recognized throughout the civilized world' – the US treaty campaign	43
3 'Catching Brother Jonathan in the Trap which He Laid for Us' – The Genesis of the Declaration of Paris	57
The US proposal	57
The Congress of Paris	62
Justifications and expectations	70
4 'That Moral League of Nations Against the United States' – The Declaration of Paris and the Marcy Amendment	75
5 'The United States Have a Vote in Framing the Maritime Law of this Age' – The Cass Memorandum and Bremen's Campaign for the Marcy Amendment	96
The Cass Memorandum	96
The Bremen campaign	100
Cobden, coal and contraband	111
6 The Declaration of Paris and the American Civil War	115
The Declaration of Paris and the North: Seward's scheme	116
The Declaration of Paris and the Confederacy:	
The end of privateering	129
Northern privateering?	134
Britain and the blockade	139
Britain and neutral rights	143

Part VI: The Declaration of Paris and the American Civil
War: A case for reform?   150

7 'Announcing Our Withdrawal from the Declaration' – The
Declaration of Paris and the Franco-German War of 1870   154
The 1866 Austro-Prussian War: A precedent for the
Marcy Amendment?   154
The French way of blockade   157
France's global war on German trade   161
Bismarck's challenge to the Declaration of Paris   164

Conclusion: The Rise and Fall of the Declaration of Paris 173

Notes   197

Bibliography   238

Index   245

Tables

2.1 UK imports of hemp, flax and tallow from Russia
     and Prussia, 1853–4   27

2.2 Overall value of Russian imports and exports, 1853–7   35

Acknowledgements

My greatest gratitude is to my former supervisor, Prof. David Stevenson, who gave me all the intellectual freedom (and occasional deadline extensions) that I needed to complete my research, but pushed relentlessly for ever more primary evidence and a more refined and precise argument. I also want to thank my first supervisor, Prof. Detlef Junker, for taking me on when no one else thought my topic made sense, and for showing great grace when I decided to leave Heidelberg and write my thesis at the London School of Economics (LSE). At that time, Jens Hainmüller showed great determination to persuade me to follow his lead into the promised land of the Anglo-Saxon school of academia. Even more important was the influence of my wife, who insisted that I turn the thesis into a book that does not just please a small number of historians but reaches out to a wider audience and has the ambition to further our understanding of the human condition.

The extensive research for this book would have been impossible without the financial support of a number of organisations, but the most important one was the Studienstiftung des deutschen Volkes (National German Merit Foundation). It supported me throughout my studies, granted me a PhD scholarship and allowed me to take it to a different country almost immediately afterwards. Moreover, the great trust and belief that the foundation has for every one of its scholars provided me with the confidence to choose the academic path, and to go my own way without compromising on my research. Essential financial support also came from the LSE's International History department; I am also grateful to the Central Travel Fund of the University of London for funding research in US archives, and the Institute of Historical Research (IHR) for granting me the Royal Historical Society fellowship that enabled me to complete the thesis. I would also like to thank Prof. Hew Strachan and Dr Robert Johnson of Oxford's Changing Character of War programme for effectively giving me a sabbatical from my post as Director of Studies to complete this book.

I have presented this research at many seminars and conferences over the years and would like to thank all those colleagues who praised my work and provided encouragement. But I owe an even greater debt to those who challenged me, questioned my evidence and conclusions, and forced me to raise my game. With apologies to those I have omitted here, I would like to thank scholars at the LSE, the IHR's international history and military history research seminars, King's College London, the German Historical Institute London, Oxford University, MIT's Security Studies seminar, Hull University's Maritime History Research Institute and the Arbeitskreis Militärgeschichte in

Germany. I also owe special thanks to Prof. Anthony Howe for allowing me to use the database of the Cobden Letter Project.

Finally, I have to thank the Earl of Clarendon for kindly permitting me to cite from the Clarendon deposit at the Bodleian Library, Oxford, and staff members at various archives for not following their initial instinct that the type of files I was asking to see could not possibly exist, but just letting me plough my way through their precious collections.

Abbreviations

ABCC:	Archive of the Bremen Chamber of Commerce, Germany
AGKK:	Akten zur Geschichte des Krimkriegs (source collection organised in four series: Austria, Prussia, Britain, France)
AMAE:	Archive du Ministère des Affaires Étrangères, Paris, France
APP:	*Die Auswärtige Politik Preußens 1858–1871*
BFSP:	British and Foreign State Papers
BL:	British Library
Bodleian:	Bodleian Library, Oxford
Bundesarchiv Lichterfelde:	Federal Archive Berlin-Lichterfelde, Germany
CLP:	Cobden Letters Project; the citations in brackets are taken from the project's letter transcriptions and are either from the British Library (BL) or the Cobden Papers in the West Sussex Record Office (CP)
CP:	Cobden Papers in the West Sussex Record Office
FRUS:	Papers relating to the Foreign Relations of the United States, with 'FRUS' referring to the first volume of the series (1861) and other volumes being specified by year
GStA Berlin:	Geheimes Staatsarchiv Preußischer Kulturbesitz, Berlin-Dahlem, Germany
HHStA Vienna:	Haus- Hof- und Staatsarchiv Vienna, Austria
House of Commons or House of Lords:	*Hansard's Parliamentary Debates, Third Series*
Martens NRG:	*Martens Nouveau Recueil Generale des Traites*
NARA:	National Archive and Record Administration II, College Park, Maryland, USA
RSC:	Roosevelt Study Centre (microfilm archive), Middelburg, Netherlands
StAB:	State Archive Bremen, Germany
TNA:	The National Archives, Kew Garden, London
Vincennes:	Centre Historique de la Défense Vincennes, Archives Centrales de la Marine, France

Introduction: Power, Law and the Declaration of Paris

Despite being an inherent part of international relations for more than four centuries, the relationship between power and international law is still poorly understood.[1] We all know that international law has spectacularly failed to restrain power on a number of occasions in the past. However, in contemporary international relations, states and international organisations grant a larger role to international law than ever before, which implies a hope that it might somehow work. It is just as clear that powerful states still succumb to the temptation of ignoring a rule that they find exasperatingly inconvenient, while also expecting other states to respect their rights under international law. This puzzle is rarely, if ever, addressed in contemporary academia, or indeed elsewhere. All too often the level of analysis is limited to either a pious wish that all states will be well behaved, civilised and law-abiding at some undefined point in the future, or the more cynical view that when states disagree, 'might makes right'. The latter interpretation is very common but can mean two very different things: either the right of the powerful to ignore the rules if they wish, or the ability of the powerful to write the rules as they please. Both directly stem from the one feature that makes international law different from any national system of law: there is no central agency that can set the rules and enforce them upon unwilling states. But this crucial feature of international law should be the starting point and not the end of a debate: if it is so inherently weak, why have states spent so much time and effort creating and enlarging the edifice of international law? And why did so many of these rules refer to restrictions in war, which are by far the most difficult ones to enforce?

This book is a detailed study of how the first global norms on the laws of war were created and enforced. It will explain the creation of the first treaty uniting almost all existing states, the mechanisms by which it was enforced for many decades, and the reasons why the Declaration of Paris was dismissed so casually at the beginning of the First World War. Before we enter into the precise reasons why the power constellation at the beginning of the Crimean War led to an unprecedented experiment with the rights of

1

neutrals, this introduction will explain why the relationship between power and law is so rarely explored, and why the Declaration of Paris marks such an important moment in its development. It will also suggest a new analytical framework for understanding its mechanics, based on the analogy of international law as 'House Rules' for the global community of nations. Despite being used so widely, the nature of international law and what this term actually means is much more disputed than is commonly acknowledged.

The problem begins with the name because, without a central authority setting and enforcing the rules, international law is not actually law.[2] 'International law' as a composite term was popularised by Jeremy Bentham in the late 18th century, replacing the older term 'laws of nations'.[3] International law is not law as applied to international affairs but the set of rules and conventions that has been established between nations as legally independent entities in frequent intercourse with each other. Hence 'laws of nations' is arguably the more accurate term – it makes it clearer that if the rules set by nations for themselves are not respected, this is a failure on the part of the nations and not a failure of 'the law'. It also highlights the fact that these rules exist because states made them, presumably because they seemed to be the answer to a problem. This problem is that solving disputes by force when adversaries are roughly evenly matched is very costly and dangerous, potentially leading to the complete demise of a state. Using mutually agreed rules of behaviour to manage the inevitable disputes between states can be an elegant and cheap solution. For a long time it was called the 'European law of nations', and it is no coincidence that none of the ancient empires of Rome or China ever developed such a concept, but messy early modern Europe with its multitude of independent territories did, and redoubled its efforts after the experience of the Thirty Years War.

As elegant as the solution seemed, it involved telling kings and princes that they could not do certain things that they wanted to do, which many of them found highly infuriating and hard to accept, given that their power had been awarded to them by God. Therefore it is unsurprising that the international lawyers of the time saw their work as an assembly of 'best practice' rules that a wise ruler would respect, and that was in full harmony with God's wishes. In other words, all authors of treatises on the law of nations saw their works as recommendatory in nature, setting out how international relations ought to be conducted based on the principles of 'natural law'. Naturally, the precise requirements of natural law were constantly debated, and were often heavily influenced by an author's stance in the incessant infighting of European Christianity over the proper role of God and the state, or their involvement in political struggles such as who should control the oceans, rather than a meticulous observation of what states actually did.

When the idea of state authority being placed within one person by God was increasingly challenged in the late 18th century, a broad intellectual movement called positivism emerged with it, arguing that only facts for which positive proof existed should be accepted in all fields of science. This transformed legal thinking in the early 19th century by challenging and eventually overthrowing the dogma of natural law, replacing it with a firm emphasis on what international law is, not what it ought to be. This new approach led to a much more precise and compelling system of norms, no longer based on philosophy but firmly rooted in documented precedent and evidence that states acted because they felt compelled to do so by the law of nations. By the mid-19th century this double standard of proof became known as the combination of 'state practice and *opinio juris*', the latter a convenient shorthand for the difficult task of establishing that states believe a certain rule to be law. This must not be confused with trying to measure a nation's moral convictions: *opinio juris* could be proved by the example of a state complying with a norm despite protesting about its injustice or political inconvenience. If one state puts such pressure on another state, we describe it as 'power politics'. If the community of states forces a state to comply with a given rule, this action becomes a source of international law. But proving the *opinio juris* of one state is not enough: to establish a norm of customary international law, all states, or at least an overwhelming majority, should have expressed such consent. But at what point does a majority become overwhelming, and whose vote counts? In short, positivism had dismissed natural law and exposed the lack of authority in 'customary' rules that do not have state consent behind them, but in doing so it raised the bar for the proof of new customary law almost impossibly high, and greatly increased the importance of formal recognition as a state.

The solution to this problem was found almost by accident in 1856, for reasons that this book will expose for the first time. The Declaration of Paris was a distinct document from the Peace of Paris that ended the Crimean War two weeks earlier, and it was the first major great power treaty that was intended to work like a global opinion poll, asking all nations to sign up to its content and thus create almost instantaneous customary law. Since the norm is clearly codified and each state's accession formally recorded, proving *opinio juris* becomes child's play. This tool that today we call a 'multilateral law-making treaty' was the answer to the positivist's challenge of how to create truly binding international law. Moreover, it could create new norms at unprecedented speed. Soon, states began to hold conferences specifically for the purpose of creating new laws, the best-known example being the 1864 Geneva Convention for the Amelioration of the Condition of the Wounded in Armies in the Field. Occasionally states would even create new international organisations to oversee the observance of the new rules, such as the International Committee of the Red Cross, founded in 1863, the International Telegraph Union, founded in 1865, and the General Postal Union, established at the Congress of Berne in 1874. Within a few decades the repeated application of the multilateral law-making treaty had created a spider web of legal obligations, amounting to a step-by-step codification of what states believed was international law. Therefore the main reason international law was codified so suddenly in the second half of the 19th century is that the necessary tool had been invented in 1856.

It is no wonder that this was also the precise moment when international lawyers began to form a distinct profession, establishing the Institut de Droit International in 1873 and, frantically trying to keep up with all of this new state practice, a special academic journal entitled the *Revue de Droit International Public* in 1894. Their role as legal advisers to the state delegations at the norm-setting conferences even enabled some members of this new profession to influence the creation of new international law. Unsurprisingly, modern international lawyers with an interest in the history of their subject invariably find this aspect to be the most fascinating of the 19th-century developments: most of the research on the history of international law looks at the history of the profession or the academic discipline, not its role as a tool of international relations.[4]

Likewise, most general works looking at the relationship between war and law are written by international lawyers with a strong interest in history, such as Stephen Neff and Alexander Gillespie.[5] Impressive in scope, they try to cover the subject from antiquity until today, providing an overview of the norms as they were created. Written from a lawyer's perspective, they rarely probe deeper into the politics of either their creation or their enforcement. To be fair, even if Neff and Gillespie had the strongest possible interest in the background of each of the thousands of documents and treaties that they cite, they would struggle to find any appropriate literature, since historians of international relations usually shy away from a field perceived as infuriatingly complex and mildly dull. For the same reason, even the few brave political scientists who venture beyond 1945 have very few archive-based studies to enlighten them on the reasons why states chose to make changes to international law. As a result, they can describe how norms are created in a world where every state is a member of the United Nations (UN) but are less comfortable in explaining why states seem to have an incessant urge to limit their freedom of action and create new complex international organisations and norms, an urge that demonstrably pre-dates the present international system and was in full swing by the second half of the 19th century.

Then as now, there is very little serious study of how these laws work, in what circumstances states chose to respect or disregard them, and with what intentions they expanded or changed the body of international law. From a positivist point of view, the question of what the purpose of international law is makes no sense: the fact that states engage in it is all that a positivist needs to know.[6] This is why the dramatic expansion of international law in the mid-19th century and the increasing entanglement of law and international diplomacy did not raise any probing questions as to what consequences that might have. But once there was a whole body of precise rules that were undoubtedly binding, the question of their enforcement became much more critical to the legitimacy of international law than it was in the days of natural law.

Instead, contemporaries celebrated the development as the sure harbinger of a breakthrough to a more peaceful, more reasonable and altogether more civilised stage of human development. Whenever the new treaties or norms were ignored, liberal enthusiasts bemoaned the return of medieval barbarism. Inevitably, the heydays of Manchester liberalism were soon dismissed as being somewhat on the naive side when it came to matters of peace and war, but from the late 1870s onwards their passionate embrace of the rule of law in international affairs was also seen by some as downright dangerous. Parts of a generation heavily influenced by social Darwinism had a fundamentally different vision of how a nation state could secure its long-term prosperity in the age of high imperialism, and believed that encouraging trust in international law undermined the necessary preparations for serious conflict. Rarely dominating the rhetoric of international politics, this dismissive view of international law never went away and has recently experienced a revival following the 2003 invasion of Iraq. The problem with this perspective is that it assumes that every state on earth is engaging in a collective charade designed to resemble a rule-based international society, and wasting considerable time and effort on this rather pointless activity. In short, it starts from the premise that the world went mad at some point in the mid-19th century and never fully recovered.

However, this is not the only criticism that modern international law has to bear: while ridiculed for its lack of real power, it is just as often vilified for its close association with power. Those emphasising the second interpretation of the 'might makes right' critique – the ability of the powerful to create rules for all – point towards the prominent role of the world's leading nations in both writing and enforcing the norms of international law. Powerful states impose their rules while suppressing the wishes and needs of smaller states, and in extreme cases even demand the right to break the rules with impunity. There are practical counterarguments to this position. First, as a system of repression, international law is rather poorly thought out, with its formal notion of state equality and its practice of including even the smallest states in multilateral negotiations with full voting rights. Second, it opens up avenues for smaller states to pursue claims that their rights have been violated that great powers might once have dismissed with a shrug. But the critique that sees international law as tainted by the interests of the powerful is not focused on practical issues. Especially in US universities, these scholars describe themselves as 'idealists' fighting for 'human rights', in opposition to the 'realists' arguing that international law has no power and thus no legitimacy. However, nobody has yet offered a credible alternative enforcement structure for international norms in the absence of a prominent role for the most powerful states. There is a strong temptation to abandon the grim realities of state practice and enforcement, and to return to a discussion of what international law ought to be to best promote global justice without bowing to the realities of power and influence. In other words, what is consciously or subconsciously demanded is a return to the natural law tradition of finding international law, with a much diminished role for the Christian God.

Yet there was never a time when the creation of international law was completely detached from state interests. Political, strategic and commercial interests have always shaped global norm-making, and enforcement relied on the cooperation of the world's most powerful states – if they were opposed, who else would have the power to enforce the rules? To describe this as corruption at the heart of international law means confusing it with the idea of justice. Its aim is not to ensure complete justice in international relations but to find the best possible common guidelines in a community of states that are in the unfortunate position of having to share the same planet. But this aspect is rarely discussed in studies of the history of international law, although even those institutions set up with the explicit goal of achieving international justice, such as the International Criminal Court, are erected by states upon the foundations of the international system and have no legal authority except that granted to them by states.

This book argues that international law is best understood from its starting point as a set of rules created and respected by nations in their relations with each other. It fulfils the function of 'House Rules' for the global community of nations, and the purpose is to enable the smooth functioning of the constant interactions of their citizens or agents within the constrained space shared by all. A useful analogy is the set of House Rules agreed by all flat owners in an apartment block: they are all legally equal and independent entities, but they share part of their living space and all live under the same roof. Inevitably there will be conflict and disputes, and one approach would be to attack and either suppress or eliminate all others. If the attempt to control the apartment block is successful, a form of empire is created, changing the concept from 'House Rules' to 'my house, my rules'. But the number of empires is infinitely smaller than the number of attempts to create an empire, as most such attempts will inspire an overwhelming alliance of others to stop the would-be empire-builder, now perceived as the most dangerous troublemaker.

Hobbes famously argued that anarchy is the natural state of human society – in truth, human beings have always tried to avoid the violence and anxiety that is the consequence of competition for shared resources in the total absence of rules. The greater the number of individuals sharing a territory or resource, the greater a problem such anarchy becomes. It is no coincidence that the number of rules, norms and international institutions exploded in the mid-19th century, when global interactions became more intense, more numerous and more regular. States and their citizens increasingly felt that the world had become a smaller and more constrained place. Whatever their differences, humans tend to prefer commonly accepted rules over anarchy and arbitrary on-the-spot decisions, and international law provided some of the answers to the questions raised by the 'first wave of globalisation', the quantum leap in international commerce and communications marking the second half of the 19th century. But the issue remains a puzzle: while states set up or agreed to large numbers of new norms, they never agreed to install a central authority for enforcing them, but they still expected the system to work. And why did it then work so well that the international system today is built on essentially the same legal framework?

A study investigating the origins of international law and its stunning aspirations must therefore begin and end with the obvious question: can international law actually deliver on its lofty promises, can it ever restrain the furies of war and will reminders of its norms stop powerful nations pursuing their interests? The answer is yes, it can. Most belligerent nations observe most of the laws of war most of the time, especially in interstate warfare. Most states respect the judgments of international courts or arbitration tribunals, and the bitter opposition of the US government against the International Criminal Court in the first term of the Bush administration can only be understood as an implicit admission that once established, the world's most powerful nation would find it difficult to prevent the court from deciding against its wishes. On the other hand, examples abound where the laws of war have been trampled upon, particularly in both world wars, and court decisions were simply ignored. So why are the rules sometimes respected and enforced, and sometimes broken with impunity?

The enforcement of rules in a community-based system is possible if the rules are perceived as legitimate and a sufficient number of members feel so annoyed by a violation of the rules that they decide to confront the norm-breaker. In turn, the legitimacy of the norms depends on the fairness with which they are enforced, as well as the perceived justice of the process by which they were originally created. The more legitimate and the more important for international security a norm is, the stronger and quicker the attempt to enforce it will be. There is thus an unspoken hierarchy of norms when it comes to their enforcement: in our imaginary apartment block, the rule banning noise after 10pm will be enforced in a different way from the rule prohibiting open fires within the building. Here a violation is likely to trigger an immediate and forceful response. The enforcement of lower-hierarchy norms will tend to be more subtle, perhaps involving the naming and shaming of offenders to undermine their place within the community. There is also a likelihood that the community will overlook some transgressions and then lose patience with a persistent offender, while a flat owner with a bad reputation (whether well deserved or not) might face harsher treatment. On the other hand, a particularly powerful or well-regarded member of the community might be approached in a different way: it will take time and serious offences to attract a coalition strong enough to enforce a rule, but public shaming should be more effective in the case of someone who commands and desires a position of respect.

With some justice, this form of enforcement might be described as inherently unfair, but the problem is that in the absence of a central authority, enforcement carries a much greater risk for those that take it into their hands, and it would be naive to expect them to fulfil this function with the total neutrality demanded (at least in theory) of the police, prosecution and judicial organs within a well-organised national system. If perceived as too arbitrary or in prosecution of a norm widely seen as unfair or illegitimate, the offender might even assemble a coalition of like-minded friends and try to oppose the enforcement. In any such confrontation, the legitimacy of both enforcement and rules will influence the outcome, and in this way the process of creating legitimate rules and the power of enforcement are inextricably linked. But these links do not establish a straightforward legal relationship, but a political one, which means that it is likely to be much more complex, and more prone to change over time. However, without understanding these links, both community-based enforcement and the occasional organised opposition to it must remain puzzling and invite allegations of arbitrary behaviour. It is in this sense that this book will strive to explore the true relationship between power and international law, and there can be no better example than the Declaration of Paris.

The treaty was once regarded as the foundation stone of modern international law, but it is now almost forgotten due to its inability to prevent the escalation of naval conflict that marked the First World War. Signed on 16 April 1856 (the original signatories being Britain, France, Russia, Austria, Prussia, Sardinia-Piedmont and the Ottoman Empire), the declaration was part of the Congress of Paris following the Crimean War (1853–6), and the delegates agreed on four articles: the first one banned privateering, the second and third regulated the rights of neutrals during war, and the fourth banned paper blockades by stipulating that a blockade had to be 'effective' to be lawful.[7] Its extension of neutral rights to trade undisturbed in peace time was a radical reversal of the centuries-old British tradition of extensive belligerent rights and an aggressive interpretation of the right of search. The Declaration of Paris did not just strive to make life easier for international merchants; its purpose was to secure the flow of trade in times of war. In other words, it had the audacity to tell belligerents what they were allowed to do while conducting hostilities at sea. No longer would navies have complete freedom to harass neutral commerce and thus drive it from the enemy's coastline, and the privateers who had provided many a heroic tale in the early modern era were assigned to the dust heap of history.

Both the idea of private entrepreneurs outside any chain of command joining a naval war in the hope of capturing a valuable prize and the freedom of belligerents to search any neutral vessel they encountered no longer fitted into a world that was about to embark on revolutionary changes in the way it conducted international trade. Where once every journey had been an adventure, and a ship sent to Asia to buy spices might return with a fortune years later or not at all, by the 1850s a one-day delay of the steamer from New York had become newsworthy. Trade had become a network running on schedule and within tight margins, controlled by telegraph. Crucially, all nations depended on this network to some extent – and the most advanced ones now critically so – for much of their food, their industry and any dreams of future prosperity. The generation running politics now had vivid memories of the dislocation brought by unrestrained economic warfare in the Napoleonic Wars, when Britain controlled the waves and Napoleon tried to quarantine an entire continent. It understood what repeating this form of great power warfare would mean in a globalising world, and that the network of trade had to be protected from the impact of minor or even major wars.

To achieve this goal, there had to be common rules protecting trade everywhere, respected by all nations and equally valid on every ocean. International law did know the idea of customary law, ancient rules that had been accepted by legal scholars and states alike over a long period of time, usually several decades. But such unity had never been achieved regarding the rules of maritime warfare. The innovation marked by the Declaration of Paris was to begin with a solemn declaration by the great European powers that called upon every nation in the world to declare its accession to the agreement with a simple announcement, instead of the usual ratification process. If most of the world's states followed this call within a couple of weeks, there would be an instant case for a new norm of customary law. For the first time ever, the vast majority of nations were united under the same treaty. As an answer to the problem of how to govern the world with the means of the 19th century, this was a masterstroke.

However, it did have important implications for a process that is today referred to as the 'universalisation' of international law, the development leading from a clearly European law of nations to a global legal order.[8] Part of that extension process was achieved by colonialism: any British or French port anywhere in the world applied British or French laws and, of course, the rules of international law when dealing with foreign merchant or naval vessels. However, if international law is used to regulate oceanic trade, it has to apply in every port of some significance. In a time of rapid global expansion of maritime trade, this meant that Latin America and the Ottoman Empire had to be included (in East Asia, the problem was partially solved for the time being by having ports with special jurisdiction). So the European powers reached out and for the first time invited every nation to join this new treaty, and began to apply real diplomatic pressure if states somewhat adrift of the main thrust of European politics were slow to grasp what was demanded of them. Some of the smallest states, such as the Sandwich Islands

(Hawaii), found this process completely baffling, while others, such as Brazil, embraced the new development and attached reform proposals of their own to their accession declarations. Therefore the universalisation of international law was not simply driven by colonialism. Moreover, the confident embrace of the system of international law by lawyers from countries in the periphery was a second step, after the great powers had granted full access to the system to protect the newly created global network of trade and communications.[9] The Declaration of Paris, as the first treaty uniting Europe, the Ottoman Empire and South America as signatories to the same document, marks the very moment when the European law of nations became truly international.

The frequent repetition of the same process created a network of multilateral treaties, and once global interactions were increasingly conducted on the basis of such treaties, the vision of one international society with an agreed rulebook became possible. In turn, this process made it much harder to be a 'barbarian' – a state outside this system – and still enjoy the privileges of independence and sovereignty. Increasingly, being fully sovereign meant being recognised as such and being allowed to actively sign up for the privileges of modern statehood. It is no coincidence that the doctrines of state recognition were formulated shortly afterwards, and the increasingly international nature of the First and particularly the Second Hague Peace Conference in 1899 and 1907 demonstrate how far this process had advanced before the First World War.

The originality of the Declaration of Paris and the vastness of its intended reach were clearly apparent as radical departures from existing practices, both for the tiny group of international statesmen that created it and some shrewd contemporary observers. In a newspaper comment in 1856, Karl Marx called it 'one of the most remarkable surprises of the English-French-Turkish-Russian War that has been so rich in surprises'.[10] Its remarkable history is a prime example of the power of law effecting radical change and protecting it for decades, and both its endurance and its sudden end make it an invaluable case study for the mechanisms which underpin international law in a world of community-based enforcement. To make best possible use of it, we must understand the very different world of maritime law before the Crimean War, and the extent of confusion and ignorance which marks the existing literature on the subject.

For centuries, Britain had claimed the right to search for enemy property on vessels flying any neutral flag. Unsurprisingly, that stance was never popular among neutral maritime nations that were eager to benefit from the inflated transport prices in wartime. On two occasions, neutral outrage about what they perceived as a despotic attempt to enforce British rules on the commons of the high seas persuaded several nations to form an alliance to defend the inviolability of their flag as one powerful bloc – the so-called Armed Neutralities of 1780 and 1800. In 1780, Tsarina Catherine II announced that further attempts by the Royal Navy to interfere with Russian vessels trading with the seceding USA would be met with armed force. By the end of Britain's war against the USA, Denmark-Norway, Sweden, Prussia, the Netherlands, Portugal, the Kingdom of the Two Sicilies and the Ottoman Empire had all joined this League of Armed Neutrality, causing Britain to tread much more carefully in its inspections of neutral vessels. An attempt to revive this league in 1800, again led by Russia, was less successful in isolating Britain and forcing the Royal Navy to change its tactics. Nelson's victory against the Danish fleet at Copenhagen in 1801 removed Denmark from the alliance, and the league fell apart after the assassination of Tsar Paul II.

Both armed neutralities were a battle cry for a permanent reform of international law, firmly establishing the so-called free ships, free goods principle in international law, ensuring that enemy goods sailing under a neutral flag would be free from capture. The second largest naval power, France, endorsed this 'flag principle', although French cruisers also took neutral goods found on enemy vessels. British prize courts protected the latter as neutral property under the 'ownership' principle. But from a neutral trader's point of view, 'free ships, free goods' was by far the most important rule since it would allow them to pick up the transport trade of the belligerents while only being liable to capture if they carried arms or war supplies (called contraband goods). But few in Britain felt a need to revoke the old principles that had long been celebrated as a pillar of British naval mastery and one of the reasons for the eventual triumph over Napoleon.

Yet, on 28 March 1854, more than 70 years after the first armed neutrality, Britain and France declared that they would apply both the 'free ships, free goods' principle and the freedom of neutral property on enemy goods (as in the ownership principle) for the duration of the Crimean War.[11] Two years later, at the conference that ended the war, Britain signed a treaty that made this concession permanent. Despite this sudden reversal of a policy maintained over centuries, we have no convincing explanation as to why Britain signed the treaty and lobbied for its global acceptance. Quite unusually for a major decision taken by the likes of Palmerston, the consensus among historians was long based on the premise that the Cabinet had no idea what it was doing. In 2005 an article in the journal of the Royal United Services Institute even dismissed the Declaration of Paris as 'one of the biggest blunders in British diplomacy'.[12] So why did Britain sign away its sea power?

It is no coincidence that real historical study of the question began during the First World War. The course of the war seemed to be final proof that sea power and international law were best left separate, and made the question as to why Palmerston and Clarendon had signed the declaration even more vexing. Inevitably, the first study published by Sir Francis Piggott in 1919 blamed plain stupidity: at the pinnacle of the Manchester School's influence, the Cabinet had been intoxicated by a liberal ideology that saw trade and mutual material gain as the surest path to global peace and civilisation.

As even great minds succumbed to the empty promises of liberal ideology, the Foreign Secretary, Lord Clarendon, signed away Britain's ancient maritime rights without considering the consequences.[13] Piggott's account was supported by an article written by Charles Stockton of the US Naval Academy one year later, although with a stronger condemnation of the malign forces of liberalism. Despite writing from a rather different ideological vantage point, British historian of ideas Bernard Semmel confirmed this view in his 1986 study of the relationship between liberal thought and naval strategy in Britain. While finding that the circumstances leading to the Declaration of Paris were 'not fully clear', he concluded that the Foreign Secretary, Lord Clarendon, heavily influenced by radicals such as Richard Cobden and John Bright, urged his views on a hesitant Palmerston, but these were the heydays of liberal optimism, and even Palmerston was moved by the prospect of contributing to the progress of civilisation.[14]

This view was first criticised in 1927 by William Malkin, later to become the Foreign Office's Senior Legal Adviser. He described Britain's adhesion as a conscious decision of the Palmerston government, motivated primarily by fear of American privateers.[15] Thus the real goal was the abolition of privateering to weaken the USA in case of war, and neutral rights were the price to be paid. But was it worth it given that the USA never joined the treaty? Malkin's article never replaced Piggott's book as the standard interpretation, and it was directly challenged 33 years later when Olive Anderson published an alternative account. Anderson claimed that while the abolition of privateering was discussed by the government, 'it was not the only, or even the chief, motive for its actions'. She argued that liberals like First Lord of the Admiralty James Graham persuaded the Cabinet that Britain's economic interest was now demanding the protection of neutral trade in wartime. For that reason, Britain agreed to grant generous neutral rights for the duration of the Crimean War. Following the triumphant victory over Russia and the successful blockade, this arrangement was then made permanent without much further thought.[16] In Anderson's 1967 monograph *A Liberal State at War*, she revised many of her own conclusions as further research revealed that there was actually considerable debate about whether the blockade of Russia had been a success or not. Nonetheless, Anderson insisted that it 'is surely significant that at the end of the war the Cabinet had no doubts about the wisdom of their policy', which was 'clear from the fact that at the peace conference Britain took a leading part in securing the Declaration of Paris'.[17] She still explicitly rejected Malkin's argument about a campaign to end privateering.[18]

Confusingly, Paul Kennedy endorses both Malkin's view of a *quid pro quo* over privateering and Anderson's argument that liberals believed that the declaration was in their economic interest, while claiming that the Manchester School's disciples were simply unable to appreciate the value of 'total blockade' as a strategic weapon, 'possibly because of the failure of this strategy against Russia'.[19] In fact, as Chapter 2 will show, the blockade was neither a triumph nor a failure: after a troubled start it succeeded in severely reducing the customs income from exports, thus hitting the fiscal capabilities of the Russian state to continue fighting.[20]

The most recent explanation was proposed by one of Britain's foremost naval historians, Andrew Lambert. He describes the declaration as an example of British duplicity, with the Royal Navy never intending to keep such restrictive rules in case of war against a major power.[21] Likewise, Avner Offer explains the declaration's longevity by claiming that no major power had been sufficiently tempted to break it until 1914. Offer further argues that international law is like a classic game-theory model, the prisoner's dilemma: mutual trust is good, but the greatest rewards go to players who pretend to play by the rules but betray those trusting them.[22] However, the Declaration of Paris was a treaty between more than 40 different parties, and withholding neutral privileges because of a war with another party would break obligations to dozens of powers with which Britain was at peace.[23] Lambert's second argument refers to the possibility of bending the rules: Clarendon secured Admiralty approval for Britain's signature by pointing out that the document lacked a definition of contraband, which could thus be stretched very wide.[24] However, the letter that Lambert refers to was sent on 16 April 1856, after the declaration had been signed, and could also be read as an attempt to soothe concerns in the Admiralty about a decision that had been taken for very different reasons.

This book argues that what motivated the Cabinet was neither liberal ideology nor the (positive or negative) experience of the Crimean War blockade, nor sheer mendacity. Instead, it realised that any return to the old right of search would interfere with the new realities of British-dominated globalised trade, and greatly upset a large number of countries. On the other hand, these states would all be willing to pay a price for a British guarantee of neutral rights, especially if the price were as small as cooperation in an attempt to end privateering. For most states, privateering had indeed become an irrelevance; but for the USA, currently engaged in a number of potentially explosive disputes with London, it was the main strategic weapon in case of war with Britain. The US merchant navy was now the second largest in the world, and many of these ships could easily be converted into privateers. American politicians were not shy in pointing out what consequences this would have for British commerce worldwide. If either France or Russia chose to join this dispute on the US side, even the Royal Navy's superiority might not suffice, which made banning privateering a clear strategic interest for London. Seen from this perspective, the decisions that led to the Declaration of Paris are all perfectly plausible. The declaration was then less about granting rights to deserving neutrals and more about abolishing the institution of privateering, well established since medieval times, in one fell swoop.

It should be noted that this argument about the Declaration of Paris as the decisive factor ending privateering is challenging all other explanations put forward to explain the demise of private enterprise in naval war. Some scholars embracing a neoliberal political agenda have blamed navies as national bureaucracies for inhibiting their more efficient private competitors, while Marxist sociologists have seen 'hegemonic class interests' at work.[25] The most common explanation is that privateering lost its relevance after the introduction of steam and other advances in naval technology.[26] Nicholas Parrilo has claimed that the true end of privateering only came in the 1890s when the USA adopted a programme of naval expansion to enable a more ambitious and imperialist foreign policy.[27] However, this argument cannot explain why the US delegation at the Second Hague Peace Conference insisted on the right of privateering as late as 1907, and why the Confederate privateers attempted to use letters of marque and then abandoned the idea forever.

As this book will show, the privateers of the early American Civil War embraced steam technology, but their downfall was that most states that had signed the Declaration of Paris (and with Spain even one that had not) accepted the corollary principle that supporting the abolition of privateering had created a requirement to no longer admit privateers into the nation's ports. Therefore the Confederate privateers found no friendly neutral ports for buying supplies or selling prizes. Once the Confederate coastline was effectively blockaded, the privateers simply gave up and turned to the safer and much more profitable business of blockade running. Privateering ended in 1862, and the success of the *Alabama* one year later highlights the reason: the ship was very similar to those used by the privateers, but as an official vessel of the Confederate Navy it was granted port access by neutrals. Moreover, the *Alabama*'s habit of burning prizes (instead of risking an attempt to sell the vessel and diminish the ship's company by sending a prize crew) made no economic sense for a private individual. That is why no one accepted a letter of marque again: not having access to neutral ports made the activity a logistical nightmare, and a very risky and probably unprofitable one at that. It's not that no letters of marque were offered: Chile and Bolivia both tried to tempt foreign adventurers (in 1866 and 1879, respectively) but found no takers, for the reasons outlined above. Later attempts to return to privateering by European states such as Prussia and Russia were faced with the other fundamental mechanism underpinning the authority of the Declaration of Paris: the threat of overwhelming armed force. We will return to these examples in the Conclusion, but for now the book will explain the circumstances that led to the adoption of this most extraordinary treaty.

Chapter 1 explores the reasons behind the Crimean War compromise of 1854, revealing that the Scandinavian powers did indeed prepare a new armed neutrality in case Britain decided to apply the old right of search.

Chapter 2 investigates the application of the new neutral rights in the Crimean War, concluding that while the blockade of Russia was fraught with difficulties and caused domestic embarrassment, it still contributed to Russia's defeat, as did the improved relations with neutrals caused by the concession. More relevant for the origins of the Declaration of Paris, however, were two campaigns: first a British attempt to ban privateering and secure the closure of all ports for privateers; then a US attempt to secure the wartime concessions as permanent customary law without any restrictions on privateering.

Chapter 3 shows that it was in response to a renewal of the latter campaign in 1855 that Britain for the first time considered a linkage between granting neutral rights and the end of privateering in one treaty. France used the opportunity of the European Congress in 1856 to secure a multilateral treaty on maritime law, meant as the starting point of a universal codification of international law. The only doubt the Cabinet in London had was whether the prospect of binding America was concrete enough to warrant a concession.

Chapter 4 contains the first detailed study of the US response to the declaration, the Marcy Amendment. This shows that the proposal was not actually William Marcy's idea but forced upon him by the unilateral action of his minister in Portugal. Still, Britain seriously considered accepting it, and the reasons why it never did can now be clarified, particularly by presenting a draft rejection note that was never sent.

Chapter 5 explores a widely unknown follow-up initiative by US Secretary of State Lewis Cass in 1859, which in turn inspired a truly international campaign by private activists in the tiny German city-state of Bremen. The momentum created by their campaign caused even the great powers to consider isolating Britain over the Marcy Amendment at the next European congress, while many small states signed up to the campaigners' vision of the European congress as a forum for debate and international legislation. While these attempts were ultimately unsuccessful, France's reaction to the Cass Memorandum was to make Britain accept that coal could not be contraband as one of the conditions for signing the Cobden–Chevalier Treaty in 1860.

Chapter 6 shows how the USA was desperate to join the Declaration of Paris after the Confederacy had begun its secession with the issue of letters of marque, but withdrew this offer after it emerged that Britain and France were unwilling to endorse operations against Southern privateers by their own navies. The Southern privateers still failed, and the comparison with the successes of the later commerce raiders shows that it was the lack of port access in signatory states of the Declaration of Paris that caused their demise, proving that privateering had become unviable. Not least because of European opposition, Lincoln rejected strong demands for Northern privateers. The chapter also offers a re-evaluation of Britain's position regarding neutral rights in the conflict, showing that claims of self-interested duplicity are greatly exaggerated.

Chapter 7 explains how and why both Austria and Prussia tried to employ the fratricidal war for control over Germany in 1866 to establish a precedent for the Marcy Amendment, and why things went very differently in the Franco-German War of 1870–1. Besides investigating the global French campaign against German shipping for the first time, the chapter also reveals how minor violations of maritime law provoked a furious and aggressive response from Bismarck, ultimately leading to the first threat by a major power to withdraw from the declaration. Finally, the Conclusion will summarise the argument, outline the declaration's role and significance until its downfall in 1915, and suggest lessons that can be learned from its history that might be relevant to contemporary international relations.

1
'More Serious than the Eastern Question Itself' – The Crimean War Compromise

The story of the Declaration of Paris begins in Sweden, where a well-timed piece of political blackmail triggered a flurry of diplomatic activity that resulted in the most liberal set of rules ever granted to neutrals. When it became increasingly likely that an Anglo-French coalition would be fighting Russia in early 1854 in what is now called the Crimean War, the Swedish government realised that the Baltic would be a warzone, and that the substantial shipping of the Kingdom of Sweden-Norway was under threat of belligerent interference, particularly by the Royal Navy under its controversial interpretation of the right of search. While Britain and France hoped to secure Sweden as an ally, Russia demanded that all Swedish ports should be closed for belligerents. That would have made it extremely hard to supply a large allied fleet in the Baltic, and Sweden knew that the Western powers would be eager to prevent this. Therefore it joined forces with the Danes, the custodians of the narrow gateway to the Baltic, and attempted to build an alliance of neutral powers that might join them in their demand for undisturbed neutral navigation.[1] By contacting smaller maritime powers about a joint defence of the 'free ships, free goods' principle, the Scandinavians were effectively reviving the struggles over neutral rights of the Napoleonic era, and planned a third Armed Neutrality. They could offer the promise of unhindered port access, but the initiative remained a clear provocation to the British.[2]

On 2 January 1854, Sweden and Denmark set out their demands in a joint despatch to London, Paris and St. Petersburg. Going much further than the original Armed Neutrality, they insisted not only on the freedom of enemy goods on neutral vessels but also on the immunity of neutral property on enemy ships.[3] This meant an additional challenge to France, which traditionally captured such goods under the flag principle. Sweden also approached the Netherlands, Belgium, Sardinia, Spain and Prussia, but Prussia had declined to openly commit to a new Armed Neutrality before

17

war had been declared and, without Prussia, the Netherlands was sympathetic but unwilling to publicly adhere.[4] Even before the USA had responded, a surprisingly friendly despatch from Foreign Secretary Lord Clarendon reached Stockholm: after all, the Scandinavians might have challenged British principles, but the promise to keep Swedish ports open for belligerent vessels despite Russian protests meant a potentially decisive advantage for the Royal Navy.[5] The French Ambassador in London, Alexandre Walewski, also urged Clarendon to abandon the old rules and make the constant quarrels about the right of search disappear overnight. Britain could please the neutrals, avoid a dangerous conflict with the USA and serve the interests of British trade. Walewski thought that both Clarendon and Lord John Russell[6] understood the desirability of renouncing the traditional British principles but found it difficult to abandon a doctrine that had been established by renowned statesmen and virtually sanctified by generations of publicists.[7]

As the Queen's Advocate, Sir John Harding, politely put it, 'some declaration on part of Her Majesty's government' would have to be made to explain the decision to the public if the British principles were abandoned.[8] It was First Lord of the Admiralty Sir James Graham who volunteered to provide the arguments: in a lengthy memorandum, he argued that in contrast with earlier wars, Britain was now not only the most important naval power but also the greatest commercial trader. Industrial production depended on the steady inflow of raw material imports, if necessary on board foreign vessels. The traditional practice of stopping every neutral ship and searching for enemy goods would therefore now harm British industry. Moreover, Russia was the most important source of important naval stores, such as hemp or tallow. Finally, if the Royal Navy was relieved of this task, there would be no necessity to employ privateers against Russian commerce. Naval vessels could be concentrated for a close blockade of the Russian coastline, which would compensate for the loss in military effectiveness caused by the abandonment of traditional prize rules.[9]

French Foreign Minister Édouard Drouyn de Lhuys tried to build a bridge for the British Cabinet and suggested a compromise in which each side accepted the more liberal aspects of the practice of the other. The British concession in swallowing the 'free ships, free goods' principle was, of course, greater than France conceding the freedom of neutral goods on enemy ships, but a compromise this generous would secure considerable goodwill from neutrals. The idea was made even more appealing to London since Drouyn de Lhuys suggested a compromise for the duration of the war, avoiding the need to permanently give up national principles.[10] The latter restriction had been urged by French Navy Minister Theodore Ducos,[11] who was sceptical about the abandonment of established French naval traditions. Ducos would ideally have preferred a separate declaration by the Emperor to reaffirm the French principles, independent of British policy. Drouyn de Lhuys pointed out that this would guarantee a severe conflict with London and undermine the alliance before the war had even started. The need for unity in the coalition had been perfectly understood by the British and should be used to extract as many concessions as possible. In a final sentence, he told his colleague that Napoleon III thought exactly the same on this matter, strongly hinting that no further comments from Ducos were required.[12]

By late February, however, Drouyn de Lhuys became increasingly anxious as to whether Clarendon had the necessary will and political clout to achieve such a dramatic change in British policy. Repeated attempts by Walewski to obtain a decision proved to be unsuccessful,[13] and Clarendon had made a statement in Parliament implying that in case of disagreement, Britain would simply issue a separate declaration.[14] In response, Drouyn de Lhuys urged an understanding between the allies before any further announcements were made in public, and Clarendon promised to obtain a positive decision from the Cabinet within days.[15] Clarendon failed to fulfil his promise, and soon faced pressure not only from France and the neutrals but also from anxious merchants who were increasingly successful in shaping British public opinion.

These fears were fuelled by a reply given by the British Consul in Riga to an enquiry by local merchants that seemed to announce a return of the old British rules on neutral trade. The note from the Consul had been authorised by Clarendon, which raised the question of whether it was meant to be a simple restatement of the present law or an indication of the course that would be followed in the conflict with Russia. If the latter was true, Milner Gibson warned Clarendon, this 'might bring this country into a collision with the United States of America'.[16] Facing further questioning in the House of Lords, Clarendon tried to calm merchants by explaining that while the neutral flag would not protect enemy goods, even if owned by British subjects resident in Russia, rerouting them via Prussia would be legal if the ownership of the wares changed on the way.[17] Still, the only way to reassure Parliament proved to be a strong hint about future policy: Clarendon stated that in this first war alongside an ally, Britain had to be very clear about the principles to be applied and 'the departure which we shall sanction from our former law and practice'. In these matters the government would act 'with utmost liberality'.

It is important to point out that the 'liberality' so urged upon the government was not necessarily an expression of liberalism as a political ideology. One of the first newspapers to demand liberal rules to please the neutrals was *The Times*,[18] and among the first speakers to respond to Clarendon's announcement was a Conservative who represented the shipping interests of his Liverpool constituency. Thomas Horsfall demanded a quick resolution based on what Clarendon had promised: already, increased expenses were being placed upon the shipping industry, as uncertainty about the prize rules and the role of privateers in the coming war had caused insurers to demand soaring premiums. Rising prices for consumers would soon follow, and a speedy clarification was therefore in the interest of the country as a whole, as was a treaty with France and the USA that banned privateering once and for all.[19] John Bright suggested that such a treaty should also include the 'free ships, free goods' principle, because if US ships were searched for enemy property, this would almost certainly provoke war with Washington. Leader of the House John Russell finally asked for 'a few days of forbearance'.[20]

Russell was unable to reveal that a draft declaration had already been agreed by the Cabinet because the French had not yet replied after it had been sent to Paris. One day earlier, Clarendon had read it to US Minister James Buchanan, who was highly pleased to hear that the British were willing to accept the 'free ships, free goods' principle as well as sparing neutral goods on enemy ships, and assured Clarendon that the draft would be 'highly gratifying' to the US government.[21] Yet if the Cabinet believed that its concession would lead to a swift conclusion of the negotiations, it was wrong. The French demanded a number of changes, the first one being an objection by Navy Minister Ducos: while the British draft supported the permanent abolition of privateering, the French Navy had doubts about giving up this particular weapon. On 20 March, Drouyn de Lhuys reported to Ducos that Britain had backed down and now only requested that no letters of marque should be issued in the coming war, which he deemed 'acceptable'.[22] In addition, Drouyn de Lhuys demanded two changes that both further extended neutral rights.[23] The immunity of neutral convoys from searches was agreed without much discussion,[24] but the second demand almost caused the negotiations to collapse.

Drouyn de Lhuys had declared that a provision that prevented neutral vessels from taking over Russia's coastal trade was totally unacceptable. His reasons had little to do with present trade between Russian ports but instead lay in the distant past as well as in concerns about the immediate future. According to mercantilist principles, colonial and coastal trade were reserved for a nation's citizens. In the Seven Years War of 1756–63, France had lifted this ban and transferred much of its colonial trade to neutrals to circumvent British maritime dominance. Britain had replied by introducing the so-called rule of 1756, which declared all neutral trade during war to be illegal if the activity had been forbidden in peacetime. With liberal economic principles gaining more and more currency, Britain had since abolished any restrictions on its own colonial trade in 1849 and would open coastal trade to foreigners by the end of the month.[25] France and Russia, however, had not liberalised their markets, and a British concession in the war against Russia would have obvious implications for a future war against France. For this reason, the memorandum by James Graham mentioned earlier urged that the 'rule of 1756' should be maintained under all circumstances.[26]

France, on the other hand, wanted to allow neutral coastal trade if a special licence had been granted, and absolutely refused to accept a rule which it had consistently declared to be illegal ever since the Seven Years War.[27]

Furthermore, the National Assembly would have to change French laws, and in any case the government believed that an application of the rule would lead to war with the USA. Drouyn de Lhuys argued that all Russian ports could easily be blockaded, while British insistence on the 'rule of 1756' would have serious implications for commerce between the Russian Pacific coast and Russian-Alaska, as the state-owned Russian trade company would transfer its business to US vessels which had a legal right to coastal trade in wartime according to a French-US treaty of 1778. If the Cabinet in London were to stick to its position, France would not be able to assent to a joint declaration on maritime principles.

The reason why Drouyn de Lhuys was so willing to up the stakes and at the same time so certain what the US position would be was that the American Minister in Paris, John Mason, had begun to develop considerable initiative regarding neutral rights. Despite being a former Admiralty judge, he had not previously featured in the negotiations: new to his post and unable to speak French, much of the Anglo-French deliberations had escaped his attention, and unlike Buchanan in London he had not realised the potential of the British privateering scare for political blackmail.[28] Both issues were soon looked after by Vincent Rumpff, the delegate for the Hanseatic towns, who informed Mason that Drouyn de Lhuys wanted to talk to him about neutral rights and urged the use of privateering fears to exact more concessions.[29] In return, Mason promised to spearhead the efforts of other neutrals in pressuring the British.[30]

In an interview with Drouyn de Lhuys, Mason noted that privateering was 'the point on which most apprehension is felt', and responded with a thinly veiled threat: as long as the allies allowed for profitable neutral trade during the war, American merchants would hardly be tempted to accept Russian letters of marque. If not, his government would surely find it hard to restrain their 'bold and adventurous seafarers'. Drouyn de Lhuys emphatically agreed with Mason's assessment that the USA would never accept harassment of its merchant fleet and suggested a bilateral treaty that would guarantee extensive neutral rights, although Mason suspected that it might also include a bilateral ban on privateering: 'I have *indirectly*, from the Minister of Foreign Affairs, an assurance that he will send out, by the steamer which will take this, a proposition to the United States, to regulate these interesting questions by convention.'[31]

Shortly afterwards, Cowley went to Mason to find out whether he would be as delighted with the British proposal as Buchanan in London. Unlike Buchanan, Mason felt strongly about the inclusion of the 'rule of 1756' and declared the draft to be totally unacceptable. Cowley was surprised and found Mason suspiciously well prepared, and assumed Drouyn de Lhuys had seen the American before him. As Drouyn de Lhuys had also casually mentioned a US proposal for a commerce and navigation treaty with France, Cowley now urged Clarendon to make a further concession, since only forgoing the 'rule of 1756' would secure a successful conclusion to the negotiations, while a treaty between France and the USA on neutral rights would be most unwelcome.[32]

The Cabinet in London now had to make a decision. The two governments had already agreed on the wording of their declarations of war but still lacked a common position on how maritime law should be applied in the upcoming conflict. Two letters written in Paris on 27 March persuaded the British government that the only way out of the situation was to yield, and both documents emphasised the importance of the USA. In the first despatch, Cowley urged Clarendon to avoid a confrontation:

> The neutral question will, if we do not take care, end by being more serious than the Eastern Question itself. It contains the germs of much future discontent, and I cannot help thinking that the government should consider seriously whether to settle it once and for all. Unfortunately there appears to be no means of settling it but by abandoning those principles to which we have stood until now, for since it is a question that unites the pygmies against the giants, it is not likely that concessions will be made on the pygmy side.

In his view, the situation involved a trade-off between the benefits of retaining the present system and the risk of 'giving the maritime powers next in order to ourselves a "point de ralliement". France, Russia, and the U.S. would form a powerful combination against us.' The US treaty allegedly submitted to the French was, he admitted, the crucial factor in his reflections.[33]

On the same day, Drouyn de Lhuys instructed Walewski in London to remain firm and play the US card. He was told to ask Clarendon how France could reject the treaty offered by the USA if at the same time the British Cabinet was so uncooperative. Should France and Britain find a solution, however, there would be no need for the French government to rush in its evaluation of the US proposal.[34] The game that Drouyn de Lhuys played here was quite remarkable. There had been negotiations about a new commerce and navigation treaty with the USA but these had primarily been about reductions in customs.[35] The idea of using an imaginary US proposal on neutral rights to put pressure on his alliance partner was as perfidious as it was effective.[36] Moreover, he sidelined Navy Minister Ducos, who wanted to preserve the French principles as applied since 1543 and found the neutral rights about to be granted 'exaggerated'.[37] Drouyn de Lhuys assured him that the agreement with the British contained a reservation regarding the necessary concurrence of the French Navy, but since it was a fixed package deal requested that he would be so kind and assent as quickly as possible.[38]

On 28 March, Clarendon first read Cowley's despatch and then received Walewski. At 2pm he presented his draft to the Cabinet, and four hours later he reported to a relieved Walewski that the British government had decided to agree to the proposed declaration – against the recommendation of its legal advisers. In the evening, Britain formally declared war on Russia; and, during her speech, Queen Victoria announced the prize rules that would be applied in this conflict.[39] In an ironic turn, Drouyn de Lhuys now complained to Ducos about being tricked, as the British had made last-minute changes to the joint declaration.[40] It no longer included any reference to the 'rule of 1756', leaving open the possibility that it might be applied later in the war. Since the British declaration had already been made public, Napoleon III could do little else but accept the inevitable.[41]

Still, the joint declaration was a French triumph, and Drouyn de Lhuys expected to receive the thanks and sympathies of the commercial nations of the world.[42] He did not forget to inform his envoy in Washington, Count Sartiges, that a formal treaty with the USA was now no longer necessary, while relations with Washington were better than ever before.[43] In London, American Minister Buchanan was equally pleased: 'It has given great satisfaction to the diplomatic representatives of neutral nations in London, and to none more than myself. Indeed it is far more liberal than I had reason to expect it would have been.'[44]

In France, even the conservative newspaper *La Presse* hailed the declaration as a great and unexpected advance in international maritime law, wondering whether a future peace congress might bring the complete immunity of private goods in wartime.[45] The US press was pleasantly surprised and soon speculated that British generosity was motivated by fear of a possible involvement of American privateers in the present war.[46] Given the concerns of Clarendon and Russell, the most astonishing fact about the response to the Queen's declaration is that there hardly was any. *The Times* noted with surprise that no government minister had been asked to justify the abandonment of ancient principles in Parliament.[47] Most newspapers discussing the issue agreed that the new policy was 'no slight monument of the policy and strength of Great Britain', and consistent with the needs and sentiments of a more enlightened age.[48]

Only in early July did the Conservative opposition finally raise the question of whether the temporary abandonment of traditional principles might have lasting consequences. The motion put forward by the MPs J. G. Phillimore and Thomas Mitchell stated that while a relaxation for the duration of the war might be justifiable, a permanent surrender of these important rights 'would be inconsistent with the security and honour of the country'.[49] The main argument employed by the Conservatives was that the new doctrine would unnecessarily prolong wars by granting the enemy precious supplies. The government sent its only Radical member to respond, and First Commissioner of Works Sir William Molesworth came to the startling conclusion, based on an analysis of 130 bilateral treaties, that the 'free ships, free goods' principle was a rule of customary law. For him the ancient British principles were something that should be overcome rather than preserved:

> For if the precedent set by this war should lead to the abolition of private war on the ocean, and to the establishment of the maritime rights of neutrals on the firm and solid basis of reason and justice, whatever other results this war may bring forth, it would be noted for these results in the history of nations – as a step in civilisation, and as a benefit to the human race.[50]

Robert Phillimore, a well-known international lawyer, insisted that treaties could never create customary law, but then recommended to his brother that he should withdraw the motion, allegedly because the temporary nature of the prize regulations had already been articulated in the Queen's declaration[51] More likely, he had realised that so many Conservative MPs were absent that a vote might well have turned into a triumph for the government and thus undermined the aim of the motion.

Hence historians have to explain why such revered rights were abandoned with so little public interest and debate. The best-known current interpretation is that of Olive Anderson, who saw the decision as an expression of the power of liberal ideology, focusing on the motives of leading British politicians, such as Lord Clarendon and James Graham. However, this chapter has shown that while both men certainly shared a liberal mindset, they rather responded to domestic pressure from commercial interests. Moreover, Graham's memorandum, which according to Anderson is the crucial document for understanding British policy, was simply ignored on the question of the 'rule of 1756'. Clarendon had to respond to obvious attempts to organise a new Armed Neutrality that might deny the Baltic to the Royal Navy and play off the French against the British, and American privateers in Russian services were a real danger. The sources presented here also show that American diplomats were willing to link these two issues and use the threat of tacit approval to US privateering activities in Russian service in order to extract British concessions on neutral rights. Britain had to yield to secure its alliance with France and avoid US involvement in the Crimean War. Based on his liberal convictions, Clarendon had wanted to reform Britain's approach to maritime war all along, but only the considerations set out above persuaded the Cabinet to follow him. Therefore Warren Spencer is right to emphasise the importance of US influence, although he somewhat overstates the importance of a memorandum by Mason that had been given to Drouyn de Lhuys after the British decision to grant 'free ships, free goods' had already been made.

The USA was emboldened by its success, a rare feat of determining the course of European great power politics, and would soon exhibit even more initiative regarding neutral rights. However, the question that next occupied the minds of contemporaries followed directly from the compromise presented to the British and French public in March 1854: boasting about unprecedented neutral rights was another way of saying that no navy had ever attempted to vanquish a powerful enemy while operating within a legal straitjacket this tight. Naturally, this begged the question whether it would serve as a shining example of how war was waged in a more enlightened age, or whether it would all go horribly wrong.

2
The Crimean War and Maritime Law

When Britain and France began their naval blockade of Russia under the new rules, neutrals enjoyed the most generous set of regulations ever granted by belligerents. The first part of this chapter will investigate to what extent the allies and the neutrals were satisfied with the new regime, and whether it matched the expectation of protecting British and neutral commercial interests while at the same time throttling Russia into submission. The second and third parts will show that rather than the Crimean War experience, two further strands of wartime diplomacy were crucial to the later decision to accept the Declaration of Paris. Britain made the end of privateering a priority, while the USA attempted to grasp what it perceived as a unique opportunity to secure the new neutral rights permanently, and without any concessions over privateering.

'The dawn of a better day in warfare': The new rules in practice

In 1854 it was obvious that a global web of trade by fast, ocean-going steamers had emerged, but nobody really knew how classic naval action would interfere with it. Moreover, the extent of the privileges granted to neutrals surprised many, and liberal journals such as *The Economist* or the *Edinburgh Review* hailed them as a breakthrough into a more modern and enlightened age, 'the dawn of a better day in warfare'.[1] Other observers wondered whether a blockade under the new rules would have any effect at all, since neutral smugglers would simply divert trade through the land borders and then ship Russian goods under neutral flags.[2] Free traders like Richard Cobden believed that Britain would soon go much further since any blockade satisfying the criterion of effectiveness would necessarily interfere with Britain's and France's interests as the powerhouses of an increasingly interdependent global economic system and 'would be speedily felt as a serious injury to our trade as well as that of France, & we might probably tire of such anti-commercial policy sooner than Russia'.[3]

From the outset, the British approach to maritime law during the Crimean War was shaped by a complex double strategy.[4] On the one hand, the Royal Navy was supposed to cripple Russia's trade and economy by preventing it from exporting its produce. On the other hand, the control of trade would have to be skewed in such a way as to secure the continued importation of vital naval stores, such as hemp, tallow and flax. Russia was by far the most important exporter of these goods, and this could only be achieved by allowing the rerouting of that trade through neutral Prussian ports. This proved highly successful, but as we shall soon see there was more of a debate about whether the blockade under the new liberal setup achieved its main aim, harming Russia.

Once the war had begun, hemp, flax and tallow were moved overland to the nearest Prussian ports for export by sea. Due to the new rules of maritime law, the further transport of this Russian produce in neutral vessels was left entirely unmolested by allied cruisers. A memorandum compiled by the Director General for Taxes in the Prussian Ministry of Finance reveals that during the first year of the Crimean War the exports of flax, hemp and oakum from Prussian ports rose by more than 1 million hundredweight, from 238,764 in 1853 to 1,386,814 a year later.[5] Exports of tallow rose by nearly 40,000 percent, from 1140 hundredweight to 454,781. A memorandum by James Wilson, the Financial Secretary to the Treasury, confirmed that as a 'natural consequence' of granting the 'free ships, free goods' principle Russia's trade continued 'much as it had done before', with Prussian ports replacing Russian ones. Customs Office figures showed that imports from Prussia of hemp, flax and tallow had risen by almost the same proportion as they had declined from Russia (Table 2.1).

Thus Britain was successful in its ambition to sustain imports of important naval stores while closing down Russian ports. However, those were not the only goals that the blockaders wanted to achieve. The most distinctive feature of the Crimean War was how far Britain and France were

Table 2.1 UK imports of hemp, flax and tallow from Russia and Prussia, 1853–4[6]

Imports into UK, in cwt	Russia	Prussia
Tallow 1853	163,314	34
Tallow 1854	36,086	62,643
Hemp 1853	180,394	2,048
Hemp 1854	20,803	113,633
Flax 1853	319,736	133,722
Flax 1854	103,545	495,297
Flaxseed and Linseed 1853	262,328	35,298
Flaxseed and Linseed 1854	145,492	99,619

prepared to go to accommodate neutral interests, placate their own merchants and prevent differences with the practices of their ally. The blockade began with a number of further concessions that substantially limited its effectiveness in the first year. When Britain and France established a joint set of regulations to guide the squadrons at sea, France refused to accept the category of conditional contraband (comparable to modern 'dual use' goods), and, under additional pressure from Sweden, London accepted that coal would not be regarded as contraband.[7] In a circular, the Admiralty made clear that this even applied to ships heading for hostile ports, as long as these were not blockaded.[8] Neutrals would only face prosecution if they transported to Russia any goods that had no other use than to supply the military – for example, arms and ammunition, gunpowder, saltpetre or marine engines.[9]

Moreover, the Russian export trade had a number of unusual features. Foreign merchants would usually buy the entire crop after the harvest from the estates of often cash-strapped noblemen before it could be shipped out of Russia after the Baltic ice melted. While profitable for all concerned in peace time, in war it meant that an early blockade in the Baltic would only hurt British or neutral merchants, since their Russian business partners had already received their advances.[10] Therefore an abundance of time was given to allow these goods to be shipped away, and even Russian-owned vessels were free to join if they left port before 15 May.[11] In addition, the Americans had received a special assurance from the Admiralty that the blockade would be held up further to ensure that any US vessel would have ample time to pass.[12]

Before the Baltic blockade began on 2 June, the allied governments had been in close correspondence about the wording of the blockade announcement to prevent neutral complaints.[13] However, they failed in the admittedly difficult task of satisfying the Americans. While the allies thought that stating individual ports as well as exact geographical details of the blockaded coastline would avoid confusion, a furious James Buchanan appeared in Clarendon's office, protesting that a blockade that applied not only to individual ports but also to hundreds of miles of coastline was rather 'a general interdict of all neutral trade and communication with Russia, than such a blockade of particular ports as had hitherto been usual in the practice of nations'.[14]

While all affected neutral nations were watchful, the representatives of the USA obviously braced themselves for a confrontation over neutral rights. In March 1854 the US Minister in Russia, Thomas Seymour, called for a US frigate to be sent to the Baltic and, unsurprisingly, the Tsar supported the idea, hoping that allied vessels would be 'held in check by the presence of the American flag'.[15] On the day when the blockade began, Seymour was already reporting from St. Petersburg that it was ineffective and therefore possibly illegal.[16] In fact, it put a halt to the commercial activities of the major trading ports, at least until it was realised that the allies had brought very few gunboats that could enter the shallow coastal waters of the Baltic.[17] Soon, enterprising Hanseatic merchants had set up a new company using small steamers to organise regular trade between Memel (today Klaipeda, Lithuania) and the Russian port of Libau (today Liepaja, Latvia).[18] Unable to follow those small steamers into the dangerous shoals and coastal waters of the Baltic, the allied fleet preferred the high seas, but that in turn provoked a further US protest about illegal blockade.

Traditionally, maritime law required the presence of a blockading squadron close to the blockaded port, and, in contrast with the other complaints that Seymour raised, this point was valid and marked the beginning of a controversy that would continue well into the next century: 'Can a line of battleships along the gulf of Finland be a blockade of all ports to the north? Should they not be *actually invested* by a sufficient naval force to make a blockade effective?'[19] His allegation was vindicated by the warning given to the Admiralty by Queen's Advocate John Harding in March 1855: while the two navies had succeeded in blockading the entire Russian coast from Riga to the Prussian border with (at times) only four steamers, it had been plain luck that no neutral had challenged the effectiveness of the blockade because of that 'hazardous and doubtful operation'.[20] Rather than luck, the reason was that no US warship had been available for operations in the Baltic, and Seymour was unable to corroborate his suspicions with first-hand accounts of allied fleet activity. Coupled with the concessions to neutrals that continued throughout the war, this fact enabled the allies to prevent a clash over neutral rights that US diplomats were eager to have. On the other hand, the British government had taken so much care not to offend any foreign or domestic interests with its blockade that it had opened itself up to public ridicule.

A good example is the (non-)blockade of the White Sea coast: while the French had received a Swedish request not to blockade Archangel[21] and the Admiralty was happy about sending only a small squadron to prevent the fitting out of privateers,[22] the *Hull Packet* complained that Britain was 'too polite' in making war and far too concerned about appearing 'civilised', while a major port like Archangel was left unblockaded for no good reason.[23] When the port was finally blockaded on 1 August, most of that year's commerce had been done due to the short shipping season, and there was some justice in the *Daily News'* claim that the blockade had been a complete farce, having begun only once the warehouses had been emptied.[24]

In the Black Sea the situation was even worse: the local commanders had decided – in apparent ignorance of basic rules of maritime law – that the easiest way of blockading the Russian Black Sea coast was simply to close off and control the Bosporus. Fearing an eruption of neutral protest, the British Ambassador in Constantinople, Stratford de Redcliffe, alerted London, and while the Admiralty supported the plan, Queen's Advocate John Harding rejected it as illegal, an interpretation accepted by the Foreign Office. Although Andrew Lambert blames Harding for adopting a 'narrow legalistic interpretation', Harding's intervention prevented a conflict that Washington would have loved to have had.[25] After it had been decided that the army would attack the Crimean peninsula, reducing the navy to a supporting role, Admiral Dundas decided not to blockade the Russian coast at all[26] and instead sent a blockading squadron to the mouth of the Danube.[27] Although under Russian control early in the war, the area was soon evacuated by the Russian Army, and the blockade prevented local Austrian merchants from selling off their grain while *The Times* wondered what the navy might possibly want to achieve.[28]

Thus when the Admiralty announced in January 1855 that the blockade would be renewed and actually extended to all Russian ports in the Black Sea, it committed a serious public relations error.[29] Next to prolonging the pointless Danube blockade, the statement also confirmed that the Russian coast had never been blockaded at all, contrary to what First Lord of the Admiralty James Graham had led the British business community to believe. He had therefore done them serious financial harm and had 'revive[d] the mischievous and exploded system of paper blockades'.[30] The blockade of the Danube was lifted four weeks later, but public criticism of blockade policy had long transcended this issue.[31]

The unpredictable nature of the blockades had so infuriated business circles that by June 1854 the merchants of Hull were collecting signatures for a petition, begging the government to blockade every Russian coast, and preferably at the same time.[32] Later, MP Robert Collier forced Graham to publicly apologise for having told the House of Commons on three separate occasions that the Black Sea was blockaded when it was not.[33] The busy overland trade through Prussia had also astonished the public, and *The Economist*, which had earlier called for continuing Russian imports,[34] changed its stance: a sudden stop of imports would have caused economic turmoil, but now that Russia had withdrawn its troops behind its frontiers and Britain controlled all Russian coastal waters, economic warfare offered 'the only means that will be left open to us to bring the war to a close'. Traders about to pay advances to Russian producers for next season's imports should think twice before doing so, a warning that would certainly have impressed those merchants who knew that the paper's editor, James Wilson, also worked for the Treasury.[35]

Armed with a research paper arguing that the effect of the blockade on the Russian government's finances was minimal, the *Morning Chronicle* concluded that the government's effort to punish Russia while allowing its export trade to remain open was misguided, and that nothing would be achieved as long as Russia could divert its trade through Prussia.[36] *The Times* defended the government, reminding its readers that the diversion of Russian trade was intentional, and that Britain was effectively using Memel as its warehouse for Russian goods that it desired. More stringent efforts to interfere with Russian trade would also hurt the British economy, 'damaging the social interest'.[37] Later, the newspaper even attempted to distil its new philosophy on these matters into a golden rule for belligerent rights at sea: 'That belligerents are not to do anything that shall have a greater tendency to incommode neutrals than to benefit themselves.'[38]

The only politician who publicly demanded a return to the old maritime rights was the Conservative Lord Colchester, later to become Postmaster-General, and he was immediately rebuffed by Granville, Earl Grey and the Earl of Clanricarde, who all argued that it 'would deprive us of that sympathy which is at the present stage of so much importance' and could drive the neutrals towards Russia. Clanricarde even stated that no maritime nation would ever apply them again, 'unless she was prepared to go to war with every civilised nation in the world engaged in commerce'.[39] This was not an attempt to deflect public criticism, but matched what these politicians said in private. Lord Granville believed that if Britain and France had not made the concessions, 'their cooperation as Maritime powers would have been impossible, and they would have justified the expectations of the Czar, who fully expected England getting embroiled, on account of her pretensions as belligerent, with the United States and other neutral powers'.[40]

While there was never a discussion about a return to the old right of search, businessmen began to demand a complete import ban on Russian goods.[41] This solution was also urged upon Clarendon by James Wilson, and in combination with his editorials in *The Economist*, his memorandum on the blockade would shape the public debate.[42] He too agreed that a return to the old rules was impossible, since otherwise 'we should run great risk of embroiling ourselves with other friendly states, and in place of ending the war, we should be likely to extend it'. Nonetheless, the continuing Russian trade via Prussia was the 'natural consequence' of granting the 'free ships, free goods' principle: British imports from Prussia of hemp, flax and tallow had risen by almost the same proportion as they had declined from Russia. However, when it came to harming Russia, the blockade as carried out in 1854 was 'a farce and a dead letter'. Wilson urged an import ban on Russian goods, while British and French consuls in German or other ports would grant certificates of origin to those merchants who could prove that their wares were not originally Russian.[43]

Senior Cabinet ministers and the Committee for Trade of the Privy Council disagreed because they believed that the system of certificates of origin was unworkable. British consuls in Prussia would fight a hopeless struggle trying to police the issue of certificates while Prussian traders were busy cooking up concoctions of Russian and Prussian tallow.[44] Further opposition came from the merchants of Dundee, whose textile industry was the principal importer of Russian flax and hemp, a point that they made in person in Clarendon's office.[45] *The Times* concurred, claiming that a ban would be 'extremely oner-ous' on the British consumer, who would have to pay the higher price. It concluded that 'nothing can be done to increase the restrictions imposed on the trade of Russia, except by rendering the blockade, especially in the Black Sea, far more effective than it has hitherto been'.[46]

This was exactly the line that the new government presented to the public in early 1855. The Aberdeen ministry had fallen because of its incompetent conduct of the Crimean campaign, but in his last weeks as President of the Board of Trade, Edward Cardwell insisted that the blockade of Russia had been a success. There may have been an element of ineptitude in the abortive blockade of the Black Sea, but the Russian merchant navy was annihilated, and the non-existent risk of capture by Russian vessels had caused the marine insurance rate to sink to normal levels. English trade continued as before, while Russia had lost 52 percent of its trade, despite the overland trade through Prussia.[47] In May, his successor, Lord Stanley of Alderley, promised that that year's blockade would overcome all the known problems and surely have the desired effect on the Russian economy.[48] On that day, an import ban was finally rejected by a margin of 16.[49] And so it happened that a debate which had begun because of the universal feeling that the first year of blockade under the new maritime rules had been a complete shambles, and not harmed Russia in any major way, ended with a new government announcing that everything would remain as it was, just better.

The most disconcerting problem that had emerged during the debate was that when the decision to reroute Russian imports through Prussia had been made, nobody had considered that if the overland trade worked one way and gave Britain much-wanted naval stores, it might just as well work the other way and enable Russia to obtain modern rifles and ammunition. Belgian and German arms merchants transported their goods to the Hanseatic towns and then shipped them to East Prussia before they reached Russia by land. This was more than a nuisance, since the technological superiority of their infantry rifles was the only major advantage that the allied armies had against the Russians.[50]

After receiving reports that more than 50,000 rifles were being prepared for export to Russia, the allies first engaged the Belgians.[51] Britain threatened to re-introduce the old right of search for vessels under the Belgian flag or calling in Belgian ports, and the Belgian government implored its merchants to think about the consequences of their new lucrative business 'should the practice of exportation of arms cause England and France to bring into strict exercise their rights at sea as belligerents'.[52] The Netherlands applied additional pressure, fearing that possible punitive measures would be extended to the Dutch flag.[53] The Belgians finally provided detailed lists that named all ships leaving Belgium with arms, and their destinations.[54] Since 10 out of 20 vessels on that list were bound for Hamburg or Bremen, the Hanseatic towns became the next priority.[55] After a letter threatening 'serious measures' if nothing was done against the contraband trade had been ignored, Britain sent a ship to the Elbe estuary to control the papers of all incoming vessels bound for Hamburg, particularly if mentioned on a certain list.[56] But such pinpricks would not suffice to stop the trade through Prussia, and the problem had to be dealt with in Berlin. However, the Prussian case shows that while Britain threatened tough measures, it was unwilling to actually apply them if a neutral remained stubborn.

Clarendon had complained about Prussian arms smuggling to Russia since the first days of war, but without much effect.[57] His diplomat in Berlin, Lord Bloomfield, suggested a blockade of Prussia but admitted that the 'experiment would of course be a highly doubtful one', with potentially dangerous consequences for Britain's chances of winning the war.[58] Clarendon agreed, but also felt that the current state of affairs was intolerable.[59] Three weeks later, French Foreign Minister Drouyn de Lhuys also demanded a blockade of all Prussian ports.[60] However, Bloomfield now warned Clarendon that 'it would be unwise to take a step which would assuredly set the whole Country in a flame'.[61] Wilson warned that even if the hawks in the Cabinet were right and Prussia would accept the blockade without declaring war, the other neutrals, with the USA in the lead, surely would protest against the blockade of the ports of a country with which Britain was at peace.[62]

Early in 1855, the idea of a blockade was revived, this time by Hatzfeld, the Prussian delegate in Paris, who believed it to be the best way of frightening his King into listening more closely to the pro-Western diplomats in the Prussian foreign office.[63] At the same time, Bloomfield reported from Berlin that the contraband trade via Prussia had recommenced earlier than expected.[64] Prussian Prime Minister Manteuffel knew something had to be done to calm the allies, so he bullied the Cabinet into banning the transit trade for contraband goods. However, he only persuaded the pro-Russian sceptics by pointing out that the ban would induce the Russian government 'to more than hitherto meet its needs in arms and ammunition by purchasing from Prussian factories'.[65]

The British press immediately suspected that the trade would carry on, just with more weapons produced in the Zollverein, the German customs union.[66] Soon, naval commanders operating in the region reported that it continued unabated, but Clarendon could do little but send further protests.[67] In his desperation he even turned to the Austrian Foreign Minister for advice.[68] Unfortunately, Vienna was nearly as exasperated with Friedrich Wilhelm IV as London and Paris were, since threats of war were hollow as long as the fighting in the Crimean continued. Hinting at a re-introduction of the old British right of search had frightened the Belgians, and in 1855 it was also considered against the Dutch,[69] but it was never intended to carry out these threats. The problem was that unlike the Belgians, the Prussians knew this: Bernstorff reported from London that while a resort to the old rules had been suggested, 'the opposition of France against this maritime principle and the English concern about risking a rupture with the United States always stand in the way'.[70]

After Sevastopol fell in September 1855, it became clear that the British would sooner endorse outright war against Prussia than confront the Americans on maritime law. After a drastic warning by Bloomfield, Manteuffel promised to double his efforts, but such assurances no longer impressed Clarendon, who dryly retorted that if what the Prussians were doing was neutrality, 'some new definition of it must henceforward find its place in the Law of Nations'.[71] The Prussians asked the Austrians how they intended to fulfil their obligations under the Austro-Prussian alliance treaty of 20 April 1854 in the case of allied action against the Prussian coastline, but they were told that Vienna felt a stronger attachment to its more recent alliance with the allies.[72] On 6 January, Friedrich Wilhelm IV sent a strong warning to the Russian Tsar, pointing out the dangers that Prussia was facing,[73] and one day later Clarendon openly threatened war: 'the neutrality which Prussia for a time maintained is now considered by H[er] M[ajesty's] G[overnment] to be at an end'.[74] Only days after receiving this message, the Prussian government announced that in case of a rejection of the Austrian ultimatum by St. Petersburg, Berlin would follow Vienna and prepare its entry into the war on the allied side.[75] On the same day, Alexander II[76] decided to accept defeat, realising that Russia would have to fight four great powers in 1856.

So did the blockade under the new rules play a part in Alexander II's acceptance that Russia's position in the war was hopeless? Historians have disagreed on this question, some arguing that it was 'not very significant' while others hold that it 'had a very important effect on the war', if only by tying Russian troops at the coast.[77] Most recently, Andrew Lambert has argued that a limited blockade like the one employed against Russia could never have been decisive, but did do the Russian state substantial financial harm. The more compelling reason to accept defeat, however, was Russian fear of an allied onslaught in the Baltic in 1856, supported by new allies.[78] In fact, both of Alexander's motives were closely connected to the new system of neutral rights.

First, the Russian government concluded that Russia had to get out of the war before the campaign of 1856, which was sure to involve major allied naval operations and landings in the Baltic,[79] and all the neutrals in the region had indicated that in that case they would join the allied side.[80] This was not exclusively a consequence of the many concessions that Britain and France had made with regard to neutral rights, but without them these developments would have been highly unlikely or outright impossible, and they certainly came as a shock to the Russians. The second reason why the Tsar decided to end the hostilities was that he was informed by the Minister of Finance that the war would soon cause national bankruptcy.[81] This was a direct result of the loss of revenue caused by the blockade, and it proved that even under the new rules, blockade was still a powerful tool if applied effectively.

Even the rather porous blockade of 1854 led to shortages of strategic goods, such as lead, coal and sulphur,[82] and caused considerable losses for the Russian treasury: the Prussian memorandum cited earlier noted that the Russians must have suffered massive losses in export tolls, since even the vastly increased exports via Prussia only added up to about half of the Russian exports of naval stores in 1853.[83] Equipped with more gunboats that could reach the shallow coastal waters, the second year of blockade in the Baltic was much tighter than before, and in the Black Sea the allied squadron even succeeded in entering the Sea of Azov, conducting a highly successful campaign in that part of the Black Sea to the north of the Crimean peninsula.[84] The 1855 campaign also hurt Russia much more than the first, as Russian export and government revenue figures demonstrate. Although the American Minister in St. Petersburg reported that the Russian economy seemed stable,[85] the financial situation was actually quickly deteriorating, for Russia continued to import goods from abroad while exports were declining (Table 2.2).

Russian export figures divided by country reveal that even without an import ban the trade with France and Britain collapsed completely.[86] Apparently, British traders simply did not believe that the route would remain open when they made their orders for the next year, and so they sought alternatives.[87] Russia's exports could not make up for the shortfall, resulting in a loss in customs revenue in 1855 that was far more significant than in the previous year.[88] Without the possibility of borrowing abroad or raising taxes like more developed economies, these losses made the conduct of war increasingly difficult. Thus, when the new trade figures arrived in the summer of 1855, Clarendon concluded that while the Russian economy appeared unhurt, the impact of the blockade was felt directly in the coffers of the Tsar's treasury.[89]

The new type of blockade achieved exactly what it was meant to: it hurt Russia's capability to wage war by depriving it of important goods and reducing trade revenue while interfering as little as possible with international trade. Remarkably for countries at war, government customs income rose

Table 2.2 Overall value of Russian imports and exports, 1853–7[90]

Russian trade, in million roubles	Imports	Exports
1853	102	148
1854	70.4	65.3
1855	72.7	39.5
1856	123	160
1857	152	170

significantly in France, while it remained stable at a high level in the UK.[91] Furthermore, merchant navy statistics showed that the new rules did not mean an automatic transfer of tonnage from belligerent to neutral merchant navies. Despite the fears evident in commercial circles early in 1854, neither of the two countries experienced a significant decline in merchant shipping registered under their flags.[92]

This section has answered three questions. First, it has established that the new form of blockade allowed Britain to receive strategic goods through neutral ports. The second part revealed that Britain and France were hugely annoyed by the arms smuggling to Russia via the same route, and threatened to re-introduce the old right of search to Belgium and Prussia. However, the Prussians knew that Britain would never dare to confront the USA over this issue. No important politician in Britain advocated a return to the old rules throughout the Crimean War, although the many concessions to neutrals and domestic business interests had exposed the Cabinet to public ridicule. On the other hand, allied generosity paid off in 1856 when Russia surrendered before the threat of a vast Baltic coalition assembled against it. The third section showed that the second year of blockade caused serious damage to Russian finances, proving that a blockade under the new rules could still be effective. However, that does not mean that Olive Anderson is right to argue that liberal neutral rights were made permanent because Britain was pleased with their impact on the naval side of the Crimean War.[93] Russia was always recognised as a special case, and the lessons from the blockade could not necessarily be applied in a war against the USA or France. Sympathy for the new rules came largely from the fact that the alternative was out of the question while the drawbacks seemed manageable. The real motives behind Britain choosing to sign the Declaration of Paris were its desire to end privateering and the rather proactive US diplomacy on neutral rights, as the second and third section of this chapter will show.

'The total suppression of privateering': Britain and letters of marque

Chapter 1 shows that the fear of US privateering was an important reason why Britain compromised on neutral rights. As the neutrals were surprised by and thankful for British generosity, the Cabinet now pondered how to translate neutral goodwill into cooperation to end privateering for good. To understand this concern about a practice that according to many historians had lost all relevance after the end of the Napoleonic Wars,[94] it is important to point out that the strategic threat of American privateers employed against British commerce was not the only bugbear caused by the continued existence of the right to issue letters of marque. The mere possibility that a ship sent on a long voyage now might find itself crossing oceans swarming with privateers upon its return disconcerted British merchants and, crucially, insurers.

This privateering scare began as early as September 1853, when it became evident that the Eastern Question could soon spark a war with Russia, in which Russia would most likely attempt to grant letters of marque to American captains. The well-known New York publisher and politician J. Watson Webb responded to these rumours in a letter to *The Times*, arguing that US neutrality laws were sufficient and American citizens abhorred the idea of privateering missions in foreign service. The editorial comment added to the letter reveals what – from a British perspective – would be the ideal solution: it misrepresented Webb's views as a general condemnation of privateering and expressed the hope that 'to the United States might be reserved the honour of putting down a practice which had so long been a stigma on European civilization'.[95] But when war became a certainty in early 1854, the *New York Times* warned that any laws existing against Russian attempts to fit out privateers in the USA would be subverted: 'The hopes of profit held out will be tempting, the very spirit of adventure, seductive.'[96] Together with the unavoidable clashes about neutral rights, the privateering scare might even undermine London's position as the financial capital of the world and allow New York to benefit while Britain struggled to finance both present and future wars.[97]

British newspapers feared that privateers could endanger British trade worldwide,[98] and in early March, Queen Victoria declared that attempts were under way in several British cities to convert steamers to lightly armed but fast privateers, and exhorted her subjects to refrain from such activities.[99] While the successful fitting out of a Russian privateer in Belfast or Liverpool seemed unlikely, the British and French instructed their consuls to keep an eye on suspicious activities in every harbour worldwide.[100] A striking example of how seriously this threat was taken was the commission of a permanent guard to watch Stanley Harbour on the remote Falkland Islands and defend it against Russian privateers, in particular Americans accepting Russian letters of marque.[101]

While Britain and France had promised not to use letters of marque, the declaration by the Tsar had been silent on the issue.[102] The *National Intelligencer* concluded that this could only mean that Russia aimed to grant letters of marque to 'citizens or subjects of neutral nations, as the inordinate lust of gain may induce to accept this odious and piratical mode of inquiring wealth'.[103] This assessment was shared by the Admiralty: the commander of the Pacific Squadron, Rear-Admiral David Price, told his officers in March 1854 that the main enemy of the squadron were not only Russian frigates in the area, but also the 'numerous privateers it is known will be there'.[104] These fears were no fantasies: when Russian officials pondered their naval options, they quickly agreed on an attempt to use privateers to attack British trade in the Pacific. As the Tsar's military adviser later wrote, 'at bottom, it was the only weapon at our disposal against the naval superiority which England so rigorously exerted against us'.[105] Given its large merchant fleet, huge coastline and traditional anti-British stance on neutral rights, it seemed logical to focus any such attempts on the USA. Earlier plans also included encouraging US merchant vessels to load cargoes for Russia in the hope that British searches of these vessels would ignite conflicts over neutral rights,[106] but these were shelved after Britain and France had granted generous neutral rights.

The man coordinating the attempts to fit out privateers was the Russian Minister in Washington, Eduard Stoeckl, but he found his mission unexpectedly tricky. Although several requests for letters of marque had been received by Russian consulates in San Francisco, New York and New Orleans, the US government did not show the tacit approval that had been hoped for, and the presence of British consuls actively on guard for such ventures made the equipment of Russian privateers in US ports rather difficult. Stoeckl remained optimistic about his eventual success, and believed that a privateering expedition might easily be equipped in San Francisco if the Royal Navy were to attack Russian-Alaska and the 'interests of some American capitalists [were] united with our interests'.[107] Obviously, the reason why there was no Russian privateering in the Crimean War was not that Russia never tried. Rather, Britain and France prevented its success with a series of intelligent measures. The first of these was the British decision not to attack Russian Alaska, but to broker a neutrality agreement between the Russian-American Company and the British-owned Hudson Bay Company, with both governments guaranteeing the inviolability of the two companies' US possessions for the duration of the war.[108] With this clever move, London forestalled Russian attempts to register the entire company as a US business in San Francisco, which were clearly aimed at drawing the USA into the war.[109]

Second, the consistent concessions towards neutrals and in particular the USA meant that the tacit support that Russia had been counting on was never forthcoming. A frustrated Stoeckl was willing to risk fitting out a privateering mission anyway, counting on the support of the pro-Russian Senator of California, William Gwin, but Foreign Minister Nesselrode refused to send the necessary funds because Secretary of State Marcy had made it clear that he would regard such Russian activities in US ports as an unfriendly act.[110] But even in October 1855 the head of the Imperial Navy, Grand Duke Constantine, still hoped to draw on 'American genius and enterprise' for his scheme to break the allied blockade of Russia.[111] However, next to placating neutrals, Britain had also begun to adopt policies that were specifically designed against privateering.

In March 1854, Sir James Graham revived the idea first expressed in *The Times* in October 1853 and suggested a total ban on privateering, to be achieved by a British treaty initiative modelled on the success of the anti-slave trade campaign.[112] The neutrals' goodwill created by granting 'free ships, free goods' should be used to enlist support against privateering, particularly since the neutrals were likely to be receptive. Privateers were not only prone to abuses and tended to cause disputes wherever they operated, but the practice of neutral citizens joining wars against states that their nation was at peace with also entailed considerable diplomatic risks. However, neutral nations could not simply be ordered to ban privateering, and Britain should try to link privateering with piracy as a first step towards supporting efforts to eventually achieve a treaty banning letters of marque. Graham's memorandum was inspired by mid-Victorian disgust for the medieval habits of earlier days, and it ended almost like a sermon:

> We have abolished slavery in the British dominions. We have done more to suppress the Slave Trade than any other nation on the earth. Let us lead the way to extirpate privateering, and to prevent, even during hostilities, the entire suspension of commerce; we then shall have stripped war of a portion of its miseries; we shall have done much in our day and generation to alleviate human suffering and to promote the concord of nations. When will the greatest jurists or the most successful warriors achieve a nobler triumph?[113]

Historians should be careful to avoid the conclusion that such language implies that Graham had lost sight of British interests. The phrases he chose were meant to resonate with a widespread feeling among liberals that privateering was morally wrong. Almost forgotten after Napoleon's defeat put an end to the excesses of French and other privateers, this conviction had re-emerged in Europe following the use of privateers in the Mexican-American War of 1846–8[114] and was gaining strength as liberal ideas entered the political mainstream. Now the *Daily News*, the mouthpiece of political radicalism, singled out letters of marque as a particular evil, claiming that a privateer was 'merely a pirate with a pardon in his pocket'.[115]

However, the political pressure on the government to act against privateering did not come from high-minded moralists but was caused by the fact that the privateering scare damaged business prospects. Conservative MP for Liverpool Thomas Horsfall was the first to demand a global ban on privateering in Parliament, responding to a resolution by the Liverpool Chamber of Commerce.[116] The resolution emphasised that privateers joined wars primarily for private gain and were traditionally perceived as far more prone to violations of neutral rights as vessels under the command of navy officers. Therefore waters in which privateers were known to operate were regarded as particularly dangerous by merchants and, crucially, insurers. The Bordeaux Chamber of Commerce highlighted the convergence of moral and commercial motives in its petition to the French government: the 'total suppression' of letters of marque was the 'demand of humanity, and a commercial interest'.[117] Some French insurers even excluded all risks related to war from their policies,[118] leading to calls and petitions for a state insurance system for the risk of maritime capture.[119] Although the American Minister in London, James Buchanan, personally thought that the privateering scare in European commercial circles was overblown, he too observed that insurance rates were abnormally high because of it.[120]

Meanwhile, Clarendon had followed Graham's suggestion and instructed Foreign Office staff to draft a treaty to ban privateering. He could be sure of support from the French Foreign Ministry, where an internal memorandum investigating the privateering scare also came to the conclusion that letters of marque should be permanently abolished.[121] Clarendon further suggested treating privateers of non-cooperating nations as pirates (which meant execution upon capture) while justifying his initiative as an effort to tame the evils of war:

> We further propose a convention with foreign powers for putting an end to privateers but the Draft of that is not quite ready. [...] Those powers, such as the S[outh].A[merican]. states, who won't join us must expect to be treated as neutrals & to have their subjects dealt with as Pirates. We further intend to bring a bill in to make privateering Piracy. In short we go the whole hog & pay hommage to the civilization of the age by using our best efforts to humanize the barbarous practice of war.[122]

The success of Clarendon's scheme depended on obtaining US consent, but British journals at the time were confident that the USA would accept an end to privateering since US commerce was now so large and exposed, and *The Economist* noted with satisfaction that, even in California, 'generally the abode of violence and wickedness', a local newspaper had proposed a multilateral treaty to ban privateering.[123] When Watson Webb, who had spoken out against privateering by neutrals in October, visited London in March, he was persuaded to endorse the project of a trilateral treaty against privateering, stating that 'if I do not greatly mistake the public sentiment, in Europe and the United States, the day has at length arrived when this relic of barbarism may be even more summarily dispensed with than was the right to traffic in human flesh'.[124] *The Times* enthusiastically supported the idea, but when both items were published in the USA it became obvious that London had gravely misjudged the 'public sentiment' on the other side of the Atlantic.[125]

In an editorial the *New York Times* endorsed privateering as an established belligerent right and rejected any treaty against it because 'any such step would put the United States at a tremendous disadvantage in case of war'.[126] Webb was accused of having allowed himself to be made the 'instrument of his noble dinner friends' in London who had used him for a 'covert attack on American interests'. They had no interests in promoting civilisation and humanity, but simply aimed at furthering British interests in the case of a conflict with the USA.[127] Clarendon's attempt to persuade Buchanan that accepting the treaty would add to the prestige of the USA was met with a similar attitude. During the meeting in which he revealed that Britain had accepted the 'free ships, free goods' principle, he hinted at his ultimate goal and compared privateers to pirates. The American strongly rejected such notions:

> In short, although His Lordship did not propose a Treaty between the two Governments for the total suppression of Privateering, it was evident that this was his drift. In response, I admitted that the practice of Privateering was subject to great abuses; but it did not seem to me possible, under existing circumstances, for the United States to agree to its suppression unless the great naval powers would go one step further & consent that war against private property should be abolished altogether upon the ocean, as it had already been upon land. There was nothing really different in principle or morality betweens the acts of a regular cruiser & that of a Privateer, in robbing a Merchant vessel upon the ocean & confiscating the property of private individuals on board, for the benefit of the Captor.

Buchanan advised Secretary of State Marcy not to accept any possible future treaty proposal, since in a war between the USA and Britain, privateering was Washington's sole hope of success: the Royal Navy vastly outnumbered the US Navy, and the only chance to strike back on the oceans would be to convert parts of the huge US merchant navy into privateers preying on British commerce. But perhaps there might even be a chance of an agreement granting immunity to all private commerce on the oceans if Clarendon really was as animated by noble feelings regarding the future safety of global shipping as he had claimed. In that case the USA should happily accept, since 'the genuine dictate of Christianity & civilization would be to abolish war against private property upon the ocean altogether & only employ the navies of the world in public warfare against the enemy, as their armies were now employed'.[128] Marcy, however, was determined not to abandon privateering under any circumstances:

> Both Great Britain and France, as well as Russia, feel much concerned as to the Course which our citizens will take in regard to privateering. The two former powers would at this time most readily enter into conventions, stipulating that the subjects or citizens of the party, being a neutral, who shall accept commissions or letters of marque, and engage in the privateer service, the other party being the belligerent, may be treated as pirates. A stipulation to this effect is contained in several of our treaties, but I do not think the President would permit it to be inserted in any new one

[...] This Government is not prepared to listen to any proposition for a total suppression of privateering. It would not enter into any convention whereby it would preclude itself from resorting to the merchant marine of the country, in case it should become a belligerent party.[129]

Even though the New York Chamber of Commerce followed Liverpool's lead and demanded US efforts to 'extinguish privateering',[130] the Foreign Office realised that a treaty with the USA was out of the question, and the plan to label privateering as piracy in an official declaration was also dropped, since executing American citizens with Russian letters of marque would cause serious diplomatic complications. However, Clarendon then hit upon an idea not included in Graham's memorandum, but mentioned in the Dano-Swedish declaration of neutrality made in January 1854: it was, as Queen's Advocate Harding had noted, the first of its kind to not only pro- hibit the fitting out of privateers but also to categorically refuse privateers access to the nation's ports, except in the case of duress.[131] After war had been declared, King Oskar of Sweden-Norway confirmed the closure of his ports to privateers and also banned the sale of prizes captured by privateers.[132] Soon, Buchanan reported that he had been pressured by Clarendon to name the exact steps that the US government had taken to prevent the possible use of its ports by privateers.[133]

A number of states followed the Scandinavian recommendation to adopt the new rules[134] and, within a month Spain, all three Hanseatic towns, Oldenburg, Mecklenburg-Schwerin and the Kingdom of the Two Sicilies all closed their harbours to privateers.[135] The Netherlands' declaration even equated privateers with pirates.[136] At first glance these states were acting against their immediate economic interest, since money could have been earned from Russian privateers. But for the same reasons that persuaded the British business community to speak out against privateering, those neutrals following the Swedish model had a sound economic as well as moral case, trying to ensure lower insurance rates for their shipping and keeping the lawlessness associated with privateering away from their doorsteps.

Yet not all neutrals acted on their own initiative, and Britain began to apply pressure on those who were slow to learn. In a circular sent to all maritime powers, Clarendon praised the generosity of the allied govern- ments in limiting their belligerent rights, but then demanded 'in the spirit of just reciprocity' that neutrals should not only prevent the fitting out of Russian privateers but also adopt the new Swedish rule and deny privateers access to their port facilities.[137] This letter inspired a second wave of neu- trality declarations banning privateers from entering national ports, among others Austria, Belgium, Hanover, Portugal, Brazil, Argentina and Chile.[138] Belgium and the Kingdom of the Two Sicilies even issued special regula- tions against privateers.[139] The Austrian case is particularly revealing since the problem of privateering was not even mentioned in the initial internal deliberations over the neutrality declaration.[140] The clearest example of British involvement was the Kingdom of Hawaii: the first neutrality declaration of King Kamehameha III only prohibited the participation of his subjects in privateering ventures, but following discreet British pressure the Royal Council proclaimed that, irrespective of the actual wording, this ban of course also referred to the admittance of privateers into Hawaiian ports.[141] The combined effect of these port closures was swift, and soon the first commentators began to wonder whether privateering had lost its viability. The French *Journal du Havre* directly addressed the insurers who had been so quick to increase their premiums for the war risk of merchant vessels and pointed out that the recent port closures had made successful privateering virtually impossible. Privateers needed access to neutral ports to sell their prizes and obtain supplies, but the closure of most neutral ports to privateers meant that privateering had become much more difficult than during the Napoleonic Wars. Moreover, privateers needed vessels that were fast enough to evade enemy cruisers, which by 1854 meant steamers. These, however, would be much more dependent on port access for coal and maintenance than a sailing ship.[142]

In conclusion, even though the attempt to ban privateering by treaty was abandoned early on, the allied attempts to prevent Russian privateering worked. Clandestine Russian attempts to fit out ships in US ports came to nothing and, against all expectations, no Russian privateers ever made it to the open sea. The new, unexpectedly liberal rules agreed in March 1854 meant that Britain and France had not only prevented a third Armed Neutrality and persuaded the Americans not to give tacit approval to Russian privateering, but could also point towards their enlightened stance on maritime law to demand favours in return. The initiative to close ports to privateers came from Sweden, but Clarendon was quick to adopt the idea and ensured that a majority of neutrals acted likewise. Rumours about Russian corsair captains continued to be spread throughout the war[143] but no longer affected insurance rates like the earlier privateering scare. The danger and disruption to British and French commerce had ended because of the neutral port closures, which also acted as powerful precedents in Britain's campaign to ban privateering as piracy. In a speech given in October 1854, Prime Minister Lord Aberdeen was already talking about privateering in the past tense: 'we have, by our example, put an end to privateering, a most intolerable relic of a barbarous age, and which the world will now probably never see revived'.[144] From a US perspective, such views were rather disconcerting.

'Recognized throughout the civilized world' – the US treaty campaign

Whereas Britain pondered possible strategies to achieve a global ban on privateering, the US government was determined to attain global recognition for the liberal neutral rights granted by the allies at the beginning of the Crimean War. The Scandinavians had been instrumental in forcing these concessions but seemed satisfied when they were promised that the Royal Navy would not apply the right of search to their ships for the duration of the war.[145] If Americans wanted to secure these rights on a permanent basis, avoiding insecurity and renewed negotiations between neutrals and belligerents before every war, they would have to do it themselves. American Minister in Paris John Mason urged Marcy to grasp this unique opportunity:

> The combination of circumstances is most auspicious to the establishment of our cherished principles of neutral rights [...] There is, in my opinion, an anxious desire to avoid any collision with us [...] I feel an anxiety, which I have difficulty in adequately expressing, that the opportunity should not be lost.[146]

The problem was how to actually create a new rule of international law. Traditionally, this process was a painfully slow one: consistent state practice of the major powers was finally confirmed as 'customary law' by the leading jurists if they could also agree on a philosophical deduction of the new norm from established principles of the law of nature. In an age when the 'progress of civilization' was increasingly perceived as the supreme guideline, there had of course been attempts to speed up this process. Britain had pioneered the idea of creating unanimous state practice more quickly by establishing a spider web of bilateral treaties, designed to enforce the ban of the global slave trade as an international norm. Secretary of State William Marcy agreed that there was a window of opportunity to achieve the same for the 'free ships, free goods' principle without any concessions in the field of privateering, which Britain would surely demand in a bilateral treaty.[147] By early April 1854, he was already negotiating a treaty with Russia that included the two principles granted by the allies in March.[148]

The official invitation to start an international campaign was clothed in invocations of the common struggle for the principles of the Armed Neutrality, and, unsurprisingly, Tsar Nicolas I responded.[149] Next to the obvious benefits of securing principles that Russia had proclaimed since 1780, it was a rare opportunity to demonstrate that he still had powerful friends. The Russians were even willing to throw diplomatic convention over board when the Americans suggested dropping the usual formalities of joining a treaty between sovereign nations, instead 'requiring from other powers nothing but a formal declaration that they accede to it'.[150] In a private letter sent on 14 April, Marcy revealed the full scheme to Eduard Stoeckl, Russia's Minister in Washington:

> We are going to ask France and England to sign this convention; if they refuse, as I have every reason to think, we will conclude it with you alone

in the first instance. We will then put forward the same proposals to the maritime powers of the second rank. Having less means of defending their rights, they are, because of that very fact, interested in seeing them determined by rules in a definitive manner; and we have no doubt that they will give their consent to them, provided that they succeed in escaping English influence.[151]

An added benefit of the initiative was its potential to split the Anglo-French alliance.[152] This alliance was a major obstacle to the expansionist foreign policy of the Pierce administration, which aimed at extending US influence at the expense of European nations holding colonial possessions in the Western hemisphere, primarily the Spanish in Cuba, but, because of the Central American Mosquito coast, also the British.[153] Washington was afraid that the two European naval powers would react by asserting their US interests in close cooperation. In this situation the Crimean War was a godsend, since British military resources would be tied up by the struggle against Russia. For all ambitions that could only be fulfilled against British opposition, now was the time to act, whether in Central America or regarding neutral rights. Because of France's traditional stance on neutral rights, maritime law seemed the most promising issue over which the USA could drive a wedge between Britain and France.

Russia was a natural choice as the first treaty partner because it was an established great power, and Marcy could point to the role of Catherine the Great in organising the Armed Neutrality that once fought for the same principles. However, Russia's prominence in this venture made it rather obvious that what was intended was an unfriendly act against Britain. Thus Marcy needed to reassure potential signatories that joining the initiative would not cause negative repercussions for them, and emphasised the Queen's proclamation of 28 March. Here, Britain had recognised the justice of the 'free ships, free goods' principle, and the allies would be in an awkward position if they granted the principle in the spring but rejected its endorsement in the summer, and once they joined the new treaty all other nations would follow.[154] Furthermore, Marcy tried to forestall allegations of organising an anti-British alliance in secret by informing both Britain and France first. For that reason, the official US reply to the notification of the new rights granted by the allies was not the simple expression of gratitude that was expected in Paris and London.[155] Instead, Marcy explained why his government would seek to turn the rules into permanent norms of international law by signing agreements with other powers:

> Notwithstanding the sincere gratification which Her Majesty's declaration has given to the President, it would have been enhanced if the rule alluded to had been announced as one which would be observed not only in the present, but in every future war in which Great Britain shall be a party [...] To settle the principle that free ships make free goods, except

articles contraband of war, and to prevent it from being called again in question from any quarter under any circumstances, the United States are desirous to unite with other Powers in a declaration that it shall be observed by each, hereafter as a rule of international law.[156]

Clarendon's initial reaction only enhanced Marcy's optimism; when Buchanan announced that the USA would seek to secure the neutral rights by treaty, Clarendon interrupted him and declared that 'this will make no difference, the precedent has now been set & it will not be departed from in future wars'.[157] Perhaps intended to discourage the USA from fervent campaigning, it only provided further encouragement. The French government deplored the move, not least because it put it in a very uncomfortable position.[158] Having repeatedly referred to the perfect agreement between France and the USA regarding neutral rights in his attempt to put pressure on Britain, Drouyn de Lhuys now could hardly argue against the US proposition. Therefore a later report by the Prussian Minister in Paris that Drouyn tried to informally discourage the Americans from sending a draft convention to France is entirely credible.[159] It also underlines what an unpleasant surprise it must have been for the allies once they learned that the first treaty that the USA had signed in its quest to change international law had been with Russia. The treaty signed in Washington on 22 July 1854 contained both the 'free ships, free goods' principle and the guarantee that neutral goods on enemy vessels were free from capture, but the really innovative part was the third article:

> It is agreed by the high contracting parties that all nations which shall or may consent to accede to the rules of the first article of this convention, by a formal declaration stipulating to observe them, shall enjoy the rights resulting from such accession as they shall be enjoyed and observed by the two powers signing this convention. They shall mutually communicate to each other the results of the steps which may be taken on the subject.[160]

Intending to invent a new procedure by which states could be assembled as supporters of neutral rights as quickly and informally as possible, the treaty pushed the boundaries of international law, since it did not state that a new treaty partner needed to formally ratify the agreement, or procure assent from the original parties. Any state unilaterally announcing its intention to join 'by a formal declaration' would *ipso facto* be entering a treaty agreement with the two original signatories as well as any other state deciding to do likewise in the future. Obviously the two signatories to this novel type of treaty aimed at an international campaign of unprecedented scope and speed. The treaty was ratified by the US senate only three days after it was signed, and, even before the official copy of the treaty had arrived in St. Petersburg, invitations were sent to selected nations in several waves.[161]

In this new form of international law-making, every state counted as long as it was generally recognised as such, but if important powers joined early on, their example would convince smaller nations. Therefore the first invitations sent out in early August went to a select few. All of the chosen states were traditional supporters of liberal neutral rights, had a large merchant navy and had signed similar treaties with the USA in the past. Furthermore, it was hoped that the Netherlands, Prussia and the Hanseatic towns[162] would not be deterred by English pressure, and in the case of the former two the pro-Russian sympathies of the courts were well known. The other invitations of the first wave went to France and Britain, but Marcy never expected these states to join. Rather, it put the allies under pressure to name good reasons why the European neutrals should not join after they had granted the principle earlier.[163] The second wave of invitations was sent out a month later, and went to all other European neutrals that had some commercial significance, such as Denmark and Portugal.[164] The idea was that negotiations with these states would be eased by the previous accession of either the Netherlands or Prussia. Yet the campaign was not an exclusively European one, and one day later Marcy sent out invitations to the states of the Western hemisphere.

Still, the Americans pinned their greatest hopes on the Prussians. A treaty concluded with Frederick II in 1785 was the most liberal commerce and navigation treaty of its age, not only abolishing the category of contraband but also granting the vessels of one party freedom to trade 'as in full peace' if the other was at war with a third power. These rules had been carried over to the later treaties of 1809 and 1828, but it can safely be said that the Prussian elite were not overly concerned with maritime law of warfare in the decades afterwards, and when the US treaty arrived in Berlin, Prime Minister Otto von Manteuffel was mystified.[165] Clearly a diplomatic game unknown to him was being played here, and he asked his senior diplomats in Paris, London and Vienna as well as some of his Cabinet colleagues for advice. Manteuffel's first instinct was to sign, because the principle that neutral goods were immune from seizure on enemy ships was not included in the former bilateral treaties, and it might work in Prussia's favour in case of war. Furthermore, the USA could abrogate the commerce and navigation treaty of 1828 at any time, whereas the new proposal was a permanent commitment.[166] Still, he told his three senior diplomats that he suspected further unknown implications and asked them to find out 'whether and how such a treaty has been directed to the local government and what the reception has been'.[167]

From Paris, Count Hatzfeld reported that American Minister John Mason had mentioned an international campaign on neutral rights and asked whether Prussia would join. However, Hatzfeld was unsure about the details because the Prussian's English was, by his own admission, 'as good as that of a Spanish cow' and the American was unable to converse in French.[168] Later conversations with Drouyn de Lhuys and Cowley only revealed that both claimed to have never heard about any US campaign,[169] and the same was reported from the court in Vienna.[170] Clarendon also claimed that no US offer had been submitted, but he seemed suspiciously well briefed on the issue. He gave the Prussian Minister Bernstorff a lecture on English liberality and benevolence, highlighting that in its desire to humanise warfare, Britain had not only granted unprecedented neutral rights but also supported a more important principle: the abolition of privateering. War had to be waged by governments, not private individuals; and letters of marque were nothing but licensed piracy and a relapse into barbarism. The USA had chosen to accept only one of the two principles and ignored the other. Clarendon went on to claim that 'countless' American adventurers were already waiting for their chance to prey on British merchant vessels, but did not forget the Prussian interest in the abolition of letters of marque:

> When Prussia was engaged in war with Denmark [in 1848/50] the North-American government suggested to the Danish government to issue letters of marque to its merchant captains. If Copenhagen had not declined, Prussia would soon have witnessed an immense number of American pirates in the Baltic and other seas which would have destroyed its commerce.[171]

This was clearly news to Manteuffel, who put three big question marks next to this paragraph.[172] Still, the story impressed Bernstorff, who recommended banning privateering because 'this barbaric custom could be very dangerous for Prussia'. However, the most important benefit would be the prospect of achieving Britain's permanent acceptance of neutral rights by supporting the quest to end privateering. Manteuffel's Cabinet colleagues were less inclined to support London. Minister for Trade August von der Heydt saw the US offer as a request for assistance in its attempt to break Britain's supremacy on the oceans, and argued that it would be in Prussia's interest to cooperate:

> If the core of the matter is, as may be assumed, the struggle for supremacy on the ocean, if the intention is to break British power with the self-evident prospect of succession, then Prussia indeed has no interest to wish that England's supremacy should be left untouched. At all times, the minor maritime powers [...] have been united in the interest of neutral rights, if not in action then in their aims and wishes, against the mightiest maritime power that would molest and oppress their seaborne commerce in the case of war.

Next to joining the informal coalition that secured the 'maritime balance of power' against the strongest sea power of today, Britain, it would also be wise to sign a treaty with the USA since the latter would be the strongest sea power in the future.[173] Finally, Britain could hardly condemn Prussia for embracing principles that it had itself proclaimed a few months earlier. In short, not following Prussia's long-term interest because of a fear of offending Britain would amount to 'stupid self-effacement'. That position was later backed by Minister for War Count Waldersee.[174]

Manteuffel accepted both arguments and attempted to outplay both Britain and the USA, while appearing to be a willing partner to each of them. In his instruction to the Prussian Minister in Washington, Baron von Gerolt, he wrote that Britain and France were fully justified in viewing the proposed convention as the 'seed of a coalition opposing them'. Furthermore, it was unforeseeable who would later join that agreement and enter into treaty obligations with Prussia. Nonetheless, the government had concluded that it was in Prussia's best interest 'to see the crushing naval superiority of England reduced to a level corresponding to the relative power of the other states participating in navigation'. Thus, Gerolt should begin negotiations by stating Prussia's general concurrence. If the US reply revealed that no important power had signalled consent so far, Gerolt should convey how valuable it would be if Prussia was the first to commit, and then extract concessions, in particular a bilateral ban on privateering. Thereby, Prussia gained a lever to win time, and Britain could see that Prussia was not an enemy but a friend: 'Irrespective of the predominant interest Prussia itself has in this matter, it will presumably correspond to the wishes of England if we take the initiative vis-à-vis the United States regarding privateering.'[175]

Naturally, Manteuffel also informed London about Prussia's stance on privateering, while on the same day drafting full powers for Gerolt to sign a convention without this addition.[176] He also wanted to know who else was negotiating with the Americans and sent instructions to sound out the governments in Stockholm, Copenhagen, The Hague, Lisbon, Turin and Naples.[177] Finally, public opinion had to be prepared for this double-edged approach to foreign policy, especially since Prussia's elite were largely unaware that their nation abhorred privateering.[178] An article in the widely read semi-official *Preußische Correspondenz* hailed the treaty concluded between Russia and the USA, with one exception:

> We miss the solemn renouncement of the right to issue letters of marque, a practice that debases that character of naval war by confederation with licensed piracy [...] We hope that after the conclusion of the present war this matter will be – like the interesting questions regarding the exercise of the right of search – satisfactorily resolved in a joint agreement of all major maritime powers.[179]

Soon, Manteuffel learned that most nations had been much more cautious than the Prussians. The Dutch had already rejected the US offer on

22 September because in the present situation a treaty with the USA was much more likely to create tensions with the allies than to secure any gains for the Netherlands.[180] Accordingly, they received a commendation from Paris for their 'excellent sens de politique'.[181] The Hanseatic towns adopted the same position, but also found it opportune to lie to the Prussians and claim that they had never received a US offer.[182] Thus all of the states that Marcy had included in the 'first wave' of invitations had refused to cooperate, and the replies from the states approached in the 'second wave' proved to be even more disappointing. The Spanish King expressed his sympathies for the proposal, but wanted to consult other powers before making a decision.[183] Portugal stated the same, but made it clear that it would have to find out, in the words of the American Minister in Lisbon, 'whether the local English minister would put obstacles in the way or not'.[184] The Swedish government argued that after Britain had surprisingly yielded to its demands, 'it might look discourteous in the Northern Powers to say more upon the subject at present'. Further pressure only resulted in a formal statement that Sweden rejected an immediate accession to the treaty.[185] The Danes feared that the US initiative might mean the beginning of a new Armed Neutrality. If Britain returned to the old principles during the present war, would the coalition gathered around the US-Russian treaty be expected to fight it out? Having experienced unpleasant encounters with the Royal Navy earlier in the century, these were understandable concerns, and Foreign Minister Christian Bluhme summarised the Danish interest as 'avoiding anything that might lead to a kind of armed neutrality at sea or even to an embarrassment regarding England'.[186]

In contrast, the King of the Two Sicilies welcomed everything that might embarrass the government in London. Only a few weeks earlier, Palmerston had threatened to send a fleet to Naples after the Secretary of the British embassy had not been admitted to the box of the theatre director. No action had been taken after an appalled Queen Victoria had complained to Lord Clarendon, but the affair had certainly left an impression on King Ferdinand II.[187] He immediately accepted the US invitation and sent full powers to sign the convention in late November.[188] Furthermore, his vision of the 'maritime balance of power' certainly had an aggressive edge. When the Americans rewarded Naples with an improved commerce treaty that included most-favoured-nation status,[189] it was the Sicilian lead negotiator, Don Guiseppe Arpino, who suggested a formal Armed Neutrality, since 'if the present war was protracted, a league of neutral nations, for the assertion and maintenance of such rights, would be of the greatest importance'.[190]

While most European neutrals would have agreed, such open support for the US campaign was an exception. Most states invited by Washington asked London for a second opinion, or declined to be involved in this openly anti-British initiative straight away. Together with Naples, the Prussians were the only European state that had welcomed the US offer, and despite their elaborate double strategy they were now on record as the only great power supporting not only the principles but also the way chosen to enforce them. When London realised the crucial importance of the Prussian-US negotiations, the British Minister in Berlin, Lord Bloomfield, tried to pressure Prussia into asking for an additional article banning privateering, and was relieved to hear that Prussia had done so months earlier.[191] Nonetheless, Bernstorff warned from London that Prussia's role in the busy arms smuggling to Russia might suggest an even more conciliatory course. The *Morning Post*, a newspaper widely known to be Lord Palmerston's mouthpiece, had for the first time called for drastic action to curb the overland trade to Russia, advocating a formal blockade as the first step towards certain war with Prussia.[192] Therefore this was not the right moment to anger Britain further by signing a treaty with the USA.[193]

A few weeks later, Manteuffel learned that Washington had declined an amendment banning privateering. Secretary of State Marcy claimed that in the case of a war against a superior maritime power, the USA would have no other means of defence than to issue letters of marque to its own citizens and that of other nations. Manteuffel highlighted the last phrase, since it went beyond the position usually taken by the USA that letters of marque should only be given to nationals of the country that they were defending.[194] Fully aware of Prussia's difficult position regarding Britain, Prussian Minister Gerolt had responded with an almost Machiavellian suggestion: if the US President explained his position on privateering in his upcoming State of the Union address, all other maritime nations could consider these arguments and decide whether it was in their interest to conclude treaties without a clause on letters of marque. After Marcy had promised that President Pierce would accept the Prussian request, Gerolt wrote a note to lay out the Prussian position. He began by claiming that privateering was a barbarous practice insulting the spirit of the age, and reminded the Americans that Benjamin Franklin had suggested its abolition in 1789. Anticipating that Pierce would justify privateering with the need for self-defence against an enemy with a superior navy, Gerolt shrewdly pointed to the Prussian example during the war against Denmark, when the government had declined several requests for letters of marque even though Prussia only possessed two warships.[195]

Thus Marcy now found himself in a very difficult position. No European state had joined the US-Russian treaty except for the Kingdom of the Two Sicilies. The only important power that had not directly refused to get involved had just forced the President to elaborate on the philosophical underpinnings of privateering in the State of the Union address. The campaign had been even less successful in the Western hemisphere, where it had been undermined by the poor transport connections in many parts of South America, and in the case of Mexico by the failure of the local diplomat to grasp what it was all about. The proposal sent to Mexico simply urged the resident to 'promptly' conclude a convention, but James Gadsden explained that, happily, both principles had already been secured in relation to Mexico in a treaty more than two decades ago, and that he had instead suggested renegotiating the entire relationship of the two countries regarding commerce and navigation. A clearly irritated Marcy replied that the existence of the 1831 treaty 'had not been lost sight of' but that the intention was to affirm the principles as permanent and immutable for all nations, and that he should therefore invite the attention of the Mexican government to the subject 'at the earliest opportunity'.[196] Increasingly desperate, Marcy even sent out an invitation to the island nation of Hawaii, previously not deemed sufficiently important to be included.[197]

In November the treaty with Russia was published on the title page of the *New York Times* in an attempt to recover lost momentum for the campaign.[198] But by the time President Pierce had to lay his cards on the table in the annual State of the Union address, only Venezuela had offered its support, and even Caracas had taken care to adopt the principles, not the treaty.[199] Obviously, the task at hand was to describe the failure of the campaign as an encouraging start and persuade more nations to join the US-Russian treaty. In his speech, Pierce placed the actions of his administration in the tradition of the 'celebrated confederacy of armed neutrality' and claimed that the joint declaration on the rights of neutrals by Britain and France had offered an opportunity to make these doctrines a part of international law 'by means of special conventions between the several powers of Europe and America'. Russia and the King of Naples had acted promptly, and, while none of the other powers had signed treaties so far, Pierce saw reason for optimism in the fact that no state had spoken out against it.

Now turning to Prussia, the President warned that 'the only apparent obstacle to their general adoption is in the possibility that it may be encumbered by inadmissible conditions.' Although the King of Prussia 'entirely approve[d]' of the project, he had proposed an additional article banning privateering. The USA 'could never listen to such a proposition' since letters of marque were essential for the defence of the Union, especially when the strongest maritime power in Europe had a fleet that was ten times the size of the US Navy. The abolition of privateering was only desired by nations that owned large navies, since, if adopted as an international rule, the commerce of a nation with a small navy would be 'very much at the mercy of its enemy' when attacked by a great naval power. Pierce then added an idea that would soon develop a life of its own: the USA might be willing to consent to an abolition of privateering, but only if the Europeans took the first step: 'Should the leading powers of Europe concur in proposing, as a rule of international law, to exempt private property upon the ocean from seizure by public armed cruizers, as well as by privateers, the United States will readily meet them upon that broad ground.'[200]

This last bit of the speech received a surprisingly positive reception in Britain, where it was supported in a much-discussed paper of the Statistical Society,[201] and even *The Times* declared that it had no doubt that modern warfare would gradually develop in this direction. For the present, however, the paper found it hard to believe that 'although the example of all the belligerents in the present war has proscribed that most barbarous practice of maritime warfare', President Pierce still appeared to regard privateering as a legitimate form of defence.[202] A gleeful Lord Clarendon told Prussian Minister Bernstorff that he was wondering why Pierce had chosen to include this subject in his speech, since it had presented the Prussian government in a very positive light and his own administration in a very bad one. After all, privateering was true piracy, irreconcilable with the current state of civilisation. The examples that Clarendon chose to underline his point illustrate that he was not only appalled by privateering but genuinely afraid of it: one great American screw-propelled steamer of 300 horsepower would be capable of scaring the commerce off an entire ocean, and, if the USA was at war, all seas would be covered by privateers.[203] But had the impression created by the message really been as bad as Clarendon thought, or was Marcy right in hoping that the clear exposition of the US position would help the other nations realise that their interests were best served if they acted in conjunction with the USA?[204]

The Kingdom of Hawaii certainly thought the latter, and it became the first state to join the US-Russian treaty by means of a simple declaration.[205] Nicaragua, with its internal politics now heavily under US influence, published a similar declaration three months later.[206] Peru and Bolivia declined to join immediately and, like Mexico, preferred to use the opportunity for a renegotiation of their commercial treaties with the USA, which were eventually signed after the end of the Crimean War.[207] In Europe, the US government was even less successful. The Two Sicilies joined the US-Russian treaty by formal convention on 13 January 1855, and the US Senate rushed to ratify it on 3 March.[208] But the reports about the swift negotiations in Naples had alarmed the local French Minister, who warned Paris that the King would soon join 'an entente, a sort of collective manifestation' in favour of neutral rights, and that similar talks with Prussia seemed promising.[209] In response, France sent a circular to the major neutral powers and warned them not to join: without the signature of France or Britain, the treaty would be useless, and if states followed the Russians and joined nonetheless, it would have to be regarded as an unfriendly act against the allies. The Netherlands, Belgium, Portugal,[210] Sweden, Denmark and Sardinia all promised not to get involved, and when Naples still went ahead, the French Ambassador in London, Walewski, concluded that King Ferdinand II must have 'lost his head'.[211]

The way in which France and Britain used their influence did not remain unnoticed in Washington, and for Marcy it offered a welcome explanation as to why the Europeans had failed to embrace his initiative. Whereas, as we have seen, most states rejected the initiative before asking London, it fitted Marcy's world-view to assume that his plans had been spoiled by Britain. He was especially disappointed by the Dutch, whose swift rejection was 'unexpected', and in a letter to the local US diplomat he claimed that they were under the influence of 'some controlling power'.[212] When the American Minister in Portugal, John O'Sullivan, reported that despite a positive start he had ultimately been unsuccessful, Marcy consoled him by explaining that this result 'does not surprise the president':

> We have traced to the Allies – particularly Great Britain – an early and active interference among the European powers against the proposition which this government has submitted to them. The excuse in nearly all instances for not acting upon the subject is the same offered to you by the Portuguese Government, the pendency of the war. Nearly all powers profess favorable views of the principles presented, and indicate that, at a proper conjuncture, of political affairs in Europe, the will negotiate on the subject.[213]

Still, many observers were surprised that neither Britain nor France condemned the US campaign in a direct reply. Marcy himself was perplexed by the fact that no answer from London or Paris was forthcoming,[214] but finally Buchanan provided the explanation: he had simply not forwarded the proposal for six months. When he first mentioned it to Clarendon, the latter took it as a personal insult, disrespectful of his efforts to achieve a relaxation of belligerent rights:

> You were the first person I consulted about the adoption of this rule, and you are fully aware of the difficulties we had to encounter in adapting it. The lawyers, who are a very powerful class, were violently opposed to it and talked as if they believed it would ruin the country. We think, however, it is a rule in accordance with modern civilization, but the conclusion of such a treaty under existing circumstances is a different affair.[215]

Thus Buchanan knew that a formal proposition would be most unwelcome, although in his opinion the Cabinet as a whole was not actually opposed to the 'free ships, free goods' principle. A formal rejection, on file in the Foreign Office, might in turn make things more difficult for 'a future Ministry, desirous of pursuing the correct course'. He had therefore chosen to 'bide his time' and simply do nothing. For the same reason, no formal invitation was made in Paris after Drouyn de Lhuys had informed American Minister Mason that France would have to decline because of the English alliance.[216]

After all of these disappointments, Marcy's last hope was that the Prussians would sign the treaty without a clause on privateering. The President had responded to the Prussian wish and laid out his rationale for sustaining letters of marque in his Annual Message, and he urged Berlin to drop these 'inadmissible conditions' and join the US campaign. The Prussian Minister, Gerolt, supported that call, arguing that even without London or Paris signing up, a treaty between Prussia and the USA would have a certain moral effect.[217] But Trade Minister von der Heydt, earlier the most hawkish Cabinet member, now counselled caution since signing the treaty might escalate the increasingly serious Anglo-Prussian conflict over Berlin's neutrality. Instead, the negotiations should be kept pending for as long as possible. Thereby Prussia would be in a position where it could quickly sign the treaty without the privateering clause 'as soon as our position regarding the present war or the relationship between the United States and Great Britain should let it appear desirable'.[218]

Manteuffel shared these sentiments and had been unimpressed by the President's message. Most maritime nations had a smaller navy than the USA, but like Prussia favoured an abolition of privateering. Prussia now appeared in the best possible light, and Gerolt should avoid being pushed towards a clear decision to accept or abandon the treaty as it was but continue to negotiate.[219] With this reply the US campaign to establish the 'free ships, free goods' principle by means of a treaty campaign came to an end. Marcy could have no interest whatsoever in protracted discussions with the Prussians. Had it become known to him, he would have been much more pleased by an idea floated internally by the Prussian Admiralty: as the President had also mentioned the complete immunity of private property at sea in wartime in his speech, why should Prussia not use the upcoming peace congress to promote it and put it on the conference agenda? As a first step, a motion at the Diet of the German Confederation might be used to gather the support of the other German states, and then all maritime nations would most likely join the bandwagon.[220] As this book will demonstrate, the idea of using a European congress for a reform of maritime law would soon become a recurrent theme.

Marcy's attempt to exploit Britain's weakness had ended in a coalition with the Tsar of Russia, the equally autocratic King of the Two Sicilies and the notoriously erratic King Kamehamea III of Hawaii. The fundamental mistake was to use a treaty with Russia as the starting point of the campaign. Drafting a convention that allowed for a swift and simple accession was innovative and worked with some American states, but for the Europeans it meant that they would have to take sides in a war between European great powers, and choose the weaker party. Hence it was unsurprising that most nations were rather cautious. The second drawback of choosing Russia was that the Tsar proved to be a very passive ally. Russian diplomats were instructed to support the local American diplomats in their efforts,[221] but were only to formally invite nations to join the US-Russian treaty after the Americans had done so.[222] This led to the absurd result that, for nearly a year, Belgium was not invited at all because it had been forgotten by the US State Department. Only after the Americans discovered their mistake and submitted a formal invitation in April 1855 did the Russians follow, sending an invitation of their own in May.[223]

Another important reason for the failure of the campaign was that the two mightiest sea powers actively sought to thwart it. Clarendon later remembered that all nations immediately asked London how they should respond, and followed his advice to ask for a clause against letters of marque.[224] That is an exaggeration, since many states declined without asking London or Paris, while others forgot to ask and had to be reminded. But it is true that the discreet work of the British and French diplomats ensured that all nations knew that an embrace of the US proposal would be viewed very unfavourably by Europe's leading powers. However, they knew as well as the Americans that most of the smaller nations had only rejected the invitation because they feared a collision with Britain and, like the Portuguese Foreign Minister, 'would very much like to come back to the idea once the war was over'.[225] A second US campaign was a certainty, and would be much more difficult to undermine.

As Chapter 3 will show, the British decision to accept the Declaration of Paris was motivated by the fear that a second US initiative might be successful, and the wish to at least secure a global ban on privateering in return for the abandonment of British maritime rights. The Crimean War experience, briefly dealt with in the first part of this chapter, provided an example that concessions to neutrals could pay off while still allowing for an effective blockade. Still, when French Foreign Minister Walewski (who had replaced Drouyn in May 1855) suggested a permanent convention on maritime rights, the British reaction was primarily determined by the prospect of stripping the Americans of their most dangerous weapon.

3

'Catching Brother Jonathan in the Trap which He Laid for Us' – The Genesis of the Declaration of Paris

In this chapter the inquiry into the history of the Declaration of Paris proceeds to the actual document, from the first drafts to the final treaty and its subsequent signature by the seven most important European powers. The US attempt to utilise maritime law to split the Anglo-French alliance, combined with the prospect of imminent war between Britain and the USA in 1856, persuaded the British government to consider signing a treaty granting neutral rights permanently if it also included US acceptance that privateering was banned. Getting rid of privateering seemed more important than ever because letters of marque would have been a pillar of the US war effort. Crucially, Britain informed the French government of these deliberations, leading to France's proposal for a multilateral treaty at the European congress that ended the Crimean War. The second part of the chapter will describe the negotiations from the French draft presented as a consequence of the British idea of a 'package deal', to the final document signed on 16 April 1856 and its subsequent justification in Parliament.

The US proposal

Chapter 2 showed that most observers suspected a second US treaty campaign after the Crimean War – which had prevented the success of the first one – was over. When Sevastopol fell on 9 September 1855, the end of Russia's resistance seemed imminent, and on 26 October, American Minister in Paris John Mason presented a new treaty proposal, accompanied by a note to Walewski that emphasised the shared naval traditions of the USA and France, and the common struggle against England in the past.[1] Under pressure, Walewski 'hesitatingly acknowledge[d]' that the French and US positions on these questions were indeed almost identical, but declared that it was not a favourable time for such negotiations. Mason argued that there had never been a better time: England had accepted the declaration of 1854 only because of French pressure, and France's influence on Britain could not be any greater than it was now. Forcing the British to accept the compromise as permanent would mean a significant and lasting progress in human history, while the alliance with England could certainly not be expected to be perpetual.[2]

This last comment hints at the real motive behind the second US attempt, its timing and the fact that this time only one country was invited: France. Instead of creating customary law, the aim now was to drive a wedge into the Anglo-French alliance. A war with Britain seemed increasingly likely, and while most European states would surely remain neutral, France might remain faithful to the Anglo-French alliance even if it meant war with Washington. The reason behind the Anglo-US crisis was that the Pierce administration had used the opportunity of the Crimean War to adopt a more expansive foreign policy, triggering a conflict with Britain in Central America over territorial sovereignty along the Mosquito Coast (modern Nicaragua). The simultaneous revelation of secret (and illegal) British recruitment activities in the USA had exacerbated the conflict. The Cabinet had so far remained passive, but after the success at Sevastopol, Palmerston suggested a substantial transfer of warships and troops to North America.[3] The generals in the Crimea prevented the transport of soldiers, but the first men-of-war soon sailed westward.

When the American Minister in London, James Buchanan, complained about the fleet movements, Clarendon told him; 'the fleet has not been sent with the least unfriendly intention'.[4] After enquiries in New York confirmed that the British pretext of a fleet of Russian privateer steamers allegedly being fitted out there was unfounded, Buchanan openly accused Clarendon of hypocrisy.[5] Meanwhile, the new First Lord of the Admiralty, Sir Charles Wood, undertook to assemble a substantial fleet in British waters to be ready to cross the Atlantic 'if Brother Jonathan becomes saucy'.[6] In Paris, Mason asked Walewski directly what France thought about the British fleet movement to the USA, and whether France had done the same. Walewski's reply added to US apprehensions: France had not sent ships and did not want war with the USA, but might be drawn into one because of the British alliance.[7]

Walewski was a firm believer in Anglo-French cooperation,[8] which is why he also forwarded the US proposal to London and asked Clarendon for his opinion. Clarendon was not surprised because Buchanan had offered an identical treaty to the British only two months earlier. Buchanan had pleaded with Marcy to allow him to hold up the original proposal sent to Europe in 1854, arguing that a formal proposal at that stage would only lead to a British rejection being formally placed on the record. Marcy had agreed 'that this note should be presented at such a time that an answer to it in the negative would not be received during your mission'.[9] Now, with his posting in London due to end soon, Buchanan sent it off; given the worsening bilateral crisis the proposal might have been interpreted as a deliberate provocation if presented any later.[10] Thus Clarendon received the original invitation of 1854 shortly before Walewski approached him with the new proposal submitted to the French in October 1855.

Clarendon's response to the French came as a major surprise: while no reply had been given to Buchanan, the Cabinet had decided that it 'would not be unwilling to agree to some such Treaty as the United States Government propose, if the United States on their part will consent to forego the right of issuing Letters of Marque'.[11] Until then, Clarendon had suggested this addition to all neutrals being offered a treaty, primarily to thwart US efforts to build a league of neutrals. Now, London had indicated for the first time that Britain would be willing to sign if the USA gave up privateering. Palmerston had shown earlier that he was willing to adopt drastic measures to counter the threat of US privateering; during Cabinet discussions about an appropriate response to the US bombardment of Greytown (Nicaragua), the then Home Secretary had counselled a rather aggressive despatch:

> In dealing with Vulgar-minded Bullies, and such unfortunately the people of the United States are, nothing is gained by submission to Insult and Wrong [...] The U.S. have no navy of which we need be afraid, & they might be told that if they were to resort to privateering, we should however reluctantly be obliged to retaliate by burning all their Sea Coast Towns.[12]

Like Clarendon, Palmerston was genuinely afraid of American privateers, and this new strategy of discouraging their use seemed much more promising than his own earlier suggestion. Clarendon had long believed that a reform of maritime law was in the best interest of civilisation, but, now that it had become a matter of naval strategy, he was ready to fight the proposal past the Cabinet. As British Ambassador in London Lord Cowley pointed out, the idea had the added advantage that if the USA declined, it would no longer be the British who stubbornly defended outdated belligerent rights. Instead, London could take the moral high ground, isolate the USA on the issue of privateering 'and catch Brother Jonathan in the trap which he had laid for us'.[13]

Having learned of this shift in the British position, Walewski considered his options. Should the French government offer the same deal to Washington, and mention confidentially that London thought likewise? Walewski asked Navy Minister Hamelin for his opinion, who rejected the notion that the Crimean War had proven the feasibility of maritime war under the new rules. The Russian merchant navy had been practically non-existent, so privateering had never been an option for want of potential targets. Furthermore, the Russian coastline was particularly easy to blockade. Neither of these conditions would be present in the case of a war against the USA. If enemy property were safe on neutral vessels and letters of marque banned, it might prove impossible for France to win a naval war against Washington. Therefore this treaty would not be in France's interest. However, Hamelin promised that he would not oppose a different policy in the Cabinet since the USA would surely reject any treaty banning privateering.[14]

Meanwhile, Mason pressed Walewski for a speedy reply, since he firmly believed that splitting the Anglo-French alliance should be a priority of US policy. As Britain's maritime strength was not only dangerous to US interests, but because of its rejection of fundamental principles of justice also endangered the future prosperity of the whole world, splitting the alliance by exploiting the principles that Britain rejected but France shared with the USA would be a service to the greater good: 'with the firm but temperate maintenance of our rights, we shall contribute to the happiness of the world, because our success will be that of all other nations'.[15] Walewski knew that an outright rejection of the proposal would have been hard to justify, given the common history of trying to force a more liberal interpretation of maritime law on the British. On the other hand, he could not delay his answer as Clarendon urged him to do.[16] Since Buchanan had left London and his successor Dallas not yet arrived, silence was possible for Clarendon, but with Mason regularly enquiring about the French position, Walewski had to act. He chose to disregard Hamelin's advice and proposed to support the US initiative, as long as a ban on privateering was added to the document.[17]

At their next meeting, a disappointed Mason declared that he was happy to see that the French government 'still appreciates the principles for which [it] always stood', but claimed that he had no instructions to speak about privateering. Privately, Mason advised Marcy not to yield, since letters of marque were a necessary attribute to sovereignty.[18] Marcy reassured him that the reasons that had prevented the USA from accepting a similar treaty with Prussia in 1854 'remain in full force', and that he would not accept such a treaty with France.[19] Mason now wanted to find out whether there was any possibility for a treaty on neutral rights without banning privateering, but Walewski was busy chairing the Congress of Paris that ended the Crimean War.[20]

Just when the European powers gathered in Paris to negotiate peace, the crisis between Britain and the USA escalated further. Buchanan was now convinced that Britain's 'arrogant and belligerent' leader, Palmerston, wanted to add to British military prestige after the disappointing Crimean campaign by provoking a war with the USA.[21] The Pierce administration, however, had just published the correspondence on the recruitment affair, exposing blatant British violations of US neutrality. Clarendon was dumbstruck: 'by publishing the papers and continuing to inflame the popular passions, it would seem as if their wish was to render a peaceful solution impossible'.[22] Palmerston now found it easy to persuade the Cabinet to follow his more aggressive course, and, on the day the Crimean War ended, he ordered the transport of 5,000 soldiers from the Crimea to Canada.[23]

After the US government also recognised William Walker and his filibustering associates as the legitimate government of Nicaragua, Clarendon's latent anti-Americanism came to the fore, and in private letters he railed against 'the rascals who call themselves the government of the mob which governs them' and even dreamt of a global alliance against the USA:

> That nation of pirates [...] is every day becoming a more formidable nuisance and there is no country which will not in turn be exposed to American insolence and encroachment unless the commercial and dollar-making classes there are made to feel that their government will end up by turning all mankind against them and that there will be a universal league to compel them to observe the usages of civilized nations.[24]

The new US Minister in London, George Dallas, realised very soon after his arrival that Anglo-American relations were not what they could be and dryly wrote home that his 'longing for historical fame' would certainly be satiated if he were to be the last ever American minister at this court.[25] However, the idea of a war with the USA was never popular in those papers not controlled by the government, and major commercial bodies such as the Manchester Chamber of Commerce began to pass resolutions demanding an amicable solution to the various disputes. During this debate it became clear why British merchants feared this war: British trade as a whole might 'become the victim of privateers, and the whole Atlantic would be as completely ravaged as the Sea of Azoff had been by our own cruisers'.[26] *The Times* agreed: the recent victory against Russia was meaningless since the theatre of war in the next conflict could span Central America, the USA and Canada, in a struggle that would be fought 'against no fleet, but an ocean swarming with privateers'.[27] The *Leeds Mercury* warned of the wider consequences once the USA had turned its commercial marine into privateers that would

> cruise in every sea, capturing all English vessels which did not sail under convoy, thus inflicting on English commerce and Navigation losses such as have never before been known. Of course our intercourse with India, Australia, Canada, the West Indies and all our other possessions would be exceedingly interrupted, and the price of all colonial and foreign produce would be greatly enhanced.[28]

So far, this chapter has shown that a US attempt to split the Anglo-French alliance by offering a treaty on neutral rights to France had led to Anglo-French discussions that resulted in Britain proposing to accept the new neutral rights permanently if the USA accepted an end to letters of marque. US privateering was also a much talked about danger to British trade. What was unclear at the beginning of the congress was whether Britain would be willing to accept a package deal if the USA was not even at the table, but the multilateral nature of the gathering offered a reasonable prospect that Washington might face international isolation and subsequently lose privateering as an option without even being asked for agreement. Walewski was determined to find out.

The Congress of Paris

When the Congress of Paris finally met on 25 February, the maritime law question was temporarily overshadowed by the more immediate business of peacemaking. One of the open questions was whether there would be peace at all since Palmerston was keen to continue the war, but Clarendon implored him to accept the peace. Fighting alone would surpass Britain's capabilities, especially since it would mean isolation in Europe and a possible entry of the USA into the conflict.[29] Finally, Palmerston accepted this logic and agreed to the peace treaty.[30] Throughout the congress, France was very much in control of proceedings, exemplified by the admission of Prussia: in British eyes, Prussia had excluded itself from the Concert of Europe, but Napoleon III was keen on the added legitimacy of a congress involving all great powers.[31] After the Prussians had accepted the invitation, Walewski clarified that they would not be asked to contribute towards the negotiations but merely to sign the final documents.[32]

For that reason, Prussia was among the powers present at what was called the 'after-congress', in which the French intended to open a discussion that prepared the ground for Napoleon's ultimate aim, a revision of the treaties of 1815 that would redraw the map of Europe in France's favour and solve the problem of nationalism with one stroke.[33] The session of 8 April was especially noteworthy, since in one long speech Walewski laid out the vision of his Emperor for Europe as whole and the suppressed nationalities in particular, with a strong emphasis on the plight of the Italians. Yet, at the end of the speech, Walewski surprised nearly everybody in the room by proposing a fundamental reform of maritime law of warfare.[34] However, laying the foundation stone for a new maritime code, subscribed to by all other nations, perfectly matched Napoleon's overall aim of a new, more just order in Europe and the world, drafted under French leadership.

What surprised the delegates, and would perplex later historians, was that Walewski was so sure that the British delegation would agree. Chairing the proceedings, he would never have taken the risk of being embarrassed and losing face in front of the elite of Europe's diplomats. Historians were loath to believe that a treaty of this dimension could have been agreed between France and England in a matter of days, and in complete secrecy. Even the completely unfounded theory put forward by Friedrich Martens that the declaration was essentially a Russian proposal drafted in highly secret negotiations was still considered possible by eminent historians such as Winfried Baumgart.[35] But as this chapter has shown, the idea of a new treaty on maritime law had been discussed for months. Still, what was to become the Declaration of Paris was first drafted only on 2 April, six days before it was presented.[36] In this short time, fundamental decisions had been made, particularly on the British side.

The best available insight into French thinking is an undated Quai d'Orsay memorandum written shortly after the Declaration of Paris had been signed. Entitled 'England and the Declaration of Paris', it was archived alongside the original drafts, and shows that the original motivation for the treaty had a strong anti-British element. In the March 1854 declaration, Britain had only waived the exercise of its ancient belligerent rights for the duration of the conflict. Although unlikely at the time, London seemed to think that those rights could be revived whenever it pleased the British. The congress was a perfect opportunity to extract a binding and permanent waiver of the British government's right to take enemy property on neutral vessels.[37] But the settling of old scores from the Napoleonic Wars went further, since the Declaration of Paris had four points, not three: the question of how to determine the 'effectiveness' of blockades had not been mentioned at all in the Anglo-French correspondence up until this point. The memo shows that the added clause claiming that only 'effective' blockades could be legal was meant to ban not only paper blockades, which were simply announced but not backed up by a meaningful naval force, but also 'cruising blockades'. These were blockades by a squadron cruising along the enemy coast, but without a stationary blockading force at the entry of every port. According to the British understanding, the latter were entirely legal as long as the naval force was powerful enough. Thus, although the fourth point seemed like a mere confirmation of the customary principle that paper blockades are illegal, the French diplomats actually planned to secure Britain's approval to the French definition of 'effective', namely a close blockade with a stationary squadron at the entrance of a blockaded port.

Walewski must have felt that the British were so eager to see privateering banned that they would not demand a close definition of this article. He was right, and after Walewski had informed Clarendon of his ideas on 4 April, the British Foreign Secretary added a single line to a long letter to Palmerston: 'Do you see any objection to a resolution of Congress against privateering in time of war?'[38] Palmerston was, of course, well briefed on the subject, and the logic of using the congress to put an end to privateering immediately appealed to him:

> Privateering is a practice most inconvenient to the Power which has the largest number of merchant men at sea, and the least useful to the Power which has the largest war navy. England is that Power and we should therefore willingly agree to abolish that Practice in regard to all Powers which would enter into the same Engagement towards us. The United States have hitherto declined, but if all the Powers of Europe, and those

not represented in Congress might be invited to join were to unite in such an agreement the United States could scarcely refuse to accede, and the Engagement might ultimately like the abolition of Slave Trade become universal among all maritime states.[39]

In a letter to Queen Victoria of the same day, Palmerston also mentioned the danger of French privateers, who, having proved to be such formidable enemies during the Napoleonic Wars, would now never threaten her realm again. The Queen was more interested in the 'spirit of the age': she deemed privateering a disgrace to civilisation and declared that she would consider its abolition to be a great victory for human progress.[40]

However, Palmerston needed the approval of the Cabinet, and while some of its members shared the Queen's feeling that banning privateering meant a vote for progress and morality, others would surely question the wisdom of giving up belligerent rights for which the nation had fought more than one war. After all, had it not been explicitly stated at the beginning of the war that the neutral rights granted then were privileges, meant for the duration of the conflict? Clarendon, however, argued that these 'ancient rights' were an illusion, as their actual exercise would unite 'all mankind' against Britain. Furthermore, he reminded the Cabinet of how Britain had responded to the US campaign aimed at establishing these principles as a part of international law:

> It is quite clear that we can never again re-establish our ancient doctrine respecting neutral rights, and that we must in any future war adhere to the exception to our rule which we admitted at the beginning of the present war, under pain of having all mankind against us. I am, therefore, for making a merit of necessity, and volunteering as a benevolent act of the Congress to proclaim as permanent the principle upon which we have lately acted, adding to it a resolution against privateering [... the USA] sent a Circular to all Maritime Powers asking their assent to the neutral flag covering the goods. Most of these Powers consulted us as to the answer they should give, and we suggested that they should not agree unless the United States at the same time gave up the system of privateers.[41]

Using this logic of making a merit out of necessity, Palmerston presented the draft to his Cabinet. Secretary for War Lord Panmure was among the first to agree because he believed that this was a very promising way to isolate the USA, even if the latter did not join the treaty. Colonial Secretary Henry Labouchere proposed an addition: since it was very likely that the USA would not join, a clause should be added that explicitly restricted the benefits of the rights granted to neutrals to those states that had signed the declaration as a whole. This rule could discourage any US attempt to enjoy a free ride regarding neutral rights and still retain the right to issue letters of marque. The idea was accepted as a welcome addition by most colleagues, most notably First Lord of the Admiralty Sir Charles Wood.[42] Others, such as Granville, did not think that US consent should be a *conditio sine qua non*, and the Lord Privy Seal, the Earl of Harrowby, neatly summarised Cabinet thinking in one sentence: 'I should be disposed to run all risks as to the non-concurrence of the United States in the Declaration against Privateering, trusting to the effect of opinion in the long run, but confining the effect of the several Resolutions as far as possible to those who concurred in the whole.'[43]

The fact that the Cabinet's decision on the Declaration of Paris was primarily about the USA is underlined by the arguments of the only minister who refused to submit to Palmerston's proposal. Baron Stanley of Alderley, the President of the Board of Trade, accepted that Britain could never return to its ancient principles but warned that under the new rules a war against France or the USA would be a very dangerous affair. Therefore Britain should secure Washington's signature before entering into any obligations: 'Without their assent we shall be the only losers.' He was outvoted by his colleagues, and Britain's approval was telegraphed to Paris on the same day. Palmerston summarised the Cabinet consensus to serve as an instruction for Clarendon:

> We agree with you that it is scarcely probable that in any future War, we should abstain from the same Declaration of our former Rules about neutrals which we thought it right to adopt at the beginning of this War, and we think that a formal Renunciation of an old Doctrine, or at least a formal Adoption of a new Practice, might be advisable as a General Engagement by maritime Powers, if accompanied by a Renunciation of Privateering. Of course such Engagements would be binding only, as between the Countries which might be parties to them, and if for instance the United States refused to join, neither England nor France would think that the Engagements they had contracted with each other, could bind either as regarded the United States.[44]

When Walewski presented the idea of a declaration on maritime law to the congress on 8 April, he already knew that Britain would be on his side. Walewski reminded his listeners that all great European congresses had left a particular legacy of progress: the Westphalian Congress had given the world freedom of religion,[45] and the Congress of Vienna had abolished the slave trade and secured the freedom of navigation on international rivers. Would it not be a fitting end to the great Congress of Paris if the participating powers laid the foundation for a universal code of maritime law of warfare? After Walewski had ended, Clarendon rose to second the proposal and make it clear that there would be no negotiations: France and Britain had suspended their traditional principles at the beginning of the last war, for the benefit of the neutrals. Now, Britain was willing to abandon its ancient rights as long as privateering was permanently abolished at the same time.[46] Making the case for abolition, Clarendon never mentioned the USA. Instead, he denounced privateering as legalised piracy, one of the worst evils of war and unworthy of the current state of civilisation. This was no lie: Clarendon truly abhorred privateering. But the reason behind the British decision to propose this package deal was a different one, and all participants understood what Clarendon was aiming at when he explained that the liberal rights for neutrals would only be granted to states that had joined the treaty, and that no state could demand to receive this favourable treatment if it had not.

None of the other delegates had been involved in the Anglo-French discussions and most declared that they had no instructions to enter into obligations on maritime law, including the Russian delegate, Orlov, a fact that has always cast a certain doubt over Martens' claim that Orlov initiated the declaration. Only Prussian Prime Minister Manteuffel, now well briefed on these matters after his earlier negotiations with Washington, declared that Prussia had always supported these principles, and he would be willing to sign any document intending to elevate them to the status of international law. Not long ago he had even considered signing a treaty with the USA to force them on Britain, and now he was offered a British guarantee. Naturally there was no need to ask his sovereign whether Prussia could do without letters of marque.

The deliberations of the Austrian Cabinet are instructive as to the thinking of the other European powers. Following the request of Foreign Minister Buol-Schauenstein that he be authorised to sign this 'déclaration utile',[47] Emperor Franz Joseph presented the case to his Cabinet and asked whether any of the ministers had concerns. None were forthcoming. The Emperor's reasoning was remarkable since it did not even mention privateering. All that counted was that Britain presented on a silver platter all of the neutral rights that the continental powers had desired for so long:

> His Majesty remarked that from Austria's point of view the acceptance of those principles of the laws of war at sea [...] only deserved approval [...] The members of the [Cabinet] conference unanimously deemed it an important benefit for the law of nations if the terms proposed in Paris achieved formal universal recognition, [...] and in particular that such appraisal under international law would completely correspond to the direction which the imperial Austrian government has reason to maintain in questions concerning the rights of neutrals at sea.[48]

Unlike the French or Dutch, none of the other signatories had a history of successful privateering, and they merely abandoned a right that they had never used. The USA was unique in placing such an enormous importance on privateers as a means of self-defence, and Palmerston had not given up hope that even Washington might be tempted by the chance of finally securing the 'free ships, free goods' principle: 'Perhaps [the] United States might accept the Privateering condition in order to get the engagement about Goods and Ships.'[49]

As the signature of the final document came closer, the Cabinet now took a close look at the French draft and suggested changes to the text as well as to the preamble. As Clarendon wrote to Walewski in his request for the draft, Palmerston was 'naturally anxious about the *rédaction*. We entirely agree, but in adopting *as permanent* a principle which is new in England & to which *all the English lawyers are opposed* we must be careful about words.'[50] The preamble stated the signatories' belief that as far as they were concerned the new rules would become 'part of the law of nations'.[51] Palmerston felt that it was unfortunate to announce changes to the law before every state had had a chance to accept or reject the new rules, but his request of a formal invitation to all states underlines the British commitment to creating new universal law:

> It will be better not to say that we make our new principles Part of the Law of Nations because no Declaration of a few Powers can alter that law, and it will be enough to say that those Rules shall be binding on those Parties who sign the Declaration, as between each other, and as between them and any other Powers or States who may afterwards accede to them; and it will be well to add to the latter Part that the declaration shall not only be communicated to other Powers, but that other Powers shall be invited to accede to it.[52]

A day later, the Cabinet sent a second wish list of changes. First, Palmerston suggested dropping the fourth point on 'effective' blockades, arguing that it merely repeated customary law and was therefore superfluous. Regarding the preamble, the Cabinet had taken offence that it hinted at the problems that the British approach to maritime law had caused in the past, and which would now be overcome. Palmerston wrote that he would not sign the document in its present form as it would amount to inappropriate criticism of his predecessors in office and would make the motivation of the present government all too obvious: by signing it, the government would 'admit that the course which they are prepared to take upon a balance of advantages and disadvantages is forced upon them by necessity'.[53] Palmerston also reinforced his insistence that the declaration should explicitly describe itself as a treaty between states, not a universal reform of international law. Just a few days earlier, he had praised the effectiveness of a concerted effort of states to secure universal recognition for individual norms, citing the example of Britain's endeavour to achieve a global ban on the slave trade. Now it had dawned on him that a method that worked for Britain might work for everybody else, and that a powerful nation such as the USA could use the same ploy against Britain:

> Again, it would not be correct to say that a declaration of principles such as now is proposed could alter the Law of Nations. That Law rests upon foundations wider and deeper than the occasional declaration of a few States, and it could not be altered except by some agreement much more general and much more formal than the proposed Declaration; and it would be dangerous for Great Britain to admit that such a declaration issued by the representatives of a small number of states could alter the Law of Nations. An example thus set and a precedent thus established, by the consent and participation of Great Britain, might hereafter upon other occasions be used for the purpose of establishing doctrines of International Law to which Great Britain might have the strongest possible objection and repugnance.

Despite his concerns, what Palmerston had just agreed to was the invention of the multilateral law-making treaty, today the most important tool of international legislation. Essentially it was an amalgam of the traditional European practice of passing universal reforms of European law (before it claimed to have widened its outreach) at the major European congresses, and a British innovation developed during the campaign for the abolition of the slave trade: creating a spider web of bilateral treaties to force certain principles into the international code, and isolate and ostracise those who still held out and refused to join. The USA had unsuccessfully attempted to follow this model by inviting other nations to join its bilateral treaty with Russia. The French innovation was to begin with a multilateral document that was cloaked with the dignity and legitimacy of a European congress.

When the Congress of Paris re-assembled on 14 April, all delegations reported that they were now fully authorised to sign the declaration.[54] The new French draft of the preamble was passed unanimously: in response to Britain's concerns, it avoided an explicit condemnation of Britain's traditional maritime law, but pointed towards the potential for violent conflict in the 'divergence' of current practice and therefore strived to create a 'doctrine uniforme'.[55] This elegant phrase also avoided a clear statement as to if and when the declaration would create new norms of international law. After this session, Clarendon wrote home that the decision on the declaration had now been made and that the deal was done. In a letter to the Queen, he expected a very positive reception for the declaration back in Britain.[56] Palmerston responded with a last-minute request for a further change that once again highlighted the difference between the stated motive and the true motive:

> I forgot to say in my last letter that if it is not too late to do it I think it would be best to leave out in the Declaration about Neutral Rights

the words 'et même des conflits'. Those words seem to imply that the new principles are adopted in order to avoid giving offence to the United States, in short out of fear of a conflict. This may be a true and justifiable reason but one which perhaps is better kept as the motive of conduct rather than a ground to be publicly assigned for it. If it is too late to make the change, no matter.[57]

It was indeed too late, since on the following day, 16 April 1856, the delegates of the seven nations signed the Declaration of Paris.[58] For the French diplomats, it meant a glorious ending to the congress, a historic triumph against British pretensions and an example of French efforts on behalf of liberality and civilisation. Yet, when Charles Iain Hamilton says that the search for easy prestige was the main motivation behind the declaration, he misses the point of the serious negotiations that were still continuing on the very day that it was signed.[59] In response to the British request for additional rules to prevent potential US countermoves, Walewski proposed that none of the signatories would in future be allowed to sign a convention on maritime law that did not contain all of the four points of the declaration, in order to preserve its unity.[60]

In other words, no nation however small should dare to accept a probable new offer from the USA that included generous rights for neutrals but maintained privateering as a belligerent right. It was fitting that Russia raised its voice at this point, being the only state at the table having actually signed such a convention with the USA. Would his colleagues agree, delegate Orlov asked, that this new rule was not retroactive and thus inapplicable to treaties signed in the past? They agreed, and the amendment passed without further discussion, although it meant a substantial limitation on the freedom of action of sovereign states and was not even part of the treaty, but was only mentioned in the protocol of the 24th and last session of the Congress of Paris.

Walewski was willing to go far beyond the normal diplomatic and legal procedures to accommodate British requests, but a previously neglected letter sent by Clarendon to Palmerston on the day after the declaration was signed shows where he drew the line, and why. The letter reveals a discussion at the last congress session that was not included in the official protocol: shortly before Walewski presented the document for official signature, Clarendon suggested that the fourth point declaring ineffective blockades illegal should be dropped. Echoing Palmerston's instruction, he argued that it was merely declaratory of existing customary law, and therefore pointless. As has been shown above, the inclusion of the fourth point was an attempt to smuggle the French definition of close blockades into the law of nations, which is why Walewski was ready to silence Clarendon by referring to British practices during the Napoleonic Wars and declaring that the fourth point included an important principle that had been violated as recently as the present century.

Yet, Walewski also gave a second reason which clarified the French intentions behind the declaration. He argued that even though the rule was already part of international law, it should still be a part of the declaration because it was meant to be 'the foundation of a New Maritime Code in Time of War'.[61] While for the British government the Declaration of Paris was first and foremost a package deal in which the abolition of privateering was gained by granting certain rights for neutrals, Walewski had a more ambitious vision. The century-old conflict between Britain and the neutrals (often led by France) would finally be settled in France's favour, and the document could form the beginning of a global code of maritime law. Future problems would not be resolved by confrontation and war, but in multilateral negotiations, with the French Emperor presiding and moderating. Therefore Walewski was ready to accept the abolition of privateering against the misgivings of his own navy, and accept every British proposal that was aimed at securing near-universal recognition of the ban on privateering, even if presented at short notice, but he quite aggressively snubbed Clarendon's polite question as to whether it was really necessary to include a point that was no longer controversial.

By presenting new sources on the genesis and drafting history of the declaration, this chapter has shown that the document cannot be understood without appreciating its nature as a package deal, forced on Britain by the danger of a new bilateral treaty campaign by the USA after the end of the Crimean War. Before late 1855, Britain had only recommended the linking of a ban on privateering with neutral rights to those states that had been presented with a US proposal. After receiving a formal offer in late August 1855, the British government intimated to the French Foreign Minister that it would consider signing such a treaty with the USA. Later, Lord Cowley added the idea of a treaty campaign aimed at isolating the Americans. After lengthy internal deliberation, the French government decided to take up this British idea and turn it into a formal declaration that could form the foundation of a global law of maritime warfare. The proposal was presented to the conference as the result of close coordination between the two governments, and only after the British side had previously signalled its assent.

Justifications and expectations

The reasons why Britain decided to accept the French proposal were discussed in public for the first time after the government was challenged to defend its decision in Parliament. Historians have tended to ignore the reasons presented by the government on this occasion, preferring to discuss those parts of internal letters concerning the conditions under which a signatory would not be bound to follow the new rules. However, as has been shown here, these discussions did not refer to the prospect of extricating Britain from the commitments, but rather to the prevention of US attempts to benefit from individual parts of the package deal without accepting the whole. Following an aggressive attack by the Conservatives, Clarendon emphasised with astonishing honesty the need to respond to the reality of US power.

The Conservatives had picked the House of Lords for their debate, probably believing that avoiding the strong commercial representation in the House of Commons gave them a better chance of defeating the government. The Earl of Hardwicke began the attack by questioning the legality of the form in which the new principles had been signed: by calling it a declaration and not a treaty, the need for ratification had been avoided. Still, it was not only legally binding between the parties like a ratified treaty but even strived to create new international law: 'This declaration places the Government in the position of judges and exponents of the international law of Europe.' Entering such commitments without even a consultation of Parliament's views was stretching the royal prerogative in a dangerous way: 'Whatever arguments of theory or expediency might be put forward in reference to ameliorating the evils of war, and other rubbish of that sort, it [is] impossible that a proceeding so extraordinary could be passed over without serious comment.'[62]

Unsurprisingly, the Conservatives also found fault with the contents of the treaty. The 'free ships, free goods' principle had already prolonged the war against Russia by allowing the diversion of Russian trade, and this new declaration would cause unnecessary grief and bloodshed by prolonging every future war.[63] The Conservative leader Lord Derby even claimed that Britain had 'hacked off her right arm' and was now powerless to employ its former maritime prowess against a powerful rival such as France. Never before Had a British Secretary of State walked into a trap so eagerly, and, when the delegates in Paris had informed their governments of the planned declaration, the answer must have been 'Good heavens! Is England so weak to consent to this! We have been trying for the last eighty years to find a British Minister who would surrender this point, and here we have found one at last!' Thus the best description of the new document was the 'Clarendon Capitulation of Paris',[64] and the motion asked Parliament to censure the government because an important right had been 'suddenly abandoned, without the previous Sanction or Knowledge of Parliament'.[65]

At first, the government responded much as it had done in the 1854 debate and countered the presentation of numerous eminent international lawyers who had testified what highly esteemed principles British maritime rights had been by citing equally eminent (and even more numerous) lawyers who asserted that human civilisation might experience the occasional incident of progress. But this attack had been much more severe and dangerous, and this time the Cabinet revealed the true reasons why it thought a good deal had been struck. Citing the classics of international law was all very well, Clarendon argued, but since Vatell wrote, there has arisen a community of Anglo-Saxons on the other shore of the Atlantic, numbering almost as many millions as their elder brethren on this side of the sea, addicted like them to commerce, consequently possessing the same means of making a powerful military navy, and imparting the same morbid jealousy of interference in their affairs. The existence of this people changed the whole thing.[66]

This fundamental fact had determined the Cabinet decision in 1854, and nothing had changed since then. Clarendon implored the House of Lords to understand and recognise the necessity of what the government had done:

And now, my Lords, let me ask: having once waived these rights, was it possible, or was it prudent, for us to return to them? This is not a question of law, but of policy. If your Lordships could be aware, as I was, of the strong feeling – of the intense anxiety – of the neutral powers at the commencement of the war, to know whether we meant to adhere to the rule which we had hitherto maintained, you would then fully comprehend the importance of the question. Almost daily inquiries were addressed to me by representatives of the neutral Powers, and though I certainly cannot say that the maintenance of the rule would have led to another 'Armed Neutrality', it was quite plain that we should have stood alone in the world – we should have had every other maritime power against us, and most properly so – because we should have been maintaining a law which was contrary to the public opinion of the world, which was hostile to commerce, and as unfavourable as possible to a mitigation of the evils of war. We should not only have stood alone in the world, but it was quite clear that we should have been at war not only with Russia, but with every other maritime Power in the world; or, if not actually at war, in a position of a most unpleasant character with other nations, and especially with the United States.

But if that were the state of things in 1854, I would ask your Lordships whether we have any reason to suppose that there will be any change of public opinion on the subject, that civilisation will retrograde, that humanity will diminish, or that anything is likely to occur to render less stringent or less obligatory the motives which imposed upon us the necessity of passing the Order in Council of 1854? Those who know the mode in which that Order in Council was received by most of the neutral Powers, and how much importance they attached to it, would at once see how dangerous it would be to do anything to check the friendly feeling which was then created by saying that we would adhere to the principle of our old rule.[67]

It would have been impossible to stage a big debate in Parliament while the congress was meeting, and doing so would also have made it more difficult to achieve the biggest advantage of the treaty: 'Abolition of privateering is more than an equivalent for the abandonment of a claim which I know it would be impossible to sustain.' Getting rid of privateering was 'of far greater importance now than at any former period', since trade was still primarily done with sailing ships and a handful of fast privateer steamers could capture as many ships as they liked.[68] Right before the vote, former Secretary of State for War and the Colonies Earl Grey reinforced this message by pointing out the consequences of a continued celebration of Britain's ancient principles: those who claimed that it was appropriate to force arbitrary measures on neutrals to harm an enemy would also have to prepare for a war against the whole world. It was fine to talk of Britain's greatness and the glory of confronting powerful opposition in eloquent speeches, 'but it was not the language of a cool and reflecting statesman. Neither England nor any other nation could stand against the world in arms.'[69] In the end, the motion to censure the government for signing the Declaration of Paris was rejected by the House of Lords with a clear majority (156 to 102).

Before Chapter 4 discusses the reactions to the news of the Declaration of Paris in the USA, Europe and the world, this chapter will end by discussing its effect on the 'maritime balance of power'. How did the fact that these seven states had signed this treaty affect the rules of the game? As described most recently by Rolf Hobson, the 'maritime balance of power' was profoundly anti-British.[70] United under the leadership of the strongest 'neutral', the maritime nations of the world confronted the biggest sea power to ensure that the actual exercise of Britain's supremacy on the oceans remained within certain limits. But now, Britain had committed itself to defend the neutral rights that it had previously claimed did not exist, provided that the neutrals cooperated in suppressing a practice of maritime warfare that had been criticised in the past but was still considered a traditional right of every belligerent. This was not just a victory for the neutrals; it turned the 'maritime balance of power' on its head. With the advent of the Declaration of Paris, it was transformed from a permanent, if not always manifest, stand-off between Britain and the rest of the world over the rights of neutrals during wartime into an international, even global, regime.

Now that Britain had committed itself to respect and defend this regime, its sea power was certain to be the foremost force upholding neutral rights against belligerents. Any signatory of the Declaration of Paris who did not respect its generous terms for neutrals and thereby violated the interests of neutral shipping could not avoid hurting the interests of British merchants and ship-owners. If British citizens suffered because a privilege protected by an international treaty was not granted, a reaction by the British government and ultimately the Royal Navy would surely follow. In return, the other signatories agreed to cooperate in setting up what modern political scientists have called a global abolition regime against privateering.[71] Such a regime tries to impose a certain set of norms that ideally should be applied universally. Thus it is not a simple exercise in balancing the strongest power, but its aim is to exert 'global governance' over the outcasts of the system.

French journalist Jean-Baptiste Labiche fully understood this change when he commented on the new maritime law and pondered what would happen if the USA challenged the new rules. He emphasised that in contrast with the Armed Neutralities of 1780 and 1800, which defended neutral rights against Britain, the new alliance could rely on Britain as 'its primary pillar'. The original signatories and the states that joined the declaration formed an 'armed league', which unlike the earlier alliances against Britain was now an 'irresistible' force.[72] To hasten its eventual success in the upcoming struggle against the USA, Labiche suggested that the maritime powers should include an additional article that made it clear that signatories not only forfeited the right to issue letters of marque themselves but also promised not to recognise privateers as ships of war, irrespective of the flag that they were flying. Just as pirates were banned from entering any port, so should privateers be treated as international outlaws. In Britain, *The Economist* believed that by signing the declaration, the European powers had already accepted this new status for privateers:

> Privateering having become piracy in the code of the civilised nations of Europe, those nations cannot acknowledge or countenance American privateers even in the most indirect manner. They cannot admit them into their ports for the purpose of disposing of their prizes, or for refitting, or for victualling, or for shelter. They become *hostes humani generis* everywhere except within the ports of the Union. It will most probably, therefore, be found practically that the retention of a practice discountenanced and abandoned by all the civilised States of the East cannot permanently be continued by the one nation of the West which clings to this congenial relic of a barbarous age.[73]

But all of these ideas depended on the adherence to the declaration by the large majority of the world's states. Moreover, what would the USA do to counter this Anglo-French move so clearly aimed at Washington?

4
'That Moral League of Nations Against the United States' – The Declaration of Paris and the Marcy Amendment

As Chapter 3 shows, the intention behind the Declaration of Paris was to create new universal rules of international law that would first isolate the Americans and then force them to accept the abolition of privateering. This chapter will examine the success of that attempt, and the counterproposal that the USA made to thwart the Anglo-French ambition to ban privateering. While scholarly research on the Declaration of Paris is limited, it is almost non-existent on the USA's response, although the proposal made by Secretary of State William Marcy in July 1856 remained official US policy until the Second Hague Peace Conference. Based on a wide selection of previously neglected US and non-US sources, this chapter will examine the USA's attempts to prevent the declaration's success as well as the origins and global impact of the Marcy Amendment.

Alan Dowty dismisses the importance of the proposal, claiming that it was doubtful whether Britain ever seriously considered the idea.[1] Bernard Semmel agrees, quoting a speech by Prime Minister Palmerston in which he spoke out in favour of the principle in Liverpool in November 1856, but then explains that Palmerston changed his mind after this trial balloon was not well received in the press.[2] Charles Iain Hamilton also uses the term 'trial balloon' with regard to several newspaper articles that he believes were sponsored by the French government, but concludes that upon further reflection the Marcy Amendment 'was too much even for Quai d'Orsay'.[3] As for the position of the British government, Hamilton also cites the Liverpool speech, yet in contrast with Semmel he regards it as proof that the idea was nearly accepted, and that the Cabinet later changed its mind for unknown reasons. This question will be resolved towards the end of this chapter.

While the Declaration of Paris surprised even the keenest observers of European politics, it was a particular shock for the US government. At the time when the French proposal was first discussed, American Minister in

Paris John Mason reported to Marcy that the continuing discussions of the congress would be limited to details of the peace treaty, 'whatever may be said in the newspapers'.[4] News of a declaration on maritime law only reached the USA on 13 May when the full text was published in the *New York Times*.[5] Not least because the Americans had been kept in the dark, the US government perceived the Declaration of Paris as a slap in the face. The US Minister in London, George Dallas, even saw the declaration as the first step towards a major war between the USA and Europe:

> We have kept at peace, and I hope we may continue so. It is barely possible, however, now that the late Congress at Paris intended their declaration abolishing Privateering as the groundwork of a coercive movement by a confederation of European sovereigns against America. If so, have it ye all, my lads![6]

Mason was first informed by Walewski himself, who mentioned a French proposal on maritime law accepted by the congress and allegedly made 'with no unfriendly feeling' towards the USA. Moreover, it included no 'stipulations or purpose to enforce it against those who might not choose to agree to it'. When Walewski followed up on these rather obvious lies by asking Mason whether the USA might be interested in joining this exciting new declaration, Mason angrily responded that Walewski knew full well that the belligerent right he wanted to abolish was valued very highly by the US government. Since France and the USA were actually still engaged in negotiations over a proposed convention on neutral rights, he would have expected at least an enquiry about whether the USA had anything to suggest. But Mason went beyond complaining and surprised Walewski with a counterproposal that was taken from President Pierce's speech in 1854: the USA would accept an abolition of privateering if it was coupled with a complete immunity of peaceful commerce in wartime, irrespective of a vessel's flag. Walewski found the idea worthy of 'serious consideration', and Mason urged Marcy that it was not too late to make a formal proposal on this basis:

> It may not be adopted, by one, perhaps by more of the great powers, who have united in the agreement adopted in the Congress. But if rejected, and the United States, isolated though she be, shall be compelled to decline to surrender her right of self defence, without any equivalent, she will stand justified before the world, for maintaining her rights, which she is willing to surrender, if other nations will agree with her.[7]

When this letter reached Marcy on 17 May it was the first suggestion of how the USA might respond to the declaration's challenge. Days later he received a letter from Dallas in London, who had been given the full protocols of the conference proceedings. Dallas highlighted the unusual provisions in protocol 24 which prevented signatories from granting the rights under the declaration to non-members or signing any different convention on maritime law. Publicising them would make the mischievous intentions behind the declaration potently obvious and 'arouse the counteracting throes of liberal and enlightened opinion, wherever it exists in Europe'.[8] Thus the advice from Marcy's top diplomats in Europe amounted to exposing the anti-American intentions behind the Declaration of Paris, and escaping isolation as the sole defender of privateering by making an even more liberal counterproposal. But if Marcy wanted to prevent other nations from joining the declaration, he would have to act quickly, and it is interesting to note that he did absolutely nothing at this point. Meanwhile, the French Minister in Washington, Count Sartiges, tried hard to dispel US doubts over the declaration.

Sartiges argued that in the age of steam, privateering had become completely obsolete, as half a dozen Navy steamers would be sufficient to chase all privateers off the oceans. No private individual anywhere in the world could fit out a steam privateering ship, and any steam privateer would not be permitted to enter ports along the coasts of Europe, and thereby be unable to load fresh coals. If the USA decided not to accede, on the other hand, it would not enjoy the liberal neutral rights granted in the declaration. Yet Sartiges' assessment of privateering as an anachronism was countered by President Pierce's laconic remark that this was most interesting news which he would attend to at the first opportunity, and Marcy made it clear that for him privateering was still the USA's most powerful weapon. The influential Attorney-General Caleb Cushing was more sympathetic and praised the Declaration of Paris as a huge step in the right direction, but ultimately all merchant vessels should be allowed to pass freely in time of war. Sartiges was unsure whether Cushing had presented him with a Cabinet decision or his private opinion on the matter, but it was clear that some ministers favoured a plain rejection and others preferred Mason's counterproposal. In his final assessment, Sartiges concluded that even a US accession to the declaration remained a possibility.[9]

But the first priority of Britain and France was to increase the pressure on the USA by persuading as many other nations as possible to join. It had been agreed at the congress that all seven signatories should address all other states, but in individual invitations.[10] Walewski coordinated these efforts and urged the British to include an instruction in their circular that asked all ministers to invite states jointly with the ministers of the other signatories, especially after the Austrians had already sent out instructions that were silent on coordination.[11] Clarendon's priorities were equally clear: he demanded that the French instructions should emphasise the indivisibility of the four principles, just in case there might be a government wishing to benefit from the neutral rights but unwilling to give up privateering.[12] As it became clear that the Russian and Turkish governments were less than eager to act swiftly, he authorised individual ministers to go ahead and issue invitations jointly with those ministers who already had instructions.[13] In an angry letter to his representative in Hanover he also affirmed that the invitation was meant to be extended to all states, regardless of whether they had a maritime tradition or not.[14]

The Prussians did not actively participate throughout Europe but sent an invitation to all states of the German Confederation that came close to an order, and resulted in the swift accession of all of its members.[15] Sardinia did the same for Italy, and during June and July other European states, such as Belgium, the Netherlands, Denmark, Sweden-Norway, Switzerland and Greece, followed. According to the US Minister in the Netherlands, August Belmont, the smaller European states were well aware of the punishment for non-adherence:

> I am told that the language of the British circular is very pressing, and contains an implied threat that those powers, which will not adhere now to these conditions are to be deprived hereafter of the privileges granted to the neutral flag.[16]

While it had been assumed that Washington might launch a counter-initiative to prevent the declaration's success, none of the powers involved expected that the centre stage of this diplomatic stand-off would be Lisbon, capital of the small kingdom of Portugal. The Pierce administration had appointed John Louis O'Sullivan as its local representative, after the influential Democrat publicist (and inventor of the phrase 'Manifest Destiny') had narrowly escaped a guilty verdict for supporting a filibustering expedition to Cuba and was in urgent need of a new position, preferably far away from New York.[17] However, if Pierce believed that sending O'Sullivan to his rather remote new post would force him to maintain a low profile, he was wrong.

Like Mason in Paris, O'Sullivan immediately responded to the news of the declaration by advising a modification guaranteeing freedom of commerce in wartime, but he also suggested a clause securing port access for American privateers in case of war. Later he informed Marcy that the Europeans had already begun to put pressure on Portugal. If he had full powers to conclude a convention on maritime law, he would do it immediately 'before this potent *injunction* should be served by the great master powers upon this feeble little one'. Upon hearing that full instructions for the British Minister had arrived, he went to the Portuguese Foreign Minister to warn him of the grave implications of protocol 24, which would enjoin him from signing a convention on the immunity of private commerce with the USA. But just when he was certain that he had made an ally, the Portuguese government fell.[18]

O'Sullivan was eager to repeat his success with the new Foreign Minister, Soulé, but found his efforts increasingly ridiculed by his European colleagues.[19] Hurt in his pride and convinced of certain success if he acted quickly enough, O'Sullivan decided on a truly remarkable course of action. On 12 June he sent Soulé a treaty proposal that only had two articles, one guaranteeing the immunity of private maritime commerce in wartime and the other affirming the principle of 'effective' blockades.[20] He informed Marcy that he had stayed as close as possible to the wording of the US President's speech in 1854, and pleaded with him to understand the necessity of his highly unusual step. Had he waited for formal instructions from Washington, it would have been too late to prevent what O'Sullivan felt was one of the great injustices of the age:

> I feel no small degree of indignation at this attempt, made by the great naval powers at Paris, to combine the community of nations in a sort of moral league against the United States, which shall thrust us outside of the circle of their general agreement upon our own principles in regard to neutral maritime rights, and which shall create an atmosphere of universal opinion to stigmatize as piratical a weapon of maritime self-defence peculiarly our own, & peculiarly indispensable to us, unless we shall succumb to their dictation on the subject, and consent thereby to redouble their effective naval preponderance against us.[21]

Furthermore, his unorthodox action had already yielded its first success: Soulé had declined to pledge Portugal's immediate adherence to the declaration during a joint visit of the British, French, Russian, Austrian and Sardinian ministers because O'Sullivan had submitted his proposal right before their visit. At Soulé's specific request, the ministers also confirmed that adherence to the declaration without accepting protocol 24 was impossible. Now Soulé pondered whether he could simply accede to both the declaration and the US proposal at the same time, hoping that the congress powers would find it too embarrassing to censure a sovereign state on the basis of a congress protocol.

More importantly, the Prussian, Dutch and Russian ministers had already asked O'Sullivan for copies of this new 'American' proposal to forward them to their home countries. The British representative, he wrote to Marcy, had simply grabbed one without asking, 'I presume for the same purpose'.[22] Marcy received this despatch on 24 July and must have realised that his options were now very much restricted. If he publicly declared the proposal to Portugal to be unauthorised, this would mean a huge embarrassment, particularly since President Pierce had supported the idea in 1854. The alternative was to pretend that O'Sullivan's convention had not been unauthorised at all and quickly send out a formal proposal to all states. The latter, however, was not Marcy's preferred course of action, since he had done nothing to further the idea suggested to him in early May, and in letters sent to selected nations on 14 July he had simply urged them not to sign the Declaration of Paris, without any reference to the immunity of belligerent commerce. The abolition of privateering, Marcy argued, would make small states powerless to oppose orders given by the great maritime powers. The maritime balance of power would be practically abolished and the freedom of the seas put in grave danger.[23] In the letter sent to the Netherlands, Marcy referred to the nations endorsing the Declaration of Paris as the 'Confederated States' and expressed his sincere regret that some governments had 'promptly, and this Government cannot but think unadvisedly, accepted [the declaration] without restriction or qualification'.[24] He warned that this might have 'fatal consequences' for commercial nations and wondered how some signatories could reconcile their new commitment with existing treaty obligations with the USA, which guaranteed a friendly reception for American privateers. Thus Marcy's preference was to simply reject the Declaration of Paris and to advise other nations to do the same, in a tone that can only be described as aggressive and threatening.

Four days after receiving O'Sullivan's letter, however, Marcy sent out a very different despatch, which would become famous as the forceful and enlightened proposition of what contemporaries soon called the Marcy Amendment. This letter, addressed to Sartiges but also forwarded to the Russian, Austrian, Prussian and Sardinian (but not British) ministers, began by describing the Declaration of Paris as an attempt to deprive small nations too poor to maintain a substantial navy of an important means of self-defence. Up until this point the right of privateering had been undisputed, and just as every state would boost the ranks of its army with volunteers in case of war, states should be equally free to enlist the support offered by their merchant navies. Without the right to employ privateers, all nations would be at the mercy of the maritime powers, and the power with the biggest navy would automatically become the absolute ruler of the seas, able to cut off the trade of other nations as it pleased. To preserve the freedom of the seas, privateering must be maintained.[25]

So far, this was exactly the argument that he had made two weeks earlier, but Marcy now included the counterproposal suggested by Mason and O'Sullivan. Giving up privateering could be considered if the vital sea trade of smaller nations was protected from the encroachments of the maritime powers by a complete immunity of private property, with the exception of contraband. Then Marcy laid out the US position in case his proposal was rejected, and officially declared his nation's adherence to the second, third and fourth principle of the declaration. In addition to this attempt to undermine the indivisibility of the four principles of the declaration as laid down in protocol 24, Marcy included a further demand: even if states had abolished privateering for themselves, the USA still demanded unhindered access to their ports for its own privateers, based on international law as it was 'before the attempted modification of it by that Congress'.

The assessment of Marcy's action by foreign diplomats in Washington confirms that his intentions were considerably more aggressive than was evident from the despatch: according to British Minister Savile Lumley, Sartiges had persuaded Marcy to erase the most offensive parts, including a condemnation of the declaration as 'inconsiderate'. Sartiges was now so frustrated with Marcy's attitude that he suggested coercing the US into acceding: if the US government was officially informed that its privateers would no longer be granted entry into any European port, privateering would be impractical and the right to issue letters of marque worthless. Regarding Marcy's proposal, Sartiges was convinced that it was 'an attempt to create a maritime league against England'.[26] Lumley's view was similar: in his opinion, the intention was 'to place the United States' Government in the light of a protector or advocate of the rights of the secondary and third rate Powers, as opposed to the great maritime Powers'.[27] Yet if the USA really wanted to undermine the success of the Declaration of Paris, valuable time had been lost.

The only American diplomat unaffected by the delay in Marcy's reaction was, of course, John Louis O'Sullivan, who had meanwhile presented a new draft convention to the Portuguese. The ministers of the congress powers had stated categorically that an accession to the declaration without accepting protocol 24 was out of the question to maintain the indivisibility of the four points, so O'Sullivan wrote a draft that repeated all four points, with an additional sentence about the immunity of private property in the article one.[28] However, O'Sullivan conceded that confronting Britain and France at the same time might be too dangerous for Portugal: 'The alarm about a possible outbreak of war between us and that power [Britain], with vague uncertainties as to the extent of the alliances which such a war might involve, tells against us at this moment.' Furthermore, since Portugal was almost bankrupt and utterly dependent on French and British credit, 'they are even more to be pitied than despised for not being able to call their soul their own'. O'Sullivan made the latter point brutally clear in two despatches to Soulé that ended with an appeal to national pride, but he could report more promising news from Britain since the British government 'respecting my proposed projet for a convention, *does not show itself entirely opposed to the idea*, though it does to its present adoption by Portugal'.[29]

Although he dismissed O'Sullivan's efforts as hopeless, British Minister Henry Francis Howard had not only forwarded the draft convention to London but also lectured the Portuguese about how unwise it would be to sign a convention including fundamental changes to maritime law 'without having first learnt the views of Her Majesty's Government concerning it'.[30] To everyone's surprise, these views turned out to be much more positive than expected. Clarendon wrote that 'Her Majesty's Government do not pronounce an opinion decidedly hostile to the principle of such a Convention' and only insisted that a reform of this magnitude should be discussed by more than two powers, 'and after the fullest deliberation upon all the bearings of a step which would be irrevocable'.[31]

The French Minister in Portugal was also in favour of the idea, although he remarked that some in Paris had taken offence that when sending the proposal to Europe, Washington had 'first specifically addressed [it] to this despised point of the circumference', instead of to the 'moral centre of the European political system' – that is, Paris.[32] That had obviously been O'Sullivan's fault, but at least he could report that his energetic appeal to Portuguese national pride had not been without effect. The Portuguese Parliament (the *Cortes*) formally accepted the Declaration of Paris, but during a reception Soulé declared that Portugal's adhesion only concerned the four points of the declaration, not protocol 24.[33] Thereby, Soulé informed O'Sullivan, he could proudly demonstrate 'that no amount of foreign pressure upon him would make him forget what was due to the honor of his country. This passed rapidly in a crowd.'[34]

Led by the French and Russian ministers, the European diplomats now admonished Soulé that this was unacceptable, some even considering a straightforward rejection of the adhesion without even passing it on to their governments. In the end, this was considered to be a step too far, but it was clear that Portugal would be made subject to considerable diplomatic pressure 'for the mere reason that Portugal has declined to bind herself to enter into their *grand moral league against us for the benefit of the British and French Navies*'. However, O'Sullivan was hopeful that continued US support might result in preventing Portugal 'from being "roped in" with the rest into that moral league of nations against the United States'.[35] To his great relief, O'Sullivan also finally received ex-post authorisation for his actions and was now able to propose a third, official draft convention, but Soulé had indicated that Britain was likely to put him under more pressure than he could resist.[36]

It was only at this point that the 'Marcy despatch' finally reached Europe, and when O'Sullivan wrote that 'it fully comes up to the expectation with which I had awaited it', that was another way of saying that it was about time.[37] If the intention was to prevent European states from joining the Declaration of Paris, the initiative simply came too late. Denmark, for example, expressed sincere sympathy for Marcy's ideas but had already joined the declaration more than six weeks earlier,[38] and while the Swedish press were unanimously in favour of the Marcy Amendment, the government was unwilling to act so soon after adhering to the declaration.[39] The reply from the Netherlands was similar, but also pointed out that asking the small states to reject the invitation to join the declaration meant asking them to confront the Anglo-French alliance: 'As long as the present alliance between England and France remains undisturbed, it is hardly likely that any measure of general policy proposed by them will meet with a serious resistance on the part of the smaller powers.'[40]

The Anglo-French alliance hampered US diplomacy even in the Western hemisphere. The USA should have had an advantage here, and accordingly made it much more explicit that continued port access for American privateers was expected.[41] Nicaragua announced its emphatic support of the Marcy proposal and promised a cordial welcome for any American privateers,[42] but the response from Venezuela, for example, mirrored that of the small European powers: the Marcy Amendment was viewed as highly favourable, but the government did not wish to go so far as to actually sign it.[43] As usual, the most honest answer came from Hawaii, which guaranteed port access for privateers and dispensed lavish praise on the US proposal, but likewise failed to mention any form of official accession.[44] When asked what kept Hawaii from a formal assent, the Foreign Minister explained that Hawaii could not afford an opinion of its own on such a controversial question because it depended on the benevolence of the great maritime powers. Hence his government had decided not to endorse the Marcy proposal while at the same time granting port access to American privateers to make sure that nobody was displeased.[45]

The Anglo-French alliance had to be split in order for the Marcy Amendment to succeed, and it did not seem hopeless at all: from the Netherlands, Belmont reported signs of a Franco-Russian rapprochement, and in the case of a new European congress, these two powers might be persuaded to take the US side on maritime law.[46] Russian support was certain: only months after concluding a treaty with the USA that was directed against Britain and its domination of maritime law, Russia had signed the Declaration of Paris, leading to inconvenient questions from American diplomats.[47] Keen to make amends, Russia was the only signatory of the declaration promising unrestricted port access for American privateers,[48] and the first great power to announce wholehearted support for the Marcy Amendment. Later the Tsar even offered to take the initiative in adding this proposal to the agenda of European great power politics.[49]

Marcy also knew that Prussia and Austria would be supportive of his amendment. If France decided that further liberalisation of maritime law was more important than absolute faithfulness to the Anglo-French alliance, Britain could be facing four great powers supporting the US proposal. The attempt to prevent the success of the Declaration of Paris had turned into a campaign for its reform, and the stance of the country that had drafted the declaration would be decisive for any chance of success. The US President, Marcy wrote to Mason in Paris, was 'looking with much anxiety' for the French reaction to the proposal: 'Should it meet with favor in that quarter there can be scarcely a doubt of its general adoption.'[50]

Mason went to see Walewski straight after the Marcy Amendment had reached Europe, and he reported a veritable gathering of ministers who all wanted to know what Walewski's position was. Walewski, however, countered Mason's questions by reminding him of the precarious position that the USA might find itself in if it was at war with Britain and the Royal Navy might not accept that the French flag covered US cargo. Mason coolly replied that this would simply be an insult to France, as a violation of an existing treaty between Britain and France, and thus 'would probably have the effect of bringing about a better understanding between France and the United States'.[51]

Walewski realised that the USA could not be pressured into acceding, and that he would soon have to take a position on the US proposal. Therefore he needed to know more about the British stance: the first response to the proposal to Portugal had been remarkably positive, and the British press had shown great interest once news of Marcy's proposal had reached Europe on 20 August.[52] However, when the *New York Times* claimed that the entire British press except for the Palmerston-controlled *London Post* was in favour, that was not exactly true.[53] The article in *The Times* revealing the official government line that the proposal deserved to be discussed with 'earnestness and good faith' was widely reprinted,[54] and newspapers from across the country enthusiastically supported Marcy's idea.[55] However, just as many papers rejected it – some because they believed that it would prolong wars, and others because it was not in Britain's interest as the largest naval power.[56]

More cynical commentators believed that the USA would never give up privateering, especially when a war with Britain was so likely,[57] and the *Saturday Review* reminded those of its readers not well versed in 'Yankee phraseology' that to an American mind, 'humanity and justice' were simply synonyms for US national interests.[58] The *Glasgow Herald* recalled the recent experience of the Crimean War and concluded that it would be 'sheer Quixotism' to go to war with Russia while its ports were all open. The paper was unsure whether Marcy's proposal was meant to include a ban on blockades (it was not) but nonetheless concluded: 'If this had been the law of nations we would in all probability have been in war with Russia at this hour.'[59] Understandably, Walewski asked for more precise information about the intentions of the British government before revealing his own position.[60]

The British Cabinet had already consulted the Law Officers. Queen's Advocate J. D. Harding considered the British adhesion to the Declaration of Paris to be a mistake, but now that this step had been taken, the Marcy proposal would have to be judged by the difference it made compared with the current regime. The new rules had been applied once during the Crimean War, mainly to secure the import of Russian hemp and other naval stores. The situation would have been more or less identical under the Marcy Amendment because blockades against specific ports or coastlines would still be legal. In return, accepting the Marcy proposal would bring Washington's abandonment of privateering, 'a concession of the greatest political advantage to Great Britain', but also to the wider world since private warships were a 'somewhat barbarous weapon'. The example he chose reveals Britain's nightmare scenario: a war in which Britain had to face the combined naval strength of France, Russia and the USA. In this case, the Royal Navy would be checked by the three opposing navies and be unable to offer any protection to British merchant vessels chased by American privateers. Then the British position would be better under the Marcy Amendment.[61]

Palmerston combined this assessment with the lesson learned during the Crimean War, namely that neutral trade would benefit immensely at the expense of the belligerents. Echoing Palmerston's views almost verbatim, Clarendon's reply to France was quite remarkable: Britain was not indisposed to accept the US proposal because it was 'a natural complement to the Rules and Principles established for Naval Warfare by the Congress of Paris'. Already, enemy property was free on a neutral ship, so it could just as well be free on an enemy's ship. Maintaining this distinction would have no military advantage but would allow the neutrals to benefit from taking over the belligerent's trade, 'for which there is no good reason'.[62]

Armed with these arguments, Walewski now openly opposed the French Navy Minister who had spoken out against the amendment. War, Hamelin argued, had to be waged aggressively and rigorously, and the abandonment of commercial warfare could lead to endless wars, which is why the US proposal was 'tout à fait inadmissible'.[63] Emperor Napoleon III decided that the decision-making process should involve a formalised consultation of other ministers, and several memoranda were commissioned to shed some light on the matter.[64] The memorandum from the Foreign Ministry pointed out that under the rules of the Declaration of Paris, the seizure of a hostile ship by a privateer was unlawful, while the same seizure by a navy warship was perfectly legal. It was therefore hardly surprising that Washington found this 'distinction très difficile' hard to understand, especially since it only benefited the great maritime powers. Of those powers, Britain was in favour of the Marcy Amendment because the Paris rules were too generous to the neutrals, and Russia had already signalled to Paris that it was willing to accede as well. Should France disagree, Paris might find itself isolated.[65] This memorandum silenced internal opposition, and Walewski signalled French support for the amendment to the British by the end of October.[66]

At the same time, Clarendon received a second memorandum from Stephen Lushington, the judge of the High Court of Admiralty. Lushington stated that Britain was not only the biggest naval power but also the biggest trader, and could ill afford to use its maritime prowess in the same way that it had half a century earlier. Liverpool would be plunged into misery if a war with the USA stopped all shipments of cotton. Thus only limited pressure on enemy trade was in Britain's interest, and the traditional right of blockade was sufficient for that end. In return for yielding nothing that had practical value, Britain would receive total security of its trade if it accepted the US proposal.[67] With this second memorandum also favouring the amendment, Clarendon was convinced that his own liberal instinct matched the results of sound strategic analysis.

But would Napoleon III act on his knowledge of British sympathy for the US proposal and make it his own? US Minister Mason believed that he would, since news of Russian support had spread and all smaller powers in Europe and the USA would support a French initiative. In late October, Napoleon and his Cabinet withdrew to Compiègne to make a decision.[68] Marcy's patience in waiting for the French decision showed that he had learned a lesson from the US treaty campaign during the Crimean War, and no longer placed any hopes on securing the support of individual small states. When John O'Sullivan, zealous as ever, pressured Soulé into promising that Portugal would accede to the US proposal if the Netherlands and Belgium did the same, and sought permission for a special diplomatic mission to these countries,[69] Marcy simply ordered him to stay at home. Marcy now placed all of his hopes on a new European congress:

> The obstacles which lie in the way of getting our proposition adopted, are not placed there by the minor powers, nor can they afford us much aid in overcoming them. The concurrence of three or four of the great powers will secure that of all others [...] It will undoubtedly be made a subject of collective deliberation among the principal if not all the powers represented at the late Congress at Paris and the fate of the measure will depend upon their decision. The earnest advocacy of the minor powers, may perhaps have some influence on that decision and I do not doubt our representatives will act efficiently in giving a proper direction to the course of these powers. Isolated proceedings on their part are hardly to be expected and would be of no avail unless concurred in by the leading maritime States of Europe.[70]

Mason shared these views, and believed that the crisis between Prussia and Switzerland over Prussian rights at Neufchatel might soon lead to a new European congress, which in turn would facilitate a great power consensus on the US proposal.[71] Then Walewski informed him that 'some difficulty had arisen': expecting the US proposal to be accepted soon, Quai d'Orsay officials had begun to ponder the legal form of a new change in maritime law, and had realised that the new instrument of a multilateral law-making treaty also meant that it would be very complicated to change a treaty with so many parties. Walewski suggested that the original signatories of the Declaration of Paris could pass the amendment in a new annex to the declaration, to which the other states could then accede. That approach, mirroring the original procedure after the Congress of Paris, would also solve any problems with protocol 24, since all parties bound by it would agree to the changed rules together.[72]

Russia declared its agreement with Walewski's plan and pointed out to the British that it also guaranteed that no great power would sign a separate convention with the USA without the consultation of the declaration's other signatories.[73] Marcy, however, was less pleased with Walewski's idea, since supporting it could be read as US agreement to the new approach of using European congresses to legislate reforms of international law, binding for all, even without the ratification procedures used for bilateral treaties: 'A mere declaration by a Congress of the Representatives of a few powers, would hardly be a proper instrument to send to the Senate for ratification.' In other words, a congress might be the means of choice to pressure Britain into accepting the amendment, but, once agreement was reached, the actual business should still be done using bilateral treaties. Therefore he instructed Mason to continue pushing for a formal convention with France: if Paris accepted, all other states would surely follow.[74] France's attitude, however, depended on whether Britain would oppose or condone the reform, and the Cabinet had refrained from speaking out on the matter in public. But by November, Palmerston was ready to launch a trial balloon and surprised the ship-owners and merchants of Liverpool with a remarkable election campaign speech:

> I cannot help hoping that these relaxations of former doctrines which were established at the beginning of the war, practised during its continuance, and ratified by formal engagements, may perhaps be still further extended; and in the course of time the principles of war which are applied to hostilities by land may be extended without exception to hostilities by sea, and that private property shall no longer be exposed to aggression on either side.[75]

While Palmerston's conversion was celebrated,[76] Richard Cobden threw his weight into the debate and re-established his position as the nation's foremost liberal with a forceful statement that was reprinted in dozens of newspapers.[77] His argument centred on the protection of British commerce: in a war with France, Britain would have four times as much property afloat as France, but, under the rules of the Declaration of Paris, all belligerent shipping was likely to be replaced by neutrals who enjoyed the privileges of the neutral flag while belligerent vessels would have to pay an additional war risk premium of 10 or 20 percent. In a war against the USA, British commerce would also be crushed, for at least 1,000 American privateers would swarm out to search for British prizes. Since the arrival of widespread railway networks had 'virtually put an end to blockades' as a weapon of naval warfare, Britain had little to lose and much to gain: 'It is then our interest especially, and beyond all other countries, to go forward in the path to which the Americans have invited us.'[78]

While liberal newspapers were full of praise for Cobden,[79] the *London Standard* wondered why it had taken him so long to take up Marcy's cause, given the appeal that the idea must have for the 'Manchester mind'.[80] Still, the amendment was asking Britain to make a sacrifice that it could ill afford to make: 'If America have no sufficient fleet we have no sufficient army.' In case naval war really was reduced to a duel of navies, the French and Russian fleet would simply hide in their stone forts and condemn the Royal Navy to inaction.[81] This argument was taken from a leader in *The Times* that marked a remarkable change in that paper's stance: it conceded that it had been sympathetic to Marcy's idea at first but now warned of the danger of the slippery slope: 'the truth is indeed, that carrying this principle of Mr. Marcy to its legitimate conclusions, we should in the end have to abolish blockades'. Then the Royal Navy would be next to useless, only allowed to engage in hopeless battles against stone fortresses such as Cronstadt, and Britain would have to rely on its weak army when confronted by the continental powers. It was true that Britain had four times as much property afloat as France, but the strength of the Royal Navy also meant that 'it would be in the same proportion better protected'. *The Times* finally feared that war would be more, not less, likely, since it could be had on easier terms for many nations which no longer had to fear destruction of their trade.[82] The *Aberdeen Journal* was unimpressed by *The Times'* new position. The right to blockade enemy ports was not touched by Marcy's proposal, which simply protected private property from capture. Thus the rules for warfare at sea under the amendment would be virtually identical to what was already practised on land: 'It cannot affect the supremacy of the British fleet, but it will save its flag from many an unworthy stain.'[83] Clearly, the public debate had not resulted in a consensus that might guide the British government. However, a renewed effort by the US President meant that it would soon have to make a decision.

In the last State of the Union address of his outgoing administration,[84] President Pierce pointed to the Marcy proposal as one of his few foreign policy successes and revealed that the initiative enjoyed the full support of both the Russian and the French Emperors.[85] At the same time, Walewski inquired when British support for the Marcy Amendment would be made public. He was much surprised to hear that no such decision had been taken at Cabinet level, especially since he had just told Cowley that the French stance 'had been mainly taken in deference to that of Her Majesty's advisers'. Walewski suddenly found himself in an uncomfortable position: assuming British support, he had informed the Americans about Napoleon's and Clarendon's sympathy for the reform, only to be told by Cowley that Her Majesty's Government 'had been much vexed when they found [...] that his Excellency had informed Mr. Mason of the nature of the communications which were passing between the two governments'.[86]

Partly to save face, Walewski now urged the British to come to a positive decision. He pointed out the 'contradiction flagrante' between land and sea warfare and called for a coordinated reply to the Americans by France and Britain.[87] But although Richard Cobden was certain in early December that the House of Commons would vote unanimously in favour of the Marcy Amendment if it were given the chance,[88] British politicians became increasingly cautious. The available evidence suggests that this was largely due to one man: Lord John Russell. Russell had left the Cabinet due to a rift with Palmerston in 1855, and the former Leader of the House of Commons was now just a plain MP. But after Palmerston had associated himself with the cause of liberal maritime reform, the chance to prove to the electorate that the Prime Minister was acting against the best interest of the country to please certain audiences proved irresistible. In his ambition to undermine Palmerston's position, he began by raising doubts about the Marcy Amendment in the USA.

In mid-December 1856 the British Minister in Washington, Lumley, informed Clarendon that several articles by Russell in the New York magazine *The European* had been sufficient to turn around the US press, which were now in a majority against the amendment.[89] The *New York Journal of Commerce* summed up the prevailing opinion by stating that if the USA were to join an amended Declaration of Paris, its article four should also be changed to abolish blockades against peaceful commerce, leaving only contraband goods and armed and unarmed belligerent vessels for lawful seizure. Russell replied in *The European* and argued that, as it stood, the proposal was acceptable to Britain, 'but she would not consent to abolish the law of blockades even if the whole civilized world were to unite in asking her to do so, for that would be a mere abandonment of her advantages as a great naval Power without any adequate equivalent'.[90]

While Russell and *The Times* shared the concern that the Marcy Amendment might lead to an abolition of the right of blockade, it was unclear to what extent they spoke for the Cabinet. In Paris, senior diplomats remained convinced that the signatories to the Declaration of Paris would soon agree on a new supplement to the original document, as proposed by Walewski.[91] However, those who had expected that the follow-up conference to the Paris Peace Congress taking place in Paris in January would be used to settle the maritime law question were disappointed because the discussion remained focused on details of the peace treaty with Russia.[92] With only weeks of its term remaining, the Pierce administration now sent new proposals for bilateral conventions to Britain, France and other European powers.

Ultimately, Marcy would have liked to see blockades banned, but President Pierce had decided not to mention the issue in order not to 'embarrass' the British government.[93] When Dallas asked Clarendon for his response to the new proposal on 20 February, the Foreign Secretary was evasive and pointed towards the 'great difference of opinion' on the Marcy Amendment in US newspapers. Still, Dallas believed that, privately, most politicians, including Palmerston, leaned towards it and would support it once Cobden's expected motion had been discussed in the House of Commons.[94] According to Mason, the French government believed the same,[95] and the official proposals made by Dallas and Mason coincided with the opening of the new session of the British Parliament.[96]

Unaware of these high expectations, Cobden tried to persuade the unwilling William Schaw Lindsay to propose a motion in Parliament, arguing that Lindsay could speak with more authority on maritime matters due to his position as one of the country's foremost ship-owners.[97] While Lindsay hesitated, John Russell used the opportunity of a House of Commons debate on income tax in early March 1857 to explain why the Marcy Amendment 'would greatly cripple the energies of this country in time of war'. Already, the right of blockade had been restricted by the Declaration of Paris and its new definition of effectiveness, which he referred to as the 'French rule'. This new tighter interpretation of blockade had forced the Navy to temporarily lift the blockade in the Black Sea during the last war. With the right of blockade alone, it would be possible to close off Boston or New York in a war against the USA, but the remaining ports along the US coastline would happily continue to trade, knowing that they enjoyed the protection of the Marcy Amendment. Therefore the proposal would mean the end of British sea power, and Cobden and Palmerston should reconsider their position.[98]

He was supported by J. G. Phillimore and Sir Charles Napier, who had commanded the Baltic Fleet during the Crimean War and now warned of the difficulties of a possible war with France under Marcy's rules, since the last war had shown that effective blockade was impossible during winter. At this point, Richard Cobden raised his voice for a short statement. Instead of engaging with the arguments proposed – for example, pointing out that the government understood 'effective blockade' as defined by the declaration rather differently than Russell, or wondering whether blockading France and Russia in winter really were comparable endeavours – Cobden simply remarked that he disagreed with Russell and would make a full statement in support of Marcy's amendment at a future date. His intervention failed to affect the course of the debate, and further opposition speakers criticised the concessions that the Palmerston government had made in the Declaration of Paris. The opposition also demanded a full debate before any definite obligations were entered into, instead of another *fait accompli* as in March 1854 and April 1856. Under pressure, Chancellor of the Exchequer George Cornewall Lewis assured the House of Commons that no decision had been taken by the government, and he promised that none would be taken without a debate.[99]

It must have been clear to any Cabinet member that a positive vote for the Marcy proposal was not a matter of course. Observers agreed that Russell's speech and the debate that followed had turned the tide, and that Palmerston would attempt to avoid the issue until after the elections in April. If Palmerston lost, Russell could expect to play a prominent role in the new Cabinet.[100] In Paris, Walewski even began to worry whether the new US administration under President Buchanan would still support Marcy's proposal, now that there was strong opposition against it in US newspapers.[101]

Palmerston won the elections, but Walewski's concerns had been justified. Soon the new US Secretary of State, Lewis Cass, formally suspended the negotiations with Britain and all other countries.[102] Unlike his predecessor, President Buchanan could not imagine abandoning privateering under any circumstances until the US fleet had reached the size of the British Navy.[103] Rumours spread in New York had predicted that Buchanan would add the abolition of blockades to his demands before giving up privateering,[104] but when Palmerston revealed in Parliament that the president had completely abandoned Marcy's proposal, the US press was stunned. The *Chicago Tribune* criticised the move as 'one of the evil consequences' of handing the State Department to Cass: since Britain had seriously considered the idea, a perfect opportunity to achieve a major triumph for US diplomacy had simply been thrown away. Perhaps, the paper speculated, *The Times* had a point when it blamed the withdrawal on a sudden fear that Britain might actually accept the offer.[105]

This comment raises two questions: first, whether *The Times* was right to assume that British acceptance remained a serious possibility; and second, whether the US offer was made in bad faith. The first question has puzzled historians. Francis Piggott seemed to be completely in the dark about whether there was any reaction to the proposal, and Stockton could only add his assumption that France made no objections, while Britain was directly opposed.[106] William Malkin was more careful and concluded that no official reply was sent as the US government had changed in March 1857.[107] Most recently, Andrew Lambert asserted that the Cabinet seriously considered entering negotiations but ultimately abandoned the idea 'because it undermined blockade'.[108]

In fact, Clarendon had already drafted the outlines of a formal reply to the proposal. The rejection of the amendment was based almost verbatim on the argument made by John Russell and *The Times*, namely that it was doubtful 'whether the principle of blockade could long be maintained as a fixed rule of war, if the principle of allowing the private property of a belligerent to pass free and unmolested were carried out to its legitimate limits'.[109] Thus the result of continued US pressure would have been a formal rejection of the proposal by Britain, and the fulfilment of Marcy's wishes: Britain had to justify its decision to singlehandedly scupper a major liberal reform, while the USA retained the right of privateering. But one question remains: was the previous US government, as *The Times* alleged, secretly afraid that Britain might accept? In other words, to what extent did Marcy actually support the Marcy Amendment?

The best evidence of Marcy's intentions is to be found in his despatches to Dallas in London, who opposed the amendment and pleaded with Marcy to withdraw the proposal. Even if it did secure US trade in time of war, Dallas argued, it would also mean that the British fleet was no longer tied by the need to protect trade routes and could be concentrated along the

US coastline instead. At any point, troops could be landed to 'countenance servile insurrection or separate the states'.[110] Additionally, the abolition of privateering meant the loss of the only offensive weapon that the USA could employ or threaten to employ against Britain. If the USA made this sacrifice, then it should make additional demands, not only the right of free trade with blockaded ports but also the abolition of all rules on contraband.[111]

Marcy disagreed and explained that in making the proposal he was criticised both for being too timid by not also demanding the abolition of blockades and contraband, and for being too reckless by not simply insisting on the right of privateering. But both options were not in the US interest: first, 'Had we declined concurrence in the declaration simply because it abolished privateering, we should have been placed in a state of isolation'; and second, demanding an end to all blockades 'would be going to an utterly unattainable extreme, and had we proposed it, would have subjected us to the imputation of resorting to a subterfuge by way of extricating ourselves from the embarrassment in which we were placed by the Paris declaration'. Both would have led to the USA being isolated but, because of his counterproposal, this was now Britain's lot. However, even though part of the motivation was tactical, that did not mean that he did not believe in the idea: 'I would not put forth a proposition which I did not think was right, in itself, and in its general operation, favorable to the interests of this country.'[112]

But there is more to this story. Towards the end of 1856, many ministers in Europe complained that Dallas was not doing enough to put pressure on Britain at this historic moment, and he defended himself by reminding Marcy of a private letter that the Secretary of State had sent to him on 4 August 1856, just days after making the proposal, and said that he 'felt restricted' in his support of the amendment by Marcy's private order.[113] In that letter, Marcy had indeed instructed Dallas not to formally inform Clarendon of the proposal but to leak it to the press instead and only discuss it with Clarendon if he introduced the subject.[114] So did Marcy instruct Dallas not to push too hard to minimise the danger of Britain accepting the idea? Given that Marcy's best hopes for success lay with a European congress, the order actually made sense. Too much pressure on London before the next congress might result in a negative answer being given in public, which in turn would make it much harder for any future British government to achieve a resolution at a meeting of Europe's great powers and present it to the British public as an achievement. If, however, nothing was said officially, the British Cabinet would enjoy much greater freedom of action. For the same reason, the Cabinet never published its decision to reject the amendment after it had been withdrawn.

While Marcy had secured a comfortable position for the USA, he was less successful in achieving his second goal because his efforts failed to undermine the success of the Declaration of Paris. When Count Walewski gave his official report regarding the status of the treaty to Emperor Napoleon III two years after it had been signed, most of the world's sovereign states were parties to the declaration.[115] Only the USA, Spain, Mexico and Venezuela had explicitly declined the invitation by the congress powers, all explaining that they were unwilling to give up privateering.[116] In the case of Venezuela, the reason seems to have been discreet US diplomacy,[117] while in Mexico and Spain the pressure not to sign also emanated from the USA, albeit in a less direct way. Spanish Foreign Minister Zavala was initially sympathetic,[118] but upon further reflection he declined to accede. He pointed to Spain's Cuban colony as the main reason, saying that Spain did not want to forfeit the possibility of using letters of marque 'so long as the USA reserved the faculty of sending them out from every creek and port in the Union', and would never accede if the USA did not.[119] That decision had been made even before the USA began to lobby the Spanish government not to accede,[120] and, while the Council of Ministers struggled to come to a decision on whether or not to support the Marcy Amendment, the government fell and Spain never officially stated its opinion on that matter.[121]

But all other European states joined, and, crucially, the Declaration of Paris also ultimately prevailed in South America. Here, only New Granada (modern Colombia) and Uruguay had joined straight away, but between August and October 1856, Chile, Guatemala, Haiti and Argentina followed. After Peru and Brazil signed up in October 1857 and March 1858, respectively, for the first time all important South American trading nations and almost all European states were united as parties in a single treaty.[122] The original intention to create an almost universal regime and isolate the USA had succeeded, but that did little to endear the Declaration of Paris to the British public.

That was largely due to the Conservatives' attempts to give their opposition a populist spin, as angry 'citizens of Leeds' presented a motion on the 'illegal abandonment of rights at Paris' to Parliament.[123] Like Russell in March, the opponents of the declaration had once again pre-empted a motion by the radical liberals. Lindsay had rejected Cobden's repeated prompting, arguing that a more competent MP should take the leading role, until Cobden insisted that it was his duty to raise his voice and counter 'what twaddle was uttered by Lord John [Palmerston] & that old Pirate Charley [Napier] (your own protégé) in the late Parliament upon this subject'.[124] Confronted with Conservative claims that the declaration had been an unwise decision taken without proper consultation, Lindsay finally spoke out and used the arguments that Cobden had prepared for him. He warned that British trade was doomed if Britain was a belligerent: even if the Royal Navy promised to protect every single British vessel, merchants would still place their goods on neutral vessels, with their flag being better protection than any convoy. Therefore Britain was bound to support a reform of the Declaration of Paris, since in case of war it could only honour the agreement if it accepted the ruin of its economy: insurance premiums for British vessels would reach 10 percent, the merchant navy would rot in the ports and neutrals would take over Britain's share of world trade.

Cobden frequently used this argument to explain the necessity of the Marcy Amendment, but the way in which Lindsay used it in Parliament did little to further their cause. Encouraged by Lindsay's portrayal of a Britain doomed by its signature under the declaration, Conservatives such as George Bentinck now openly demanded its abrogation. Since honouring it in war would be tantamount to the destruction of the British merchant navy, and thus its maritime supremacy, 'we must recede at any cost, even at that of the reputation of this country for integrity'. Even John Russell felt the need to affirm that whatever his personal opinion might be, a treaty had to be honoured as long as it existed, but for Charles Napier this was not an excuse but a problem to address: 'Diplomacy had drawn us into a very impolitic engagement, and it was for the noble Lord, or some clever diplomatist, to get us out of it.'[125]

Establishing a pattern that would continue for decades, potentially dangerous calls in Parliament to simply disregard the treaty and ignore the legal obligation entered into with dozens of other states were met with a more sober editorial in *The Times*. Unlike the government, the paper sought to disprove the arguments brought by the declaration's critics. Lindsay, for example, referred to the historic heights that the insurance premiums had reached during the Napoleonic Wars, and it was unlikely that they would ever reach similar percentages again now that privateers were banned and neutrals exempted, and only government vessels chased enemy merchant vessels. When Russell said that the old maritime rights had been abandoned, he went way too far, since the concession by the other states who all gave up privateering 'furnished more than an equivalent for the concession that free ships make free goods'. The Conservatives' claim that the declaration had been assented to illegally was an obvious pretext, with the Queen and both the House of Commons and the House of Lords having supported the treaty. Instead of relishing the memories of a naval supremacy that never existed, they should have realised that the Declaration of Paris was a remarkable achievement. In startling contrast with its earlier statement, *The Times* went on to deplore the fact that the Marcy Amendment had been withdrawn by the new US government, as it should have been immediately accepted when it was proposed.[126]

Obviously, assessing the implications of the Marcy Amendment was far from easy, and, as Palmerston stated, 'whatever might be the opinions at the first blush, one way or other, no one could fail to see on reflection that the question is one deeply affecting all the great interests of the country, commercial, political and naval'.[127] Palmerston himself had first favoured the idea, believing it to be 'a greater innovation in sound than in reality' despite concerns about the recruitment of sailors for the Navy if commerce continued unhindered.[128] By December he was 'more cautious' but his reasons were about politics, not the policy itself: 'I just launched the matter at Liverpool to see how the wind blows but it would be hard to know. I am inclined to think that on the whole we should have the best of it, but public opinion in this country I am inclined to think is not yet ripe for it.'[129]

In conclusion, the internal US government documents presented in this chapter confirm the assessment of the declaration proposed in the previous one as an essentially anti-American package deal. Second, although the proposal made by the USA in response is called the Marcy Amendment, numerous new sources indicate that neither was it Marcy's idea nor did it represent his initial wishes. Marcy ignored the suggestion by Mason and was only forced into making his proposal because the news of O'Sullivan's unilateral action in Portugal had spread all over Europe. His primary intention was to overcome the USA's isolation as the sole defender of privateering and once again occupy the moral high ground, leaving Britain to explain why further liberal reform was uncalled for.

To everybody's surprise, the British government, in particular Clarendon and Palmerston, seriously considered accepting the proposal. Upon hearing that the idea was not dismissed straight away, France, Russia and several smaller states openly expressed their support for it. The general expectation was that the matter would be discussed, and most likely resolved, during the next European congress, and Marcy thought that this was the most likely route to success. However, John Russell succeeded in creating a highly negative perception of what the Marcy Amendment would entail, whipping up the Conservative campaign against the Declaration of Paris in the process. Fearing that if the right to maritime captures was given up, the right to blockade might soon follow, the British Cabinet decided against it and prepared a negative response. The decision by Buchanan to cancel the negotiations meant that it never had to be sent, but the USA was still in a much better position than if it had simply insisted on privateering. The British attempt to isolate the USA and force it to sign the declaration had failed, and since all other states that still held out had made it clear that they would not join before the USA, further isolation seemed unlikely.

Crucially, this also meant that the declaration had failed to reach the status of undisputed international law, and, in a European war with Britain or France as a belligerent, it was unclear whether the neutral rights granted in Paris would also be extended to the US flag. While this was a minor concern to Buchanan in the first years of his presidency, the invasion of Italy by Napoleon III in 1859 suddenly made a general European war appear very likely. Two years after he had suspended negotiations on the Marcy Amendment, Lewis Cass decided it was in the best interest of his government to make a new proposal on maritime law, with consequences that neither he nor anybody in Europe would foresee.

5

'The United States Have a Vote in Framing the Maritime Law of this Age' – The Cass Memorandum and Bremen's Campaign for the Marcy Amendment

While the Marcy proposal discussed in Chapter 4 has not received much scholarly attention, some historians at least acknowledged its existence. The same cannot be said for the memorandum on maritime law sent by Marcy's successor as Secretary of State, Lewis Cass, in 1859. However, it was actually much more successful in influencing British thinking on maritime law. Crucially, it ruled out any attempt to undermine the new rights of neutrals by extending the contraband list. The memorandum also inspired a remarkable campaign to revive the Marcy Amendment started by citizens of the tiny German city-state of Bremen, which would have global implications and facilitate attempts by smaller powers to isolate Britain as the sole opponent to maritime reform.[1] Their use of the European congress as an instrument to influence great powers was innovative and – though ultimately unsuccessful – points towards an alternative development of this element of European politics that seemed entirely possible at the time and was supported by most members of what is now called 'international civil society'. However, the most important theme of this chapter will be the constant and often decisive influence of the USA.

The Cass Memorandum

After Marcy's initiative had overcome US diplomatic isolation over privateering without making any firm commitments, the Buchanan administration had reason to be satisfied with the outcome and turn its attention to domestic matters. As long as Europe was peacefully recovering from the Crimean War, not having a written guarantee of enjoying the new neutral rights in case of war seemed no reason for concern. However, when the Austrian-Sardinian dispute over northern Italy escalated and France entered the conflict on the Sardinian side in May 1859, British Foreign Secretary Malmesbury was not alone in fearing that a German intervention to save Austria might trigger a major European war.[2] In that case, most European nations would get involved, and merchants were likely to shun all European flags and opt for the security of the US colours. That potential windfall for US commerce, however, rested on the merchant's belief that the US flag would enjoy the neutral privileges guaranteed by the Declaration of Paris. Disturbingly, newspapers reported that France had promised to respect the Declaration of Paris 'especially for those states that signed it'.[3] Since the French note to the Americans did not mention this distinction, Secretary of State Cass instructed John Mason in Paris to find out what the French intentions were.[4]

When Mason obtained the official instructions for the navy, article nine was an unwelcome surprise: the rights under the Declaration of Paris would only be granted to member states, while others would be treated according to French maritime law. For the convenience of French commanders, the article included a list of all non-member states, including, of course, the USA.[5] On the one hand, the practical impact of these instructions was minimal, since French law guaranteed the 'free ships, free goods' principle and the distinction would only concern US property on Austrian vessels. On the other hand, the French move established a precedent that could legitimise a future British decision not to grant the 'free ships' principle to US vessels.

This was the core motive for Lewis Cass to write a lengthy memorandum outlining the US position on maritime law. The reason Cass gave was his concern that disputes over the law of neutrality at sea might trigger a spread of hostilities from Italy to other countries. War on private property was generally hard to reconcile with modern views, but the pretension to seize hostile property on board a neutral ship stemmed from a period in which the furies of war had been little tamed by humanity and religion. Therefore it was a malicious injustice if the signatories of the Declaration of Paris attempted to restrict the waiver of this rule to those states that had acceded, and the USA would not accept this: 'It ought not to be expected that this country would quietly acquiesce in such an invidious distinction, and the expectation, if indulged, would be sure to be disappointed'.[6] Several letters to American ministers explaining his intentions confirm that Cass was determined to ensure 'under all circumstances' that US rights would not be limited by the member states of the Declaration of Paris.[7] Moreover, Cass had also identified the most promising way to achieve this goal. If it was established beyond dispute that the neutral rights in question were part of customary law and not privileges, the old British maxims of maritime law would be illegal. Obviously, the USA could not achieve this alone, and therefore 'the principal object was to bring other commercial powers to the active support of our views, and thereby cause them to be engrafted into the Law of Nations'.[8]

To avoid appearing selfish, the US demand was not only clothed in the language of liberal reform but also included some genuine new proposals. Cass revived the Marcy Amendment and declared that the USA would give up privateering if the European states agreed to grant immunity for private property on the oceans, apply the right of blockade only to those ports that were also under siege from the land side, *and* restrict the category of contraband to arms and ammunition. Essentially, Cass extended the maximum position that Marcy had dismissed as 'utterly unrealistic' in 1857. But while this may sound like a liberal proposal coupled with unacceptable conditions to secure its immediate failure, there was more to it, since by 1859 the question of contraband had become an urgent problem. As the *Leeds Mercury* established, 'Formerly war suspended commerce [...] The treaty of Paris has entirely reversed this state of things.' The new rights of British and other merchants were only qualified by the prohibition of carrying contraband, but it was unclear what would be considered as contraband in this war. Merchants should consider that their commercial decisions also entailed a national responsibility: 'It would not be the first time, if the conflict of opinion arising from these causes were to end in war.'[9]

At the root of the problem was technological change: three years after the Crimean War, steam had replaced sail in warship design, and there was a definite logic in the Austrian ordinance of 11 May 1859 that declared coal to be contraband.[10] However, it was the French Navy that dominated the naval conflict and captured enemy merchant vessels,[11] and France did not regard coal as contraband.[12] But instructions could be changed at any time: Sardinia had first granted and then withdrawn immunity for Austrian vessels in its ports, with both Austria and France reciprocating.[13] Understandably, European merchants hesitated to accept orders to carry coal into the Mediterranean. These cargoes were taken up by American captains who relied on government protection for their flag.[14] Since it was public knowledge that the US government even refused to accept that British vessels had a right to search slave traders who fraudulently adopted the US flag, these captains could safely assume that Washington would not tolerate any captures of US vessels carrying coal by the French or Austrian navies.[15]

For Britain, the easiest way to avoid trouble would have been to ban the export of coal, but, given that British commerce was still suffering from the aftermath of the 1857 global economic crisis, Prime Minister Lord Derby decided that it would be unwise to interfere with the substantial coal shipments to France, and did not include an export ban in the proclamation of neutrality.[16] However, because the proclamation did not give an assurance that Britain would not accept coal being treated as contraband, it caused 'much excitement' among British merchants, especially after *The*

Times urged traders to err on the side of caution: naval stores had always been included as contraband, and, with steam the standard form of propulsion, coal might well be placed in that category.[17]

Liberal newspapers urged the government to 'insist resolutely on a large interpretation of the rights of neutrality',[18] but, when concerned merchants asked the Foreign Office for advice, it replied 'that, having regard to the present state of naval armaments, coal may in many cases be rightly held to be contraband of war'.[19] The enraged merchants secured publication of the letter in *The Times*, and after a French guarantee that coal would not be considered contraband in the present war was followed by a (false) report one day later that France had changed its mind, the topic aroused considerable interest in the USA.[20]

The *New York Herald* urged the government to resist any attempts to extend the contraband list; Britain would certainly try to treat coal as contraband in future wars, but the USA should build on the fact that France and Sardinia did not consider coal to be contraband and push for a formal clarification of what was contraband and what was not. On the question of neutral rights, 'there virtually exists at the present moment an alliance between the United States and France', and the memorandum currently drafted should be used to put pressure on Britain.[21] Unsurprisingly, an English newspaper correspondent investigating the drafting process concluded that the Cass Memorandum was essentially an initiative to secure coal shipments,[22] and when it was finally published the *New York Herald* was jubilant: 'The promulgation of this despatch will doubtless be followed by large orders for coal in this country, and generally will have the effect of promoting the interests of American shipping.'[23]

Despite the obvious self-interest involved, the solution that Cass suggested to resolve the problem pointed towards the future, and would be taken up again decades later: instead of traditional prize courts, an international tribunal should act as arbiter in disputes over contraband goods or indeed any other neutral complaint. Taken together with the demand to drop the distinction between signatories and non-signatories to the Declaration of Paris, Cass' determination to restrict Britain's options of extending the contraband list in future conflicts was more concrete and more aggressive than anything Marcy had done.[24] However, the impact of the Cass Memorandum was limited by two crucial developments: first, Britain was preoccupied with domestic turmoil as Derby's Cabinet fell and he was replaced by Lord Palmerston; and second, the Italian war ended surprisingly early after France proved unwilling to liberate all Italian territories from the Austrians and settled for a compromise. Cass even informed governments that were eager to support the new US campaign not to rush their replies, since the matter 'will lose nothing by being carefully considered'. The memorandum had been sent too late to affect the course of the conflict, but the US viewpoint that neutral rights were customary law and coal would not be accepted as contraband had been made unequivocally clear. This, Cass hoped, would not remain without consequences.[25]

The Bremen campaign

While Cass primarily hoped to impress London, his memorandum created even more interest in the small German city-state of Bremen. A tiny state almost exclusively devoted to overseas trade, Bremen had been the most enthusiastic supporter of the Marcy Amendment. In 1857 it had even tried to persuade Cass to continue with Marcy's initiative and achieve the isolation of Britain.[26] His decision to abandon the negotiations had so angered Bremen's diplomats that the envoy in Washington, Rudolf Schleiden, openly humiliated Assistant Secretary of State John Appleton, asking whether his country was so weak that it had to resort to something as barbaric as privateering.[27] Bremen's elite believed that an excellent opportunity to attain the inviolability of private property in wartime had been wasted in 1856/7. Now they were wondering whether the Cass Memorandum was the second chance that they craved.

The Bremen Senate was first informed of the proposal by its Minister in Berlin, Heinrich Geffcken, who had obtained the memorandum from the Prussians.[28] His colleague in London, Alfred Rücker, had spotted an article in a US newspaper which reported that the US government was now willing to consider the abolition of privateering.[29] Read together with the Cass Memorandum, this seemed like a cautious attempt to set out a new initiative on the Marcy proposal. Rücker immediately went to see the American Minister, Dallas, but was disappointed:

> Concerning privateering Mr. Dallas mentioned that the views of the American Government had changed. Marcy [...] was influenced by the authority of great American statesmen such as Franklin, but Franklin had then apparently been unable to foresee the future development of American trade. General Cass seems to hold the opinion (which is also shared by Mr. Dallas) that privateers are not only an effective means of attack, but also a means of defence that was indispensable to the United States; if England could apply its entire naval force against the United States then all their coasts and ports would be blockaded immediately and they would only have the mountains as a refuge. By fitting out privateers, of which they could send out more than a thousand within a year, they would be able to threaten England's commerce on all seas and prevent the concentration of its fleet at their coastlines. As long as the United States cannot sustain a naval and land force that is up to European standards they would not be able to dispense with the right of privateering for their protection.[30]

Bremen's Senate gave up, but, in October 1859, a local commercial news-paper came up with an intriguing idea: the *Bremer Handelsblatt* urged that the Marcy Amendment should be discussed at the next European congress, which was expected to take place in a few months' time to finally settle the Italian question. It called upon the congress' powers to 'disrobe war of the barbarity of the Middle Ages', and pointed out that while there would be an outcry if a state sent booty-hungry troops into a province on a mission of pillage and plunder, the robbery of private property at sea was still per-fectly legal. Only Britain stood in the way of reform, and even its opposition was not insurmountable: 'If the four other great European powers and the United States stand together, England will hardly be able to resist such a just and humane cause for long.'[31]

In essence, the newspaper called upon Bremen's Senate to somehow per-suade four of the five great European powers to defy Britain, put the topic on the agenda of the congress and achieve a major reform of international law. Admittedly, it was a tall order for a state of fewer than 60,000 inhabi-tants, and the Senate chose to ignore it. Yet the article electrified the local businessman Hermann Henrich Meier, who was also Bremen's most promi-nent liberal politician.[32] For him the Marcy Amendment was not only the ultimate expression of liberal reform spirit and human progress, but also the panacea that might save his business from certain ruin. Meier had founded his shipping company, the North German Lloyd, in 1857. A year later it was on the verge of bankruptcy, but, in a daring attempt to prevent liqui-dation, the company established a direct Bremen–New York steamer line, which would secure prosperity for decades to come.[33] A war in 1859, how-ever, would have meant French cruisers waylaying the steamers, and would have broken the company's back. The importance of this particular steamer line is demonstrated by Lewis Cass' request to the French to spare these vessels in case of war with Germany, since they carried much of the USA's European mail.[34]

Meier did what every American or British merchant in his situation would have done: he formed a committee, which drafted a resolution call-ing for urgent action. Unremarkable in more liberal countries, this style of campaigning was highly unusual in 1850s Germany, and Meier seems to have picked up the art of activism during his commercial education in Britain and the USA. The campaign was led by a committee consist-ing of Meier and several other prominent Bremen businessmen, such as Alexander Fritze and Carl Melchers, and it organised a public meeting on 2 December 1859. Meier's invitation struck a chord, particularly since almost half of his struggling company's capital of 4 million Reichsthaler had been raised among Bremen's commercial community.[35] Attendance at the meet-ing was high, and the *Bremer Handelsblatt* celebrated the re-awakening of German liberalism and the beginning of its recovery from the defeat of 1849: 'After a slumber of ten years, a sense of public life and the belief in the victory of the power which is called "public opinion" has re-awoken in Germany.'[36] The other local newspaper, the *Weserzeitung*, emphasised the potential for liberal progress inherent in the instrument of the European congress. A successful appeal to the congress to achieve a reform of maritime law would serve as a precedent for the peaceful and multilateral solution of Europe's conflicts, and it was no coincidence that it compared the congress to the ancient council of Athens that had both legislative and executive powers:

> The peoples of Europe have no other means reliably to assert their interests in the forum of this areopagus, which holds formally unlimited powers. Acting alone, even the best and clearest issues raised by them would be cast aside as special interests that did not benefit the whole. But no power would dare to resist their unanimous voice for long, and so those unhappy nations can regain a voice regarding the highest and most general issues of mankind, which they had been deprived of by clandestine oppression.[37]

This belief in the potential of the European congress was shared by the campaigners, who understood their meeting as the starting point of a global campaign, and their resolution not only urged the Senate of Bremen to take action but called for the support of every individual or corporation interested in the safety of global shipping. Every one of them 'ought to loudly raise their voice and proclaim to their own government and the assembled council of nations the unanimous judgement of the civilized world.'[38] There is, of course, an element of hubris in such demands coming from what was effectively a town hall meeting, but this global public relations campaign was a well-organised one. Having secured a budget of 200 Thaler from the Chamber of Commerce,[39] the campaigners printed their resolution several hundred times in German, English and French and sent it to consuls, politicians and other influential individuals, among them Richard Cobden and Lewis Ricardo.[40] Originally the campaigners wanted to see the resolution distributed by Bremen's consuls as an official document, but Mayor Arnold Duckwitz suggested that the letters should be sent by the campaigners and not the Senate.[41] The foreign consuls then passed the resolution on to their superiors, colleagues and friends, and instead of being informed of the campaign by an official proclamation, foreign governments were asked to take notice by their own officials.[42] More importantly, they compiled a list of well over a hundred national and international newspapers, the majority of which printed the resolution and demanded immediate action by their respective governments. The response was particularly positive in France, but Austrian and German newspapers supported it as well.[43] In Britain, the rise of news agencies operating by telegraph meant that even the accession of Stettin's Chamber of Commerce to the Bremen campaign was widely reported.[44]

Finally, the campaigners also persuaded other chambers of commerce in Germany, Europe and the USA to lobby their respective governments. Hamburg, the old rival, made a point of changing the terms of the resolution, adding a demand for an end to blockades and contraband lists,[45] but the other maritime trading towns along the North Sea coast – such as Rotterdam, Amsterdam and Antwerp – adopted the Bremen resolution within days. The *Bremer Handelsblatt* now urged the trading towns inland to show some solidarity, and soon Prussian Trade Minister von der Heydt received petitions from all quarters of his country, from Duisburg at the Ruhr to Breslau in Silesia.[46] Even smaller landlocked German states such as Saxony received letters from their chambers (in this case Cottbus and Chemnitz), and in France the influential Chamber of Commerce in Marseille lobbied the Minister of Trade, while their counterparts in Bordeaux addressed the Foreign Minister.[47]

British Prime Minister Lord Palmerston was lobbied by the Manchester Chamber of Commerce, and President of the Board of Trade Milner Gibson received mail from Liverpool. The resolution swiftly crossed the Atlantic twice: inspired by a 'great meeting of the citizens of Bremen', the merchants of St. John's in New Brunswick urged Foreign Secretary John Russell to adopt the Marcy Amendment.[48] Surprisingly, even the vast majority of articles in British newspapers were positive, with *The Economist* writing that 'It is creditable to so small a State as Bremen that it should have sufficient courage to make so great a proposal, and sagacity enough to make one that is so good.'[49] However, *The Times* attempted to ridicule the campaigners and their goals: 'a few Burghers in a little Hanseatic town have just undertaken to promulgate, for the benefit of the world, a new Code of Maritime International Law'. Perhaps with its own earlier articles on the Marcy Amendment in mind, the paper warned of the seductive dangers of liberal rhetoric: 'Even among our own multitudes there is a very large number of weak-minded people who will echo with zeal those cries about civilisation which keener wits will for their own purposes readily suggest.'[50]

After this article had been published, Bremen's diplomats in London actively tried to manipulate the coverage. Minister Rücker wrote a letter to the editor of *The Times*, using the name 'Mercator', in which he referred to the speech in favour of the Marcy Amendment given by Prime Minister Palmerston in Liverpool three years earlier. A second anonymous letter to the editor was written by Bremen's consul.[51] Soon *The Times* published a second leader in response to a 'considerable number of letters to the editor', dismissing the views of 'Mercator' and others as the biased expression of trade interests. But what was at stake was British national security: if the Marcy proposal succeeded, an 'exclusively maritime power' like Britain would be severely disadvantaged in every conflict against a continental, land-based power.[52]

In response, the Manchester Chamber of Commerce warned that because of the rules of the Declaration of Paris and Britain's role as the primary source of the world's commercial credit, a major war might cause an unmanageable economic crisis and a credit crunch, regardless of whether Britain was a belligerent or not:

> owing to the vast extension of commerce during the last forty years, and its widespread ramifications by a system of credit through all nations, it would be impossible to say on the inhabitants of what country the losses would not fall, nor would it be possible to cover by good policies against risk of seizure, the enormous amount of property afloat, after it became known that it was exposed to imminent risk.

France had already realised that the age of prizes and seizures was ending when all captured Austrian merchant vessels were returned after the war in Italy, and Britain should follow suit.[53] *The Times* countered by claiming that a coalition of merchants from different countries all acting in their personal interest meant nothing for the question of what was in the best interest of Britain and (in an interesting extension of the argument) the world. As Britain was a benevolent force in international relations that never started wars of aggression, the demise of its sea power would be felt across the globe: 'Our power would be infallibly exerted in deterring aggressors as far as possible; in preventing the outbreak of war anywhere, or in facilitating the conclusion of peace; and we think a power so beneficial should not be impaired.'[54]

The need to preserve British world domination was felt less distinctly in New York, where the Chamber of Commerce not only wrote to President Buchanan but also published a report that called upon the US government to speak out publicly in favour of the Marcy Amendment.[55] In the USA, lobbying by Bremen's officials was even more proactive than in London: the chair of the drafting committee in New York, German-born merchant Leopold Bierwirth, and the Bremen resident Rudolph Schleiden exchanged daily letters during the drafting process.[56]

Bremen's Senate had been sceptical about the campaign at first,[57] but due to the considerable momentum generated by the campaigners it changed its mind and encouraged full support by its diplomats. After all, the Senate had a tradition of fighting for liberal neutral rights, and the Marcy Amendment offered an intriguing solution to an ancient problem. While being an independent state, the city of Bremen was also part of the German Confederation, with the status of a Free City. These city-states were an anomaly originating from old imperial privileges, and would have been even odder if Bremen had got its way. When Germany was re-ordered in the aftermath of the peace of Lunéville in 1801, the three Hanseatic towns had asked for permanent neutrality for the Free Cities, unaffected by any wars that the new German Confederation might wage. To secure its position even further, Bremen had demanded the inclusion of the 'free ships, free goods' principle in the new imperial constitution, enabling Bremen's flag to protect imports from countries at war with the rest of Germany.[58] The preliminary commission accepted their permanent neutrality,[59] but the Congress of Vienna insisted that the Free Cities would be parties to any war involving the new Confederation.[60]

This is precisely what many in Bremen feared would happen in 1859: the war of France and Sardinia against Austria in northern Italy in the summer saw severe defeats of the Austrian troops, and there were loud calls for the German Confederation to enter the war to support its biggest member. If the Confederation had joined the conflict, Bremen would have been a belligerent and its extensive trade would have received no protection under the Declaration of Paris.[61] The Hamburg Senate even asked the British for naval protection for their ships in case Germany was drawn into war with France, a request that was politely but resolutely rejected.[62] Compared with the old exemptions, the Marcy Amendment was a much more elegant solution because there was no need for a special position among the German states. That would avoid the allegations of a lack of patriotism often raised against the Hanseatic towns in the past, and might help in securing Prussian support.

Unknown to the campaigners, the Senate had even taken the first steps towards a campaign of its own. In Berlin, Bremen's Minister Heinrich Geffcken wrote a memorandum advocating the opportunity that a possible European congress offered for the reform of maritime law which took the argument regarding congresses as creators of international law even further than the *Bremer Handelsblatt*: the main reason why they were so well suited to this purpose, he wrote, was that the decisions taken by the congress powers were always explicitly or tacitly accepted by the smaller states not represented.[63] After publishing an anonymous article repeating these arguments in the influential 'Prussian Yearbooks', Geffcken approached Prussian Foreign Minister von Schleinitz for support.[64]

Schleinitz doubted whether it would be possible to raise other matters than the Italian question at the congress, but Geffcken replied that the great congresses had always devoted time and effort to questions of international law and had attained much progress in this field. He implored Schleinitz to use this window of opportunity and present a motion.[65] Schleinitz remained unconvinced, but Geffcken was confident of success after the American Minister in Berlin, Joseph Wright, promised to put pressure on Schleinitz as well.[66] Wright informed Cass that even though Prussia had never replied to his memorandum, it remained a staunch supporter of the Marcy Amendment. Schleinitz had assured him that he would propose the reform to the congress about to meet:

> If Prussia succeeds in uniting the smaller powers upon the adoption of that principle, it is probable that England, for the purpose of rebuking the pretensions of France in her threatening attitude towards the commercial interests of the world, will cordially join Prussia in this movement and with great hopes of ultimate success.[67]

Yet, when preparations for the congress had progressed and it was scheduled to meet at Paris on 5th January 1860,[68] Prussia decided against a proposal. Schleinitz had realised that both Britain and Austria would resist an extension of the congress agenda, despite daily news of new public meetings in support of the Bremen resolution.[69] However, Schleinitz suggested an alternative: the Netherlands was the biggest of the smaller maritime nations not represented at the congress and could present the motion on behalf of all of them. On 31 December, Bremen's Senate sent Geffcken on a special mission to The Hague.[70] Three days later, Geffcken met Dutch Foreign Minister Baron van Zuylen. Alerted by the Bremen campaign, Zuylen had already attempted to persuade both France and Prussia to raise the matter at the Congress. Currently, he was in talks with the Swedish and Portuguese governments regarding common action. Geffcken urged him to abandon these discussions and lead a collective motion by the smaller maritime powers, since the congress would not be able to overlook such a big initiative. Zuylen was easily convinced, and on the following day the Dutch Cabinet authorised him to draft a message to the congress powers.[71]

Geffcken moved on to Belgium, where he was less successful. While being sympathetic to the proposal, the Belgians felt that it was too dangerous to risk the wrath of Britain.[72] Upon his arrival in Paris, Geffcken learned that the Congress was delayed, probably by two months. He redrafted and finalised the 'Dutch' despatch together with the Dutch Minister in Paris and even managed to convince an important member of the French *conseil d'etat*, Michel Chevalier,[73] by finding a quotation from Napoleon's decrees that showed that Napoleon too would have supported the Marcy Amendment, before returning via Hanover, where he canvassed the largest of the German coastal states.[74]

The invitation to the small maritime nations was finally sent out on 11 January.[75] The first states to join the new movement were the other Hanseatic towns, Hamburg and Lübeck,[76] even though the Hamburg Senator for Foreign Affairs, Merck, had earlier doubted the wisdom of the Marcy Amendment, fearing that it might be worthless without a strict definition of contraband.[77] With one exception (of which more later), all of the invited states agreed to participate, most importantly Denmark and Hanover.[78] With the final draft of the Dutch-Bremen resolution approved and more than a dozen supporters enlisted, all that was left was to wait for the great powers to assemble in Congress.

Some of the great powers had not been idle, too, and, unknown to the campaigners in Bremen, their arguments had made a big impression in the merchant community of Austria's Adriatic coast. In Trieste, a local newspaper called for an initiative to secure the Marcy Amendment at the upcoming congress in early November, long before the Bremen resolution was published. The language, however, is strikingly similar, also referring to the congress as an 'areopagus', a council with both legislative and executive powers that should reform the obsolete treaties of 1815. The Paris Peace Congress had made a creditable first step, but in this summer's war, horse-drawn wagons bringing Austrian property from Piedmont to Lombardy were allowed to pass, while merchant vessels on a similar mission were hunted by steam frigates. Thus the reform of maritime law should be an essential part of the congress agenda.[79]

The call was taken up by the Central Authority for Maritime Trade, a subsidiary of the Ministry of Trade. Even though the French had been less than zealous in their efforts to chase the Austrian flag off the oceans, Austrian trade had been hit hard, and it proposed three measures to the government: fortified ports, a stronger navy and efforts to secure the assent of all major naval powers to immunity for the merchant navy of a belligerent.[80] The Ministry of Trade agreed and urged the Foreign Ministry to take action on the last point, since the success of the Marcy Amendment would be 'highly desirable' for Austria.[81] The Ministry of Finance concurred: if nobody else put the topic on the agenda, Austria should make a proposal.[82] Under pressure, the Foreign Ministry compiled a memorandum stating that it was 'very doubtful' whether both France and Britain would agree, but it made an alternative suggestion: 'perhaps Russia could be persuaded to launch the initiative it hinted at in 1856 at this moment, and perhaps its voice, supported by the 2nd and 3rd rate maritime powers and carried by public opinion, will be forceful enough to break England's resistance'.[83]

Foreign Minister Count Rechberg instructed his envoy in St. Petersburg to inquire whether Russia was still supportive of the Marcy Amendment; since Austria considered making a proclamation comparable to those made in the Hanseatic town, it would like to know Russia's position.[84] However, supporting the reform and making a proposal proved to be two different things, and Lewis Cass was proved right when he claimed that Russia would like to see maritime rights extended but did not dare to be the first to challenge the Declaration of Paris.[85] Therefore Rechberg sent a similar inquiry to Paris to ensure that France was still supportive of the Marcy Amendment.[86] Meanwhile, the influential Finance Minister, Karl Ludwig von Bruck, had already sent a reminder, adding that the Congress should also set a narrow definition of contraband,[87] but Rechberg's response shows that he no longer supported the initiative: the agenda of the congress should be restricted to Italian affairs, and allowing any extensions might prove dangerous for Austria's other European interests.[88]

Nonetheless, despite the great powers' reluctance to make a proposal, Austria, Prussia and Russia were strongly in favour of reform, and the deliberations whether to start an initiative themselves demonstrate that these states would have hardly opposed it, provided that maritime law remained the only extension of the Congress agenda. France as the host nation would have to make the decision whether to allow a discussion of maritime law, which is why Cass sent explicit orders that the American Minister to France should seek 'informal communications with the Statesmen convened at Paris' to achieve that aim.[89] Bremen had attempted to secure stronger US support by appealing to its honour, now that the Hanseatic towns had 'adopted the child cast out by its father', but Buchanan was unwilling to respond.[90] In a letter to the New York Chamber of Commerce, he stated that the reform would only be acceptable once an end to blockades was added, since otherwise the USA would lose too much: in case of war against a stronger naval power, 'we should then be in a comparatively helpless condition without the aid of privateers'.[91] This unwillingness in turn reinforced his desire for the European Congress to endorse the Marcy Amendment: if Europe agreed on the new rules, the USA might once again reap the benefits without actually signing anything.

Combined with the alliance of small states assembled by Bremen and the Netherlands, the global public relations campaign and the Austrian coordination of those great powers in favour of the reform, the US determination to urge the Congress to adopt maritime reform meant that a perfect trap had been set up for Britain: once France could be persuaded to admit discussion of the proposal, Britain would be isolated and face considerable pressure to endorse Marcy's Amendment. However, the reason why this impressive campaign is virtually unknown today is that none of this ever happened. In late February, Cass was informed that the Congress was not only delayed but would never meet at all.[92] It collapsed because Britain and particularly Austria were afraid that the agenda would not remain limited to the Italian question.[93] While Austria favoured a discussion of maritime law, it feared that the French idea of open discussion of many other topics, such as those suppressed nationalities that had similar grievances as the Italians, would mean opening Pandora's Box, and it decided that it was safer not to hold a congress at all.[94] Under-Secretary of State for Foreign Affairs Lord Wodehouse confirmed to Bremen's Minister that Britain opposed an extension of the congress agenda for the same reason, not because of the call to discuss maritime law.[95]

Ironically, the disappointment was felt most distinctly in the Austrian Cabinet: Finance Minister Bruck argued that even though the attempt to isolate Britain at the congress had failed, Austria should at least try to achieve the Marcy Amendment by normal diplomatic means, using the momentum generated by the Bremen campaign.[96] Foreign Minister Rechberg admitted that the amendment was highly desirable, but, since France was so closely aligned to Britain at the moment, Paris was unlikely to take the lead. Therefore it was better to wait for the right moment.[97] Close coordination with Russia and Prussia would be vital to act immediately once an opportunity arrived.[98] Bremen's plan had failed, but the small powers that it had assembled and many of the great powers that it had tried to influence were only waiting for the next European congress to finish what had been begun.

Despite its failure, the campaign begun in Bremen and endorsed in The Hague offers important lessons about the potential inherent in the instrument of European congresses, and the hopes attached to them by small states. When the great powers began using multilateral law-making treaties, open for accession to all, to establish new norms of international law in 1856, they had not realised that they were empowering small states. In the formally egalitarian world of international law, these had more influence than in international politics. As Dutch Foreign Minister van Zuylen put it, 'the Congress powers invited the smaller states to join the Declaration of 16 April 1856, and now in turn those smaller states call upon the Congress to finish its work by proclaiming the freedom of all private property at sea'.[99]

This is also what was meant by the use of the term 'areopagus' for the European congress, which became increasingly common.[100] Instead of being a simple gathering of great powers ruling European affairs, it was now viewed as a semipermanent institution open for appeals by disaffected small powers or nationalities.[101] Ironically, the term used by liberals had been coined by a staunch conservative thinker, Friedrich von Gentz.[102] While Gentz had wished to make the point that small states and ethnic groups should wait in silence while the assembly of the major powers passed judgement on their fate, the liberals of the 1850s now demanded that the congress should turn to 'its actual task' as the 'appellate court of international law' and prevent future conflicts by securing progress in the law of nations and becoming a forum where international affairs and problems could be discussed openly.[103] The reply of Mecklenburg-Schwerin to the Dutch note – the only one to decline the invitation – is particularly interesting as it highlights the novelty of the approach taken:

> It seems hardly appropriate to the status of sovereign states to be put in a position, by the presentation of a collective motion to the Congress, where their demand might be rejected or ignored, not even mentioning the concerns regarding the recognition of the Congress as an authority or agency of international law, with the competence to manage all sorts of questions.[104]

All other maritime nations addressed by the Dutch Cabinet, such as Denmark and Hanover, welcomed the idea. Instead of only looking at the Concert of Europe from the perspective of its overall failure, historians should also note its successes (such as the peaceful resolution of the Neufchatel crisis in 1857) and the potential that was seen in this instrument by contemporaries. When reporting these new developments to the State Department, the American Minister in Portugal, John Louis O'Sullivan, wondered whether they would one day have profound implications:

> Much attention is now drawn to the approaching second session of the European Congress of Paris, which really is looked to as a sort of legislative body for a good number of pending international questions, such as those of Italy, Greece, the Danubian principalities, Neufchatel etc. Is this the embryo beginning of what may, (fifty) years hence, be a periodical Amphictyonic congress of the confederated European republics?[105]

In an early reference to the problem of reconciling European unity and democracy, some British newspapers criticised the 'areopagus' idea because it meant too much authority for a congress dominated by despotic powers, which was dangerous for Britain and humanity as a whole, but this fear was not shared on the Continent.[106] The failure of the congress plan was, of course, a setback, but it would take more wars ending without a congress to convince Europe's liberals that it would be 'iron and blood' that settled the fate of its peoples, not an 'areopagus'.

That being said, it needs to be added that while the Bremen campaigners were at the very forefront of the liberal reform movement in this respect, it is questionable whether the term 'liberal' is an adequate description of their ideological foundation. Their motivation was not pure self-interest, although it was an important factor. They had internalised the ideas of economic liberalism and concluded that what was good for them and merchants in other towns must mean progress for humanity. Yet the merchants of the Hanseatic towns always had an uneasy relationship with the mainstream German liberal movement, as they combined the economic principles of the Manchester School with strict social conservatism and anti-Semitism when it came to the political structure of their hometowns, still heavily dominated by patrician houses.[107] Nonetheless, the campaigners considered themselves to be part of the liberal *avant-garde* defying the old order restored in 1849, in Germany as well as in Europe as a whole. The uniqueness of the Hanseatic campaign in 1850s Germany was not caused by financial constraints (the campaign cost a mere 74.80 Thalers)[108] but shows that Europe's largest nation still had a long way to go until confident political campaigning by private individuals would become as natural as in Britain or the USA.

Cobden, coal and contraband

Not least for that reason, those who continued Bremen's campaign after the failure of the congress were British. The campaigners had concluded that only Richard Cobden could persuade the British Parliament to accept the Marcy Amendment and contacted him in Cannes,[109] but even before they reached him he had urged Lindsay to have a resolution ready to raise the problem of maritime law in case of a new European congress.[110] W. S. Lindsay had, as was shown in Chapter 4, been somewhat reluctant to step out of Cobden's shadow. But as with H. H. Meier, an economic slump in the shipping business provided a powerful inspiration to redouble his efforts. Even before the Bremen campaign, Lindsay had addressed a letter to Foreign Secretary John Russell suggesting that Britain should support the Marcy Amendment at any future European congress.

Lindsay used many of the arguments that he had employed two years earlier, but he could now point towards the troubled merchants of Lancashire and their anxious correspondents in India or China who had been deeply concerned about peace in Europe during the last summer. Moreover, Lindsay responded to the sentiments expressed, not least by Russell, during the 1857 parliamentary sessions, which betrayed a longing for a return to the days when the Royal Navy's determined interpretation of naval warfare humbled Britain's continental enemies, and questioned the logic that British naval clout alone could overwhelm continental enemies: 'I find it recorded as a historical fact that even after our great naval triumph at Trafalgar [...] Napoleon carried on, for nine years, the most fierce, aggressive and devastating wars, and pushed his conquests to the confines of every state in Europe.'[111]

The Foreign Office responded with a short note stating that the proposal appeared 'liable to grave objections',[112] and, when Lindsay's letter was published, these objections were discussed more widely. The *Morning Chronicle* argued that if Lindsay really believed that British trade would be ruined in the case of war, why did he not demand the repudiation of the Declaration of Paris, but instead called for the same reform as the 'sundry' merchants of Bremen? Just like those traders, Lindsay and his ship-owning friends wanted a war that was as light a burden on their profits as possible, while others paid with their lives. The nation would, of course, reject those notions, and if necessary solemn treaties; in a real struggle 'it will fling such engagements to the wind and strain every nerve for victory'.[113]

After *The Times* repeated these allegations of selfishness, claiming that the case that Lindsay made 'is not the case of the British nation, but of British ship-owners',[114] he responded in a letter to the editor, pointing out that once the strength of Britain's maritime commerce was gone, that of the Royal Navy would follow soon. Furthermore, colonial settlers who found their shipping unprotected might opt for independence to escape the British flag and benefit from neutrality. Clearly the Marcy Amendment was in the best interest of the nation as a whole. Those who suggested that Britain's obligations under the Declaration of Paris could simply be broken once war with a great power like France had broken out had forgotten that all great powers were parties to that declaration, and, if Britain violated its rules, 'any non-belligerent neutral might hold us to their observance by forming an armed confederacy to enforce them'.[115]

The latter argument pre-empted a critique by Richard Cobden, who had accused Lindsay of seemingly offering an alternative between reform and abrogation. The ancient maritime rights had been abandoned due to US pressure, '*not from choice but from necessity*', and it was in Britain's interest to even go as far as accepting the Cass Memorandum's demand of a limitation of the right of blockade. The real danger was a Britain harbouring illusions of past maritime greatness: 'With European law as it now stands, it merely offers the carrying trade to the United States in case of a war between England & any other maritime state sufficiently powerful to keep a few fast steamers at sea...'.[116]

In his capacity as a member of the Select Committee on Merchant Shipping, commissioned to investigate the problems of the industry, Lindsay succeeded in including many of these points in the final report. British shipping had been depressed in 1859 since US vessels were preferred to British ones 'upon a mere rumour of war', and maritime law could not remain as it was because of its potential to 'cause incalculable embarrassment at the outbreak of a war'. Although conservative members such as Cavendish Bentinck insisted on the option to 'revert to our ancient rights', the committee as a whole recommended the Marcy Amendment.[117]

Cobden was equally successful in securing the acceptance of another important argument, namely that the 'Anglo-French alliance' on naval law which so hampered the reform efforts of small powers and great powers alike might not hold forever, and was not unconditional. Napoleon III had been worried by reports that Britain did not rule out treating coal as contraband and immediately stopped the use of foreign coal in French Navy arsenals. He also gave orders to build flat-bottomed boats that could travel on canals to link the French coalfields and the naval ports.[118] When the Cobden–Chevalier commercial treaty was negotiated, France insisted on a clause that explicitly prohibited export bans for coal.[119] Britain accepted the demand, although the rule not to ban coal exports made treating it as contraband virtually impossible.[120]

Since the clause did not really fit in with the rest of the treaty, it was singled out for questioning in Parliament. Several members of the House of Lords pointed out that the clause meant that if Britain was a belligerent, a neutral France still had the right to buy British coal and potentially export it to the enemy, whereas if Britain was neutral, it no longer had the option of banning coal exports to prevent it from being entangled in a conflict.[121] Here, and one day later in the Commons, the government offered a variety of explanations: coal exports could not be prohibited anyway because this would damage an important export industry, belligerents might obtain coal elsewhere (although British coal enjoyed a near-monopoly for naval steamers) and the treaty would be suspended automatically in the case of war with France. Furthermore, continued French dependence on British coal was a powerful safeguard to preserve peace. Therefore, Russell claimed, it was 'quite a delusion to attach any great importance to this article'.[122] Now, Cobden urged Bright and Gladstone to make the rationale behind Article 11 brutally clear: 'You must take care to remind the House that the United States have a vote in framing the maritime law of this age, & that they will not acquiesce in our dogmas about coal being a contraband of war.'[123] The government, however, found it more convenient to proclaim that the treaty in no way affected Britain's right to declare coal contraband.[124] That, however, was the precise reason why France had suggested the article, and it represented a late triumph of the Cass Memorandum.

Britain had effectively granted the US demand never to treat coal as contraband, and would soon also give up its insistence that the neutral rights as laid out in the Declaration of Paris were privileges only available to signatories. When France and Britain went to war with China in early 1860, this distinction was quietly dropped, and the Order-in-Council guaranteed those rights for 'any neutral power'.[125] However, the erosion of the anti-US rules included in the Declaration of Paris stopped short of the most important one: the end to privateering. The French instructions of 1859 explicitly say that any Austrian privateer should be treated as a pirate, and the Austrian regulations confirmed the ban.[126] The neutrals cooperated as well: Belgium, once home to the dreaded privateers of the English Channel, duly informed its citizens that a privateer will be executed as a pirate wherever he sails.[127] Yet there were signs that the neutrals were beginning to demand a higher price for their assistance: a motion in the Prussian House of Representatives claimed that since the small states had made the 'enormous concession' of giving up privateering as a means of self-defence, the major naval powers now had a moral duty to grant the Marcy Amendment.[128]

In conclusion, the events of 1859 had confirmed the worst fears expressed in 1857. British shipping had suffered because of a mere rumour about a European war, and continued US pressure had – with French assistance – forced Britain to accept that undermining the declaration by extending the contraband list was not a viable option. Despite being withdrawn by Buchanan, the Marcy Amendment was alive and kicking, and the continental powers demanding it had shown surprising initiative. While the *Morning Post*, closely associated with Lord Palmerston, celebrated the fact that the Declaration of Paris had been scrupulously observed in its first war and had 'fully answered the expectations of its authors and promoters in obtaining for the commerce of the world a larger share of freedom and security than it ever enjoyed in time of war before',[129] Richard Cobden came to a very different conclusion, based on the success of Britain's attempt to influence the USA: 'As we stand we have acknowledged the rights of Neutrals in Europe, & we have *not* got rid of privateering in America [...] It seems to me something very akin to idiocy to allow matters to drift into such a mess.'[130] For the moment, Britain was not keen on a renewed Anglo-US conflict over neutral rights, but entirely unrelated debates about the privileges of slaveholding states in the USA would soon ensure that all these questions were discussed with a much increased sense of urgency.

6
The Declaration of Paris and the American Civil War

The first major war that was fought under the rules of the Declaration of Paris was the American Civil War, a confrontation between two parties who had both not signed up to the treaty. The theatre of the conflict was closely connected to Europe by transatlantic commerce, so the laws of neutrality became the field where the European states first had to define their positions vis-à-vis the belligerents. Nearly all of the decisive questions regarding the recognition of the Confederacy first arose in a naval context, and maritime law assumed an exceptional importance in the diplomacy of the early Civil War. Because of this prominent position, the American Civil War is the only mid-19th-century conflict for which the importance of maritime law has been recognised by many, though not all, diplomatic historians.[1] However, the best specialists in this field, such as Warren Spencer, Lynn Case and Frank Merli, were first and foremost Civil War historians and knew little about the laws of neutrality in the decades before or after 1861–5. Therefore they never claimed to be able to explain the significance of the Civil War to the wider history of neutrality. As Frank Merli put it, 'the precise relationship between that 1856 declaration of neutral rights and the American war has never been properly defined'.[2]

This chapter will attempt to fill this gap. Next to describing the history of the USA's attempt to join the declaration, it will demonstrate that it was not the advance of technologies such as steam which caused the demise of Confederate privateering but the regime of the Declaration of Paris, persuading the states of Europe and Latin America to close their ports. Furthermore, while it is well known that a problem of maritime law brought the USA and Britain to the brink of war in the *Trent* affair, the question as to why Britain chose not to confront the North over the rather patchy blockade that it had established has been less well covered. The concerted diplomatic pressure by the Europeans applied to prevent the North from evading the rules of block-ade by closing the Southern ports by decree, or issuing their own letters of marque when public opinion demanded their use, will also be unfamiliar territory for most historians. Yet these events not only shaped the debate over the future of the laws of neutrality but also deserve to be part of the historical narrative of the American Civil War.

The Declaration of Paris and the North: Seward's scheme

After the South had confirmed its secession with the attack on Fort Sumter on 12 April 1861, what remained of the Union soon regretted the decision of the Pierce administration not to join the Declaration of Paris. One of the first acts of the new Confederate president, Jefferson Davis, was to announce the issue of letters of marque, authorising their holders to attack Northern commerce. That did not come as a surprise: the *Chicago Tribune* had called upon Lincoln as early as January to ignore the confrontation over Fort Sumter and instead strengthen Fort Pickens near Pensacola, since this port could be 'the depot of piratical and privateering exhibitions [sic] to prey upon the commerce of the Gulf of Mexico and the Caribbean Sea, and our trade with the Pacific states'.[3] By February the paper demanded that rebel privateers should be treated like pirates and executed immediately: 'A short rope and a quick shrift for the buccaneers!'[4] After Davis had made his announcement, shares of the Pacific Mail Steamship Company and similar companies plummeted on the New York Stock Exchange, 'mainly on account of the apprehension of privateering'.[5] Undoubtedly, a tight blockade of the southern ports was needed, since at that time no vessel was safe.[6]

However, the *New York Times* also saw the positive side: Jefferson Davis had now thrown off the mask of legitimacy and justice, and his announcement exposed the Confederacy to 'the scorn and indignation of the civilized world'. Thereby the conflict might also add momentum to the creation of a new norm of international law guaranteeing the immunity of private property on the oceans, a cause that the USA had always supported:

> Under any circumstances, privateering has become an odious, indeed an infamous weapon of warfare [...] It is universally felt that the destruction of private property, in case of war, is a relic of barbarism, and that hostilities ought to be restricted to the public forces of the hostile powers. And although this principle has not yet secured recognition as part of the code of international law, the practice of nations has been towards its adoption.[7]

Two days after the Southern declaration, President Lincoln announced two important decisions. First, these letters of marque were invalid since they were issued by an illegal administration. Therefore holders of such letters would be treated no better than pirates. Second, he declared the entire coastline of the seceded states to be under blockade, 'in pursuance of the laws of the United States and the laws of nations in such cases provided'.[8] This deliberately murky phrase referred to both the rights of a legitimate government to subdue rebels and the traditional belligerent right of blockade under the law of nations. However, if the intention of the wording was to prevent the recognition of the Confederacy as a legal entity, it would turn out to be a costly mistake. Moreover, British newspapers immediately pointed at the obvious weakness of the plan. The *Bristol Mercury* wrote:

> The president further declares all the ports of the seceded provinces in a state of blockade, but no country in Europe will recognise a proclamation which is directly contrary to the law of nations. A port cannot be termed blockaded unless a sufficient force is placed at its mouth to maintain the blockade, and Mr. Lincoln is wholly destitute of means to carry out such a provision.[9]

The definition used by the paper to determine a blockade's effectiveness was the one traditionally advocated by France, and was also how article four of the Declaration of Paris was interpreted by the French. Furthermore, this definition was the one used internally by the US government.[10] Given that strict standard, Secretary of the Navy Gideon Welles knew that the force at his disposal was 'inadequate for the work required', but he hoped that by buying every half-suitable vessel and enlisting it for blockade duty, the force could be sufficiently enlarged before the small size of the navy caused embarrassment to the USA. By December 1862 some 358 new vessels had been put into naval service, 180 of them former merchant vessels.[11] Nonetheless, the *Liverpool Mercury* warned that while a blockade of the major ports of the South might be achieved with some difficulty, a close blockade of over 3,000 miles of coastline was impossible. The paper was acutely aware of where the blockade's effect would be felt most: in the port of Liverpool and the cotton industry of Lancashire, but also in Rouen and Le Havre and the textile industry of France. Given the importance of this industry for both nations, their governments would hardly submit to an ineffective blockade.[12]

At the same time, privateers would embark from Southern ports before a blockade could be installed, and with the US Navy stretched beyond its limit with blockade duty, hardly any vessels would be available to protect Northern commerce. Had the USA joined the Declaration of Paris, its signature would have been interpreted as binding for the seceding states.[13] If the USA joined now, and before any European government had recognised the Confederacy, privateering would be abolished for all citizens of the Union, and the British and French navies would have to chase American offenders against that treaty. Five days after the blockade was announced, Secretary of State William Seward sent a circular to his ministers in those states that were original signatories of the Declaration of Paris and instructed them to begin negotiations about a US accession immediately. In the past, Seward explained, there had been good reasons for not adhering to the document, but now it was in the national interest to join as quickly as possible after the rebels had taken 'the bad resolution to invite privateers to prey upon the peaceful commerce of the United States'.[14]

Meanwhile in Britain, *The Times* saw the Northern rhetoric used against the Southern privateers as reason for concern, and feared the worst for the freedom of the seas. Britain, it advised, should learn the lessons from the restraining effects that the Armed Neutralities had had upon the Royal Navy in the past, and seek an alliance of neutrals to counter future US pretensions.[15] The British government did not harbour such grandiose schemes, but it had agreed to solve these questions jointly with the French.[16] The Cabinet struggled to come to terms with a situation that was in many ways unprecedented, especially since most neutrals were eager to learn about the British position before making their next move. In all of the minor conflicts since 1856, the Declaration of Paris had served as the rulebook, and privateering had never been an issue. Now, the first major war since the Congress of Paris turned out to be a civil war between two non-signatories, one party being an insurgency handing out letters of marque. The Declaration of Paris did not specify how such privateers should be treated, but an answer had to be found before a Southern privateer actually met a Royal Navy cruiser for the first time. The expectation on the US side was clear: no government had accepted the Confederacy's claim to be an independent state, and therefore no nation should accept their letters of marque as legitimate. The *New York Times* even clothed this demand in the vocabulary of a joint crusade of both Europe and the USA, since in both continents 'all nations are deeply interested in banishing privateering from maritime warfare'.[17]

Unsurprisingly, the first question asked in Parliament about what was to become the American Civil War concerned privateers. Would their letters be recognised, or would Britain treat them as pirates and ultimately execute them when captured, as the Americans wanted? Foreign Secretary John Russell admitted that regarding Britain's interpretation of international law in the conflict, 'some of the points are so new as well as so important that they have been referred to the Law Officers of the Crown'. But he hinted at his ultimate goal for Britain's role in the conflict: 'for God's sake,' he called upon his fellow MPs, 'let us if possible keep out of it!'[18] That, however, was easier said than done, and it all came down to the question of whether Britain should accept the US claim that the Southerners were rebels, which would entail a duty to pursue them as criminals, or not, which would greatly irritate the North. The Law Officers were still led by Queen's Advocate J. D. Harding, who faced the most momentous task of his career: finding a relevant precedent, and preferably one which allowed Britain to remain as aloof as possible. Harding proved up to the task, and Russell greatly surprised the House of Commons on 6 May when he began to elaborate on Britain's position in the Greek War of Independence in the 1820s.

Then as now, Russell explained, Britain's stance would be guided by the actual situation on the battleground: if an insurgency is strong enough to form an entity that is *de facto* independent and defend it by waging war, then they should be treated as belligerents. Russell chose not to mention that Britain had only accepted the Greek's belligerent status four years into the conflict, in 1825, and two years before intervening militarily on their behalf in the battle of Navarino. He also avoided mentioning the Latin American rebellions occurring at roughly the same time, where Britain had used early recognition to undermine the Spanish campaign to maintain its empire and thus keep Britain out of the trade with Latin America. Instead, Russell emphasised the two yardsticks of *de facto* independence and the ability to wage war, and reported that the Law Officers found that both conditions were met in the case of the Confederacy. They were, however, uncertain regarding other questions that followed from the recognition of belligerent status, in particular about the 'alterations which are to be made in the law of nations in consequence of the Declaration of Paris'.[19] If the Confederacy was a lawful belligerent, their letters of marque were legitimate as well, but how should signatories to the Declaration of Paris deal with the privateers whom they had sought to abolish?

Harding advised that they should not be treated as pirates; pirates were outlaws, whereas privateers, even if commissioned by a *de facto* state, set out to capture a prize legally and secure an award in a prize court.[20] That assessment was shared by many, and the wish not to execute Southern privateers in English coastal towns was an important reason for granting belligerent rights to the Confederacy.[21] But that was not the end of the matter: what would the government do, the opposition asked, if a British subject was captured on a Confederate privateer and condemned to death by the North? Granville responded for the government and made it clear that no British privateer could expect diplomatic support or protection.[22] The Royal Proclamation of 13 May, in which Britain declared its neutrality and recognised the Southern states as rightful belligerents, thus contained no surprises but merely summarised the various announcements that the government had made in Parliament.[23] It also called upon British subjects to respect the Foreign Enlistment Act and enjoined them from fitting out privateers or taking part in their cruises and, since there would be a blockade, also warned them not to engage in activities 'designed to break a lawful blockade'. None of this seemed inappropriate, but next to its toxic effect on Anglo-American relations, the proclamation also entangled the government in an unwelcome discussion as to what it meant exactly when it described a blockade as 'lawful'.

The Declaration of Paris demanded that a blockading force should 'actually prevent access to the coast', but the Earl of Ellenborough claimed that this strict standard was impossible to match if taken literally. In his opinion, what the declaration really meant was to prevent access 'by establishing such a degree of danger to those who attempt to violate the blockade as to induce them to desist from doing so'. The real meaning behind his question was obvious: had Britain, in the opinion of the current Cabinet, accepted the stricter French standard of lawful blockades when it signed the Declaration of Paris, or was it free to stick to its traditional, more flexible approach? Granville's reply was unequivocal: the Declaration of Paris might be 'likely to form an epoch in the history of international law', but it had not changed the laws regarding blockades, except that it banned mere paper blockades. The standard used by the government to ascertain whether or not a blockade was lawful was whether it was 'very difficult' for vessels to leave or enter a blockaded port.[24] But rather than defining the terms of the Declaration of Paris, the government was more interested in securing their acceptance by the Americans, and was in close discussions with the French as to the best means to achieve that goal.

In Paris, the Foreign Ministry lawyers favoured recognising the South as belligerents, relying on two arguments. First was the precedent established during the American War of Independence in 1776, when initially Britain treated privateers with US letters of marque as rebels and pirates, but soon had to accept the inevitable and grant their enemies belligerent status. As an abstract principle, the memorandum suggested to always recognise an insurgent faction as lawful belligerents when it was so strong and organised that from a neutral point of view it was unclear what the result of the revolt would be. Realising that this reasoning would be somewhat unpopular in Washington, the French lawyers added a second argument: by imposing a blockade on the South that explicitly referred to the law of nations, President Lincoln had implicitly recognised the Confederacy as belligerents and so could not demand that neutrals withheld them a form of recognition already granted by the North. Regarding the question of neutral rights in the coming war, the memorandum suggested to simply remind the Americans of the various treaties that they had signed or proposed during the Crimean War, implying that they were honour-bound by these previous statements in favour of liberal neutral rights.[25]

London, however, was seeking something more official, not least to calm the concerns in business circles. Russell first suggested a joint endeavour to procure a formal recognition of the second and third principle of the Declaration of Paris by both belligerents,[26] but then changed his mind, presumably impressed by the relentless questioning on privateering in Parliament. He sent French Foreign Minister Thouvenel a draft of a despatch that called upon Washington to recognise all four principles of the declaration and asked whether Paris might be willing to cooperate in that effort 'to the great benefit of commerce, humanity, and ultimately of peace'.[27] Thouvenel was unconvinced and raised two concerns: first, the action might be perceived as an attempt to exploit the emergency in the USA to obtain an important concession; and, second, it might entangle Europe in the war. If the North accepted the Declaration of Paris but the South insisted on privateering due to its lack of alternatives, what would be the legal position of these privateers?[28]

Russell accepted these arguments and changed the instructions for Lord Lyons, his Minister in Washington. The new draft merely asked the USA to respect the rights of neutrals and the principle of effective blockade, preferably in a binding agreement with France and Britain, but not to abolish letters of marque. Russell only stated that in the past, privateering had attracted all sorts of outlaws and robbers, and that every government would be held responsible for illegal acts committed by the privateers whom they had licensed.[29] Thouvenel, on the other hand, accepted the fact that privateering was a real danger and needed to be addressed, so in his instruction to Mercier he copied Russell's warning that ultimate responsibility for the actions of privateers lay with their governments.[30] It said nothing about how Mercier should respond to a US offer to join the Declaration of Paris, and, as a confidential letter to Lyons reveals, Russell intended to make the most of that leeway.

Thouvenel, Russell informed Lyons, was sceptical regarding a full US accession to the Declaration of Paris, but his instruction to Mercier had left his Minister in Washington with some 'freedom of action' that Lyons was ordered to exploit. The British government would be very happy to see privateering abolished, so if the US government showed any signs of willingness to join the declaration, Lyons should 'encourage' it as best as he could. However, he was also warned to proceed with caution; the abolition of privateering could not be accepted if it was coupled with the condition that Britain and France would enforce it on the Confederate States. As long as the Southern privateers accepted the rights of neutrals, Britain did not wish to interfere with them.[31]

Thus it was just when Russell tried to outplay his French colleague via Washington that the American Minister in London, Charles Francis Adams, arrived with Seward's instruction to join the declaration in London. Adams asked for an appointment to sign a convention, but Russell informed him that he had just sent instructions on the Declaration of Paris to Washington, without mentioning that the official part of his instructions to Lyons did not amount to a full invitation to join.[32] This omission would add substantially to the air of confusion and mistrust that marked the Anglo-US negotiations, but it seems to have been motivated by the desire to improve the chances of a US accession to the declaration in Washington. In the Union capital, however, things did not go as planned.

After consulting with Mercier, Lyons wrote to London that both agreed the best chance to prevent a war with the USA was to act in perfect union, and that it would be a mistake to rush a US accession to the declaration. Adams was very likely to present instructions to join in London, but 'there is no doubt that this adherence will be offered in the expectation that it will bind the governments accepting it to treat the privateers of the Southern Confederacy as pirates'. Furthermore, it was unclear whether the US Congress in Washington would ratify an accession, or whether the USA would honour the treaty after it emerged that they would 'gain nothing towards the suppression of Southern privateering'.[33]

The first priority was to explain the granting of belligerent rights to the Confederacy, since it was known that Seward was fuming about this decision. After all, it raised the possibility that both French and British ports worldwide might serve as bases for rebel cruisers. Lyons and Mercier privately braced themselves for the worst: 'A sudden declaration of war by the United States against Great Britain appears to me by no means impossible.'[34] When both presented their instructions to Seward in a joint meeting, he refused to look at them since he knew that they would contain the official information that belligerent rights had been granted to the rebels.[35] The purpose of this 'averted glance' policy was to maintain the US position that no civil war existed, only a domestic rebellion that would soon be crushed. Instead, Seward wished to begin negotiations regarding an accession to the Declaration of Paris, but he was informed that neither minister felt authorised to open such talks, contrary to what Adams had written from London. In an angry despatch to London he repeated Washington's desire to join the treaty as quickly as possible.[36]

Meanwhile the new diplomats whom the Lincoln administration had sent to Europe gathered in Paris. In the absence of Adams, the Minister to Belgium, Henry Shelton Sanford, and the Minister in Paris, William Lewis Dayton, led the discussions, and they persuaded their colleagues that the current situation was an excellent opportunity to exert pressure on the Europeans to accept the Marcy Amendment. Britain was more afraid than ever of the thousand privateers that the North could unleash at any time to prey on British commerce, Sanford argued, and there was a good chance that London would no longer resist the amendment.[37] Ignoring his instructions to seek a mere accession to the Declaration of Paris, Dayton made an official proposal to sign a convention including the Marcy Amendment to French Foreign Minister Thouvenel.[38] When Thouvenel wanted to discuss the offer with his British counterpart, he discovered that no comparable proposal had been made to Britain. A direct question by Russell to Adams in London on 12 June also confirmed that the USA had no intention of submitting one. Inevitably, Russell and Thouevenel concluded that a rather clumsy attempt had been made to split the Anglo-French concert:

> The intention of the United States' Government in thus attempting to make a distinction between Great Britain and France, and endeavouring to engage France in hostilities against the so-styled Confederate States, is sufficiently obvious.[39]

Thouvenel informed Dayton that such a far-reaching reform would have to be discussed with all signatories of the declaration, while the British made sure that those 'discussions' would not be unduly intensive by asking the other European nations not to sign any convention with the USA that included the Marcy Amendment, a wish that even great powers supporting the amendment, such as Austria, respected.[40] There were, however, disturbing rumours that Bremen would soon sign a convention including the amendment in Washington, and that Prussia might follow suit.[41] Assuming that the Americans were not negotiating in good faith, Russell ordered Lyons to no longer push for an agreement on all four points of the declaration but only sign a document that contained principles two to four.[42]

At the same time, Seward and Dayton were engaged in the sort of confrontation that distinguished the US understanding of diplomatic service from its European counterparts: Dayton simply refused to act on his instruction to propose a plain accession to the Declaration of Paris, arguing that Seward's course was highly dangerous as well as unnecessary – dangerous, he claimed, because Britain and France would surely add a reservation precluding interference in the Civil War to any convention that they signed with the USA,[43] and unnecessary as Britain had just closed its ports to privateers:

> The late annunciation of the course of the British government, shutting their ports against privateers, (which so much limits the belligerent rights of the so-called Confederate States), you will consider, perhaps, renders the accession of our government to the treaty of Paris at this time of less importance than it otherwise would be.[44]

Indeed, the Cabinet had decided on 30 May to close its ports completely to privateers and ban the sale of prizes for other warships, and quickly asked the Law Officers whether such a sweeping prohibition was in accordance with international law. Harding saw no problem, pointing out that many neutrals had done the same during the Crimean War, and raised the question as to whether it might actually be a duty for every signatory of the Declaration of Paris to close the national ports to privateers.[45] The policy was announced in Parliament on 3 June, and Russell added that France would adopt a similar course: instead of closing ports completely to privateers it admitted all warships, but only for 24 hours, and prohibited the sale of prizes or captured goods.[46] Seward was elated and considered the new proclamation to be the 'deathblow to Southern privateering', especially since most European neutrals would copy the Anglo-French decision.[47] Spain followed swiftly despite not being a signatory to the Declaration of Paris, denying the Confederate privateers important ports in the Caribbean.[48] The Netherlands, Prussia and Italy did the same, and Seward duly thanked all of these states individually, not even forgetting to commend the 'enlightened' Senate of

Bremen.[49] The *New York Times* suggested, like Dayton, that the USA might well content itself with a situation where the Southern privateers might have belligerent rights but would not find a port in which to exercise them. The *New York Herald*, on the other hand, argued that a US accession to the Declaration of Paris, combined with Britain's commendable fight against privateering, would virtually eliminate the practice from the oceans 'west of China' and expose the Confederates as the archaic barbarians they were: 'It throws well earned disgrace upon those insurrectionists who have not scrupled to resort to this relic of barbarism, and it may be accepted as a final quietus to the infamous system throughout the world.'[50]

Seward was inclined to the latter view, since he still believed that his signature would also be held to condemn the Confederate privateers. If the USA concluded a treaty, he wrote to Dayton, they did so in the name of all of their citizens, loyal as well as disloyal ones.[51] Unwilling to follow his instructions, Dayton suggested on 5 July that the talks should be transferred to Washington.[52] Three days later, Sanford and Dayton were informed by Seward that he had ordered the talks to be held in London, entrusting them to the more reliable Charles Francis Adams.[53]

After a bitter dispute about who was to blame for all the confusion, Adams and Russell agreed that a convention by which the USA joined the Declaration of Paris would be signed on 16 July.[54] Historians have been mystified why Russell only informed the French Minister in London on the day before the planned signature, asking Flahault which day the signature in Paris had been arranged for. Lynn Marshall Case claims that Russell simply forgot the French misgivings about the US accession and had to be reminded at the last minute.[55] Given his special order to Lyons not to sign an accession agreement in Washington, this seems unlikely. Instead, the move put pressure on Dayton in Paris, whom Russell suspected of scheming to split the Anglo-French concert by proposing the Marcy Amendment. Dayton's reaction would reveal more about Seward's real intentions, and force him to forsake what might have been a new initiative to promote the Marcy Amendment worldwide. In any case, it was in these discussions that the French for the first time suggested that an identical written reservation should be added to the conventions in Paris and London to clarify that there would be no intervention in the Civil War.[56] Russell agreed to be the one who broke the news to the Americans,[57] but for the moment he gained time by simply informing Adams that conventions should be signed in London and Paris simultaneously.[58]

Dayton made a final effort to dissuade Seward from authorising a simple accession, warning that the North might lose its right to issue letters of marque while the South could retain it, and that a reservation to a convention between the USA, Britain and France was already being discussed in European newspapers.[59] Dayton then rushed to London and convinced

Adams that he should at least propose an adoption of the Marcy Amendment. If Britain declined, the USA would then have an official record of the negative and unconstructive British position and could point towards it in the future.[60] Russell provided the official rejection of the Marcy Amendment in a letter to Adams, expressing his delight about of the imminent US accession to the Declaration of Paris. Yet he concluded the letter with a cryptic remark:

> I need scarcely add that on the part of Great Britain the engagement will be prospective, and will not invalidate anything already done.[61]

Russell had let the cat out of the bag, and it was only because he had a later publication in mind that Adams played the fool when he forwarded the letter to Seward and Dayton, claiming to be unable to fathom the meaning of that sentence.[62] Dayton, less concerned about the impression that his written record might make, reminded Adams that he had told him so, and that Russell was simply looking for ways to extricate Britain from the duty to act against the Confederate privateers, just as he had warned Seward more than once.[63] However, now that the Marcy Amendment had been officially rejected, Dayton also had to live up to his promise and propose a convention in Paris.

Dayton's proposal meant that France and Britain finally had to decide whether they actually wanted to sign the agreement. Thouvenel was opposed, claiming that in his opinion 'the whole transaction was a scheme of the Washington Government to bind Great Britain and France to a declaration which they hoped to turn to account afterwards against the privateers of the Southern states'.[64] Cowley convinced him that it might be worth seeing whether the Americans would sign a convention if an official reservation was included.[65] The signature in both cities was arranged for 21 August, but both Adams and Dayton refused to sign the convention if it included the reservation. The reason for that, Cowley wrote, was no longer secret: 'Mr. Dayton hardly concealed from Mr. Thouvenel that the object of his government in agreeing to sign the Convention was to force the Western Powers to treat the Southern privateers as pirates.'[66]

Some historians have doubted whether the US offer really was in bad faith, and Seward was playing that blunt a game. One even goes so far as to argue that it sprang from a sincere desire to protect neutral commerce.[67] Lynn Marshall Case and Brian Jenkins argue that Seward attempted to prevent the recognition of the South as belligerents by offering to give up resistance to the Declaration of Paris. Since the maritime powers were keen on the permanent abolition of privateering, they might have been persuaded not to award the status of belligerency, which after all would primarily benefit the Confederate privateers.[68] As prime evidence for his argument, Case relied on a statement made by Seward to Dayton in July about his motivation for the offer: 'In this way we expected to remove every cause that any foreign power could have for the recognition of the insurgents as a belligerent power.'[69]

However, it seems more plausible that Seward invented this argument *ex post facto* to justify his decision to a highly sceptical subordinate. There is even a source where Seward himself admits as much. Like other maritime states, Bremen had been invited to sign a convention regarding the Declaration of Paris and, characteristically, decided that this was a prime opportunity to secure the Marcy Amendment.[70] Confronted with so much honest idealism for an amendment that would mean so much to Bremen's commercial community, Seward felt that he could afford plain language. He informed Bremen's Minister Schleiden

> that the main purpose of his proposal was to label the Southern privateers as pirates in the eyes of the whole of Europe as quickly as possible. As long as the Southern Confederacy was not recognized [...] every treaty concluded by the government in Washington would also bind the southern states, and if such a treaty banned privateering, the death verdict would be passed over the privateers fitted out by those states.[71]

Schleiden was undeterred, and, armed with full powers from three Hanseatic towns, he insisted on concluding a convention.[72] Seward then told him plainly that the deal was off because of 'changed conditions', and that he would not sign any treaty including the Marcy Amendment.[73] Schleiden still tried to point to the advantages of a convention, and together with his Prussian colleague, Gerolt, claimed that it would isolate the opponents of the amendment in the long term.[74] Lyons, on the other hand, passed the happy news back to London, relieving Russell of the fear that there might be a renewed treaty campaign to promote the Marcy Amendment.[75]

Thus Seward's plan really was to undermine the Confederate privateers by joining the Declaration of Paris to enlist the support of France and Britain against them. Britain might be so eager to finally bury privateering that it would sign a convention without making an explicit reservation, and, as he told the startled Lyons, in that case the accession would be valid for the entire USA 'and the effect of it with regard to the States in revolt be determined afterwards'.[76] When it emerged that his scheme would not work, he lost interest in it, informing Dayton that 'the President is not impatient about the negotiations concerning neutral rights'.[77] Russell, however, was determined to force Seward to show his hand and pressed for joint signatures in London and Paris. Confronted with Russell's remark that a convention would not invalidate anything already done, Seward resorted to philosophical speculation about what Russell might have meant, without stating the obvious.[78] In that form, the correspondence could be used as propaganda material in the case of conflict with Britain, which in Seward's opinion was highly likely.[79]

Having manoeuvred himself into a corner, Seward was left with little choice but to suspend the negotiations.[80] Thouvenel, Cowley and Lyons all thought that his reaction was final proof of how right they had been in including a reservation, and that a dangerous conflict had been avoided.[81] In Mercier's opinion, Seward's scheme was one of several mistakes caused by his inexperience and lack of diplomatic acumen.[82] Further evidence for the bad faith behind the proposal is the way in which Seward reacted when news arrived that his country had just acceded to the Declaration of Paris by a convention with Russia. The treaty had been signed in St. Petersburg on 24 August, and Russian Foreign Minister Gorchakov praised his own achievement in front of the city's diplomats. Telegrams from London and Paris soon revealed that the negotiations with the principal maritime powers had broken down. Fortunately for Seward, Gorchakov cooperated in silently burying the treaty by not forwarding it to the Tsar for ratification.[83] Needless to say, the US Senate never ratified it either, and no correspondence mentioning it can be found in the National Archives.

From a European point of view, the negotiations could still be regarded as a success. Seward had made an official statement that the USA respected the other points of the Declaration of Paris, which had been the core demand of the European neutrals.[84] Prussia and Austria had even threatened to use force to defend neutral rights.[85] On the other hand, the US non-accession to the Declaration of Paris meant that for the neutrals, all of their rights and privileges were only secured by US promises which could theoretically be revoked at any time. Even before a comparable pledge could be extracted from the South, the European neutrals had to respond to an open challenge to the entire system of the laws of neutrality, emanating from Congress in Washington. The representatives of the Union had realised that announcing a blockade under the law of nations implied a much higher degree of recognition of their opponents than they could wish for, and that neutrals were likely to challenge the effectiveness of the blockade very soon.

Therefore Senator Charles Sumner sponsored a motion that promised to solve both problems at once: by a simple change to the Customs Act, the Union could declare the ports of the South no longer to be ports of entry, and any attempt by US or foreign vessels to trade there would be a violation of US laws. Since it was a matter of purely national legislation, the requirement for effective blockade under international law would not apply, and the US Navy could cruise along the coast as it saw fit. When the news of the planned bill reached London, the Law Officers were consulted again, and their reply was unequivocal: the measure proposed was nothing but an evasion of the requirements for lawful blockade, and plainly illegal. Any measure against a British ship under such laws would amount to a hostile act. Unusually, the Law Officers even called upon the government to immediately protest against the act in concert with the other European powers.[86]

US newspapers brushed off Lyons' complaint, affirming that declaring ports closed to foreign traffic was part of national sovereignty, and asked how Britain would respond if it declared the Irish ports closed to suppress a rebellion and the Americans insisted on a blockade under the law of nations.[87] On 9 July, Congress passed the act as law, raising the question of whether President Lincoln would enforce the act by proclamation and risk a confrontation with Europe.[88] Both France and Britain instructed their ministers in Washington to protest in the strongest terms; French Foreign Minister Thouvenel compared the act to the paper blockades of the Napoleonic Wars, while Russell stated that it was entirely illegal and could never be accepted. Once again, Mercier and Lyons feared the worst and warned Seward that an enforcement of the act would have 'serious consequences'. They found Seward surprisingly understanding, and, after listening to their protests, he asked both ministers for excerpts from their instructions.[89] His intention was to use this material to convince the Cabinet that enforcing the act would mean war, but he had to face an equally determined opponent.

Navy Secretary Gideon Welles implored Lincoln to realise that his announcement of a blockade had been a mistake, made 'on the impulse of the occasion'. A blockade under the law of nations presupposed that those blockaded were a different legal entity, not illegal usurpers as in the case of the Confederacy. Furthermore, a blockade meeting the requirement of effectiveness was next to impossible, since the entire US Navy was insufficient for that purpose. If, as Welles feared, US prize courts would soon begin to release captured vessels because of the blockade's ineffectiveness, 'the Treasury will be exhausted under the demand that will be made upon it'. A confrontation with Britain would surely follow, so why should the USA now accept that it cannot close its own ports simply because London claimed that that would be illegal?

> Were there no fear of Great Britain, no threat or apprehension from foreign powers should we hesitate for one moment on this question of closing our own ports? If not, shall we, in our misfortune submit to the arrogance and dictation of foreign governments in relation to our domestic affairs?[90]

After protracted discussions, Lincoln decided to submit to European pressure. By late August, Seward responded to repeated Austrian complaints by defending the USA's right to close its own ports only in the abstract, hinting that Washington would remain committed to blockade.[91] Lincoln's decision to ignore Congress and simply drop the idea of closing the ports by decree was unpopular but wise, not least because Britain had already begun to assemble other European neutrals in a united front in case Washington insisted on enforcing the act.[92]

The Declaration of Paris and the Confederacy: The end of privateering

With respect for the provisions of the Declaration of Paris having been established in the North, the attention of the European diplomats turned to the Confederacy. Unlike the North, it had never confirmed its recognition of the rights of neutrals, not least because there were no official channels of communication. The first contacts with Britain had taken place in December 1860, when the future Confederacy approached the British Consul in Charleston, Robert Bunch, to make inquiries about the conditions of port access for Southern ships in case of secession.[93] For the Confederacy, close cooperation and even a possible alliance with London seemed to be a foregone conclusion: 'King Cotton' would not fail to exert his power over the Cabinet, since the entire prosperity of the English textile industry depended on uninterrupted supplies from the cotton fields of the American South.[94] Instead, Britain was primarily concerned about the security of its merchant shipping, and the first despatch sent by Russell to the Confederacy in May plainly asked it to guarantee the rights of neutrals as expressed in the Declaration of Paris.[95] Thouvenel agreed that neutral rights were so important that some form of contact with the Confederacy had to be established, but he was optimistic that their assent to the second and third principle of the declaration could be obtained by using the French and British consuls in Charleston.[96] Mercier and Lyons pointed out that a full accession to the declaration seemed out of the question because the South had already issued letters of marque and would hardly recall them.[97]

Meanwhile in London, Russell panicked when he learned how the recognition of Confederate belligerency had been received in Washington and asked Lyons not to contact the South. If, however, he had already initiated a negotiation, he should proceed with it to the end.[98] Lyons had, and informed Russell on the same day that he and Mercier had sent identical instructions to Charleston.[99] Bunch was informed that his object was to obtain the recognition of the second and third principle of the Declaration of Paris as well as a formal declaration that the Confederate government would be liable for any damages caused by illegal acts of its privateers. He was told to proceed with utmost caution, never go to Richmond himself and most importantly never to raise the question of recognition of the Confederacy as a state.[100] Bunch and his French colleague de Belligny used a former official of the state department, William Trescott, as an intermediary to contact Confederate President Jefferson Davis. Davis listened to Trescott's report and told him that an accession to the declaration was impossible because of privateering, but he would be ready to accept the other three articles as customary international law.[101]

The Confederate Congress accepted principles two to four in a formal resolution on 13 August 1861,[102] but the report sent by Bunch made it clear that for Jefferson Davis the negotiations were the first step towards recognition, and if Britain and France were so keen to ensure respect for the Declaration of Paris from one party to the conflict, they would surely display the same vigilance regarding the other:

> They also confidently expect that the same anxiety for the mitigation of the evil consequences of the present war which has rendered the accession of the Confederate States to the Declaration of Paris a matter of interest to France and England, will induce other nations to insist upon the rigorous fulfilment by the United States of the principle contained in the fourth article, viz., the effectiveness of the blockade instituted by that power.[103]

From the Confederacy's perspective, Britain and France had just implicitly guaranteed that they would enforce the principle of effective blockades and confront the Union in case its blockade did not meet that standard. Before Russell could reflect on this development further, he was facing more immediate problems: the special messenger used by Lyons had been searched, and Russell actually received the despatches from Bunch in a bag given to him by US Minister Adams.[104] For the Confederacy, this was the best possible outcome of its negotiations, since it confirmed its hopes that Britain and the North would soon clash over the question of neutral rights. Until then the Confederates would have to rely on their privateers to challenge the North on the oceans.

In many ways the naval situation of the Confederacy was similar to that of the USA in the wars against Britain in 1776 and 1812, with privateers being the only means of confronting the enemy before more powerful naval cruisers were commissioned. Regarding their administration, the Confederate government simply copied the relevant regulations of 1812, including a warning that neutral rights would have to be respected. To encourage their righteousness, applicants had to submit a bond payment of $5,000 for ships with a crew of fewer than 150 men, and twice that amount for larger vessels.[105] But neither bond payments nor Lincoln's announcement that captured privateers would be executed as pirates deterred the adventurous.[106]

Dozens of applications for letters of marque arrived within a few weeks, and although historians have often argued that the arrival of steam technology meant the end of privateering, this is simply wrong. Instead of being overtaken by technological change, the potential privateers embraced it, joined forces with other investors or even founded privateering companies to finance the fitting out of powerful modern steamers. The largest privateer, the 1,644 ton-steamer *Phoenix*, carried seven modern guns and a crew of 243.[107] Many privateers relied on fast sailing vessels and their guns were often outdated, but their early successes in the Gulf of Mexico proved that even these vessels could capture dozens of prizes and bring them back to port. The success of the New Orleans privateers proved to be brief since the port was one of the earliest to be blockaded (26 May), but by that time the first privateers had begun to operate in the Atlantic.

Although there were successful cruises lasting several weeks, such as that of the *Dixie*,[108] the procedure of the Hatteras privateers was more typical: lying in wait in one the many creeks and bays, they dashed out to capture a merchant vessel and brought the prize straight into the nearest port.[109] While the US Navy quickly gained control of the high seas, it proved impossible to control the vast coastline of the South, and the consequences of the successful Atlantic privateering were quickly felt in the port cities of the North. As the *New York Herald* pointed out, the damage was not primarily in the loss of dozens of vessels:

> The worst effect is not the loss of the vessels and their cargoes, but the destruction of our trade. Our commerce with the West Indies was immense before the pirates commenced their depredations. Now no Northern vessel will get a charter or can be insured for any reasonable premium. English bottoms are taking all our trade.[110]

This panic about losing trade to the British was not unjustified, and, like the merchants of Bremen or Trieste before them, the ship-owners of New York and Baltimore realised the effect of the 'free ship, free goods' rule on belligerent shipping. Neutral competitors took about 40 percent of the foreign trade that was formerly conducted by US merchant vessels.[111] The claim that many US vessels changed register and were now flying the British flag was also taken up by modern historians.[112] However, it is hard to discern any significant effect of the Civil War in the register of British merchant shipping.[113] On the US side, it is true that several hundred thousand tons of shipping tonnage were lost, particularly in steamer tonnage,[114] but given that hundreds of ships were enlisted in the US Navy for blockade duty, it seems that this claim was overblown: the privateers did severely harm US foreign trade but there was no significant flight of US shipping towards neutral flags. Still, Lord Lyons was right when he claimed that the small numbers of Confederate privateers had enjoyed 'considerable success',[115] but their effect was almost exclusively felt in the business circles of the north-eastern commercial towns. These circles did, however, control the New York newspapers. When the crew of the first captured privateer, the *Savannah*, arrived in chains at a New York prison, the *New York Herald* compared Jefferson Davis and his privateers to Satan, and many of its readers were just as eager to see Lincoln's announcement that they would be executed as pirates acted upon.[116] Jefferson Davis immediately warned Lincoln that he would order the execution of a high-ranking prisoner of war for every privateer hanged as a pirate.[117]

To make matters worse, the case of the *Savannah* was not exclusively an American affair. Just as Lord Derby had feared in May 1861, there were British subjects among the crew, and Lyon's dispatch informing Russell of the fate of these four men was most unwelcome in London. In Parliament, opposition leader Derby had demanded strong warnings to the Americans not to execute British subjects as pirates, and Lord Chancellor John Campbell, keen to deny the opposition any weak spots, had concurred that any state that executed a privateer under these circumstances would be 'guilty of murder'.[118] Lyons had acted accordingly and warned Seward that the plan to execute privateers as pirates was 'unacceptable'.[119] Now, London would have to live up to its rhetoric, and the Cabinet must have felt relieved when the trial of the *Savannah* crew ended in a hung jury. Apparently, some jurors struggled to see the difference between the *Savannah* and those privateers who had heroically fought for independence back in 1776. The crew of the privateer captured next, the *Jefferson Davis*, was not as lucky and was sentenced to death in late October 1861. Fortunately for the Europeans, this crew was all-American, and they could simply watch the drama unfold. Davis reacted by singling out individual prisoners of war for execution in case the verdicts were enforced. After a protracted stand-off, Lincoln finally backed down and the privateers were granted prisoner-of-war status.[120]

But even though the South was successful in securing the recognition of their status as belligerents from the North, the problems that their privateers faced abroad proved insurmountable, although the status of belligerents had been granted straight away by the Europeans. As Seward had foreseen, the British decision to close its ports to privateers really was the deathblow to the whole operation. Only days after news about the port closure had reached the USA, the insurance premiums for Northern vessels began to decrease.[121] The Confederates hoped that the Europeans might somehow be persuaded to open their ports, and Jefferson Davis used the first contacts established by Consul Bunch to urge them to reconsider their decision.[122]

The Europeans resisted these attempts – not because they wanted to disadvantage the Confederacy but to end privateering for good. The Netherlands even explicitly informed the North that it was happy to condemn the Southern privateers as pirates if the Union joined the Declaration of Paris now.[123] Denmark sent cruisers to the Caribbean, not only to protect its small island colonies but also to 'prevent privateering' and chase any privateers off Danish waters.[124] The British government asked Queen's Advocate Harding how far precisely it could go in the new instructions for Admiral Milne, the commander of the American squadron: was it legal to order the cruisers to keep such a close watch on the notorious privateers that they were even asked 'in a clear case of piracy on British ships, to deal with the aggressor as a pirate', instead of waiting for the decision of a prize court?[125] This approach went far in equating them to pirates, but Harding deemed the instructions to be just about legal. He added that it was highly unusual to treat privateers in this way even before there had been any reports of misdemeanour.[126] Russell, however, thought that it was 'quite right to anticipate piratical acts and outrages, and to put them down, if they should occur, with a strong hand'.[127]

Jefferson Davis was aware of the privateers' reputation and the need to avoid any incident implicating European neutrals. For that reason, great care was taken to emphasise all cases in which neutral goods were returned to their owners, or even Union ships released because their cargo was neutral.[128] Likewise, Confederate prize courts ruled against the instincts of their compatriots, who had claimed that black crew members found on captured Union vessels should be considered part of the cargo and sold as slaves.[129] Davis also refused to issue blank letters of marque for use by Confederate agents on the Pacific coast, even though their use would have in all probability enabled the South to carry its commerce raiding to the Californian coast. Without blank letters to aid clandestine operations, all schemes to equip privateers in the West failed, their only success being the creation of continuous privateering scares throughout the war.

Yet, despite all of these efforts, the Europeans remained hostile to privateering. Furthermore, the blockade was getting tighter, and it became more and more difficult to bring in even small prizes. Many investors decided to cash in on their profits and not risk new privateering ventures. A typical example is that of the *Sallie*, whose owners sold the vessel after one successful cruise in December 1861.[130] Most but not all privateers switched to the less dangerous and far more profitable profession of blockade running. Those who stayed on wanted to claim rewards for sinking Northern naval ships with technologically superior crafts, and letters of marque were granted to an ironclad steamer (the *Manassas*) and an experimental submarine (the *Pioneer*). Both, however, were taken over by the Confederate Navy before they first set to sea.[131]

By mid-1862 it had become clear that privateering was now completely unviable, but it had successfully spread terror among Northern merchants, and while Spencer Tucker claims that they were 'not much use' in the war,[132] privateers had filled a crucial gap. Without them there would have been no Confederate commerce raiding at all until 1862. Moreover, the success of the later commerce raiders, such as the *Florida* or *Alabama*, showed what vessels of this type could accomplish if they had port access, since these were hardly more sophisticated than the earlier privateers. Both used fast steamers that were also good sailing vessels to preserve coal, and while Sartiges had indeed argued in 1856 that progress in technology would make privateering obsolete, by 1863 the US Minister in London, Charles Francis Adams, came to a somewhat different conclusion:

> The great improvement made in steam navigation had given facilities for this kind of piracy never before known, especially in favor of those who had nothing to lose, and against those who had commerce spread over every sea.[133]

The reason why the commerce raiders enjoyed such spectacular success while the privateers had failed to make a comparable impact was that they were treated differently by neutral nations, who closed their ports to Confederate privateers but treated Confederate cruisers as legitimate warships. Although Seward lobbied hard with each and every neutral that every Confederate vessel should be branded a privateer (and thus denied port access), even small neutrals stood their ground and made a clear distinction. This attitude is expressed most clearly in the Dutch reply to Seward's complaints, who confirmed that since they were not privateers, Confederate vessels were free to use Dutch ports (including those in the Caribbean) like all other belligerent warships.[134] All other neutrals, and most importantly Britain and Spain, followed the same policy despite numerous US complaints.[135]

Northern privateering?

Following the Anglo-American crisis during the *Trent* affair (of which more below), the Europeans began to discuss whether they could apply similar restrictions to US privateers. Replying to a French request about its stance regarding maritime law in case of a war, Sweden confirmed that it was already pondering how to treat Northern privateers: the government was inclined to close its ports to all privateers since it had pioneered that approach in 1853. However, an old commerce and navigation treaty with the USA guaranteed American privateers the right to bring prizes into Swedish ports. The government was wondering whether it should risk a confrontation with Washington and sincerely regretted not having formally renounced the treaty when it had acceded to the Declaration of Paris.[136] Despite its satisfaction when the European states had closed their ports to Southern privateers, the USA had pointed out that it did not expect any such obstructions to its own privateers.[137] There was no question that the USA would resort to privateering in the case of a war against Britain: in an interview with Bremen's Minister Schleiden in summer 1861, Seward explained that the need for privateers in a war with Britain was the real reason why the Cabinet was unwilling to sign any treaty including the Marcy Amendment at that moment.[138]

In late 1862 the panic and outrage caused by the *Alabama* led to public calls for the use of letters of marque. Consistent rumours about more vessels being built for the Confederacy in Britain only fanned the flames, and the enraged Northern ship-owners began to promote the idea that instead of lying idle, their ships could solve the problem. In December the National War Committee, an organisation of New York notables, petitioned Congress to authorise the use of letters of marque as the 'the surest and best way' to hunt the Confederate raiders. Any privateer capturing a Confederate man-of-war should receive a 'liberal reward' for his efforts.[139] The petition was passed on to the Senate Committee for Naval Affairs on 18 December, and in his annual message of 5 January the Mayor of New York, George Opdyke, added his weight to the demands, describing letters of marque as 'the best and only weapon' against vessels like the *Alabama*.[140]

The Committee for Naval Affairs supported the idea but added an important amendment: the new version of the draft authorised the President to issue letters of marque in *foreign and* domestic wars.[141] Thus the President would need no further consent from Congress to use this authority in the case of war against Britain. The Senate passed the bill including the amendment, but the subject proved to be controversial, and senators did not vote along party lines. Senator James Wilson Grimes, Chairman of the Naval Affairs Committee, argued that this was a good time to 'reaffirm our maritime rights', whereas his fellow Republican, Senator Charles Sumner, a close advisor of President Lincoln, strongly argued against it: if additional cruisers were necessary to hunt the *Alabama*, the Navy should hire them and man them with naval officers; 'self-regulated' privateer cruisers were highly dangerous and might bring about a war with the great powers in Europe 'who had solemnly declared against this system of privateering'.[142]

Now the question was whether the House of Representatives would agree with the Senate. Despite condemning privateering as barbaric at the beginning of the war, the *New York Times* became the most active lobbyist on behalf of the north-eastern commercial community. In the first of a series of highly opinionated editorials, it questioned Sumner's patriotism and urged the House to pass the bill immediately to ensure that the USA was prepared for a foreign war. The recent mediation initiative of Napoleon III, it argued, was a sure sign that France would soon attempt to break the blockade to procure much-needed Southern cotton. Just days later it advocated the bill as a good warning to Britain, reminding it of the potential costs of a conflict with the Union and its numerous privateers, and a third editorial claimed that Britain was rapidly taking over the US shipping business. The loyal merchants of New York had of course not reflagged their vessels, and provided with letters of marque they could clear the oceans of all Confederate commerce raiders.[143] The New York Chamber of Commerce also urged the House to authorise privateering to stop the *Alabama*, against the vote of a certain Leopold Bierwirth who opposed privateering as a matter of principle.[144] The House passed the bill without much discussion on 2 March 1863.[145]

The news was not received well in Europe, and *The Times* feared that the bill might be the first step towards war with Britain. Parts of the Cabinet, it speculated, might be willing to promote privateers because they would inevitably cause a conflict, and the unavoidable final break-up of the Union could then conveniently be blamed on the Europeans.[146] Lord Lyons warned Seward that the bill might be 'misapprehended' in Europe, and Seward instructed Adams to make it clear in London that the decision as to whether the President would use his authority had not been taken yet.[147] For the French government, this seemed to be a foregone conclusion, and it sought legal advice on the consequences for France. The memorandum written by a clerk of the Foreign Ministry suspected that the deeper motive behind the act might be an attack on the lively contraband trade that British merchant vessels were conducting around Bermuda, but it saw no problems for France since French trade with the USA was depressed already. Not being bound by any inconvenient treaties, the French ports would remain closed, just as they were to Southern privateers. Further measures against privateers holding letters of marque by a state that had not joined the Declaration of Paris were unlawful since the prohibition of privateering was not yet customary law.[148] The British agreed that the privateers were still entitled to be treated as rightful belligerents but would close their ports as well.[149]

Meanwhile the Cabinet pondered whether the President should actually use the authority granted to him by Congress. Seward was preparing the ground in Europe, informing Adams that the President would soon announce the adoption of letters of marque, although 'not without great reluctance'. Lincoln, Seward wrote, felt compelled to act in this way because of the depredations caused by British-built vessels such as the *Florida*. If there was no 'improvement' in Britain's neutrality, public opinion in favour of letters of marque would be 'unanimous and exacting'.[150] Naval Secretary Gideon Welles thought that the bill had been a ploy to frighten and deter Britain, and was now stunned to see that Seward and Treasury Secretary Salmon Portland Chase were keen to implement it without even waiting for a reply from Britain, wishing to placate the 'whole commercial community [which] is greatly exasperated against the robbers'. Welles begged Lincoln to abandon the idea, calling it an 'idle attempt to spear sharks for wool', and claimed that if the scheme was actually carried out it would 'leave a stigma upon our country'.[151] A similar combination of moral and practical arguments was employed by Charles Sumner, who wrote a private letter to Lincoln in which he presented eight reasons why privateering was not in the national interest:

1. It is not <u>practical</u>. It is not the agency best calculated to do the required work.

2. It may possibly involve us with Foreign Nations.
3. It is counter to the opinions & aspirations of the best men in our history.
4. It is condemned by the civilization of the age.
5. It will give us a bad name.
6. It will do this – without any corresponding good.
7. It will constitute a precedent which we shall regret hereafter & the friends of Human Progress will regret every where.
8. It will pain our best friends in Europe.[152]

Apparently it emerged that some members of the Cabinet were arguing against letters of marque on moral grounds, and the *New York Times* ridiculed the critics as 'old ladies weeping for poor pirates': Confederate commerce raiders had even destroyed some of their prizes and caused overall damage of many millions of dollars, not least by triggering an exorbitant rise in insurance premiums. The government had failed to address the problem, and the New York merchants were impatient to take the matter into their own hands. Those Europeans who were complaining because of their commerce should consider that these letters would be issued not against commerce, but against destroyers of commerce. In any case, they had only abolished letters of marque out of self-interest. Soon the time would come to issue them against Britain as well, and if one further *Alabama* left a British wharf to sail against Northern commerce the President, who was a real man, would no longer listen to the weaklings surrounding him: 'The President, instead of being persuaded to put his letters of marque into the fire as the rubbish of a bygone age, we trust will always have them within arm's reach.'[153]

In the following weeks the Cabinet struggled to make a decision, and the majority against it presented an additional argument: if letters of marque were issued against the Confederacy, this would imply its recognition as a sovereign entity. The *New York Times* was quick to counter: the North was taking prisoners of war, which already implied their recognition as belligerents.[154] Welles fought hard to convince the Cabinet that the proposal was anything but effective, and that its adoption would entail an irresponsible risk of conflict with foreign powers:

> To clothe private armed vessels with governmental power and authority, including the belligerent right of search, will be likely to beget trouble, and the tendency must unavoidably be to abuse. Clothed with these powers reckless men will be likely to involve the government in difficulty.[155]

Welles' concerns were shared by the new French Foreign Minister, Drouyn de Lhuys, who informed Dayton that in the eyes of the French government it was 'an act uncalled for in present circumstances'.[156] Together with the apprehension of unwillingly granting additional recognition to the Confederacy, the fear of instigating a foreign war seems to have convinced the President not to follow (published) public opinion. With only a handful of Confederate cruisers or merchant vessels sailing the world's oceans, privateers would sooner or later target blockade runners, which were predominantly British. Furthermore, if a violation of neutral rights by a privateer brought conflict with one state, the Europeans were very likely to form a united front. Finally, many European states would close their ports, and there would be endless disputes about the right to take coal or make repairs once the privateers ventured off their New York base. In early April, reports emerged that some Cabinet members were still putting pressure on Lincoln, but that he had refused 'lest he should increase the difficulties of the republic and imperil its friendly relations with the maritime powers of Europe'.[157] Of these Cabinet members, Seward was certainly the most vocal, and the one who had the greatest influence on Lincoln. On 7 April he informed Adams and Dayton that the matter had not been decided yet, and that would-be privateers were already sending in applications.[158]

Adams, meanwhile, had passed on the threat to Russell, and warned him that if those in the USA wanting to preserve amicable relations with Britain did not receive some evidence of British benevolence that they could point to, 'it seemed impossible to resist the force of popular reasoning'.[159] But in his despatch to Seward he also made it clear that in his opinion the measure of using letters of marque 'was one very distasteful to the government' and that he had personal doubts regarding its efficiency and expediency. Shortly after this letter arrived in Washington, Seward wrote back to inform him that a final decision had been made and that the President would 'pursue the course of prudence and moderation which you have suggested'.[160] Crucially, Seward added that the news from Britain regarding its position towards naval construction for the Confederacy was inconclusive, and did not represent the decisive change in British behaviour that the Washington Cabinet had hoped for.

This is an important detail because Sumner's biographer, David Herbert Donald, explains the privateering bill as a ploy by Seward to frighten Britain into action against ship-builders suspected of constructing ironclads for the Confederacy.[161] Evidently, Lincoln and his ministers did not simply wait whether the threat with letters of marque had worked, but decided against privateering before positive news like the seizure of the *Alexandria* in Liverpool had reached the USA.[162] *The Times* speculated that the reason why the idea was dropped was a combination of the fear that privateers could provoke an unwanted foreign war with the danger that it might provide an excuse for the Europeans to recognise the Confederacy not only as belligerents but also as a state.[163] As the evidence presented here shows, this was remarkably accurate, except for the omission of the argument that resorting to letters of marque meant a moral defeat for the Union.

Britain and the blockade

The Declaration of Paris undermined Union as well as Confederate attempts to revive the privateering heydays of the Napoleonic Wars. However, American Civil War historians have usually portrayed the US efforts to bend or disregard the rights of neutrals as firm evidence that in war, might makes right, and that a British government will always claim to defend the laws of nations but privately file the precedents for later use.[164] While later criticism centred on the issue of prize law and continuous voyage, which will be discussed below, the first allegation of foul play against Britain was raised by the South, accusing London of recognising a blockade that was clearly illegal under international law, instead of challenging it for the benefit of neutral commerce.[165] This chapter argues that this and later criticism is unfounded, and that Britain consistently applied the same doctrine on blockade before, during and after the American Civil War, and found after extensive investigation that the Union blockade met that standard, if only just. Other neutrals, notably France, were more belligerent, partly because their definition of 'effective' blockade was narrower, demanding stationary vessels at every port. The original 'misunderstanding' about what article four of the Declaration of Paris actually meant was finally exposed, and the realisation that the requirement of 'effectiveness' was not the triumph of the Armed Neutralities that many thought it had been came as an unwelcome surprise to the French government. Since the North switched from promoting the French definition to the widest possible interpretation of the more lenient British standard while at the same time the Confederacy insisted that it had an agreement with the maritime powers that included the strictest possible application of the French definition, this meant that the precise meaning of article four became a crucial issue in the diplomacy of the American Civil War.

Suspicions that a blockade of the entire Southern coast would be problematic had been raised from April 1861, and after the Northern attempt to avoid this issue by declaring the ports closed had failed, the efforts of the US Navy would have to pass the standard demanded by international law. Lyons was not alone in thinking that it might fail, and began to ponder the possibility of concerted efforts with the principal foreign diplomats in Washington.[166] In London the opposition was keen to establish the blockade as a political issue since it was sure to be injurious to British business. As early as May 1861, Lord Derby urged the government never to recognise a mere paper blockade, and tell as much to the Americans.[167] Obviously the Cabinet needed to obtain as much precise information as it possibly could to determine the effectiveness of the blockade. In addition to the consuls, the government instructed every naval captain cruising along the US coast to collect and report data on the US blockade squadrons.[168]

The reports from the USA were inconclusive: some consuls, notably Robert Bunch from Charleston, sent daily updates on blockade runners, and Bunch concluded that 'the blockade is utterly ineffective, and can, in my judgement, be properly resisted by foreign powers'.[169] On the other hand, his colleague William Mure reported from New Orleans that the blockade was effective and all British merchants had left the city.[170] The investigations by the navy confirmed the mixed picture: some ports were blockaded more tightly than others, but the squadrons cruising along the coast meant that every blockade runner risked capture.[171] In the following weeks the information became more nuanced. The Gulf of Mexico was blockaded effectively,[172] but the blockade of the main Atlantic trading ports in Charleston and Savannah was only effective for larger vessels. The coastal trade continued and many of the smaller ports remained open.[173] This assessment was confirmed by the French Navy.[174]

The Confederate delegates in London and Paris tried to persuade the Europeans that this meant a violation of the law of nations. Consul Bunch was easily convinced, writing that the 'blockade is the laughing-stock of the Southern mercantile marine' in official correspondence.[175] At the same time the first British traders whose ships had been captured arrived at the doors of the Foreign Office. The first case in which Russell ordered further inquiries was that of the *Monmouth*, captured before Savannah: Russell wanted precise information about the blockade force before that port, but also instructed Lyons to avoid mentioning the issue to Seward and 'not to open a contentious correspondence'.[176] The Confederates struggled to provide exact numbers of blockade runners but promised more data to support their views. These statistics, however, were slow to arrive in London, with fighting the Union being an obvious priority. However, this delay meant that Royal Navy reports had a huge impact on decision-making in London. New investigations during the autumn had shown that some stretches of the coast were undoubtedly under blockade, and even Consul Bunch had to admit that it was becoming 'more stringent'.[177] Impressed by the navy reports, Russell concluded that 'the blockade must be regarded as generally effective against foreign trade' but he wanted to learn the opinion of Lyons before making a final decision.[178]

A second factor influencing his decision was a report from the Law Officers in response to the numerous individual complaints raised by British traders. Exasperated by dozens of petitions that were strong on sentiment and weak on facts, Harding wrote to Russell that what seemed to happen was a blockade just below the requirements of effectiveness, and any gaps that existed were exploited primarily by British ships. In essence, any shortcomings in the blockade worked to the advantage of British commerce.[179] Russell copied Harding's advice nearly verbatim in his next instruction to Lyons:

> Practically British interests may profit to some extent by the imperfect manner in which the blockade may be maintained, and it is questionable how far they would be advanced by the attention of the U.S. Government being called to the inefficiency of the blockade of any particular point.[180]

The Confederate commissioners now faced the challenge of turning around this decision and finally produced a comprehensive set of trade statistics in London on 30 November. In other words, it was a list of all blockade runners and their cargoes, which they asked to be treated confidentially.[181] Again it failed to impress since most of the vessels were small coastal traders, while the list contained surprisingly little evidence of successful British blockade running. Since October, however, reports suggested that this form of organised blockade running with modern steamers was an established fact. The *Bermuda* had arrived in Savannah from Liverpool, carrying weapons and ammunition, and many more comparable deliveries were being organised.[182]

Russell was puzzled and once again turned to the Law Officers: the Americans had considerably strengthened their squadrons, but, since more and more large steamers seemed to break the blockade, what did that imply for the effectiveness of the blockade? Harding and his colleagues replied that the crucial test was not the number of vessels running it but whether the blockader made a serious effort to station more and more ships before the enemy coast and succeeded in creating real danger for blockade runners. Again, Russell accepted their advice and instructed Lyons that a neutral power should be cautious in raising complaints, 'except when it entertains a conviction, which is shared by neutrals generally having an interest in the matter, that the power of blockade is abused by a state either unable to institute or maintain it, or unwilling, from some motive or other, to do so'.[183] In other words, the only thing that was really illegal was a paper blockade, a traditional British stance that had, at least from London's point of view, been confirmed in the Declaration of Paris.

In Parliament the Conservative opposition led by Lord Derby saw the question of blockade as a useful opportunity to challenge the government for its perceived lack of determination to protect British interests. After it had even called for a public inquiry, *The Times* made a forceful case to defend the government: if Britain broke the blockade because it was evaded, and primarily by British merchants, 'we should have somewhat the appearance of taking advantage of our own wrong if we alleged such partial transgressions as a reason for not respecting the blockade at all'. Furthermore, British action would open the nation to the allegation of having finally split the USA simply to obtain cotton. Finally, the major difference to the Napoleonic blockade was that Washington obviously made a serious effort to blockade the entire coast, and the only question was how successful the effort was. Therefore Derby's demand for an enquiry was wrong-headed and might lead to war.[184]

In response to these demands for more public information, Seward and Adams tried to influence the debate in Britain: the true test, the Union government now argued, was not the number of vessels that slipped through the net but the actual economic effect of the blockade. Cotton cost four times as much in New York as it did in New Orleans, while Southerners had to pay six times the Northern price for salt. The British Parliament could not lament the severe distress brought upon poor English textile labourers by the Union blockade and at the same time complain that it was ineffective.[185] As it turned out, Parliament could; the Conservative opposition made two further attempts to make the case for challenging the blockade, but was soundly rebutted, first in the Commons by Solicitor General Roundell Palmer and then later in the Lords by Russell himself. Both relied on the navy reports and argued that there was a clear intention on the Union side to blockade all ports, and most of the blockade running was conducted in small vessels, making the number of ships running the blockade a deceptive measure.[186] The pro-Confederates, such as London merchant William Shaw Lindsay, now changed the focus of the debate and urged mediation: if both sides accepted the inevitability of separation and the good services of the European neutrals, the senseless killing might be stopped – and, presented like an afterthought, the blockade lifted. Palmerston ended this debate by pointing out that if mediation was not welcome (as it clearly was not in this case), joint European action would amount to intervention, which would inevitably lead to war.[187]

In France, the shortage of cotton caused much graver economic upheaval than in Britain, and by late summer Napoleon III described recognising the blockade as a 'great error which I now regret'.[188] Therefore he made a fresh attempt to persuade Britain to join a mediation initiative, this time based on an armistice which would of course have involved a temporary lifting of the blockade.[189] The Cabinet rejected the idea but did not rule it out at a more opportune moment, and a French Foreign Ministry memorandum argued in March 1863 that the American way of conducting the blockade was 'leaving the door open' for a later challenge on its effectiveness. However, the affair had shown that the definition of effectiveness had not been affirmed in the French sense in 1856, as everybody had thought. The British, it had emerged, only saw it as a ban on paper blockades, although from a French point of view it also outlawed the 'cruiser blockades' favoured by London.[190] Given that Washington had adopted the British definition and no longer supported the tighter French one, the 'cruiser blockade' was an important step closer to being accepted as customary law.

But this was not the last word on the blockade: inspired by a Confederate offer of a permanent duty waiver on imports from France and 100,000 bales of cotton as a subsidy in return for breaking the Northern blockade, Napoleon III tried again, this time by encouraging Lindsay and fellow MP Arthur Roebuck in a private meeting in June 1863.[191] On 30 June, Roebuck introduced a motion calling for the recognition of Confederate independence, and conveyed what he announced as a personal message from the Emperor of the French to encourage immediate and joint diplomatic recognition.[192] Naturally, the question of Confederate statehood was instantly overshadowed by a robust debate about how appropriate it was for British pro-Confederates to conduct private diplomacy on matters of war and peace. It remains unclear whether Napoleon III actually tried to send a message in this unusual way or whether he was simply misunderstood, but together with France's armed intervention in Mexico the affair ended any prospect of a joint Anglo-French intervention in the Civil War, and thereby any chance of a challenge to the blockade.

Still, modern historians have doubted the effectiveness of the blockade, and Stuart Bernath claimed that it 'may well have been illegal'.[193] Both Howard Jones and James McPherson imply that Russell invented the British definition of 'effectiveness' on the spot and as a deviation from the Declaration of Paris, which as we have seen is factually incorrect.[194] David Surdam concludes that while many vessels slipped through the net until the end of the conflict, the blockade still succeeded in disrupting Southern transport patterns, limiting the availability of crucial military supplies and drastically reducing Southern trade.[195] This argument is a faint echo of Seward's demand that the 'true test' of the blockade should be its economic impact, but under the contemporary French and US standard of 'effectiveness' that demanded a stationary vessel at the entry of every port the blockade was in violation of international law, at least in its first year. What confused contemporaries and later historians alike is the difference between the French and British interpretation of 'effectiveness', with the latter allowing for cruising blockades as long as they created real danger for any blockade runners and thus frightened off honest merchants who were too timid for smuggling.[196] The Declaration of Paris only specified that a blockade has to be maintained by a force 'sufficient for actually prohibiting the access to the enemy's coast', which sounds closer to the French version but does not rule out the British understanding.

Thus, while the blockade was not perfect, it was also much more effective than those blockades that had previously been branded as 'paper blockades', and the case for challenging it was never compelling. Based on this evidence, it is hard to sustain the notion of a secret Anglo-US collaboration to undermine the rules of international law. After all, if Washington had got its way, there would not have been a formal blockade under the rules of the Declaration of Paris at all.

Britain and neutral rights

The second argument supporting the claims of British duplicity in the Civil War relates to the prize cases decided in US Admiralty courts. Some were widely regarded as blatant attempts to rewrite the rules of maritime law, particularly the attempted re-introduction of the 'continuous voyage' doctrine, which condemned neutral vessels carrying contraband even to neutral ports if it could be established that the ship's journey was intended to proceed to an enemy port. Regarding the British response, the classic view is that London's reaction was largely dictated by the future interests of British sea power.[197] Stuart Bernath acknowledged that a strong desire not to get entangled in the Civil War was another reason why the government resisted the aggressive demands of public opinion, but insisted that the main motivation was 'reasons of precedent and future requirements'.[198] James McPherson concurs, stating that the British government 'was willing to tolerate extraordinary Northern extensions of the blockade', and instead of protesting vigorously 'the Foreign Office merely recorded the precedent'.[199] This chapter argues that while this argument was used occasionally by the press, it never formed the basis for Cabinet decision-making. Rather, the Palmerston Cabinet resisted Washington's attempts to flout the rules of international law and only dropped its support in those prize cases where speaking out for notorious British smugglers would have carried significant political risks, after earlier embarrassments.

The first time Britain made a strong statement on prize law was during the *Trent* affair, when US Navy commander Wilkes famously claimed that like enemy dispatches, enemy agents could be contraband and thus taken from a neutral vessel. Like no other event during the Civil War the incident on 8 November 1861 during which Wilkes took the Confederate delegates Mason and Slidell from the British steamer *Trent* brought the two countries to the brink of war.[200] It was finally resolved when the Union accepted that Wilkes had been wrong on a technicality (he should have brought the ship in as a prize in case of suspected contraband smuggling), relieving both governments of discussing the merits of the case.[201] The British government did, however, insist on the absolute freedom of the neutral flag, pointing out that 'contraband' was a category that could only be applied to cargo that was destined to an enemy port, not to a neutral one. France supported this position, implying that it would join Britain in a war with the Union over neutral rights.[202]

Always a shrewd observer, Charles Francis Adams in London suspected that there was even more to the French despatch: in coming to Britain's defence, France had actually gone further regarding the rights of the neutral flag, allowing few if any exceptions for belligerent search and visit. It might, he suspected, be the first step of a clever manoeuvre aimed at binding Britain to a more liberal international law for neutrals.[203] And indeed, only days after Thouvenel had written his despatch, the semi-official *Moniteur* carried an editorial which claimed that a time when Britain was speaking out for the rights of the neutrals with unprecedented fortitude was surely a most opportune moment for an international conference on maritime law.[204] A highly supportive editorial in the *Journal de St. Pétersburg* confirmed that Russia could be counted on,[205] and Dayton urged Thouvenel to formally propose a conference. At this historic moment, it could achieve three reforms at once: the Marcy Amendment, a close definition of contraband and a complete abolition of the right of blockade. If the latter was agreed by a congress, Dayton hinted, the USA would be prepared to lift the blockade of the South.[206]

The British government realised that it was in danger of being overwhelmed by its own diplomatic success in the *Trent* crisis and rushed to kill off the idea of a multilateral conference, declaring in Parliament that Britain would not participate.[207] Following an intervention by the Law Officers, Russell also hastened to point out that British prize law actually knew what was known as the 'ultimate destination' theory, meaning that a ship and its cargo could be seized when allegedly travelling between neutral ports if their ultimate destination could be proved to be hostile.[208] The entire trip is then seen as a 'continuous voyage' intended to supply the enemy. The principle had always been controversial and was not accepted by many continental lawyers, who insisted that only the physical act of breaking a blockade constitutes an illegality.[209] It was precisely this question that again became controversial when British blockade runners began to supply the Confederacy, using tiny ports nearby, such as Matamaros in Mexico (just at the border with Texas) or the British island ports of Nassau and Bermuda as a neutral stopover.

As Adams reported from London, it was no secret that most of the Confederacy's imports came from Britain, and British blockade running was 'a frequent item for newspaper gossip'.[210] While the British had grudgingly tolerated similar trade in Hamburg during the Crimean War, the difference was that Hamburg was a major European port, and the brisk business now being done in the Caribbean was in stark contrast with normal trading patterns. Annoyed by profiteers who made fortunes supplying arms and ammunition to their enemy, the US government soon decided that enough was enough. In November 1861, Navy Secretary Gideon Welles sent an order to the commander of the blockading squadron in the Gulf of Mexico that he was to make a capture whenever there was good reason to suspect that goods were destined for the enemy, even if they were sailing under a neutral flag or heading towards a neutral port.[211]

Inevitably, the captures made under this order provoked difficulties with the neutrals. The British led the protests, complaining that although the USA had officially accepted the 'free ships, free goods' principle for the duration of the war, the US Navy was harassing peaceful merchants. Impressed, Welles agreed to give an order to his squadrons to remind them of the extent of neutral rights.[212] Still, the Foreign Office pressed the Admiralty to send more ships to the region without delay.[213] When the New York District Court released one of the contentious vessels on 21 May 1862 (the *Labuan*), this episode seemed to be over. Its capture had violated the 'free ships, free goods' principle and it was the ship's right to carry a cargo of rebel cotton coming out of Matamaros. The *Will o' the Wisp* was released despite having hidden huge amounts of gunpowder in barrels marked 'codfish'. The judgement did not accept the principle of continuous voyage and stated that 'in a trade carried on between neutral nations or ports there can be no such thing as contraband of war', and only denied damages and compensation because the hidden cargo was bound to raise the suspicions of the US Navy.[214] The British government protested even against this decision, unsuccessfully demanding financial compensation for the owner.[215] Despite these legal defeats, Rear-Admiral Farragut re-affirmed the earlier order from November, clarifying that all ships calling at Matamaros would be subject to visit and search.[216] Unsurprisingly, more seizures of British vessels followed, and the British government issued its strongest protest yet, demanding full respect for British neutral rights for all vessels trading with Matamaros.[217] Once again, Welles was compelled by Seward to issue new orders, warning his commanders not to violate neutral waters (as they had done repeatedly) and only seize vessels if they found evidence of wrongdoing.[218]

However, for many American officers their suspicion that a ship might be a blockade runner was evidence enough. Whenthe *Orion* was captured on the way to Matamaros, based on the claim that since this was a smuggler's port- the ship might well be involved in smuggling, an increasingly irritated Lyons wrote to Seward that 'upon this plea every vessel that swims the ocean, and does not belong to the United States, may be captured'.[219] The *Orion* marked the start of an important pattern which saw strong British protests backfire in rather embarrassing circumstances. During the prize court proceedings, it emerged that the ship had only changed from Confederate to British register in Jamaica, just before starting the return journey with the same crew, and was therefore condemned not under the 'continuous voyage' doctrine but on the grounds of fraudulent identity.[220]

The British Cabinet had to endure a similar experience shortly afterwards, this time with a Liverpool merchant called William Joshua Grazebrook. After having unsuccessfully offered his services to the Confederacy, which declined his offer to provide ironclads at a fixed rate of profit,[221] he began to organise blockade-running ventures from Liverpool, using the tiny port of Nassau as the alleged neutral destination. When one of his ships, the *Dolphin*, was captured, he found supporters in Parliament, and the Marquess of Clanricarde raised his case as one of a succession of 'grossest violations of international law', concluding that 'a greater outrage on property, or a greater insult to the British flag, had seldom or never been offered'. What would the Government do to protect British commerce?[222] Well briefed by the Law Officers about the recent problems with blockade runners, Russell made a careful statement of British policy: the *Dolphin* had apparently been taken just outside the Danish port of St. Thomas, which was a violation of Danish neutrality. Regarding the ship, however, he asked the Lords to consider the possibility that the *Dolphin* never intended to go to Nassau. In case she was actually a blockade runner, Britain would stick to its own laws and precedents, which would be respected as belligerents and as neutrals:

> Accordingly, those persons who think, that whatever may be the destination of a ship, and whatever papers she may have on board showing that

she is about to break the blockade, or to carry arms to some one of the confederate states now in hostility with the United States, they are to be protected by the power of the British nation in contradiction to all our decisions, and in contradiction to the declared law of nations, will, I hope, know that the British government never will place itself in that position. Let us look impartially at these cases which have occurred [...] Do not let us be led by passion into anything which is not founded on justice, and which cannot afterwards be justified in the face of the world.[223]

Facing the question of whether he implied that a vessel could be legally captured if the ultimate destination of goods conveyed to neutral ports is a belligerent consumer, Russell clarified that he had meant nothing of the kind and only referred to vessels that claimed to have a neutral destination but were actually bound for an enemy port.[224] One day after the debate, Russell informed Grazebook that the Foreign Office would support him, and ordered Lyons to remind Seward of the claim that a peaceful merchant vessel had been illegally prevented from reaching Nassau.[225]

Grazebrook, however, clearly had enemies, and soon after the government intervention, his original letter calling for subscribers to a blockade running investment, a 'secure adventure' with profits of up to 2,000 percent, was leaked to the press and reprinted in several British newspapers.[226] Furthermore, the judgment against the *Dolphin* rejected the argument of a peaceful business transaction: with 2,240 cavalry swords and almost 1,000 rifles being delivered to a Caribbean port of fewer than 10,000 inhabitants, how credible was Grazebrook's claim that no further transport of the cargo was intended?[227] Using this powerful rhetorical argument, the court obscured what amounted to a reversal of the burden of proof; instead of being innocent until proved guilty, the merchant was confronted with an allegation of smuggling that he had to disprove, or lose the case. Yet because of Grazebrook's singular newspaper exposure it might have meant political suicide to challenge Washington on his behalf. For this reason, the Palmerston government chose to ignore his continued requests for assistance.

The fact that it was Russell's personal disappointment about the honesty of British traders that influenced his decision-making clearly showed when he was challenged again in Parliament by the Marquess of Clanricarde. Following the capture of first the *Labuan* and the *Dolphin* and now the *Springbok* and the *Peterhoff*, Clanricarde complained that British trade in the Gulf of Mexico had collapsed because insurance premiums were now so high that the journey was not worth it. What was the government doing to prevent the deliberate US attacks on British commerce?[228] Russell responded that while the Americans were accused of trying to unilaterally rewrite the rules of international law, Seward's statements had shown that this was not the case. Given the brisk blockade-running business in the region, Union 'vigilance' was understandable, and not every case was worthy of support. Occasionally, Russell explained, a smuggler gets captured, and then

> the owner immediately comes to the Foreign Office with all the air of injured innocence, declares that nothing was further from his thoughts than the breaking of the blockade, and asks that the strongest representations may be made to the American Government on his behalf [...] We must be somewhat slow and cautious in believing all the reports which are made to the Foreign Office by the owners of ships.[229]

Domestically, this was not a popular stance. One day later the Commons passed a motion protesting against Russell's statements in the Lords, complaining that they sounded as if the Americans had an unlimited right to capture neutral vessels going to Nassau and Matamaros. Instead the Americans should be told that this was unacceptable and that a red line had been crossed.[230] Still, Russell remained cautious and only made a firm protest when there was reason to believe that legitimate trade had been unduly interfered with. The Cabinet also continued to apply pressure on the US government, and not without success. For a final time, Welles was forced to send instructions to his officers outlining which of the principles they had recently relied on were actually illegal.[231] After a careful perusal of the new instructions, the Law Officers concluded that they no longer included any principles that violated international law, and there was hope that there would be no more comparable confrontations in the future.[232] However, these consistent diplomatic efforts went largely unnoticed in the press; what made the headlines were those cases in which the Americans had bent the rules to convict what they knew to be notorious smugglers, and Britain had avoided taking a strong position for the same reason.

So what had the prize courts actually done? As we have seen, they had effectively reversed the burden of proof and accepted circumstantial evidence that blockade running was intended. From the summer of 1862 onwards they also extended the 'continuous voyage' doctrine: it had originally been applied by British prize courts when it could be shown that a ship only claimed to go to a neutral destination but was actually intent on carrying contraband to an enemy port. But the way in which Civil War blockade running worked was to reload the goods onto small, fast steamers in the ports of Nassau or Bermuda, or in the case of Matamaros simply unload the vessel to the northern, Texan bank of the Rio Grande instead of the southern, Mexican one. The US prize courts therefore extended the principle and held that the only thing that mattered was the enemy destination of a cargo, irrespective of whether it travelled in the same ship or even by land. Moreover, it was not only applied to clear contraband articles such as arms and ammunition but increasingly to 'dual use' goods that had been prepared for an army, such as army blankets, boots or even surgeon's kits. Russell had made it clear in Parliament that this was not the British understanding of prize law, and that as stated during the *Trent* affair, Britain only condoned captures of vessels that fraudulently claimed to travel to a neutral port but in reality were heading for the enemy.[233] Since the owners appealed the decisions, it was also unclear whether the US Supreme Court would actually uphold the contentious convictions.

Politically, it helped that when pushing the boundaries the USA always chose vessels that they knew to be blockade runners. This was a not a coincidence but a success of their new secret service in Britain which supplied lists of known smugglers, including the *Springbok* and the *Peterhoff*.[234] As the British soon learned, these were then passed on to Union naval commanders, together with tip-offs from American consuls in Bermuda or Nassau.[235] As long as there was no danger of the USA's new principles being established as international law, speaking out for these smugglers seemed as unnecessary as it was politically risky. Instead, Britain attempted to secure neutral rights by concentrating its efforts on less prominent cases, and provided diplomatic support until four of the early Matamaros captures were finally released by the US Supreme Court in 1867. Those criticising Britain for colluding with the Union prize courts should also say clearly that any stronger protest or threat either faced the risk of further embarrassment if the merchant turned out to be another Grazebrook, or could lead to war between Britain and the USA. The pro-Confederates in Parliament knew this, exemplified by John Arthur Roebuck's outburst that British commerce was 'subject to the overbearing and domineering insolence of an upstart race [...] I, speaking here for the English people, am prepared for war'.[236] Russell was not, and preferred to influence the Americans behind closed doors.[237]

The Supreme Court only decided upon the 'continuous voyage' prize cases after the war had ended, and went through the evidence in painstaking detail. Vessels like the *Bermuda* and the *Springbok* were found carrying despatches destined for the Confederacy, and containing ample evidence that at least some of the cargo was intended to be smuggled to the South. Therefore the Supreme Court upheld the extensions to the 'continuous voyage' principles but released the vessels and the rest of the cargo since it could not be proved that the ship-owner or master was involved in the blockade running.[238] These decisions inspired a small library of legal pamphlets condemning them, many of which came out of London business circles.[239] They focused on the *Peterhoff* case, since the court could not rely on captured correspondence and condemned some of the cargo on much weaker evidence than in the other cases; while there were strong indications of blockade running, a whiff of victor's justice remained. However, James McPherson's recent claim that in the *Peterhoff* case 'the British government recorded the precedent and applied it a half century later against goods shipped from neutral America to neutral Holland destined for Germany in World War 1' is misleading.[240]

Britain did refer to the Civil War prize cases to tame US complaints about interference with neutral trade, but the actual scale of Britain's attempt to control neutral trade dwarfed anything that Lincoln's administration had considered. Moreover, Britain pushed aside the 1909 Declaration of London, of which more in the Conclusion. At this point the only important detail is that when summarising current prize law, the London conference came up with rules that look very much like the 'continuous voyage' principle as applied by the US Supreme Court in the Civil War: while avoiding the contentious rule by name, article 30 agreed that goods 'destined to territory belonging to or occupied by the enemy' can be captured, and that 'it is immaterial whether the carriage of the goods is direct or entails transhipment or a subsequent transport by land'. Moreover, article 37 clarified that the ship carrying such cargo can be seized at any part of the voyage, even before reaching a neutral stopover. It also accepted the extension of the contraband category, confirming that clothing of distinctly military character can be contraband.[241] The difference to the early prize court cases is that the Declaration of London and the US Supreme Court agree on strict rules for the evidence necessary to achieve a conviction.[242] Thus the legal thinking behind the *Peterhoff* and other decisions had by 1909 been accepted by continental powers such as France, Germany and Italy, and was then ignored by Britain when it simply could not provide the evidence demanded by these rules. Therefore the argument that Britain acted with precedents for the future in mind not only fails to acknowledge that Russell and Palmerston had other very good reasons to act as they did but also ignores that what Asquith and Grey wanted to get rid of was essentially the law as applied by the US Supreme Court in the 1860s.

Part VI: The Declaration of Paris and the American Civil War: A case for reform?

After 1862, outrage over the toleration of the blockade and Northern extensions of prize law dominated public debate, and was increasingly employed to question the wisdom of signing the Declaration of Paris. Both conservative opponents of the declaration and liberals fighting for its reform tried to portray the Civil War experience in the darkest possible colours to further their own goals. In stark contrast with the global congratulations which had greeted its arrival ten years earlier, the treaty now had a public relations problem. Its fate during the American Civil War could have been a narrative of triumph: the big question of 1854, whether an effective blockade in a major war was still possible under the new rules, had finally been answered in the affirmative, allowing for increased 'vigilance' near smuggler ports. Respecting the rules had not always been easy for the Americans, but the framework of the declaration had enabled peaceful relations with all neutrals. Next to securing a remarkable stability of global trade, given the extent and severity of the conflict, the declaration had prevented Northern and undermined Southern privateering, effectively ending the practice forever. None of this, however, was discussed by the contemporaries. Instead, the American Civil War convinced many that the current regime was unsustainable.

Liberals in Britain had learned to appreciate the declaration from a new perspective: during the *Trent* affair the general expectation was that Britain and the Union would clash, and vessels bearing the British flag were shunned by merchants worldwide and had to face much higher insurance premiums than neutral ships. As for their colleagues in Bremen or Austria before, the experience came as a shock and resulted in vigorous campaigning for the Marcy Amendment. Shortly after the French call for a new congress on maritime law, they made their move in Parliament. The motion was presented by Thomas Horsfall (Conservative, but representing Liverpool) and described the current state of maritime law as 'ill-defined and unsatisfactory'. John Bright seconded the motion, arguing that once the 'free ships, free goods' rule had been granted, the Marcy Amendment had to follow, or Britain would risk permanent damage to its merchant shipping in every war. It was an illusion to believe that the vast British commerce could be protected by the navy; instead, all merchants would opt for neutral vessels, and consumer prices in Britain would rise. Prime Minister Palmerston opposed the motion and warned that this additional principle would crush England's naval supremacy, since it was bound to entail the abolition of blockades, effectively depriving the nation of its only means of striking other distant nations.[243]

US newspapers took a keen interest in the debate and were sure which way the wind was blowing. The *Chicago Tribune* predicted that the push for the Marcy Amendment 'now fairly set in motion, [will] never stop this side of final triumph'.[244] The *New York Times* combined progressive optimism with a healthy dose of glee: Britain had chosen to decline the amendment in 1856; 'scarcely it had half-a-dozen years experience of the practical working of the provisions of the treaty of Paris than she begins to feel all the embarrassments which a half-recognition of truth or duty invariably brings with it'. The principle that the USA had proposed because of its humanity and justice was now gaining friends in Britain, convinced by the persuasive power of their own material interest. Furthermore, this attempt to secure the amendment had been hampered by Cobden's absence from the debate, and the push for reform would become irresistible once his health returned.[245] Seward shared this feeling and assured the Europeans that the USA would support neutral rights as strongly after the Civil War as they had done before it.[246]

Instead, once he returned, Cobden committed a major strategic error by supporting the agenda for maritime reform now promoted by French government lawyer Laurent-Basile Hautefeuille. The French initiative had already been taken up in Washington: on 3 March 1862, delegate Samuel

Cox of Ohio presented a motion in the House of Representatives calling upon Congress to summon a conference of all maritime powers. In that way the scattered neutrals could unite, create a maritime equilibrium and force Britain to accept their demands, first of all the Marcy Amendment.[247] Cox argued that now was the moment to push for a conference because France, the traditional advocate of neutral rights, was very likely to be neutral in the next naval war. This was a thinly veiled reference to the fact that it would in all likelihood be a confrontation between Britain and the USA. In that case, France would naturally form the core of a new armed neutrality to create a 'maritime equilibrium':

> The maritime equilibrium, so important for the repose and freedom of the universe, will thus be established. Formed in anticipation of war, it will subsist in time of peace, and become a lasting element in the international relations of civilized peoples.[248]

While this kind of argument certainly pleased audiences in the USA, its effect in Britain was predictable, particularly since Cox's anti-British rhetoric was a true restatement of what Hautefeuille had written. Before, those who argued for the Marcy Amendment could claim that they had the 'spirit of the age' on their side, an ephemeral force that was, at least to the better part, British. Now, any Englishman demanding new maritime rules appeared to be the lackey of an anti-British plot. *The Times* observed that Hautefeuille 'apparently believes that the destruction of English power is the final object and ruling principle of international law'.[249] Cobden, however, failed to see that the case for reform was in danger of losing its status as an idea worthy of a British patriot, and criticised Horsfall and his motion for being too tame: instead of concentrating on the Marcy Amendment, he should have called for blockades to be restricted to towns that are also blockaded on the land side, and for a final clarification that belligerents must not board a neutral vessel on the high seas under any circumstances, as Hautefeuille had demanded.[250] Instead of strengthening the case for the Marcy Amendment as a measure that was in Britain's best interest, Cobden played into the hands of those who believed that the reformers were simply walking into the trap set up by the French.

These critics were not numerous but their rhetoric became more aggressive. Conservative criticism of the declaration combined with the admission that Britain was now honour-bound to keep it, followed by a Cabinet minister explaining that it was actually advantageous for the country, had by now become a ritual.[251] The tone began to change when the former Foreign Minister, Lord Malmesbury, stated his belief that the ineffective US blockade showed that in a great war the declaration would not be respected. France, he claimed, would rather resort to privateering than lose a naval war against Britain.[252] A month later, Benjamin Disraeli, establishing for the first time what would soon become a Conservative orthodoxy, openly called for the Declaration of Paris to be annulled to restore Britain's former maritime greatness.[253]

Foreign observers noticed the change, with Adams reporting home that it seemed no longer certain if Britain really intended to honour the obligations entered into in 1856.[254] It seemed that Britain would soon have to decide what it really wanted. With all political parties agreeing that the current rules of Paris were unsustainable, were they prepared to pay the political price to extricate themselves from the treaty in the future, or would Britain finally accept the Marcy Amendment? Prussia was particularly interested, since the stand-off about the future of Germany seemed likely to result in war soon. Reflecting on the consequences of the Civil War, the Prussian Minister in Washington, Gerolt, concluded that Britain now faced a stark choice: in any future war, the USA would remember the *Alabama* experience and attempt to return the favour by providing support for foreign commerce raiders. Thus Britain either had to accept losing much of its ocean trade to neutrals, or choose the Marcy Amendment and accept losing much of its naval power.[255] Gerolt hoped that Britain would choose Marcy, and in a turn that is not acknowledged in history writing, the Prussians as well as the Austrians would soon try to make the most of their strife to fight for a reform of maritime law. Given the state of the debate in Britain, a precedent set by great powers might just be what was needed to finally secure the immunity of private trade in wartime.

7
'Announcing Our Withdrawal from the Declaration' – The Declaration of Paris and the Franco-German War of 1870

The Prussian-Austrian War of 1866 and the Franco-German War of 1870–1 have rarely been studied regarding their impact on the relationship between sea power and international law. Both wars were essentially continental affairs, a clash of the world's most advanced infantries to settle the problem of Germany's future and its position in the European hierarchy. However, both Prussia and Austria were also aspiring naval powers that had built up small but modern ironclad fleets, and France was at the time challenging British naval supremacy.[1] This chapter will describe the previously unknown ambitions of the Prussians and the Austrians to utilise the continental wars of the 1860s to establish a precedent, facilitating a subsequent reform of international maritime law that suited their interests as second-rate naval powers. In a second part, it will discuss the France's global naval war against German trade and explore to what extent a blockade under the rules of the declaration was still feasible and effective in the 1870s. The third part will demonstrate how disputes about French violations of maritime law rattled the regime of the Declaration of Paris, leading to the first serious challenge by a great power. Newly discovered letters by Prussian Prime Minister Otto von Bismarck show that this process of escalation marked an important turning point in the history of the regime of the Declaration of Paris, rendering a future reform of the system well-nigh impossible.

The 1866 Austro-Prussian War: A precedent for the Marcy Amendment?

The war of 1866 pitted Austria against Prussia and Italy in a high-stakes bid for the future control of both Germany and Italy. It is less well known that all three participants also intended to establish a powerful precedent for a more liberal law of warfare. Moreover, this astonishing policy choice was one of the few in 19th-century diplomacy that can be traced back directly to aggressive and persistent lobbying by merchants, ship-owners and various institutions interested in commerce. The key experience was the war of 1864 against Denmark, which dealt a painful blow to Austrian and Prussian trade. As the Fiume Chamber of Commerce pointed out in a petition, the rules of the Declaration of Paris meant that ships carrying the flag of a belligerent were shunned by merchants, and thus the war with Denmark had destroyed Austrian shipping in the Adriatic. Therefore Austria should do everything in its power to further the cause of a liberal reform of the declaration. In particular, they suggested that the peace conference in London (meant to resolve the Danish-Prussian-Austrian conflict) should be used to make this proposal.[2]

Both the Ministry of Trade and the Navy Ministry agreed wholeheartedly.[3] The Foreign Ministry was sympathetic but had doubts about whether it was opportune to use this conference (in which London wanted to mediate in the Danish conflict) to isolate Britain and push for a reform of maritime law.[4] The idea was dropped but the problem was not forgotten, especially since other merchants who were active in Austria's main port of Trieste started voting with their feet: 53 traders of Swiss nationality who were residents of Trieste had applied for the right to use the Swiss flag on their vessels because of their recent unfortunate experience with the Austrian flag, and the Swiss Federal Council approved the idea.[5] The *Journal de Genève* warned that having no navy at all, Switzerland would be unable to prevent abuses of its new merchant flag, but the urge to benefit – as a permanently neutral state – from the advantages conveyed on neutral vessels by the Declaration of Paris proved irresistible.[6] Switzerland informed the slightly puzzled British about its new maritime project, who then turned to the Austrians for their opinion.[7] Naturally, the Austrians were not amused, and insisted that only states possessing access to the high seas should have their own merchant flags.[8] In the end, the US decision to accept the new Swiss flag decided the matter, and thus, in one of the more unintended consequences of the Declaration of Paris, Switzerland became the first landlocked state to have its own merchant flag.[9]

This new competition for trade in Trieste explains why Austria, while embarking on what was essentially a fratricidal war for the control of Germany, proposed that this conflict should be the first to be fought under the rules proposed by Marcy in 1856. However, the offer to respect the private property of Prussian citizens would only be valid if Berlin promised to adopt the same course against Austrian merchant vessels.[10] Despite being the stronger naval power, the Prussians agreed, for two reasons.[11] First, since there was no intention to use the navy against Hanover, it would have been inconsistent to attack Austrian shipping. While the Austrian navy was in the Adriatic, the North Sea coastline of their Hanoverian ally lay open to the (recently enlarged) Prussian Navy. But when War Minister Albrecht von Roon asked whether Hanover should be blockaded, Bismarck replied: 'Better not.'[12] After all, the aim of the campaign was to turn the Hanoverians into Prussian citizens, and taking their ships and destroying their trade would not endear the idea of Prussian rule to local elites.[13] Second, the principle fitted Prussia's status as a power that was strong on land but weak on the oceans. Setting a precedent might help to establish a rule of international law favourable to Prussian interests. At a ministerial meeting in May 1866, Roon initially opposed the idea because he felt that it benefited the Austrians more than the Prussians, but he was overruled by his colleagues.[14]

The decision was praised by the usually pro-Prussian *New York Times*, which saw Berlin's embrace of the Marcy Amendment as a powerful symbol of the increasing US influence in Europe. The King of Prussia, it claimed, was 'the first European ruler who has moral courage enough to act upon the lessons taught by a republic', conveniently forgetting that the original offer came from the Austrians.[15] Not to be outdone, Bremen accepted the Marcy Amendment as well (despite not being a belligerent), and immediately informed the Americans, hoping in vain to trigger a strong official statement.[16] There was less enthusiasm in Britain, where the news was buried in the back pages of *The Times*.[17] So far, so predictable, but no merchant could predict what Italy would do. There had been reports that it would honour the agreement,[18] but when asked in Parliament the British government refused to provide official confirmation of Italy's position.[19] That only came when Italy formally declared war on Austria, making the war of 1866 the first and only conflict where all sides explicitly agreed to Marcy's rule and refrained from attacks on enemy maritime commerce.[20]

Yet the Austrian merchants who had inspired this extraordinary development were deeply unhappy, and soon fresh petitions arrived in Vienna, claiming that the agreement had failed to protect Austrian trade. Despite the declarations of all powers involved in the war, the merchants of Fiume explained, none of their ships had been chartered to transport any cargo. A fourth power not respecting the agreement might have entered the war at any time, and traders still relied on neutral flags. Therefore the only way to protect the peaceful commerce of belligerents in times of war was to secure the Marcy Amendment as a permanent reform of the Declaration of Paris.[21] Trade Minister Bernhard von Wüllerstorf-Urbair concurred and wrote to Foreign Minister Beust that having just set a powerful precedent, Austria would not remain without support from other states if it started a new initiative now.[22] Beust, however, was more concerned about the consequences of Austria's final defeat in the battle for control over Germany.

The government of the new North German Confederation in Berlin came to exactly the same conclusion on the Marcy Amendment: War Minister von Roon pointed out that because the decision whether the navy would be used against enemy trade or not had only been made days after war had been declared, this uncertainty had created severe problems for the disposition of a navy unsure about what its tasks were. Therefore reciprocity should only be granted if an enemy government had made its intentions clear well before the war, or that alternatively Prussia should push for ensuring the acceptance of the Marcy Amendment as a principle of international law. The latter option would be preferable, Roon argued, since the Prussian Navy would not be as strong as those of the other great powers 'for a number of years'. Furthermore, in a war against a naval power, the German coast would be blockaded, and prizes could not be brought into a North German port anyway. Therefore Bismarck should start an initiative to secure the international recognition of the Marcy Amendment.[23]

Just days later, Bismarck received the first of many petitions demanding the same. Like their Austrian colleagues, the elders of the merchants of Danzig complained that under the Declaration of Paris their business had come to a standstill every time Prussia was a belligerent, or seemed likely to be one in the near future.[24] Bismarck promised to Roon that he would make a serious attempt and ordered Baron von Gerolt, the Minister in Washington, to enquire whether Prussia could count on the support of the USA.[25] Gerolt replied in the negative, as Secretary of State Seward informed him that the USA had no interest in confronting Britain over an important international issue while the negotiations over the *Alabama* claims were still dragging on.[26] Without US support, Bismarck concluded, an initiative for the Marcy Amendment would be hopeless.[27] Bismarck was proved right when an Italian initiative launched a few months later achieved nothing. Although the North German diplomats had been ordered to speak out in favour of the Italian move, Britain could afford to ignore it because the support of other states was as lukewarm as that of the Prussians.[28]

The French way of blockade

Nonetheless, this history of Prussian support for the Marcy Amendment helps to explain the unprecedented declaration issued by the King of Prussia in July 1870. On the day France declared war, King Wilhelm announced that French property at sea would not be harmed, without regard to reciprocity.[29] Although the navy had been expanded and modernised, it was still vastly inferior to the French Navy, the second largest in the world. In this situation, the best option was to set a precedent and thereby increase the chances of international recognition of the reform.

The announcement attracted warm congratulations from Washington, where the decision of the 'great and enlightened government' in Berlin was received 'with great pleasure'.[30] After all, the immunity of the French flag also meant that the regular steamer lines from France would maintain their service.[31] That said, the US government chose not to act on Prussia's suggestion that it should use its 'high position and influence' to obtain the universal acknowledgement of the principle as part of international law.[32] Still, the British Cabinet sensed that this Prussian declaration, although directed at Paris, ultimately pointed towards London, and reminded Berlin that other powers might have different ideas about this principle, 'in proportion to their maritime strength'.[33] The German move was even more unwelcome in Paris. Napoleon III had supported the Marcy Amendment in the past, and the well-known parliamentarian Louis-Antoine Garnier-Pagès had recently moved for its acceptance as a French law.[34] Nonetheless, Napoleon III refused to grant reciprocity. In 1870 the French Navy was about ten times the size of the Prussian one, and France simply announced its desire to continue its 'long-standing respect for the Declaration of Paris', without explicitly rejecting the Prussian offer.[35] In a circular to all diplomats, the French government also confirmed that this respect for the Declaration of Paris included applying its privileges to non-signatories Spain and the USA.[36] Britain did not complain, and protocol 24 of the Congress of Paris was now officially history.

The original French war plan foresaw a large-scale invasion of the North German coast, with a successful landing operation facilitating Denmark's entry into the war to take revenge for 1864.[37] Yet France's naval ambitions were undermined by a slow mobilisation, and the opportunity for an invasion was lost.[38] Because of the slow build-up, the German North Sea coast was only blockaded on 15 August and the Baltic coast three days later. The fact that the blockade was only announced after the ships had arrived at their stations shows that France wanted to avoid neutral complaints about an 'ineffective' blockade right from the start,[39] but within days, the American Consul in Königsberg was already demanding an additional US warship to verify his concerns that the blockade was ineffective.[40] The British government was not keen to get involved in the conflict, and, as Foreign Secretary Lord Granville explained, he expected 'a free field for France and Prussia and a packed grandstand'.[41] The problem was that there was no grandstand on the high seas, and both belligerents expected Britain to interpret and enforce the rules of the game in the English Channel and beyond, while MPs made it clear that they expected the rights of British merchants under the Declaration of Paris to be defended.[42]

The first complaint was raised by the French, who accused the Germans of reviving privateering in disguise. The North German government had appealed to the patriotism of ship-owners (particularly Hanseatic merchants possessing fast ocean-going steamers), asking them to register their ships for the new *Seewehr*, a volunteer navy. However, in the words of the semi-official Prussian *Provinzial-Correspondenz*, it also tried to 'awaken the spirit of enterprise' by offering a cash premium for every French warship that was taken or sunk by these vessels.[43] Unsurprisingly, the French were not amused and complained to London that the *Seewehr* was, for all intents and purposes, privateering and thereby a violation of the Declaration of Paris.[44] But if Britain agreed, these vessels would be pirates and the Royal Navy would have to attack them. The government consulted the Law Officers and soon announced that the *Seewehr* did not amount to privateering. The crews were under naval discipline and command, not free agents with a licence to participate in war in the same way as the traditional privateers.[45] This despatch set an important precedent and was invoked by the Germans when they sent 'auxiliary cruisers' against British shipping in the First World War.

While the privateering controversy was unexpected, many feared that France would try to undermine the Declaration of Paris by extending the contraband list. The *Chicago Tribune* wrote:

> It is easy to see that, as France is superior to Prussia in naval force, and as all privateering is abolished, there will be a great temptation to stretch the Emperor's authority and to render the exemption clause of little effect by including everything possible under the contraband exception. We foresee much trouble from this source.[46]

However, it was the Germans who complained to London, targeting the Achilles' heel of 1870s steamer warfare, the need for regular coal supply. The bunkers of the French steamers were often exhausted after a single day of cruising and chasing blockade runners. Since the British commander at Heligoland refused to serve as a French coaling station, coal had to be shipped in small colliers from Dunkirk to the squadron every day.[47] Dunkirk received its coal supplies from Britain, and the Germans complained that since France was acquiring coal for naval use from Britain, coal should be treated as contraband and banned from export.[48] In a rather cool reply, the British government declared that it had neither the means nor the intention of stopping private enterprise just because the Germans were unable to interfere with it due to their maritime inferiority.[49]

When North Germany insisted, demanding 'benevolent' neutrality by Britain because France clearly was the aggressor and Germany only defending itself,[50] Foreign Secretary Granville gave a remarkable reply. He rejected any preferential treatment and argued that since coal was not contraband according to traditional Prussian legal doctrine, the request implied that it should only be treated as such because it was useful for France's war effort, which 'raises the question of the prohibition of all articles, not contraband of war, which might be of service to a belligerent. But if this principle were admitted, where is it to stop?'[51] Thus Britain had not availed itself of the opportunity to extend the contraband definition as a possible loophole for future wars, which ironically only served to convince the Germans that Britain was partial.

The French, on the other hand, found managing their coal supply difficult enough. Their squadrons had chosen to enforce the blockade from two semipermanent positions at Heligoland and off Travemünde, with individual vessels cruising along the coast and probing the most important harbours.[52] This meant that the blockading force did not fulfil the strict

French criteria of 'effective blockade', with stationary vessels blocking the entry to every blockaded port. Nonetheless, it proved to be effective, at least by the standards employed in the American Civil War (when a 'cruising blockade', not restricting vessels to a particular port, had been accepted). German merchants, of course, complained to British newspaper correspondents about this 'ineffective' blockade, but at the same time admitted that they did not dare to leave the harbour because 'the risk is too high'.[53]

Nonetheless, by late September the US Minister in Berlin, George Bancroft, denounced the French action as a paper blockade and claimed that 'the injury done to American commerce by the proclamation of the pretended blockade in defiance of international law has been very great'.[54] Several American consuls seconded this claim while British newspapers already feared an important negative precedent: if the blockade of the Baltic really was ineffective, this should not be allowed 'unless the Declaration of Paris is to become a dead letter'.[55] If the blockade had continued, a US challenge would have been highly likely, but to everybody's surprise the blockade was officially called off just a month after it had begun.[56] In part, this was due to the weather, as the Baltic Sea squadron had to endure repeated storms in dangerous waters while the North Sea squadron lost several colliers trying to recoal warships in rough conditions.[57] Furthermore, the catastrophic defeats of the French Army and the revolution at home affected the blockaders' morale. By September it was feared that the ports of the French Navy might be taken from the land side while the fleet's powerful artillery was lying off Heligoland, and the two squadrons returned home without waiting for an order from the new government.[58] Therefore the blockade of the Baltic Sea ended as early as 11 September.[59]

The announcement caused a flurry of maritime activity in English ports.[60] The merchants were relieved to see the blockade ended, since it had been, as one trader from Hartlepool remarked, 'a serious drawback to our prosperity'.[61] Its effects had been felt in Hull, where locals feared that the economic situation would become 'deplorable' should the blockade last over the winter, and throughout the Scottish herring industry, which had lost its primary export market.[62] Thus the French blockade had seriously hurt British trade. The question remains how damaging the blockade had been to the German economy: could a naval blockade under the rules of the Declaration of Paris still throttle an industrialised power in the 1870s, with an advanced railway network and neutral ports nearby? As it turned out, it could.

Even before the blockade began, Austrian Lloyd announced that it had started new steamer lines from Trieste to Liverpool and London, intending to ship North German goods to England.[63] Soon, British and Danish steamer companies set up new routes to the Danish port of Aarhus, conveniently located at the end of a 200 km rail track to Hamburg.[64] But even this ideally placed port could not shield the German economy from the effects of the blockade. The import trade continued, though at a higher price, but the same increase in freight costs practically stopped exports from Germany, in particular the fruit and grain that had just been harvested. Furthermore, it turned out that the port in Aarhus was much too small to handle the increased traffic.[65] Merchants and trading towns in North Germany were hit hardest,[66] but a longer blockade would have caused supply shortages throughout Germany, as well as bankrupting those producers who were dependent on overseas export markets and whose losses could not be set off by increased demand from the military. Thus, even if applied as haphazardly as in 1870, a naval blockade could still seriously hurt an opponent despite well-developed railway lines.

France's global war on German trade

The benefit of being the stronger naval power was not restricted to the ability to blockade the enemy. When war broke out, German ships had to flee into the nearest neutral port, and a German captain in New York complained that while his ship was forced to lie idle, French merchant vessels were entering and leaving the harbour as before.[67] France used this maritime advantage to import large quantities of arms and ammunition, and a German protest to London was met with a reference to Prussia's activities in the Crimean War.[68] Yet France's naval ambitions went much further, and, in an aspect of the war that has been completely ignored by historians, the French Navy tried to capture German merchant vessels all over the world.[69] This lack of interest is even more surprising since France's efforts provoked a highly unusual regional naval truce in East Asian waters, where commanders of both countries decided that showing a united front to the Chinese was more important than the war. Moreover, the global reach of France's navy and German trade provided a snapshot of how neutral and belligerent rights were implemented in a variety of countries. Some 15 years after the Declaration of Paris had been signed, France found that for belligerents, the world's oceans were becoming an increasingly regulated sphere, and that neutrals often had their own views as to how the law should be implemented.

The primary interest of the French Navy was to use neutral ports as bases for bringing in prizes and obtaining coal and other supplies, and German diplomats worked hard to prevent this. After a French Navy squadron had found itself a temporary home at Syra, one of Greece's foremost commercial ports, it was forced to leave due to German pressure.[70] When the French Navy tried to disrupt the substantial trade between Argentina, Brazil and the Hanseatic towns, there was no German warship in the region to hinder them but consistent protests by German ministers and consuls ensured that the Brazilian government republished its neutrality laws on 16 October, with new instructions that restricted the freedoms of belligerent warships and forbade telegraph offices to accept postings concerning ship movements connected to the war.[71] Moreover, the French warship *Hamelin* was banned from entering Brazilian ports for the duration of the war after it had left a prize in a neutral harbour without securing it with men from its crew.[72]

Next to the Germans, commercial interests lobbied with neutral governments: when a German diplomat complained about an extended stay of a French warship in Rio de Janeiro, the Brazilian government explained that it felt compelled to disregard the rules limiting the stay of a warship and its prizes to 24 hours to honour the spirit of the Declaration of Paris. The declaration, they argued, intended to protect the property of neutrals under the enemy's flag, so it should be unloaded straight away. After all, the ship's cargo was intended for Rio de Janeiro, which meant that the merchants protected there were residents of Brazil.[73] The Austrian Lloyd's representative at Syra had made the exact same argument earlier, so after responding to German demands to send the French away the Greek government now faced Austrian fury about the neutral cargo of 44 tons of coal on a German prize that the French had taken with them.[74] The Austrian Minister of Justice even felt compelled to warn the Foreign Ministry that the demand to unload neutral cargo before any prize court decision was actually an innovation unknown in existing law.[75]

Emboldened by the cast-iron guarantees included in the declaration, neutrals proved increasingly confident in asserting the neutrality of their ports and waters, and the most confident was, of course, the USA, which cherished the freedom of the seas at least as much as it loathed Napoleon III and his attempt to install a monarchy in Mexico. The US neutrality declaration favoured the stronger naval power by opening the ports for all belligerents, but French warships were received less than cordially.[76] After the blockade had been lifted, the French Navy tried to capture German vessels trying to leave US ports for Germany. On 24 September, the *Hermann* spotted two French men-of-war upon leaving New York and was lucky to escape back into the port. The German Consul complained that French ships were hunting for prizes in US waters, and the *New York Tribune* wondered: 'Can a nation which abandons the blockade of the ports of its enemy maintain that of vessels in neutral ports?'[77] Secretary of State Hamilton Fish told the French representative in Washington, Jules de Berthemy, that if France continued to prey on German vessels off the US coast, this would be regarded as an unfriendly act.[78] The French vessels had not violated any rule, either national or international, but only days later the US government declared its territorial waters closed to belligerent warships, turning a mere approach towards the coast into a breach of US neutrality.[79] This declaration effectively meant that the French Navy was barred from operating near US waters, and the squadron duly returned to the North Sea.[80]

If US diplomacy had been more successful, Washington could even have brokered a naval truce guaranteeing immunity for German vessels in East Asia. After news of the war had reached Japan, the commander of the North German gunboat *Hertha* suggested a deal to his French colleagues: since

Prussia had two modern steamers in Japanese waters (*Hertha* and *Medusa*), the French squadron might be able to match them but would have to withdraw most of its vessels from China. Given the recent massacre in Tientsin, this would expose French citizens in China to great danger.[81] The French naval commanders accepted a provisional truce while asking for instructions from Paris. French diplomats in Japan concurred, arguing that while fighting German trade in Asia was never going to decide the war, it was much more important to demonstrate to China as well as Japan that, even in wartime, European powers would always represent their Asian interests jointly. When Granville was informed of the deal he was 'very happy', since Franco-German hostilities in Asia could 'produce effects permanently disadvantageous to European influence in those countries'.[82]

The North German government informed Britain and the USA that it would honour the local agreement,[83] and Bismarck also supported the US proposal of confirming the Asian truce in a formal convention.[84] The new republican government in Paris, however, rejected the initiative and ended the truce unilaterally.[85] As the new Foreign Minister Jules Favre explained, Navy Minister Fourichon had rejected the idea because it was evident that Prussia did not have a sufficient naval force in the area to protect the large number of German merchant vessels trading there. Thus France could only lose by accepting the agreement, which would be interpreted as a sign of weakness by the Germans as well as the Chinese.[86]

For this reason the naval war in East Asia only began after the land war in Europe had been decided, but, because the regime of the Declaration of Paris had not yet reached the entire region, the French Navy found it a much more hospitable environment. While Japan had issued a declaration of neutrality for the first time, thus entering the system of a globalising international law,[87] China had not done so. Accordingly, the state of war in Europe had no influence on the rights of the contracting powers to enter Chinese harbours with their warships, and since German merchants were very active in the China trade, it is unsurprising that France used Chinese harbours as naval bases.[88] The German diplomats in China did not even attempt to complain. The German envoy, Rehfues, had unsuccessfully tried to notify the Chinese government of Prussia's embrace of the Marcy Amendment in 1866, only to be called in by the Emperor's ministers to clarify the meaning of the word 'contraband'. After lengthy discussions, Rehfues concluded that the Chinese were unable to understand the entire concept of neutrality.[89] Therefore, the diplomats stationed in China in 1870 could do little more than count the well over 100 North German vessels trapped in Chinese ports or captured by the French.[90] The authorities in Saigon even began selling the prizes assembled there to local merchants, without waiting for the verdicts of the formal prize court proceedings. The local officials must have known that what they were doing was clearly illegal, but felt that they could ignore Bismarck's angry telegram to stop the sales.[91] In the absence of the usual legal framework, French authorities and commanders behaved differently from anywhere else, providing negative proof of the effectiveness of maritime law where it existed.

Bismarck's challenge to the Declaration of Paris

The fourth part of this chapter will investigate the earlier claim that disputes over maritime law played an important part in escalating the Franco-German confrontation. The atrocities and violations of the laws of war committed on land are relatively well known – for example, the French *franc-tireur* guerrilla units and the brutal German counter-insurgency tactics. The war crimes committed at sea remain obscure even to specialist historians, but relatively minor naval incidents provoked a drastic and unprecedented German response.

The first issue concerned the crews of captured German merchant vessels: in letters published in the *Norddeutsche Zeitung*, several captains complained that they and their crews had faced regular abuse, including severe beatings, theft and other forms of mistreatment, by their guards as well as by street mobs during their transport.[92] Ten days later, Bismarck accused the new French government of violating international law as well as basic principles of humanity by treating merchant sailors as prisoners of war, and he demanded that all mistreatment should be stopped immediately. Otherwise, French officers imprisoned in Germany would face reprisals.[93] Unimpressed, the Government of National Defence insisted that there was no rule of international law stating that sailors of the merchant navy could not be taken as prisoners of war. The merchant navy was part of the maritime power of a state, and sailors could be drafted into the navy at any time. The latter argument, it claimed, was especially true for the North German Confederation, which drafted every able man into its armed forces. Regarding the allegations of mistreatment, Delegate Chaudordy (acting as the chief diplomat of the Government of National Defence in Tours) ridiculed the accusations and explained that the prisoners had all happily signed a declaration that they were treated well.[94]

Bismarck was furious and accused the French of barbarism, and to counter the claim that 'especially in North Germany' every man was drafted, Bismarck referred to the recent decree in which the new republican government called upon every man under 45 years of age to join the forces defending the fatherland. Accordingly, the North German government would from now on regard every French male as part of the armed forces, and Bismarck even mentioned the possibility of reprisals, namely to 'treat the male French populations as far as it is available to us as prisoners of war'.[95] In other words, he threatened to imprison the entire adult male population of the occupied French territories in special camps. It is unclear whether this despatch ever reached the French government since there is no reply in the files in Berlin. However, the simple fact that this threat was made in official correspondence shows how ready Bismarck was to escalate the war, long before the actions of the *franc-tireurs* began to affect German logistics during the winter. Soon, another French violation of international law incensed Bismarck even more.

In late October, English newspapers reported that the French cruiser *Desaix* had burned several German merchant vessels on the high seas, while another, the *Frei*, had been captured inside British territorial waters.[96] Sinking a merchant vessel on the high seas was a grave violation of international law, since a prize had to be adjudicated in a prize court before it could be expropriated. Moreover, the French had taken the English pilot on board the *Frei* all the way to Cherbourg and released him there without pay, and upon his return he went straight to the North German Embassy in London and signed a declaration that the ship had been taken in English waters, 'one and a half miles off Dungeness'.[97] The German Minister, Bernstorff, complained about the 'severe and deliberate violations of British neutrality by France' and demanded that the British government should secure the immediate release of the vessel.[98] Granville assured him that the matter would receive the full attention of the Cabinet.[99] Once the reports about burned merchant vessels were corroborated, Bismarck used them to appeal to all neutrals. By burning merchant vessels on the high seas, he wrote in a circular sent to 14 European capitals as well as Washington, France had committed a 'grave violation of international law that concerns all nations'.[100]

But did the French Navy really systematically disregard international law? The report by the *Desaix*'s commander on his hugely successful mission (eight prizes had been taken) confirmed that three German merchant vessels had been burned, while later captures were sent home with a prize crew, showing that men would have been available earlier. As for the exact location of the *Frei*'s capture, Commander Chevalier explained that it was taken 'a bit off Dungeness', avoiding the obvious question of whether neutral waters had been violated.[101] The report was immediately passed on by Chevalier's superiors, who wanted to share the happy news with the new Navy Minister, Maurice Fourichon. However, Fourichon ordered the *préfet maritime* of Cherbourg to remind Chevalier that according to his instructions, prizes could only be sunk in the case of absolute necessity, when dispatching a prize crew was manifestly impossible.[102] Thus the allegations were clearly based on fact, but represented isolated incidents not condoned by the naval high command. The Germans, on the other hand, could not know this, and further reports about burned merchant vessels suggested otherwise.[103]

The German complaint reached Paris only in late December, since the system of sending despatches to the Government of National Defence via American diplomats Washburne and Bancroft was interrupted and the first despatch returned.[104] When it finally reached Foreign Minister Favre, he turned to the navy, which quickly closed ranks to protect Commander Chevalier: Rear-Admiral Hormoz, the navy representative in the besieged capital, had to admit that he could not even say with certainty that a ship named *Desaix* existed. Probably, he suspected, one of the navy's cruisers had been renamed after the fall of Napoleon III.[105] Nonetheless, he was already convinced that the commander was innocent.[106] In a letter sent to the Navy Minister on the same day, Hormoz again admitted that he could not know which ship the German accusations referred to, but insisted that the sinkings must have been justified by the instructions, and he urged Fourichon to put pressure on Favre to ensure that he adopted the navy's stance without asking too many questions.[107]

Given the context of the catastrophic military situation, it is understandable that the French Navy did not see the need for detailed discussions about the failings of individual officers. But in German (and particularly Bismarck's) eyes, the cover-up of the *Desaix* case fitted into a pattern of French war crimes that seemed to have the authorisation of the new Government of National Defence. The implications of this assessment for the conduct of the war became obvious in the controversy about whether or not to bombard the civilian quarters of Paris. Bismarck believed that the war had to be ended quickly at all costs, and, if it meant burning villages to contain the *franc-tireurs* and bombarding Paris to force the city to surrender, then so be it. Gradually he persuaded the King to act according to his views and overrule the generals around Moltke, who were deeply sceptical about such atrocities.[108] The decision regarding how to react to the *Desaix* incident was taken at the same time, and the response was equally extreme: on 29 December, Bismarck wrote to Favre that in reprisal, his government had given orders to destroy every French vessel that His Majesty's navy could capture.[109]

Bismarck announced the decision in a circular on 9 January 1871, in which he accused the French of starting the escalation with their numerous violations of international law, whereas the German armies only reluctantly resorted to 'the more rigorous measures warranted by international law and the usages of war'. Bismarck buttressed his case by presenting an array of accusations, with the crimes committed by the *Desaix* and the mistreatment of sailors on German merchant vessels featuring prominently. The despatch shows that while the naval war was certainly peripheral for the military decisions taken by the German High Command, the incidents at sea described in this chapter were central to Bismarck's political appraisal of the new republican government. Significantly, the only concrete countermeasure against French war crimes mentioned in the lengthy circular was the announcement of 'reprisals against French ships'.[110] This phrase masked the enormity of the actual order, just like the telegram sent to Washington on 13 January, which merely stated that the immunity of French property at sea had been revoked.[111] The same phrase was used in the official proclamation of 19 January, one of the first administrative acts issued by the new German Reich founded the previous day, but the internal letters presented here show that Bismarck's true intentions went far beyond that, illustrating the potential for escalation if the war had continued.[112] Furthermore, the *Desaix* controversy also revealed that London and Berlin had a fundamentally different understanding of the rights and duties of neutrals under the Declaration of Paris, with important consequences for its future.

Since Britain had ruled in Germany's favour when France challenged the legality of the *Seewehr*, the Cabinet felt that Germany had no reason to complain about British neutrality, which led Granville to underestimate the seriousness of German complaints about the *Desaix*. Granville first said that the Law Officers needed to be consulted on French prize court procedure,[113] and he announced two weeks later that Britain would not send an official complaint to France, basing this decision on the (hardly novel) fact that the distance from the coast during the capture of the *Frei* was 'disputed'.[114] Bismarck's anger at the encroachments of French cruisers now turned against Britain, and he accused the government of inventing a pretext to dodge Britain's duties as a neutral. The English flag, he wrote, had always been present near any theatre of a maritime war to watch out for possible infringements of neutral rights, but now London pretended to be blind to violations right before its shores while the 'ineffective' French blockade was hurting British trade. Britain had a special responsibility as the guardian of the Declaration of Paris, due to its unique status as the biggest sea power. If Britain did not see it as its duty to uphold the declaration, what was it worth? Bismarck ended with a firm warning to Granville:

> I beg you [Bernstorff] to include that the four points of the Declaration of Paris are inseparable, that a general reciprocity among the signatories is assumed and that, since the biggest sea power among the signatories has been silent regarding the French blockade notifications contradicting the four points, even the concern for the co-signatories would not prevent us from announcing our withdrawal from the Declaration.[115]

This, Bismarck realised, was rather aggressive wording. After all, it was the first time that one of the signatories had threatened to leave the declaration. He crossed out the last sentence, and now announced his intention to follow the French example and simply disregard the declaration, since this had been tolerated by the other powers, and later raise the question of the declaration's future with the other signatories. In essence, Bismarck had replaced the threat of leaving with a half-hidden statement of his intention to issue letters of marque. In an unusual step for the typically obedient Bernstorff, the diplomat expressed concern that this extreme step might be a major mistake. Removing all doubt about the meaning of Bismarck's words, Bernstorff wrote that he had inferred from his conversations with Granville that the

British government 'would hardly accept that the right to issue letters of marque against France is based on the circumstance that the blockade of the North German coast was ineffective'.[116]

Bernstorff also reminded Bismarck of what had happened during the war against Denmark in 1864. Enraged at the ineffectiveness of the Danish blockade of the Baltic coast and the lack of response to his complaints,[117] Bismarck had instructed Bernstorff to declare at the London conference discussing the Danish question that if Denmark persisted with its ineffective blockade, the other articles of the declaration would equally 'lose their value' and would no longer be respected by Prussia with regard to Denmark.[118] The comment alerted British Foreign Secretary Clarendon, who asked Bernstorff repeatedly whether this meant that Prussia would issue letters of marque and told him privately that he 'could be under no delusion as to what the consequences would be if it was believed that we wanted to reintroduce privateering'. The Russian and Swedish delegates also implored Bernstorff to make an explicit statement that Prussia would not use privateering. Faced with an outcry in the British press, Bernstorff sent a telegram to Bismarck about this 'important and dangerous' matter, pointing out the mismatch between the possible advantages in using privateers against Denmark and the massive disadvantage if Britain and Sweden joined the war because of Prussian letters of marque: 'The conviction of all neutrals that privateering is abolished and that no belligerent may reintroduce it for whatever reason is so firm that the maritime powers, namely England and Sweden would undoubtedly resist.'[119]

In 1864, Bismarck refused to make a clear announcement that Prussia would not use privateers, but claimed that it had been his intention to alert the neutrals to possible consequences of their inaction regarding violations of the declaration by Denmark.[120] Obviously, Bismarck wanted to achieve the same result again six years later, but, convinced that insinuations about privateering would provoke a similar British reaction, Bernstorff rewrote the despatch and asked for permission to send his version to the British government. Bismarck agreed,[121] and in the letter received by Granville on 13 January 1871 the announcement of future disregard of maritime law had been replaced by a warning that Germany might find it difficult to respect the Declaration of Paris much longer if the British Cabinet did not challenge the French about their violations:

> The French Government has ignored the principles of international law more than once throughout this war, for example by declaring an ineffective blockade of the German ports. Still, His Majesty's government itself has maintained all rules of the 1856 Declaration of Paris until now. It will have to ask itself whether such concern for the neutral powers does not do injustice to the interests of Germany, if it cannot rely on the neutral powers to carefully guard the maintenance of the principles of international law they have accepted.[122]

However, unlike Clarendon in 1864, Granville did not realise what was at stake here. It took him three weeks to send a reply, and when it arrived it ignored all of the insinuations that Bernstorff had included and only discussed the question of what was permissible in French prize court proceedings and what not.[123] For the German government, this was no longer an issue after the surrender of Paris had settled the outcome of the war. It was interested in Britain's interpretation of neutrality (which would have important implications for the next war), and came to the conclusion that the British government was completely deluded regarding its duties as a neutral.[124] In Bismarck's view, the right of a neutral state to demand respect for its territory also placed it under a duty to defend it and demand satisfaction for violations. In other words, neutrals were obliged to secure their rights, if necessary with armed force. Failure to do so would mean granting an advantage to the misbehaving belligerent and thereby be in itself a violation of neutrality. While this interpretation of neutrality was extreme, Granville's reaction seemed to imply that Britain was willing to accept even a violation of its own territorial waters if it meant helping France against Germany. Therefore, when Granville finally announced in late February that Britain would now seriously investigate the capture of the *Frei*,[125] Bismarck had already decided to publish the correspondence to illustrate Britain's failure as a neutral.[126]

It is noteworthy that the British interpretation of neutrality as applied by the Gladstone Cabinet was met with scathing criticism in the British Parliament. The Liberal Robert Peel accused it of following a 'policy of selfish isolation' that damaged Britain's reputation in Germany, while Auberon Herbert cited the series of German complaints that had not been acted upon. Neutrality as understood by the government had meant that Britain was 'bound neither to hold nor to express any opinion whatsoever' and had prevented other concerned countries from speaking out to call upon the belligerents to moderate their violence. Gladstone rose to defend his policy and claimed that the criticism in a German official newspaper that Peel had referred to had been disavowed later by the government.[127] But as we have seen, such criticism reflected the opinions held inside the German leadership rather accurately.

How deeply this experience affected Bismarck's attitude towards maritime law is best illustrated by his reaction when Germany was asked to join the Washington Convention on the rights and duties of neutrals,[128] agreed by Britain and the USA after the lengthy *Alabama* negotiations: Bismarck wondered whether it might be possible to unite with Austria-Hungary against the new rules, in particular since 'the last war has given him severe doubts about the expediency of the four points of the Declaration of Paris'.[129] The new attitude became apparent when Bismarck dismissed all attempts to persuade Germany to include the principle of immunity of private property at sea in the peace treaty with France. Although countries such as the Netherlands and pressure groups such as the German Nautical Association suggested that Germany should impose the principle that it had supported at the beginning of the war on its beaten opponent and thereby further its acceptance as a rule of international law,[130] this only showed that many had not understood what had just happened: with a traditional supporter of the idea having turned against it while simultaneously becoming the most powerful nation on the Continent, the Marcy Amendment was practically dead. However, few realised it at the time, and campaigning for the reform continued for decades. But as the *Pall Mall Gazette* pointed out, the German decision to end the war by bilateral treaty instead of a European peace congress meant that, unlike in 1856, there would not be any progress in international law after this war because 'the very machinery for the amelioration of public law will be wanting'.[131]

Next to its relevance to the creation of future laws, many observers wondered what lessons could be drawn from the Franco-German War for the existing regime of the Declaration of Paris. After Russia had used the opportunity of the continental war to unilaterally withdraw from the obligations imposed on it by the peace treaty of 1856, the *New York Times* feared that together with the restrictions on the use of the Black Sea in the old peace treaty, Russia would also throw the Declaration of Paris overboard. In the case of a war against Britain, it would surely resort to privateers, and damage British commerce as the *Alabama* had destroyed US trade.[132] *The Times* dismissed the sceptics and hailed the declaration as a model of stability in an ever more insecure world. Although Germany possessed fast transatlantic steamers, it had resisted the temptation to use them to challenge the French command of the seas:

> What could have been more easy and more advantageous than the issuing of Letters of Marque to the ocean steamers of Bremen and Hamburg, so as to use them as privateers to stop the drawing of war supplies from America and elsewhere except under the cumbrous protection of convoys? [...] Why has Germany refrained from this step? Simply because she is pledged by the treaty of Paris to abstain from privateering, and she has a wholesome apprehension that neutral powers would not tolerate a violation of the engagement. This apprehension clothes the treaty with force, but without the treaty no neutral could have made the use of privateers a casus belli. The Treaty made privateering an international offence which the other parties to it had a right to resent.[133]

Nonetheless, for the first time since 1856, the House of Commons seriously debated whether Britain should revive privateering. Cavendish Bentinck claimed that while the Declaration of Paris offered some protection for commerce in wartime, it deprived Britain of the opportunity to completely destroy an enemy's trade with large numbers of cruisers and privateers.

Other speakers wondered whether Britain could both allow trade to continue under neutral flags and emerge victorious in a war with the newly unified Germany, with Benjamin Disraeli denouncing the declaration as 'a very impolitic step, calculated to cripple the power of this country'.[134] The government responded that whether the declaration was advantageous or not, Britain was bound in honour to the co-signatories, and Gladstone successfully cut the debate short by declaring that since it would be very difficult to extract Britain from this obligation, it would be wise to withdraw a motion calling for such delicate negotiations.[135]

However, this statement left the impression that the government would hesitate to defend Britain's adherence to the declaration on its merits, and preferred highlighting the difficulties involved in getting out. Abroad, the debate reinforced fears that Britain would hesitate to defend the treaty against powerful violators.[136] Once again *The Times* dismissed the case presented against the declaration in the motion: 'Something more powerful must be presented to the public imagination before the government can be moved to demand from Europe the undoing of a work that has stood for 15 years.'[137] But just like the debate, this comment seemed to indicate that the nation was only waiting for the right arguments to justify its withdrawal. Only weeks later, the Conservatives tried again in the House of Lords.

The new motion simply called upon the Queen to declare the Declaration of Paris null and void, echoing newspaper claims that it was not legally binding and should be ignored.[138] The Earl of Denbigh argued that the balance of power in Europe had changed fundamentally. Britain's potential enemies – Prussia and Russia – were far stronger on land, and could undermine Britain's maritime supremacy by hiding their fleets in well-defended harbours and harassing British commerce with a few cruisers. A prime example of Britain's unfortunate position was the declaration, imposed upon Britain by others to restrain its maritime power and weaken its defences. By leaving it, Britain could and should 'by a stroke of her pen recover her maritime supremacy'.[139] Furthermore, Denbigh wondered why we should believe that nobody would send privateers to fight at sea if states sent *franctireurs* to fight on land? As during the American Civil War, the former Foreign Secretary, the Earl of Malmesbury, affirmed his belief that nations in desperation would not adhere to rules if it meant defeat. But whereas he had referred to France nine years earlier, he now advised that in case of need, Britain itself should break the Declaration of Paris and use privateers. Such declarations and conventions, he claimed, 'were only meant as lovers' promises, to be broken'.[140]

Granville sensed the danger of what had just been said and openly attacked his predecessor: it was scarcely judicious, he said, that an ex-Secretary of State claimed in Parliament that Britain would break treaties once they were found inconvenient. Furthermore, the Declaration of Paris had secured the safety of Britain's commerce in the last war, and without it British neutrality would have been perfectly impossible.[141] Still, Malmesbury's statement was front-page news in the USA.[142] Once more, *The Times* defended the rules of Paris. The end of privateering was a clear gain, most of all for the country with the largest regular navy, and if an enemy partially evaded a blockade by trading with neutrals, this could be ignored as in return British commerce was safe all over the globe.[143] But from now on the defenders of the declaration in Britain were clearly on the defensive, and its opponents proved much better at shaping public discourse and eventually its historical record.

Conclusion: The Rise and Fall of the Declaration of Paris

When the Declaration of Paris was passed on 16 April 1856, the seven major European powers had agreed on a revolution in maritime law, abolishing privateering, securing surprisingly generous trading privileges for neutrals in wartime and banning 'paper blockades' by demanding the actual presence of naval forces. At its time, the treaty was hailed as a breakthrough to a brighter future, but this claim has usually been given short shrift by historians. While the judgements vary in nuance, there seems to be a consensus that the British Cabinet acted against Britain's best interests and – motivated by naivety, liberal ideology or both – accepted a document that restricted the Royal Navy while offering no guarantees against encroachments by Britain's enemies.[1] Today, many naval historians consider the question largely irrelevant, since throughout the 19th century, Britain was so dominant on the oceans that if necessary it could change or ignore any rules of international law that it found inconvenient or damaging to its interests.[2]

However, this assessment makes it even harder to understand why British politicians felt compelled to sign the Declaration of Paris in the first place. The picture that finally emerged after years of archival research is a different one: instead of oozing confidence, the political establishment of mid-19th-century Britain was acutely aware of the danger that its lead as the dominant global power was slipping away. The Royal Navy was still vastly superior to any rival navy, but Britain's position on the oceans was vulnerable to an attack by a coalition involving France, Russia or both. Crucially, both countries enjoyed very friendly relations with the USA, whose merchant navy was now the second largest in the world. In case of war with Britain, these ships could easily be converted into privateers, and American politicians were not shy in pointing out what consequences this would have for British commerce.

This was the underlying dilemma that British politicians had to face, and, seen from this perspective, the decisions they took that led to the Declaration of Paris are all perfectly plausible. As soon as a certain legal principle forms a rallying cry for an alliance of neutrals and resistance to it makes war against a strong coalition likely, accepting this norm may become the national interest. This is exactly what happened with the 'free ships, free goods' principle. What made this principle so attractive was that the opposing (British) idea – the right of search on whatever ship a belligerent thought might carry contraband – hurt so many different interests. Since it interfered with navigation on a global scale, everybody who had an interest in the affordable and predictable transport of goods would be opposed. Thus it united all neutrals against the belligerent who favoured the right of search as interpreted by the British. Faced with strong and determined resistance, the Cabinet did the sensible thing and tried to use Britain's considerable power to influence the norm-setting process in the direction that it preferred.

In 1854 the Cabinet accepted that a compromise had to be found with the French alliance partner, and that an early assurance that the right of search would be severely restricted was of vital importance to prevent a hostile alliance of neutrals, a new Armed Neutrality.[3] Instead, Britain's demonstrative generosity helped to secure the goodwill of the Baltic neutrals throughout the Crimean War. While accepting that this compromise might ultimately mean the end for the old British interpretation of the right of search as a means to control neutral trade wherever it might benefit the enemy, Secretary of State Lord Clarendon now attempted to abolish another established principle at the same time: the right of privateering. As has been shown throughout this book, the potential of the US merchant navy for swift conversion meant that privateering was more than a nuisance, and certainly not a medieval relic overtaken by technological change. On the contrary, it had profound implications for the maritime balance of power.

The idea of a convention against privateering was first drafted in the Foreign Office in 1854 in reaction to the outcry in business circles caused by rumours about alleged Russian privateering schemes in the USA and actual naval preparations.[4] These rumours were quickly spread by newspapers and shocked insurers while they were setting the war risks for certain routes. Since privateers were free agents outside any chain of command and could sail wherever they pleased, the exact risk that they posed was impossible to calculate. Therefore insurers preferred to err on the side of caution, and increased their rates for all routes when rumours about Russian privateering became more numerous. This cost to the economy as a whole by raising the cost of global transport triggered calls for abolition.

Although virtually nobody had spoken out against privateering between 1815 and 1853, the idea that this was an odious relic that urgently needed to be outlawed caught on quickly. Next to its relevance to business and shipping circles, it resonated with the belief that in this time and age, the involvement of private marauders who had merged their participation in interstate violence with their interest in personal profit was no longer acceptable, and that all military action should be conducted by state forces. Furthermore, the idea of abolishing privateering appealed not only to reform-minded philanthropists but also to hard-headed naval strategists. The prospect of stripping weaker naval powers of their only means of naval defence warmed the hearts of those admirals and politicians who were unimpressed by alleged advances in human civilisation.

In response, the US government conducted a treaty campaign aimed at elevating the 'free ships, free goods' principle to the status of undisputed customary law without losing privateering. The willingness of European states to accept these treaties once the Crimean War was over highlighted the danger of losing the old right of search without gaining anything in return. Therefore the crucial decision for the creation of the Declaration of Paris was made in late 1855. Previously, Britain had only recommended the linkage of the freedom of neutral trade with the abolition of privateering to other states that were approached by the USA. Now it informed the French that the Cabinet was seriously considering the signature of an identical agreement between the USA and Britain.[5]

French Foreign Minister Walewski immediately realised the potential of a universal code of maritime law based on this idea, and he used the opportunity of the Paris Peace Congress to broker a multilateral treaty that in many respects would have been unthinkable only a few years earlier. The fiercest resistance was domestic: the French Navy was afraid of losing a powerful weapon in the case of a war against the USA and Britain, or both.[6] However, the navy was overruled by Napoleon III, who found the chance to obtain a British signature under the 'free ships, free goods' principle too attractive and concrete to dismiss it for a mere eventuality, which seemed even more remote when considered in the light of the recent triumphs of the Anglo-French alliance.[7]

Thus the Declaration of Paris can only be understood as a package deal: Britain gave up a principle that proved increasingly hard to defend, and gained the abolition of another principle that the Cabinet was rather keen to see go. The Cabinet discussions clearly show that the Palmerston government was not concerned whether it would be able to shake off these restraints once they became inconvenient, but rather whether the prospects of fastening the restraints on the unwilling Americans were sufficient to warrant a British concession. With one exception, all Cabinet members were convinced that sooner or later the international agreement would oblige the Americans to submit, securing the Royal Navy and British commerce a vital advantage.[8]

In the process, they had committed Britain to support a revolution in international law-making. The French Foreign Minister had combined the idea of a spider web of bilateral treaties to secure the global recognition of a certain norm, as pioneered by the British regarding the slave trade and copied by the Americans during the Crimean War, with the more traditional use of a great European peace congress to legislate advances in international law. The Westphalian Congress had been the first, establishing a basic freedom of religion, while the Congress of Vienna had banned the international slave trade, and Walewski was eager to connect the name of the Congress of Paris (and his own) with the final triumph of the Armed Neutrality and the abolition of privateering.[9] However, these had been European congresses, and they had previously only claimed to set the norms regulating the 'European law of nations'. This restriction was quietly dropped in an attempt to use this classic instrument of great power policy-making to contain the reality of US influence. In turn, this meant that the system of the law of nations was now opened to a global community of states, and a declaration by the great powers of Europe calling all states to join their agreement could hardly be interpreted in a different way than also promising access to the entire catalogue of norms of the European law of nations, including its notion of the equality of states. In their attempt to use the instrument of the European law of nations to constrain the USA, the European powers extended the sphere of 'international law' first to South America and later even to Asia.

US attempts to prevent South American states from adhering to the declaration largely failed, and soon most Latin and Central American nations were party to a multilateral treaty uniting most of the world's states. It is this achievement that highlights the effectiveness of the new law-making treaty if combined with a great power congress: the treaty effectively becomes a proposal endorsed by major powers that any independent state can vote on by joining or abstaining. If the vast majority of states join within a period of weeks or months, as in the case of the Declaration of Paris, a new norm of global reach is established that almost immediately qualifies as customary international law. This was revolutionary, since creating new customary international law was an arduous process that involved consistent state practice (examples of states acting according to the norm) and *opinio juris* (proof that states acted as they did because they felt bound by law). The bar was set high because customary international law can bind states that never explicitly accepted a norm, or did not even exist when it was created. The only exceptions are persistent objectors, states that have consistently declared their opposition to a new norm. The USA would certainly qualify as a persistent objector, and could expect that other states would respect the USA's right to retain privateering. But that was a rather feeble and isolated position for the country that claimed to be more committed than most to the freedom of the seas. By using the multilateral law-making treaty as an instrument to create customary law by obtaining the consensus of the many, Britain and France had from the beginning also counted on the other mechanism that gives international law its power: the isolating, shaming and ultimately binding of the unwilling.

Only weeks after the Congress of Paris ended, US Secretary of State William Marcy presented what became known as the Marcy Amendment, the promise given to abandon privateering if private property was immune from capture at sea in wartime, even if enemy property sailing in an enemy merchant vessel. Despite coming so swiftly after the declaration, the proposal came too late to prevent most states from joining it. However, the initiative became a cherished part of the USA's traditional campaign for the freedom of the seas, and remained the official US position on maritime law of warfare until the Second Hague Peace Conference in 1907. This book has revealed that the Marcy Amendment was a half-hearted effort from the start, and was only made after one diplomat in Portugal had put forward a similar proposal without waiting for instructions. John Louis O'Sullivan, the man who had coined the phrase 'manifest destiny', could point towards a similar demand in a speech given by President Pierce in 1854, but was motivated primarily by his outrage that the Declaration of Paris could have been firmly established against the USA's wishes before Washington had had time to react, since the transatlantic cable was still only a project idea. After Marcy learned that this unauthorised proposal was already circulating in Europe, he was virtually forced to embrace it and make it his own. The British reaction to the proposal is instructive: Clarendon and Palmerston seriously considered it because of the protection that it would offer to British maritime commerce, the largest in the world, but ultimately the Cabinet decided against it because it feared that if successful, the Marcy Amendment would lead maritime law towards a slippery slope. If pressure to abolish the right of blockade became overwhelming, British sea power would be seriously endangered. That, however, is not a line of argument used by a power that is confident in its ability to rewrite the rules of the game at any given point.

The Cass Memorandum further illustrates the strategic problem facing Britain. After reports that coal might be treated as contraband in the Austro-Sardinian War of 1859 had alerted British merchants, and the Foreign Office had refused to condemn this practice, pointing to its inherent logic in the days of steamer navies, US Secretary of State Lewis Cass sent a strongly worded despatch that left little doubt that the USA would regard a comparable extension of the contraband list by Britain as a *casus belli*.[10] France made it clear that it had similar views, which shows that the argument that Palmerston only signed the declaration because it was clear that the definition of contraband (which was not restricted in the treaty) could always be extended misses the point.[11] If Britain had really tried to circumvent the declaration by extending the definition of contraband in any 19th-century conflict, this provocation would have recreated the same anti-British coalition of neutrals that the declaration was meant to prevent.

Those who argue that in war even more than in peace, might makes right, and that no state would agree to be restrained from deploying its military in the way that it sees fit by a mere piece of paper, often forget that for absolute norm-setting power, absolute political and military power is needed. After overpowering Carthage, the ancient Romans did possess that kind of power, which was why their empire knew no law of nations in the modern sense, based on the formal equality of each entity in the system. It rather resembled the Chinese Empire, which knew tributaries but no equals. Although Britain was by far the most influential nation on the planet in 1856, it was never in a position simply to impose norms on all other nations. Therefore British politicians turned to the multilateral law-making treaty to achieve their goals, and the angry US reaction, branding the Declaration of Paris 'that moral league of nations against the United States', underlined the effectiveness of the chosen method.[12]

The suppression of privateering against US wishes was achieved in two ways: first, most states in Europe and the USA immediately accepted the corollary principle that a party joining the Declaration of Paris would also declare its ports closed for privateers of all flags, in any conflict. The idea had been pioneered by the Swedish in 1854, and was immediately adopted by Britain, which in turn strongly recommended it to every neutral during the Crimean War. While Britain's motive was strategic, for the small neutrals the logic was commercial: while in earlier days good money could be made from supplying privateers and benefiting from the sale of captured vessels at competitive prices, in the days of scheduled steamer connections within a dense web of commercial entanglement, the confirmed presence of privateers would simply raise the insurance rates for everyone sailing for, or passing, a particular port. Keeping privateers away had now become a commercial interest. Although they had enjoyed practical equality with vessels of war for centuries, privateers now had to accept a new, lower status which prevented them from buying supplies or fuel and disposing of their prizes. Effectively, privateers were restricted to the ports of the nation that had issued their letters of marque. Practices such as privateering that rely upon the cooperation of other states are thus dependent upon the continued willingness of others to provide that cooperation. As states withdrew their logistical support and joined what modern political scientists have called a global abolition regime against practices such as privateering,[13] it became very difficult indeed to sustain that practice.

The second mechanism was more straightforward and ensured that states that had signed the treaty would continue to respect their obligations: in case of a threatened revocation of the ban on privateering, the powers that had subscribed to it would signal their willingness to use force to uphold the principle. When Bismarck implied in 1864 that Denmark's failure to respect the principle of 'effective blockade' gave Prussia the right to issue letters of marque, his delegate at the London conference was put under intense pressure by every other participant to reaffirm Prussia's adherence to the declaration.[14] This episode is an example of how the enforcement of international law can work in practice, showing that states can and will combine spontaneously, and threaten the use of force if met with an open challenge to an important norm of international law. As will be shown during the discussion of enforcement of international law in general, various later attempts to re-introduce privateering met with exactly the same reaction, which is why they are almost unknown.

But the Declaration of Paris was more than just a treaty to ban privateering, and for most signatories it meant that freedoms for neutral trade they had long demanded in vain were handed to them on a silver platter, provided that they cooperated in suppressing privateering. The older and profoundly anti-British concept of defending the rights of neutrals by relying on the 'maritime balance of power' had succeeded in keeping the actual exercise of Britain's supremacy on the oceans within certain limits. However, it required the strongest neutrals to take huge political risks when combining the world's maritime nations into an armed alliance joining a war on the side of Britain's enemies. Now, Britain volunteered to act as a permanent guarantor for neutral rights: any nation violating the interests of neutral shipping could not avoid hurting the interests of British merchants and ship-owners. If British citizens suffered because a privilege protected by an international treaty was not granted, a reaction by the British government and ultimately the Royal Navy would surely follow. In other words, as the freedom of neutral trade was elevated from a political principle to a global norm, British sea power suddenly became the foremost force upholding neutral rights against belligerents. But it would not have to do it all alone: the commercial nations of the world had every interest in cooperating to maintain the effectiveness of the Declaration of Paris. In an age of rapid economic expansion, ensuring the global flow of commerce irrespective of which nation happened to be at war with another became more important with every year that passed. International law was by far the most effective means of securing this freedom everywhere on the high seas, relying on its implied threat of overwhelming force against anyone who tried to defy or subvert the rules.

The American Civil War is the best example to illustrate its efficiency. By 1859, many in Britain believed that the USA had benefited from the breakthrough for the rights of neutrals without having to abandon privateering, and that the rule restricting the liberal neutral rights to member states, written into one of the Congress protocols at British insistence, had failed.[15] The two mechanisms outlined above, however, proved highly effective after April 1861. The first one, denying neutral ports to the privateers of the Confederacy, meant that this final episode in the history of privateering ended with the rather inglorious conversion of most Confederate privateers to blockade runners within 12 months. None of the signatories to the declaration argued that the issue of letters of marque by a non-party was illegal, but all cooperated to render privateering unworkable. When Congress demanded that the Union should also issue letters of marque, Lincoln knew that most states would have denied Northern privateers the use of their ports. Faced with the choice of accepting the reality of the new norm and risking domestic discontent, or overstepping it and inviting a conflict with the European powers over the right of port entry, Lincoln wisely chose the former.

The second method of securing international norms – threatening a military confrontation with a powerful alliance – not only prevented the North from evading the inconvenient requirement of 'effective' blockade by simply declaring the Southern ports closed, but was also influential in Lincoln's decision not to issue letters of marque. Both measures had already been passed as Acts of Congress, but, in the case of blockade by decree, Lincoln dropped the idea after numerous governments had announced their intention not to respect it, which was another way of saying that they would back up the right of their merchants to trade in these ports with military force.[16] Thus even in a major conflict like the American Civil War, fought between two non-signatories, the principles of the Declaration of Paris prevailed.[17] It failed to prevent all disputes about the laws of neutrality at sea, but that had never been the intention. The goal was to remove the biggest bones of contention, ensuring that the inevitable conflicts between belligerents and neutrals would be over comparatively minor issues. Seen in that light, the *Trent* affair serves as a powerful reminder of why states had chosen to set very clear rules on belligerent privileges toward neutral shipping.

It is true that the doctrine of 'continuous voyage' as practised by the USA, taking neutral vessels en route to neutral ports if the ultimate destination of the cargo was the enemy, violated the spirit if not the letter of the Declaration of Paris, but the fact that nearly all vessels confiscated actually were blockade runners made its temporary application acceptable. Here, this book argues for a re-assessment of British policy: instead of being delighted that the USA had extended belligerent rights that might one day be claimed by Britain,[18] London fought hard behind the scenes to secure neutral rights for British merchants. However, after unfortunate experiences early in the war, Foreign Secretary Russell was careful not to publicly support traders who were highly likely to be unmasked as criminal smugglers.[19]

Despite the impact of the blockade on transatlantic trade and cotton exports, global trade as a whole was remarkably stable, and even transatlantic trade continued largely unmolested under neutral flags. Whereas in earlier times a military conflict of such scale and magnitude would have disrupted shipping severely and caused insurers to ask for prohibitive war risk premiums, a war fought under the rules of the declaration was actually a godsend for neutral trade, offering handsome and secure profits for those not involved in the fighting. On the other hand, many argued that it was exactly this effect that made the declaration unsustainable. In earlier wars, the economic dislocation had affected the global shipping industry as a whole. Now the entire burden fell on the shipping business of the belligerents.

The Civil War had demonstrated to those English merchants interested in the question how quickly and permanently even the second largest merchant navy of the world could be ruined and replaced by neutrals. Likewise, the continental wars and war scares of the late 1850s and early 1860s turned entire business communities in the Hanseatic towns, the Prussian Baltic coast and the Adriatic into energetic campaigners for a reform of maritime law. The joint campaign of the Senate of Bremen and the Dutch Cabinet to gain the support of all secondary maritime powers for a declaration demanding the Marcy Amendment, which would then be presented to the great powers at the opening of the European Congress of January 1860, is a prime example of the effectiveness of international business networks and transnational actors, as they are now called: the combined diplomatic and public lobbying campaign was the brainchild of a single ship-owner in Bremen, and if the congress had not been cancelled at short notice the Dutch-Bremish declaration would have been welcomed by four great powers and effectively isolated Britain. It could be argued that they were selfish capitalists trying to shape international law to suit their commercial interests, but they were certainly more effective campaigners than idealists such as Cobden or Bright. A steady stream of petitions, sent in the name of chambers of commerce or similar bodies, ensured that the topic was never forgotten for long in the chancelleries of Europe. In the Austrian port of Trieste, personal and national interests were peculiarly intertwined after merchants had alerted the government to the fact that local Swiss traders had successfully lobbied for the creation of a Swiss merchant flag, offering the benefits of permanent neutrality.[20]

When war broke out in 1866, Austria immediately offered to apply the Marcy Amendment if Prussia promised to do the same. The Prussian government was taken by surprise, but faced with numerous similar petitions itself and no opposition from a navy keen to establish a precedent for an advantageous principle of international law, it agreed within days.[21] The war that tore the German Confederation apart thus became the first and only war to be fought under the rules proposed by William Marcy. Of course, the naval war was never likely to decide the contest, but all states involved saw it as a first step towards universal reform, in particular after Italy also agreed to honour the new principle when it joined the war.

The master plan to secure an amendment to the Declaration of Paris was the one drafted in Bremen in 1859: constantly reassuring themselves about their positions, the European states could isolate Britain at a European congress. Under additional pressure from the USA, London might then be persuaded to sign a new treaty. It seemed that time was on the side of the reformers, and that civilisation on its march only needed the assistance of one British government realising that it was in Britain's best interest to protect its merchant navy in this way. Alternatively, a European congress might find the leverage to compel Britain to give up its isolated position. All of this was seriously discussed in diplomatic correspondence between the Prussians, Austrians, French and Russians, although the Europeans were surprised by how little interest was shown in these discussions by Washington.

US desire for the amendment was significantly reduced following the country's ascent into the elite club of nations with major modern navies during the Civil War. But the USA signed the only treaty containing the principle, with the new kingdom of Italy in 1871.[22] Furthermore, a sizable group of activists, particularly in the chambers of commerce of the north-east, ensured that Marcy's legacy was kept alive. By 1870, all but one of the great powers were publicly committed to the principle. Had Britain been forced to discuss the reform at a congress, it would have fought alone. To understand why this confrontation never came about, and why the history of maritime law of warfare took a very different course, we need to look at the Franco-German War of 1870/1.

As set out in Chapter 7, Napoleon III refused to respond to the Prussian offer to apply the Marcy Amendment, instead declaring that the rules of the Declaration of Paris would govern the conduct of his naval forces.[23] Britain assumed the role of an umpire, determining whether the rules of the Declaration of Paris were respected, and successfully rejected the pretensions of both sides. The French complaint that the German *Seewehr* was essentially the return of privateering in disguise received a cool reply: the inclusion of private vessels into the official navy even under a lease arrangement with bonus payments for captures (as in the German case) did not amount to privateering, Foreign Secretary Granville argued since privateers had been abolished because they were commanded by private individuals exempt from naval discipline and free to hunt for enemy vessels wherever they pleased. As long as the ship was under the command of a navy officer, the question of who actually owned the ship was peripheral.[24] This seemed to be a rather petty difference and might have invited privateering in all but name, but the requirement to submit to naval discipline and command kept private adventurers away, and the numbers of 'auxiliary cruisers' were small in both world wars.

The declaration was first broken by the French Navy, but the deeds of the *Desaix* – burning three German merchant vessels at sea – were not on a sufficient scale to assemble a global alliance of enraged neutrals on the German side.[25] While the powers of Europe had combined to defend the declaration – for example, against Prussia in 1864 – they now did nothing whatsoever. The reason was that while some of the 'House rules' had been broken, the fundamental aim of the Declaration of Paris was never challenged, and the safety of neutral commerce was never in doubt. There was also no need to intervene to correct the wrongs committed against German merchant vessels, since the Germans had won a resounding victory and could be expected to find ways of obtaining compensation. The problem was that Bismarck never understood any of this. Enraged at the apathy towards France's violations of the rules, Bismarck ordered the sinking of all French vessels, a prelude to 1915 only prevented by the French surrender.[26]

Bismarck grasped the old idea of a maritime balance of power but failed to realise that the Declaration of Paris was much more than a normal treaty. In a bilateral agreement, party A could opt out of its obligations to party B, if B had broken the treaty earlier. A multilateral treaty, however, involved many more parties with an interest in the matter. To challenge a treaty regulating international commerce between more than 40 parties because of an alleged infraction by another party shows a fundamental misunderstanding of the state of maritime law of warfare after 1856.[27] When his protests were ignored, Bismarck concluded that the Declaration of Paris was just a piece of paper and could not be relied on.[28] He was either unwilling or unable to understand that the other signatories never felt that the rule of international law was seriously challenged. Bismarck, on the other hand, showed an understanding of international law that was based not on outcomes but on principle: either the norms were respected absolutely, or the injured party had the unqualified right to respond with reprisals, no matter how brutal.[29] This absolute stance, principled and archaic at the same time, remained a feature of the German Empire's approach to international law and would eventually persuade its leadership that unrestrained submarine warfare was morally justifiable.

At the time, most observers failed to notice the fundamental change in the prospects for reform that had just occurred. The leader of a new powerful empire forged from states that had all been traditional supporters of liberal neutral rights had just been thoroughly disillusioned by the very idea of maritime law. Thus the idea of a European congress forcing an isolated Britain to accept an even more liberal interpretation of the rights of peaceful commerce was effectively dead. Liberal thinkers in England continued to make the case for the immunity of private trade, as the only way to secure the lines of communication in Britain's far-flung empire and to save British shipping in case of war, but the secret diplomatic alignment wanting to compel Britain to accept this principle had been broken forever. Regardless of the claims by many that the status quo was unsustainable, a reform of the Declaration of Paris was now well-nigh impossible. An increasingly vocal conservative minority in Britain began to demand its abrogation, a fact that did not remain unnoticed abroad. But a British revocation of the pledge given in 1856 would have meant a return to the permanent confrontation with neutrals deemed too dangerous at the beginning of the Crimean War. With reform or abrogation both out of the question, the status quo remained unchanged. The declaration may have had far fewer friends than in 1856, but its regime would show remarkable resilience and stability for decades to come.

When the Ottoman Empire declared a blockade of the Russian coast in the war of 1877/8, the lack of respect shown for the fourth article of the declaration, demanding 'effectiveness', soon became apparent. The blockade was enforced only at the Bosporus, denying the passage of the Strait to neutral trade although no Turkish naval squadron was anywhere near the Russian ports. European and American diplomats duly reported home that the Turkish attitude to the Declaration of Paris could only be described as brazen disregard.[30] Invoking article four of the declaration, many states now demanded that the blockade be either made effective or raised completely. Otherwise they left little doubt that modern naval vessels would protect merchant vessels carrying their flag from frivolous molestation by Ottoman authorities. Faced with the unwelcome prospect of naval war against the majority of the world, the Ottoman Empire chose the sensible option and raised the blockade. It is noteworthy that the new state of Bulgaria, formed as a consequence of the Russo-Turkish war, immediately joined the Declaration of Paris in July 1878. Being part of the fabric of international law was not seen as an entanglement of unwelcome obligations, but as the hallmark of a sovereign and civilised nation.

At the same time, the Russians toyed publicly with the idea of reinstituting privateering in case the verbal sabre-rattling escalated to a full war between the Tsar and Britain. The reports about these plans did not fail to cause a privateering scare, particularly in lightly defended outposts of the British Empire, such as South Africa and Australia. The scheme, apparently approved by the Tsar, envisaged a large number of privateers operating from hidden bases in Siberia and attacking British trade with China, as well as letters of marque issued to Americans who were keen on preying on the vessels of the old mother country.[31] But even before it became clear that the diplomatic crisis would not escalate to military conflict, these plans were shelved. The Tsar seems to have realised that the tacit US support that he had hoped for would not be forthcoming, whereas an open challenge to the Declaration of Paris would have destroyed any hopes of finding allies against Britain, and raised the possibility of an isolated position comparable to the Crimean War. Furthermore, many commentators pointed out that the same military effect could be achieved with a volunteer force modelled on the Prussian *Seewehr*.

A similar pattern would re-emerge in the next Anglo-Russian crisis in 1884/5, but now the rumours of privateering schemes were almost certainly circulated to cause another privateering scare while the preparations for a volunteer navy of the *Seewehr* type were under way. Although the USA never accepted the abolition of privateering, and calls for letters of marque to be issued were not limited to Russia, the prohibition mechanism of the Declaration of Paris was intact, constituting a strong deterrent even for great powers when privateering seemed a promising way to circumvent naval inferiority. The problem was simply that with the right of port access gone, no private individual could be tempted to sign a letter of marque, despite at least two attempts in Latin America, a hotbed of privateering earlier in the century.[32] Chile was a signatory to the declaration but it tried to issue letters of marque against Spain, a non-signatory, in September 1865.[33] With a strong Spanish squadron blockading Chile's coastline and no access to other ports, it is unsurprising that the offer enraged the Spanish but found no takers. Likewise, Bolivia's attempt to counter Chile's invasion of its coastline in 1879 by offering letters of marque was completely unsuccessful: without a coastline of its own, potential privateers would have been entirely dependent on the ports of Bolivia's wartime ally, Peru – a signatory to the Declaration of Paris. Nobody was tempted, especially after Britain announced that it would treat every Bolivian privateer found molesting British vessels as a pirate.[34]

The ban on privateering withstood the test of time, but it was the issue of neutral trade and the definition of contraband that would place the declaration's authority on a downward trajectory. Contraband was never defined by the drafters, but despite hints by Clarendon to the Admiralty that the extremely short contraband lists of the Crimean War might be extended in the future, this possibility was seen as too fraught with conflict to be a viable loophole. The Cass Memorandum of 1859 made it clear that treating even coal as contraband (for being the primary fuel of warships) would be a *casus belli* for the USA. When Britain was offered the chance to widen the definition following German complaints about deliveries of English coal to the French Navy in 1870, the German argument that anything that assisted the war efforts of the enemy should *ipso facto* be contraband was laughed off: Secretary of State Granville replied that under this definition, absolutely anything might be labelled contraband – an outrageous idea at the time.[35]

The turning point came, surprisingly enough, in France's war against China in 1885. Facing more stubborn resistance than expected, the French government decided that the shipments of rice from the south to the north, a traditional form of payment that was vital for the Chinese military effort, had to be stopped. Instead of declaring the entire coastline blockaded, it chose what it thought was a less disruptive option and declared that rice would be considered contraband, and therefore liable for confiscation even on neutral vessels.[36] The neutrals protested immediately, in particular Britain and the Scandinavians, arguing that treating food as contraband was unheard of and set a dangerous precedent.[37] Since the Declaration of Paris did not include a definition of contraband, the French action was not technically a violation of its terms, but it went far towards undermining it. Perhaps that had not been the intention, but it certainly was the effect of the action, especially after Britain toned down its protests and seemed to accept the French explanation, to the dismay of other neutrals who would have liked a firm commitment that a belligerent's right to determine contraband was not unlimited. Now, they wondered, if a state could get away with declaring food contraband, where was the line? For the first time the danger that a nation might be starved out by the withholding of its food imports was seriously discussed, particularly in Germany. War planners began to adapt their strategies to the expectation that a potential enemy was likely to disregard the laws of warfare.

The war planners themselves had changed: in the past, respect for the laws of warfare had been ensured by the idea that illegal fighting methods violated the honour of an officer, and were likely to add to the number of one's enemies. At the same time as the move for codification in international law brought numerous conferences and declarations, seeking to ban more and more practices considered barbarous and irreconcilable with the 'spirit of the age', a new breed of military men emerged who showed a disregard for 'playing by the rules' that would have been alien to their predecessors. Under the influence of an intoxicating cocktail of high imperialism and social Darwinism, war between great powers was increasingly perceived as a no-holds-barred struggle for national survival, industrial in its methods but medieval in its brutality.

In the field of naval strategy, the French *Jeune Ecole* led the way, suggesting that France's best chance of beating Britain was to hit the island itself as hard as possible, bombarding coastal towns, extorting ransom and destroying British trade.[38] In their deliberations, there was little room for the Declaration of Paris. Even more influential in naval circles and beyond, Alfred Thayer Mahan studied sea power in the age of Nelson, concentrating on the brief period when Britain had actually enjoyed total dominance over the oceans. His lessons about how sea power helped to create the British Empire in its Victorian splendour were eagerly received, and after the Franco-Chinese war his advice that every nation had to defend its maritime lines of communication with a large fleet intuitively rang true.

Soon, a generation of naval officers who had welcomed the idea of reducing maritime conflict to a regulated duel between navies was replaced by officers who were hostile to the very idea of international law. Increasingly, respect for the rules of warfare had to be forced on navies by their governments, and potential opponents could no longer take it for granted that the diplomats would be successful in restraining the warriors. Accordingly, even those who were convinced that the laws of warfare represented progress planned for the worst. Moreover, the traditional strategy of responding to such a worst-case scenario, winning allies against an enemy on the basis of his lawlessness and violation of neutral interests, seemed alien to admirals like Aubé, Fisher or Tirpitz.

Nonetheless, the Declaration of Paris was still intact, and even increasing its outreach as a further unintended consequence of China's treatment: the accession to the treaty by Japan in 1886 was the first formal step of an Asian power into the sphere of international law. Throughout the Sino-Japanese War of 1894/5, Japan pointed to its strict adherence to its rules as the basis for its claim to being a civilised power, worthy of respect and equal treatment by the Europeans.[39] A few years later, two of the few nations that had never signed the declaration clashed, and both the USA and Spain confirmed that they considered themselves bound by articles two to four. Neither formally accepted article one, the ban on privateering, but both kept their written promise not to issue any letters of marque.

The Spanish-American War of 1898 also served as a reminder to the business and shipping circles of the American north-east of how the Declaration of Paris affected the interests of a belligerent's shipping during war. Brief but intense lobbying led to an act being passed in Congress that called for a renewed push to finally secure the Marcy Amendment. After a long pause, a US president once again used his annual State of the Union address to call upon the world to adopt it. This newly found impetus of the McKinley administration was the main reason why Britain chose to prevent all discussion of maritime law of warfare during the First Hague Peace Conference.

The Russo-Japanese War of 1904/5 demonstrated that technological change had created a profoundly different naval environment from the one that had been envisaged in 1856. Free-floating mines posed great dangers to neutrals trading near a warzone, while the advances in torpedo technology brought a new edge to the question of effective blockade: how close did the now highly vulnerable battleships and cruisers have to be to the coast that they blockaded? Even Britain now accepted that these matters had to be discussed, and the Second Hague Peace Conference was a major breakthrough. Wisely, the reforms or clarifications of maritime law had been split into seven different conventions: when the USA refused to sign a convention on the conversion of merchant vessels into auxiliary cruisers, complaining that article one repeated the abolition of privateering, that did not endanger the conference's successes in slowly adapting the rules of maritime war to the technological realities of the 20th century. The conference even attempted to overcome the fundamental problem of partial justice – that is, the trial of the neutral trader by the belligerents' prize courts – by establishing a new international prize court.

A follow-up conference met a year later to write a detailed rulebook of maritime law that could serve as the basis for the new court's decisions. On paper the 1909 Declaration of London marked the final triumph for the Declaration of Paris: during the negotiations, Spain and Mexico finally gave up their insistence on privateering and formally declared their adherence to the Declaration of Paris. It was at this moment, however, that the seeds for its downfall were sown as the conference drafters committed three crucial mistakes that would bring down both treaties. The first one was to succumb to the old military mistake of planning how to win the last war: by essentially accepting the US Supreme Court's way of interpreting 'continuous voyage', they adopted a solution that arguably struck a sensible balance between belligerent and neutral rights in a specific civil war in the 1860s, but was completely out of touch with reality by 1909. The Declaration of London placed enormous significance on a ship's papers to establish the ownership and destination of its cargo, which made little sense in a globalised economy where ownership of a cargo could be traded multiple times on a futures market in London or New York while the ship was crossing the Atlantic.[40]

The second mistake was to simply repeat the definition used in the Declaration of Paris to describe what is an 'effective' blockade. As has been shown throughout this book, that definition was less than crystal clear and did not acknowledge that 'cruising blockades' had become state practice in the 1860s and 1870s. By 1909 a blockading squadron had to approach a coast potentially swarming with submarine mines and torpedo boats, so simply repeating the old formula instead of providing guidance to naval commanders reduced the declaration's credibility in naval circles. Worse, it allowed those in these circles who never really believed in the utility of the laws of war to claim that there were 'differing interpretations' of these very complex issues, giving the impression that no one really knew where bending the rules ended and breaking them began.

The third mistake was that on less controversial issues, the drafters attempted to regulate every detail, leading to a final document that shirked its responsibility on blockade and acknowledged no hierarchy between the various articles, whether they were basic principles of neutrality or mere practical advice. The delegates had lost sight of the simple fact that an international legal norm is only as strong as the will of its signatories to back it up by force. While states were ready to take up arms to defend the honour of their flags and the business interests of those flying them, nobody would go to war over the question of whether belligerent vessels were allowed to stay in neutral ports for 24 or, say, 48 hours. In its eagerness to solve all existing disputes except the most important ones, the Declaration of London tightened the reins too much and paid no regard to technological change. Therefore there were good reasons why the House of Lords refused to ratify it, but, together with disparaging statements attributed to prominent admirals like Sir John Fisher, this only served to reinforce the traditional image of 'perfidious Albion', participating in setting the rules for others but never intending to keep them itself.[41]

Yet it was governments not admirals making the key decisions over whether treaties should be broken, and when it dawned upon the Foreign Office that in a potential war, Germany might undermine a blockade by rerouting trade through neutral Rotterdam, the suggestion was not to challenge the declaration's guarantee of neutral rights but rather to declare war on the Netherlands.[42] Analysing the same problem, the Admiralty came up with a very different solution: in his latest book, *Planning Armageddon*, Nicholas Lambert shows that it wanted to exploit Britain's controlling influence over global credit supply and communications not just to deprive Germany of access to the sea but to lock it out of the world economy entirely. Instead of the slow asphyxiation of a classic naval blockade, this new approach to economic warfare would work like a garrotte and strangle

Germany's economic and financial system almost instantaneously. Britain would have won the war long before the neutrals would have had any chance to organise a protest about the complete disregard for their rights, since freezing all of Germany's trade meant freezing most of Europe's trade as well. Hence they were completely ignored in planning. Lambert even presents some evidence that the Cabinet might have approved of this idea and that it amounted to Britain's official war plan. If so, it was surely one of its more foolish attempts at grand strategy.

When war came, Britain's bold scheme violated far too many domestic economic interests to ignore them for any length of time, and the plan unravelled within three weeks. It was replaced by an impromptu 'blockade' that constantly tried to find new and innovative ways of preventing the Netherlands or Sweden from supplying Germany.[43] In short, Britain had reverted to the traditional game of a belligerent taking a fresh look at the existing rulebook at the start of a conflict and seeing how far one could go in working it to one's advantage. The neutrals would surely protest, but the real question was whether they would take the next step and organise a coalition of the unwilling to undermine the infringement of neutral rights, potentially leading to a formal alliance like the Armed Neutralities of the 18th century. So why did none of this happen after 1914?

The answer lies in two highly unusual decisions taken in Washington and Berlin, both of which are easier to understand when seen in the context of the events discussed in this book. The USA was severely hit by Britain's economic restrictions, but once the initial scheme had been abandoned and US bankruptcy averted, President Wilson decided that US interests were best served by negotiating a series of compromises with Britain rather than leading a neutral alliance. John Coogan argues that Wilson feared that too much pressure on Britain might lead to the unwanted outcome of a Wilhelmian Europe; in addition, the USA's recent conversion to imperialism contributed to a much more favourable view of extensive belligerent rights at sea.[44] This book shows that the US stance on the freedom of the seas was never one of unconditional support, and never disconnected from its own naval strength. But the enforcement of international law should not lie upon the shoulders of a single country: Sweden and Denmark had proven in 1854 that Europe's neutrals alone could and would confront an Anglo-French alliance over neutral rights.

The real puzzle is Germany's reaction once it realised that Britain intended to bend the rules to the utmost. Instead of making every effort to form a coalition of neutrals against British pretensions, building on the real damage inflicted upon Dutch, Swedish or US interests, they responded by applying the logic used by Bismarck in earlier wars: if a treaty was broken by one party, the injured party enjoyed a virtually unlimited right to use reprisals. But whereas Bismarck had ordered the sinking of every French merchant vessel in 1871, demanding that each of them should be burned on the high seas after the crew had been taken prisoner, the German high command now authorised the U-boat captains to sink merchant vessels with torpedoes, ensuring that crew members would perish. Since big merchant vessels and passenger steamers were hard to distinguish, the measure guaranteed that neutral nations would complain not only about lost cargoes but also about dead civilians. By responding to infractions of the rights of neutrals in a way that exposed all neutrals to unprecedented danger and injury, Germany paradoxically managed to eventually create an informal alliance of neutrals around Britain, the original offender. The earlier examples of this pattern from the days of Bismarck described in this book make it easier to understand why they even felt that they were completely justified and operating within the accepted framework of international law.

The compounded effect of the US and the German reaction to Britain's challenge was that instead of a coordinated response based on existing treaties, the belligerents triggered a vicious circle of reprisal and counter-reprisals, linking violations and atrocities on land and sea in a cycle of escalation and indignation that left the regime of neutral rights as it had existed until the summer of 1914 in smouldering ruins, never to rise again. The Declaration of Paris had not disappeared completely: when the Admiralty wanted to bury the unloved corpse in 1918, the Foreign Office insisted that Britain could only withdraw in agreement with all other states concerned.[45] But the enforcement mechanisms that had previously sustained the declaration were gone, and would never return. Although there were plans to discuss the future of maritime law at the Versailles conference, these talks never took place. The Declaration of Paris was never abrogated; trampled upon in both world wars, it still remains formally in force, and its rules on neutral trade are included in the military manuals of the world's major navies. But unlike in the 19th century, they offer no guarantee or even reassurance that belligerents will respect the rights of those not involved in their conflict to use the oceans as they wish.

Leaving aside the obvious consequences for the safety of global transport in times of war, the destruction of the declaration's regime has made historians blind to its extraordinary achievements. The rules set up at the Paris Peace Congress regulated and restrained naval war for the next 60 years. Crucially, they helped to keep limited wars limited by setting universal ground rules that were accepted by all, avoiding the escalations that had previously occurred when disputes over the rights of neutrals turned sour. That had been the stated ambition in the preamble of the declaration, and in that respect it was an unreserved success. The very predictability of the rules that would be applied to global trade in wartime allowed insurers to charge much lower premiums, and persuaded merchants to complete transactions that they would otherwise have avoided. The benefit for the world economy is hard to express in numbers, but a glance at the insurance rates charged during the Napoleonic Wars and a comparison with the much increased volume of global trade by the mid-19th century go far in illustrating the real gains that were made because of the Declaration of Paris. Over the 60 years in which the regime of the declaration worked, these amounted to massive savings in global transport costs, adding prosperity to the world economy as a whole. This staggering achievement has never been acknowledged by historians, largely because wars that are avoided make few headlines, and costs that are never incurred often escape the attention of economic historians. But the question raised at the beginning of this book is a bigger one than why the Declaration of Paris was signed, or whether it was a good or a bad thing. The introduction also asks whether the history of the declaration can provide fundamental truths about the enforcement and effectiveness of international law in the absence of a central authority.

The declaration demonstrates how the 'first wave of globalization' transformed international law, and that the need for frequent and reliable commercial interactions across the globe provided a compelling case for increasing codification. A norm that is written down and accepted by all will be more difficult to misinterpret, and more dangerous to oppose outright. The crucial innovation of the Declaration of Paris was that it invented a means of ensuring the approval of the newly codified norm. Instead of relying on the organic growth of new customary law through coherent state practice and clearly established *opinio juris*, the simple waiver of accession ratification procedures allowed for a norm to become the internationally accepted rule in weeks and months, rather than years and decades. Consequently, the decision permanently enhanced the power and status of any entity entitled to its own vote in the process. The similarity to our own UN system with its vast disparities of power but (almost) equal voting rights for each member state shows that great powers are still glad to pay this price in order to achieve a global uniformity of agreed rules, and thus much greater legitimacy of the norms. After all, many of these norms will be inspired by them rather than the small states. In other words, the declaration is an example of how global governance works in practice in the absence of a central authority, and the solutions found have inspired more aspects of the UN Charter than is acknowledged.

The drafter's sense of the importance of universal legitimacy for enforcement is further demonstrated by their second innovation, the conscious use of a major European congress as a legislative forum for matters unrelated to the war or crisis that had inspired the assembly of the congress. For a time, even the visions of a semipermanent political and legal court, a mixture of the ancient Athenian 'areopagus' and a modern international organisation, seemed perfectly possible and even likely. The example of Bremen's extraordinary initiative to force the congress to legislate the desired change in international law, and the support that it received from the Netherlands and most smaller states in Europe, shows that the history of the Concert of Europe is not just one of great power politics. The grander hopes and expectations vanished in 1860 when Napoleon III decided to resolve his war in Italy without a congress, but the fact remained that the Congress of Paris had sought confirmation of its decision by small states for the first time, and thus formally included them in the system.

This fundamental change was almost overlooked at the time because the ambitions of the declaration were much grander: it wanted to restrain states, however big or small, in wartime. Its history shows that states indeed threaten the use of force to protect established rules for the protection of trade. The nature of international law as agreed 'House Rules' within a community of sovereign entities makes the process more unpredictable than in a national system of legislation and law enforcement, but the examples presented here, particularly from the American Civil War and the Franco-German War, highlight the existence of an enforcement system based around the community of states and the lead of its most powerful members. But while the enforcement system was real, so was the danger of failure, and since the multilateral law-making treaty is still the primary tool for creating new rules of international law today, the declaration's fate also holds important lessons for policy-makers. One of the more surprising ones is that unlike in a bilateral treaty or national legislation, more detail does not mean greater clarity or security. This is due to the fundamentally different nature of the enforcement mechanism, because a forceful response by the community of states to defend norms that have been challenged is not automatic, and has to be the negotiated result of a joint desire to act in this particular case. This joint decision is easier to achieve when the broken rule enjoys a particularly high standing and legitimacy, and the violation is especially brazen and obvious.

The Declaration of Paris outlined four basic principles, and as was shown above these were defended over many decades against powerful challenges. Some of the additional rules outlined in the protocol, such as the British demand that the privileges for neutral trade should be exclusively applied to signatories, or the even more secretive French attempt to enforce its own definition of 'effective blockade', were dropped without much ado once they became politically inconvenient. The hierarchy of rules between the document itself and the protocols allowed the community of states to avoid conflict without harming the credibility of the declaration itself. Solutions to new and unexpected problems were developed on the spot, in the spirit of the declaration and in constant interaction with affected neutrals and belligerents. The simultaneous development of the idea that neutral goods should be taken off a prize straight away in both Brazil and Greece in 1870 is a good example of this dynamic.

In stark contrast, the excessive detail in the Declaration of London hid major disagreements over fundamental principles, such as the interpretation of 'close blockade' in an age of rapid technological change. The detailed solutions that were found prompted a number of states to include ever more detailed reservations, while convincing the House of Lords that the framework as a whole was too strict and inflexible to allow for British ratification. Crucially, these rules had exactly the same rank as the core principles underwriting the freedom of neutral commerce in wartime. This proved to be a fatal flaw because instead of offering a clear rallying call uniting all neutrals at the outbreak of the First World War, these rules and reservations allowed belligerents to cite the 'confusion' of the existing law as a justification for violating its 'outdated' or 'impractical' rules. The community of states that might have spontaneously decided to confront a clear violation of neutral rights was now facing a 'dispute over alleged violations'. Within months the Declaration of London had ceased to be a guideline for naval commanders and had brought down the Declaration of Paris with it.

The swift demise of the Declaration of Paris at the beginning of the First World War leads to the final and most complex question: can international law ever restrain belligerents in a major war that is not just a great power confrontation but a war for hegemony? Or can it only ever provide partial answers to limited conflict? The example of the declaration would suggest so, but the events of the Napoleonic Wars and the world wars point not so much to a breakdown of the law itself but rather towards a breakdown of the community of states that used to uphold it. Since the enforcement of the global 'House Rules' relies on the will of the community of states to defend them, a total breakdown of that community must compromise all rules that cannot be defended by threatening reciprocity. There is no way to design a better set of laws that could withstand the removal of its primary enforcement mechanism. Therefore it seems more appropriate to ask to what extent and how international law can help to prevent such breakdowns of the international community. The drafters of the Declaration of Paris were conscious of the demise of neutral rights during the Napoleonic Wars, and the solution that they found was to focus on the limitation of existing conflicts to prevent them from spreading, codifying clear rules accepted by all and deliberately raising the solemnity and legitimacy of the document to raise the political cost of breaking it. Given its eventual fate, it is chilling to think that the only real addition to our arsenal of tools since 1856 has been the invention of international courts, and two attempts at creating a central political organisation that was meant to use the resources of great powers to solve international problems without being dominated by them.

On the other hand, the conclusion that the winners of hegemonic warfare have drawn from their experience has always been to set up a much more radical and comprehensive system of international law and organisation, be it in 1648, 1815, 1919 or 1945. In all four cases they were also seeking to include both the victors and the beaten within the new political system of organising and managing the globe's manifold political conflicts. In short, they turned towards international law to manage the inevitable disputes between nations, and it seems rather arrogant of historians or political scientists to claim that the victors of hegemonic conflict routinely fell for pipe dreams of unrealistic levels of international cooperation. Rather, these statesmen had experienced a world where might makes right, and were determined to never let it happen again. They embraced the power of law to contain the destructive side of the human spirit, and, instead of dismissing it as toothless, we should strive to understand as much about the nature of that power – and its limitations – as we possibly can.

Disputes about the nature, the source and the power of international law are not simply academic squabbles with little impact beyond the ivory tower. They have shaped the architecture of international politics, and they continue to do so today. This is most obvious in the US debate as to how the new League of Nations should be constructed after the First World War had been won. Obviously, international law would be at the heart of the new institution, but how would it be enforced throughout the world, and would the new institution take over its creation as well? Some influential senators, such as Elihu Root, and two former presidents, Theodore Roosevelt and William H. Taft, believed that if norms were not defended and ignored with impunity, this would soon endanger the entire body of international law and thus the idea of a rule-based international community as a whole.[46] Therefore states should only create rules that they would actually follow. The core of their vision of the league was a judiciary to decide international disputes, an executive to enforce the judgements and a legislative chamber charged with formulating the international legal code. This vision, promoted by the League to Enforce Peace, was explicitly rejected by President Wilson. He saw the true locus of sovereignty not in the community of states but in mankind as a whole, expressed in the 'common consciousness of mankind'. This consciousness inspires new norms based on values and principles of justice, and if they are not enforced then either the world was not ready for them or the norms themselves were flawed and deserved to be discarded: a solution blessed with the elegance unique to the world of circular logic.[47] Wilson's visionary approach to the community of states inspired millions, but it certainly repelled Republican senators, many of whom would have been comfortable with a league based on the enforcement principle.

In the end, the League of Nations was created in the absence of the nation that inspired it, and it remained a hybrid between Wilson's vision and a 19th-century international organisation. The new international order created and represented by the League deserves more credit than it is usually given, and the recent work of Patricia Clavin and others has highlighted its achievements in many fields of international cooperation and regulation. But the key legacy of Woodrow Wilson was to have removed the problem of enforcement from the core of the collective security promise of the charter. Article X of the Covenant gave the great powers assembled in the League Council the power to enforce the Covenant's rules whenever a state sought to solve a dispute by aggressive means, but it did not impose a duty on them to do so.[48]

In the absence of the USA, the burden of imposing respect for the Covenant proved too heavy for the remaining great powers, especially once the Great Depression severely curtailed their financial ability to project military power while sparking manifold new conflicts. Soon the League was faced by a challenge that objected not just to a particular rule, such as the ban on interstate aggression, but to the entire idea of a universal legal order binding on all and enforced by a community of states. The fascist power's onslaught was the most extreme form of the contempt for international law that had been inspired by the social Darwinism of the late 19th century. It was nihilistic and emphasised the primacy of power and aggression in a zero-sum game for resources, but it was not entirely irrational: both the German and the Japanese programmes for achieving autarchy through import substitution and aggressive empire-building were inspired by the illegal First World War blockade of Germany, a cruel consequence of the destruction of the regime of the Declaration of Paris.

After the Second World War had been won by the alliance that called itself the 'United Nations', the drafters of the charter of the new international organisation that would follow the League of Nations were determined to avoid the mistakes of the Covenant. The granting of a veto to permanent members of the Security Council was a price consciously paid to achieve the inclusion of all great powers. Article 25 of the Charter makes the decisions of the 'enforcement team' legally binding on all other members, giving the Security Council a power that the great European councils had never claimed in the old days of the Concert of Europe. The second pillar of enforcement was the UN's standing army, to be commanded by the Military Staff Committee assembled at the New York headquarters. Yet the relevant articles 45 to 47 of the Charter quickly became devoid of any practical meaning since the great powers assembled in the Security Council preferred to deal with enforcement themselves, on a case-by-case basis. They proved more amenable to the later invention of 'peacekeeping', special troops under UN authority (despite their absence from the Charter) that attempt to play a constructive role in interstate conflicts and even civil wars.

Yet whenever the Security Council is unable to agree who is to blame for a conflict and how to go about pacifying it, the Charter offers little guidance to member states. This is not the fault of the Charter itself; rather it is the repeated failure of the great powers assembled in the Security Council to live up to the task that they have set themselves. Whenever this happens, international society effectively reverts to the enforcement dilemma as it presented itself in the late 19th century, and states can chose whether they want to support one side in a conflict or maintain neutrality. Unlike the 19th century, there is no body of universally recognised neutrality laws that have been written with the present state of the world economy in mind. According to the Charter, neutrality as a status is a thing of the past because states have to follow the decisions of the Security Council regarding who is the aggressor or victim in every conflict. Therefore the laws of neutrality are the only body of international law that has not been developed at all since the Second World War, and the codified conventions date back to 1907 or indeed 1856.

In all other fields, the UN has proved to be an extremely active forum for the creation of new codified international law, with the multilateral law-making treaty still the instrument of choice for both the central organisation and its many sub-institutions. The complex interplay between the legitimacy of state consent and the power of ideas is now more visible than ever, with many UN conventions inspired by new concepts, such as human rights or solidarity with developing nations. What begins as a radical demand is occasionally signed into law by most of the world's states, but there is still plenty of scope for research as to how some ideas can progress towards being a codified norm. There is also no systematic research on whether the enforcement of such norms differs from that of rules that are motivated by commercial or political interests, or those that are part of a complex package negotiated to balance competing state interests. It is the enforcement dilemma that constantly reminds us that for all its progress, our present international community centred on the UN is a thin veneer, masking the fact that the basic fabric that holds our rapidly globalising world together is a cloth made in the late 19th century.

The power of international law is real, but it is what states make of it. They create new norms by using multilateral law-making treaties, and defend and enforce them using a variety of sanctions, in ever-changing coalitions of the willing and able. A functioning international community without international law is unthinkable, but, as the last instance of a complete breakdown of the international community moves further and further away from living memory, a light-hearted disregard of its importance has become fashionable again, ignoring the close link between power and law that has grown over centuries. A popular variant of this disregard often brands itself 'Realism', but the 'reality' that it describes often resembles the anarchy that the winners of past hegemonial conflicts wished to overcome. It would seem more reasonable to seek a better understanding of the power and the weakness of international law: its ability to prevent, defuse, arbitrate and even solve difficult international conflicts, and its fragility due to its necessarily politicised enforcement mechanism. This book uses the treaty that laid the foundations for the present system as an example to illustrate these mechanisms, but much more research is needed to truly understand the power of law, and its importance as our first and last line of defence against a breakdown of the international community as we know it today.

Notes

Introduction: Power, Law and the Declaration of Paris

1. Throughout this book, 'international law' refers to 'public international law' and follows 19th-century practice in seeing private international law as a separate field.
2. This argument is often known as the 'Austinian challenge' to international law, but John Austin's extreme scepticism about international law went far beyond that of his mentor Jeremy Bentham, and his argument that international law is simply 'set by general opinion' and only enforced by 'moral sanctions' was as wrong in 1832 as it is today.
3. See M. W. Janis, 'Jeremy Bentham and the Fashioning of "International Law"', *American Journal of International Law*, Vol. 78, No. 2 (April 1984), pp. 405–418.
4. The best-known example is Martti Koskeniemi, *The Gentle Civilizer of Nations: The Rise and Fall of International Law 1870–1960*, Cambridge 2004.
5. See Stephen Neff, *War and the Law of Nations: A General History*, Cambridge 2005, or Alexander Gillespie, *A History of the Laws of War* (3 volumes), Oxford 2011.
6. A modern example of this phenomenon is Mary Ellen O'Connell's, *The Power and Purpose of International Law*, Oxford 2008, which was criticised by Carlo Focarelli, for 'nowhere provid[ing] a definition of the "purpose" of international law', see *European Journal of International Law*, Vol. 20 (2009), pp. 957–961, p. 957. Her main argument is that international law is law because there are a variety of sanctions available to enforce it, but she does not discuss the politicised nature of that enforcement.
7. *Martens Nouveau Recueil Generale des Traites*, Vol. 15, p. 791.
8. See Brett Bowden, 'The Colonial Origins of International Law. European Expansion and the Classical Standard of Civilization', *The Journal of the History of International Law*, Vol. 7, No. 1 (2005), pp. 1–24.
9. For a different view, see Arnulf Becker-Lorca, 'Universal International Law: Nineteenth Century Histories of Imposition and Appropriation', *Harvard International Law Journal*, Vol. 50, No. 2 (Summer 2010), pp. 475–552.
10. Karl Marx/Friedrich Engels, *Werke*, Vol. 15/4, Berlin 1961, p. 427.
11. British and Foreign State Papers (BFSP), Vol. 46, p. 36.
12. Damian O'Connor, 'Privateers, Cruisers and Colliers: The Limits of International Maritime Law in the Nineteenth Century', *RUSI Journal*, Vol. 150, No. 1 (February 2005), pp. 70–75, p. 71.
13. See Francis Piggott, *The Declaration of Paris 1856. A Study, Documented*, London 1919, p. 128; and Charles H. Stockton, 'The Declaration of Paris', *American Journal of International Law*, Vol. 14 (1920), pp. 356–368, 358, 361. The first monograph, Francis Stark's *The Abolition of Privateering and the Declaration of Paris*, New York 1897, did not make use of archival sources.
14. Bernard Semmel, *Liberalism and Naval Strategy – Ideology, Interest and Seapower during the Pax Britannica*, London 1986, pp. 56–57.
15. William Malkin, 'The Inner History of the Declaration of Paris', *British Yearbook of International Law*, Vol. 8 (1927), pp. 1–44, p. 37.

16. Olive Anderson, 'Some Further Light on the Inner History of the Declaration of Paris', *Law Quarterly Review*, Vol. 76 (1960), pp. 379–385, pp. 382, 385.
17. Olive Anderson, *A Liberal State at War: English Politics and Economics During the Crimean War*, London 1967, p. 272.
18. *Ibid.*, p. 252.
19. Paul Kennedy, *The Rise and Fall of British Naval Mastery*, London 1976, p. 175.
20. Clarendon was fully aware of this. See Clarendon to Westmorland, 19 June 1855, Akten zur Geschichte des Krimkriegs (AGKK) III/3, No. 500, p. 762. Cf. Andrew Lambert, 'The Crimean War Blockade, 1854–1856', in Bruce Elleman and S. C. M. Paine (eds.), *Naval Blockades and Seapower – Strategies and Counter-Strategies, 1805–2005*, Abingdon 2005, pp. 46–61.
21. Andrew Lambert, 'Great Britain and Maritime Law from the Declaration of Paris to the Era of Total War', in Rolf Hobson and Tom Kristiansen (eds.), *Navies in Northern Waters: 1721–2000*, London 2004, pp. 11–40, p. 15.
22. Avner Offer, *The First World War: An Agrarian Interpretation*, Oxford 1989, pp. 271, 282.
23. In his most recent article, Lambert changes his stance slightly, arguing that 'while many British commentators have criticized the Declaration as an unwise concession [...] the reality was far less clear-cut', *Crimean War Blockade*, pp. 60–61. Also note Nicholas Tracy (ed.), *Sea Power and the Control of Trade: Belligerent Rights from the Russian War to the Beira Patrol, 1854–1970*, Aldershot 2005, which is a highly valuable source collection but not a research monograph that could replace earlier accounts.
24. Andrew Lambert, *Crimean War – British Grand Strategy, 1853–1856*, Manchester 1990, pp. 333–334.
25. Gary Anderson and Adam Gifford, Jr., 'Privateering and the Private Production of Naval Power', *Cato Journal*, Vol. 11 (Spring/Summer 1991), pp. 99–122, p. 112. Pat O'Malley, 'The Discipline of Violence: State, Capital and the Regulation of Naval Warfare', *Sociology*, Vol. 22, No. 2 (May 1988), pp. 253–270, p. 265.
26. Alexander Tabarrok, 'The Rise, Fall, and Rise Again of Privateers', *The Independent Review*, Vol. 11, No. 4 (Spring 2007), pp. 565–577, p. 575; Antony Bruce and William Cogar, *An Encyclopedia of Naval Warfare*, Chicago and London 1998, p. 293; Ulrich Scheuner, 'Privateering', in Rudolf Bernhardt (ed.) *Encyclopedia of Public International Law*, *Vol. 3*, Amsterdam and New York 1997, pp. 1120–1122. This argument is also made in the otherwise very well-informed study by John W. Coogan, *The End of Neutrality: The United States, Britain and Maritime Rights 1899–1915*, Ithaca 1981, p. 23.
27. Nicholas Parillo, 'The De-privatization of American Warfare: How the U. S. Government Used, Regulated, and Ultimately Abandoned Privateering in the Nineteenth Century', *Yale Journal of Law & The Humanities*, Vol. 19, No. 1 (Winter 2007), pp. 1–95, p. 10.

1 'More Serious than the Eastern Question Itself' – The Crimean War Compromise

1. Lobstein to Drouyn de Lhuys, 22 November 1853, AMAE, Correspondence Politique Suède, No. 325, f183.
2. Schroeder to Marcy, 30 November 1853, private, NARA, M45, Vol. 8, Roll 9; Schroeder to Marcy, 3 December 1853, No. 106; Schroeder to Marcy, 19 December 1853, No. 108, *ibid.*

3. Rehausen to Clarendon, 2 January 1854, and Reventlow Criminil to Clarendon, 2 January 1854, BFSP, Vol. 44, p. 94. See also Parliamentary Papers, *Correspondence Relative to Neutrality of Denmark, Sweden and Norway*, 1854 (1711) LXXII.601.
4. Belmont to Marcy, 20 January 1854, No. 13, NARA, M42, Roll T-19; Werther to Manteuffel, 2 December 1853, AGKK II/1, No. 86, p. 255. The Netherlands' decision was dependent on Prussia: Koenigsmarck to Manteuffel, 7 January 1854, *ibid.*, No. 112, p. 306.
5. Schroeder to Marcy, 18 January 1854, No. 111, *ibid.*; Schroeder to Marcy, 30 January 1854, No. 112, *ibid.* For the Russian demand to close the ports and the Swedish response to Clarendon's despatch, see Lobstein to Drouyn de Lhuys, 30 January 1854 and 6 February 1854, AMAE, CP Suède, No. 325, f223+f230.
6. John Russell was at this time the Leader of the House of Commons, and Minister without Portfolio in the Aberdeen government since handing over the post of Foreign Secretary to Lord Clarendon in February 1853. He continued to speak frequently in the name of the government on foreign policy matters.
7. Walewski to Drouyn de Lhuys, 6 January 1854, AGKK IV/1, No. 344, pp. 749–752.
8. Memorandum of 11 January 1854, printed in Malkin, *Inner History*, pp. 8–9.
9. Anderson, *Liberal State at War*, pp. 248–253; Spencer, *Mason Memorandum*, pp. 50–51.
10. Drouyn de Lhuys to Walewski, 12 January 1854, quoted in Spencer, *Mason Memorandum*, p. 49, and Drouyn de Lhuys, 'Les Neutres Pendant la Guerre d'Orient', *Revue Maritime et Coloniale*, Vol. 23 (1868), pp. 658–681, 663f.
11. Hamilton, *Anglo-French Seapower*, p. 169.
12. Drouyn de Lhuys to Ducos, 16 February 1854, Vincennes, CC⁴1251.
13. Walewski to Drouyn de Lhuys, 16 February 1854, AMAE, Correspondence Politique, Angleterre, No. 694, f4–5.
14. Thomas Milner Gibson had asked whether a decision to grant 'free ships, free goods' had been reached. See House of Commons, 27 February 1854, Vol. 130, Col.1353.
15. Drouyn de Lhuys to Walewski, 1 March 1854, AGKK IV/I, No. 413, pp. 898–899; Walewski to Drouyn de Lhuys, 2 March 1854, *ibid.*, No. 414, pp. 899–901.
16. House of Commons, 13 March 1854, Vol. 131, Col. 698–699.
17. House of Lords, 17 March 1854, Vol. 131, Col. 888–891. This advice in favour of buying Russian produce in neutral ports in order to import it to Britain was the official recommendation given to merchants. See Parliamentary Papers, *Correspondence between Board of Trade and House of Messrs. Martin, Levin & Adler, on Rights of Neutrals*, 1854 (146) LXI.645.
18. *The Times*, 10 March 1854, p. 8.
19. House of Commons, 17 March 1854, Vol. 131, Col. 966–969.
20. *Ibid.*, Col. 969–973.
21. Buchanan to Marcy, 17 March 1854, No. 25, NARA, M30, Vol. 65, Roll 61; BFSP, Vol. 46, p. 828.
22. Drouyn de Lhuys to Ducos, 20 March 1854, Vincennes, CC⁴1251.
23. See Spencer, *Mason Memorandum*, p. 55; De Lhuys, *Les Neutres*, pp. 667–668.
24. Cowley to Clarendon, 19 March 1854, quoted in Spencer, *Mason Memorandum*, p. 55.
25. The law was passed on 23 March 1854. See Hamilton, *Anglo-French Seapower*, p. 173.
26. Spencer, *Mason Memorandum*, pp. 51, 56.

27. Cowley to Clarendon, 22 March 1854, quoted *ibid.*, p. 56.
28. Buchanan had reported home that Clarendon was 'evidently apprehensive' about privateers and had used this as an argument to promote generous neutral rights. See Buchanan to Marcy, 24 February 1854, BFSP, Vol. 46, p. 826. Mason noticed the privateering scare, but not its political potential. See Mason to Marcy, 14 March 1854, No. 10, NARA, M34, Vol. 36.
29. The memorandum of Mason's conversations with Rumpff is attached to Mason to Marcy, 22 March 1854, No. 12, *ibid.*
30. Mason to Rumpff, 19 March 1854, printed in Gavin B. Henderson, 'Problems of Neutrality, 1854: Documents from the Hamburg Staatsarchiv', *Journal of Modern History*, Vol. 10, No. 2 (June 1938), pp. 232–241, 233.
31. Mason to Marcy, 22 March 1854, No. 12, NARA, M34, Vol. 36; an abridged version is printed in BFSP, Vol. 46, p. 829.
32. Mason to Marcy, 28 March 1854, No. 13, *ibid.*; Cowley to Clarendon, 26 March 1854, quoted in Spencer, *Mason Memorandum*, p. 60.
33. Cowley to Clarendon, 27 March 1854, printed in *ibid.*, p. 62.
34. Drouyn de Lhuys to Walewski, 27 March 1854, printed in *ibid.*, p. 62; and De Lhuys, *Les Neutres*, p. 672.
35. See Sartiges to Drouyn de Lhuys, 5 December 1853, AMAE, CP Etats-Unis, No. 110, f70.
36. Martin Senner argued that the treaty proposal did exist, relying on a handwritten notice on an undated draft sent by Marcy to Sartiges, which clams it was made in 1853. See AGKK IV/2, p.78, fn.4. The suggestion of a treaty by Drouyn de Lhuys and the fact that I have been unable to locate any reference to this proposal in the relevant files in Washington suggest that the undated draft is in fact a copy of the later US treaty proposal sent in April 1854. This discussion of neutral rights was separate from the negotiation over a new commerce and navigation treaty between France and the USA that had been begun in 1853.
37. Ducos to Drouyn de Lhuys, 26 March 1854, Vincennes, CC[4]466, No. 1011.
38. Drouyn de Lhuys to Ducos, 27 March 1854, Vincennes, CC[4]1251.
39. BFSP, Vol. 46, p. 36. On 15 April the declaration was supplemented by an Order-in-Council (BFSP, Vol. 46, p. 49) and the official instructions for the fleet (printed in Piggott, *Declaration of Paris*, p. 280). See also the Anglo-French Convention of 10 May 1854, BFSP, Vol. 44, p. 11.
40. Drouyn de Lhuys to Ducos, 30 March 1854, Vincennes, CC[4]1251.
41. BFSP, Vol. 46, p. 243. Both declarations were immediately despatched to Washington. See Mason to Marcy, 30 March 1854 und Buchanan to Marcy, 31 March 1854, BFSP, Vol. 46, p. 832.
42. Drouyn de Lhuys to Walewski, 30 March 1854, AGKK IV/2, No. 4, p. 75.
43. Drouyn de Lhuys to Sartiges, 30 March 1854, *ibid.*, No. 5, p. 78.
44. Buchanan to Marcy, 31 March 1854, BFSP, Vol. 46, p. 832.
45. *La Presse*, 29 March 1854, p. 1.
46. *New York Courier*, printed in *The Times*, 21 April 1854, p. 7.
47. *The Times*, 3 April 1854, p. 8.
48. *The Times*, 19 April 1854, p. 6; 21 April 1854, p. 6, *Morning Chronicle*, 29 March 1854; *Manchester Times*, 1 April 1854.
49. House of Commons, 4 July 1854, Vol. 134, Col. 1098.
50. *Ibid.*, 1129.
51. *Ibid.*, 1135.

2 The Crimean War and Maritime Law

1. *The Economist*, 1 April 1854; *Edinburgh Review*, April 1854.
2. *Daily News*, 21 April 1854.
3. Cobden-Bright, 3 January 1854, CLP (BL Add. 43650 f58–60).
4. Lambert, *Crimean War Blockade*, p. 47.
5. Pommer-Esche to O. Manteuffel, 19 May 1855, AGKK II/2, No. 299, p. 593.
6. Memorandum on the Commercial Policy pursued with respect to Russian produce since the commencement of the war, by James Wilson, 23 October 1854, TNA, FO/65/459. Also printed in AGKK III/2, No. 432, pp. 703–711.
7. Lobstein to Drouyn, 2 March 1854, AMAE, CP Suède, No. 352, f253; Schroeder to Marcy, 27 February 1854, No. 118, NARA, M45 Vol. 9, Roll 8.
8. Circular by Hamilton to all naval commanders, 24 May 1854, TNA, ADM/116/857, No. 25.
9. *London Gazette*, 24 April 1854, p. 1.
10. See the explanations given by Lord Stanley of Alderley in the House of Lords, 15 May 1855, Vol. 138, Col. 603–607.
11. Circular to naval commanders, 8 May 1854, TNA, ADM/116/857, No. 23.
12. Buchanan to Marcy, 2 June 1854, No. 35, NARA, M30 Vol. 65, Roll 61.
13. Drouyn de Lhuys to Walewski, 19 April 1854; Clarendon to Walewski, 1 May 1854, TNA, ADM/116/857, No. 21, 22.
14. Buchanan to Clarendon, 22 June 1854, NARA, M30, Vol. 66, Roll 62 (attachment No. 4 to Buchanan to Marcy, 2 July 1854, No. 35).
15. Seymour to Marcy, 31 March 1854, No. 1; 13 April 1854, No. 2, NARA, M35 Vol. 16.
16. Seymour to Marcy, 2 June 1854, No. 4. *ibid.*
17. Charles Napier, *The History of the Baltic Campaign of 1854*, London 1857, pp. 128–198.
18. Andrew Buchanan to Napier, 8 April 1854, TNA, PRO/30/16/5, No. 21b.
19. Seymour to Marcy, 24 July 1854, No. 6, NARA, M35, Vol. 16.
20. John D. Harding to the Lord Commissioner of the Admiralty, 12 March 1855, TNA, TS/45/139.
21. Lobstein to Drouyn, 14 March 1854, AMAE CP Suède, No. 325, f262; Drouyn de Lhuys to Ducos, 27 March 1854, Vincennes, CC⁴1251. Norwegian Finmark inhabitants were dependent on food imports from Archangel.
22. Winfried Baumgart, *The Crimean War 1853–1856*, London 1999, p. 187.
23. *Hull Packet and East Riding Times*, 2 June 1854.
24. House of Commons, 13 July 1854, Vol. 135 Col. 164; *Daily News*, 29 August 1854.
25. See Lambert, *Crimean War*, p. 108; *ibid.*, *Crimean War Blockade*, p. 55. James Graham was later forced to admit the episode after intense questioning in Parliament, see House of Commons, 20 February 1855, Vol. 136, Col. 1708. Granville confirmed this version three days later in the House of Lords, Vol. 136, Col. 1742.
26. *Ibid.*, see also *The Times*, 30 May 1854, p. 9. The exceptions were Odessa and Sevastopol; both were blockaded.
27. Notification printed in *The Times*, 20 June 1854, p. 10.
28. *The Times*, 15 December 1854, p. 8; 26 December 1854, p. 4; 28 December 1854, p. 8; 5 January 1855, p. 5, 8 January 1855, p. 7; 11 January 1855, p. 8.

29. *The Times*, 11 January 1855, p. 7.
30. *The Times*, 12 January 1855, p. 6. On Graham's role, see also Charles Iain Hamilton, 'Sir James Graham, the Baltic Campaign and War-Planning at the Admiralty in 1854', *Historical Journal*, Vol. 19, No. 1 (March 1976), pp. 89–112.
31. The blockade was lifted on 18 February 1855.See *The Times*, 12 March 1855, p. 6.
32. *Hull Packet and East Riding Times*, 9 June 1854; *Daily News*, 16 June 1854.
33. House of Commons, 20 February 1855, Vol. 136, Col. 1707.
34. *The Economist*, 25 February 1854, 1 April 1854.
35. *The Economist*, 30 September 1854, reprinted in *Manchester Times*, 3 October 1854.
36. *Morning Chronicle*, 26 August 1854; J. T. Danson, 'Our Commerce with Russia, in Peace and War', *Journal of the Statistical Society of London*, Vol. 17, No. 3 (September 1854), pp. 193–218, p. 217.
37. *The Times*, 18 September 1854, p. 6.
38. *The Times*, 12 April 1855, p. 8.
39. House of Lords, 6 March 1855, Vol. 137, Col. 616, 618, 622. *The Times* also deemed it highly dangerous, and practically impossible, 17 May 1855, p. 8.
40. Remarks by Granville on Wilson's memorandum, 29 October 1854, TNA, FO/65/459.
41. 'Mercator' to Clarendon, 4 October 1854, TNA, FO/65/459; 'Exports from Russia', 7 October 1854, *ibid*. The memo itself is unnamed, but a letter by Clarendon dated the next day makes it almost certain that the author was London businessman John Diston Powles.
42. Wilson to Clarendon, 20 September 1854, 18 October 1854, Bodleian, Mss.Clar.Dep.c19, f289, 315.
43. Memorandum on the Commercial Policy pursued with respect to Russian produce since the commencement of the war, by James Wilson, 23 October 1854, TNA, FO/65/459. Also printed in AGKK III/2, No. 432, pp. 703–711.
44. Memorandum by Edward Cardwell (President of the Board of Trade), 29 October 1854; Remarks by Granville (Lord President of the Council) on Wilson's memorandum, 29 October 1854; Committee of Privy Council for Trade to Clarendon, 2 November 1854, TNA, FO/65/459.
45. W. Duncan to Clarendon, 20 October 1854, 31 October 1854, TNA, FO/65/459. A handwritten notice gives the date of the agreed appointment as '8 November, 2.30', and the petition handed over by the merchants is in the same file.
46. *The Times*, 3 November 1854, p. 6. The *Dundee Courier*, 8 November 1854, was delighted.
47. House of Commons, 20 February 1855, Vol. 136, Col. 1684–1698. See also Granville's speech, House of Lords, 6 March 1855, Vol. 137, Col. 162–168.
48. House of Lords, 15 May 1855, Vol. 138, Col. 603–607.
49. *Ibid*, Col. 631.
50. Albert Seaton, *The Crimean War – A Russian Chronicle*, London 1977, p. 30; John Shelton Curtiss, *Russia's Crimean War*, Durham NC 1979, p. 423.
51. Drouyn de Lhuys to Barrot, 25 February 1854, No. 7, AGKK IV/1, No. 407, pp. 886–887; Barrot to Drouyn de Lhuys, 7 March 1854, *ibid.*, No. 422, pp. 918–922.
52. De Walden to Clarendon, 14 April 1854, No. 78, TNA, FO/10/181.
53. De Walden to Clarendon, 15 April 1854, No. 79, *ibid*.
54. The list was forwarded to the commander of the Baltic squadron. See Napier, *Baltic Campaign*, p. 151.

55. De Walden to Clarendon, 28 April 1854, No. 86, TNA, FO/10/181.
56. Hodges to Smidt, 13 April 1854, printed in Henderson, *Problems of Neutrality*, pp. 234–235.
57. Clarendon to Bloomfield, 22 March 1854, AGKK III/2, No. 168, pp. 295–296; Clarendon to Bloomfield, 18 July 1854, TNA, FO/356/31.
58. Bloomfield to Clarendon, 21 July 1854, AGKK III/2, No. 321, pp. 518–519.
59. Clarendon to Bloomfield, 25 July 1854, *ibid*, No. 327, pp. 530–531.
60. Drouyn de Lhuys to Boudin, 17 August 1854, AGKK IV/2, No. 202, pp. 417–421; Cowley to Clarendon, 17 August 1854, AGKK III/2, No. 353, pp. 572–574.
61. Bloomfield to Clarendon, 25 August 1854, AGKK III/2, No. 362, pp. 587–589.
62. Wilson memorandum, 23 October 1854, *ibid*, No. 432, pp. 703–711.
63. Cowley to Clarendon, 12 February 1855, AGKK III/3, No. 169, p. 318.
64. Bloomfield to Clarendon, 17 February 1855, *ibid*, No. 183, p. 336.
65. Official minutes of 8 March 1855, AGKK II/2, No.249, p. 503; O. Manteuffel to Heydt, 12 February 1855, *ibid*, No. 204, p. 424.
66. *Morning Chronicle*, 23 March 1855.
67. Edmund Heathcote (HMS *Archer*) to Hertslet, 13 June 1855, TNA, FO/634/4, f2; Clarendon to Bloomfield, 31 July 1855, AGKK III/3, No. 53, p. 830.
68. Clarendon to Elliot, 4 September 1855, *ibid*, No. 581, p. 869.
69. The British Minister in The Hague, Ralph Abercromby, suggested this in April 1855. See Abercromby to Clarendon, 12 April 1855, TNA, ADM/116/857, No. 32.
70. Bernstorff to Manteuffel, 16 January 1856, AGKK II/2, No. 386, p. 763. The Minister in Paris, Hatzfeld, had earlier expressed similar views, also emphasising the importance of the USA. See Hatzfeld to Manteuffel, 21 November 1854, *ibid*, No. 91, p. 234.
71. Walewski to Moustier, 1 December 1855, AGKK IV/3, No. 282, p. 556; Moustier to Walewski, 4 January 1856, *ibid*, No. 324, p. 637; Clarendon to Bloomfield, 26 December 1855, AGKK III/4, No. 292, p. 526; Bloomfield to Clarendon, 5 January 1856, *ibid*, No. 309, p. 551.
72. E. Manteuffel to Friedrich Wilhelm, 4 January 1856, AGKK II/2, No. 368, p. 725; E. Manteuffel to Friedrich Wilhelm, 6/7 January 1856, *ibid*, No. 370, p. 731. The treaties are printed in Martens NRG, Vol. 15: Alliance between Austria and Prussia of 20 April 1854, p. 572; Alliance between Austria, France and Great Britain of 2 December 1854, p. 600.
73. Winfried Baumgart, *Einleitung*, AGKK II/2, p. 44.
74. Clarendon to Bloomfield, 7 January 1856, AGKK III/4, No. 314, p. 558.
75. Manteuffel to Werther, 15 January 1856, AGKK II/2, No. 382, p. 757.
76. Alexander II had become Tsar after the death of his father Nicolas I in March 1855.
77. Kellow Chesney, *The Crimean War Reader*, London 1960, p. 58; Curtiss, *Russia's Crimean War*, p. 87.
78. Lambert, *Crimean War Blockade*, pp. 55–57.
79. For the plans of the allied war council for the 1856 Baltic campaign, see the memorandum by Jérome Napoléon, 16 January 1856, AGKK IV/3, No. 348, p. 683.
80. Curtiss, *Russia's Crimean War*, pp. 496–499.
81. *Ibid*; Seaton, *Russian Chronicle*, p. 222; Baumgart, *Friede von Paris*, p. 116.
82. *The Economist*, 28 October 1854.
83. Pommer-Esche to Manteuffel, 19 May 1855, AGKK II/2, No. 299, p. 593.

84. Seaton, *Crimean War*, p. 189, J. B. Conacher, *Britain and the Crimea, 1855–56: Problems of War and Peace*, Basingstoke 1987, pp. 130–131, Curtiss, *Russia's Crimean War*, pp. 419–421, Lambert, *Blockade*, pp. 48, 53.
85. Seymour to Marcy, 20 October 1855, No. 52, NARA, M35, Vol. 16.
86. *Ibid.*, p. 580. Whereas Russia in 1854 had exported goods for 12 million paper roubles to the UK and goods for 3 million paper roubles to France, exports to both countries ceased almost completely in 1855.
87. That was certainly the opinion among flax merchants, *Morning Chronicle*, 15 September 1854.
88. Mitchell, *Historical Statistics*, p. 750. Overall government revenue fell from 220 million paper roubles in 1853 to 213 million in 1854 and 209 million in 1855.
89. Clarendon to Westmorland, 19 June 1855, AGKK III/3, No. 500, p. 762.
90. The numbers are taken from Brian Mitchell, *European Historical Statistics 1750–1975* (Second revised edition), New York 1980, p. 511.
91. Mitchell, *Historical Statistics*, pp. 746–751.
92. *Ibid*, pp. 642–646.
93. Anderson, *Further Light*, p. 385.
94. See, for example, Bruce/Cogar, *Encyclopedia of Naval Warfare*, p. 293; Coogan, *End of Neutrality*, p. 23.
95. The letter by Webb was written on 29 September and was printed (with comments) in *The Times*, 3 October 1853, pp. 8–9; both pieces were reprinted in the *New York Times*, 17 October 1853, p. 2.
96. *New York Times*, 22 February 1854, p. 4; 28 February, p. 4.
97. *New York Times*, 5 April 1854, p. 4.
98. *Glasgow Herald*, 3 March 1854; *Morning Chronicle*, 24 January, 14 February and 14 March 1854; *Hampshire Telegraph*, 18 March 1854; *Freeman's Journal and Daily Commercial Advertiser*, 9 March 1854.
99. Proclamation against the Fitting Out or Equipping Vessels for Warlike Purposes, 9 March 1854, BFSP Vol. 46, p. 32.
100. Drouyn de Lhuys to Dillon, 31 March 1854, AGKK IV/2, No. 7, p. 81. Drouyn also sent a special warning to all diplomats in Latin America, see his circular of 31 March 1854, AMAE, CP Etats-Unis, No. 110, f215.
101. George Rennie to Duke of Newcastle, 14 June 1854, TNA, WO/43/961.
102. The declaration of 6 April 1854 is printed in Adolph Soetbeer (ed.), *Sammlung officieller Actenstücke in Bezug auf Schiffahrt und Handel in Kriegszeiten*, Vol. III, Hamburg 1854, p. 17.
103. *National Intelligencer*, reprinted in the *New York Times*, 18 May 1854, p. 4.
104. Barry M. Gough, 'The Crimean War in the Pacific: British Strategy and Naval Operations', *Military Affairs*, Vol. 37, No. 4 (1973), pp. 130–136, p. 131.
105. Antoine-Henri Jomini, *Diplomatic Study of the Crimean War, Volume II*, London 1882, pp. 77–78.
106. Konstatin Katakazi (charge d'affaires in Washington)-Nesselrode, 6 February 1854, cited in Norman E. Saul, *Distant Friends – The United States and Russia, 1763–1867*, Lawrence, KS 1991, p. 198.
107. Stoeckl to Nesselrode, 22 March 1854, 20 April 1854, cited in Saul, *Distant Friends*, pp. 200–201.
108. Russian American Company to Board of Directors of Hudson Bay Company, 31 March 1854 and 17 April 1854, TNA, FO/93/81/35.

109. Alan Dowty, *The Limits of American Isolation: The United States and the Crimean War*, New York 1971, pp. 82–83.
110. Stoeckl to Nesselrode, 5 February 1855, quoted in Frank A. Golder, 'Russian-American Relations During the Crimean War', *American Historical Review*, Vol. 31, No. 3 (April 1926), pp. 462–476, 470.
111. Seymour to Marcy, 30 October 1855, No. 53, NARA, M35, Vol. 16.
112. *The Economist* had earlier echoed that call and demanded a trilateral treaty between Britain, France and America. See the issue of 14 January 1854.
113. 'Privateers and Letters of Marque' Memorandum written by James Graham for Lord Clarendon, 3 March 1854, printed in Tracy, *Sea Power*, pp. 10–24.
114. *Le Siecle*, 7 June 1846.
115. *Daily News*, 10 March 1854. Similar views in *Belfast News-Letter*, 27 February 1854.
116. House of Commons, 17 March 1854, Vol. 131, Col. 968. Resolution printed in *Liverpool Mercury*, 14 March 1854.
117. Bordeaux Chamber of Commerce to Ducos, 20 March 1854, Vincennes, CC⁴1251.
118. An example of an insurance form excluding all risks related to captures is attached to Barbey to Ducos, 16 March 1854, *ibid*.
119. Minister of Trade to Ducos, 3 April 1854, *ibid*. Ducos rejected the idea.
120. Buchanan to Marcy, 17 March 1854, No. 25, NARA, M30, Vol. 65, Roll 61.
121. 'Mission des agents de la Russie aux Etats-Unis pour y armer des corsaires', Memorandum by A. G. Bellemare, 24 March 1854, AMAE, Affaires diverses politiques, Etats-Unis, Box No. 6, Vol. 43 'droit maritime'.
122. Clarendon to Cowley, 13 March 1854, AGKK III/2, No. 155, pp. 280–282; Walewski to Drouyn de Lhuys, 2 March 1854, AGKK IV/1, No. 414, pp. 899–901.
123. *The Economist*, 25 March 1854; the article from *Daily Alta California* is reprinted in the issue of 21 January 1854.
124. *The Times*, 9 March 1854, p. 8.
125. Both articles were reprinted in the *New York Times*, 29 March 1854, p. 2.
126. *New York Times*, 14 April 1854, p. 4.
127. Letter to the editor by 'G. T. P', *New York Times*, 31 March 1854, p. 5.
128. Buchanan to Marcy, 24 March 1854, No. 26, NARA, M30, Vol. 65, Roll 61.
129. Marcy-Buchanan, 13 April 1854, BFSP, Vol. 46, p. 835.
130. The New York Chamber of Commerce passed its resolution soon after news of the Liverpool resolution had reached the USA. See *New York Times*, 7 April 1854, p. 8. Not all chambers of commerce agreed, and the merchants of Marseille sent a petition to the French Navy Minister, warning him of the 'monstrosity' of British plans against privateering. See Marseille Chamber of Commerce to Ducos, 17 March 1854, Vincennes, CC⁴1251.
131. Memorandum of 11 January 1854, printed in Malkin, *Inner History*, pp. 8–9. This new provision was praised by the *Morning Chronicle*, 6 January 1854, which condemned privateering as 'legalized piracy' and would be more active than any other newspaper in campaigning against it in the following months.
132. Declaration of 8 April 1854, BFSP, Vol. 46, pp. 833–835, Art. 9. The American Minister in Stockholm immediately alerted Marcy. See Schroeder to Marcy, 10 April 1854, BFSP, Vol. 46, p. 832.
133. Buchanan to Marcy, 14 April 1854, No. 29, NARA, M30, Vol. 65, Roll 61.

134. Denmark had sent a circular on 20 December to coordinate neutrality declarations. See the declaration of 20 April 1854, printed in Soetbeer, *Actenstücke Vol. III*, pp. 11–13.
135. The declarations are printed in Piggott, *Declaration*, pp. 305–328 and Soetbeer, *Actenstücke Vol.III*, pp. 3–17. See also Royal Decree prohibiting the Outfit of Privateers in the Spanish Dominions, 12 April 1854, Art. 1, TNA, FO/881/305.
136. Declaration of 15 April 1854, printed in *Belfast News-Letter*, 24 April 1854. A copy can also be found in Napier's papers, TNA, PRO/30/16/5, f60–66.
137. The circular of 4 April 1854 is printed in Tracy, *Sea Power*, No. 2, p. 24; see also Crampton to Marcy, 21 April 1854, BFSP, Vol. 46, p. 837.
138. Austrian declaration of 23 May 1854, Belgium 25 April 1854, Brazil 17 May 1854, Argentina 16 June 1854, Chile 22 July 1854, TNA, FO/881/9315X, Soetbeer, *Actenstücke Vol. VI*, p. 14/15. For the Portuguese Declaration of 9 May 1854, see also *The Economist*, 27 May 1854.
139. De Walden to Clarendon, 28 April 1854, No. 85, TNA, FO/10/181. A special circular called upon Belgian officials not to hesitate in prosecuting any transgressors, De Walden to Clarendon, 5 May 1854, No. 95, *ibid*. The news of the second declaration by Naples of 17 May was also reported in the USA. See *Chicago Daily Tribune*, 14 June 1854, p. 3.
140. Krauss to Army *Oberkommando*, 27 March 1854, HHStA Vienna, Außenministerium, allgemeine Registratur, F36 (Schiffswesen), No. 5.
141. Declaration of King Kamehameha III of 16 May 1854, printed in *New York Times*, 11 July 1854, p. 3; Resolution of the Hawaii Privy Council, 17 July 1854, BFSP, Vol. 51, p. 933.
142. *Journal du Havre*, reprinted in *New York Times*, 20 April 1854, p. 2.
143. As late as September 1855, Clarendon received reports about a fast steamer being finished in New York to attack ships going to Britain from Australia. Anthony Barclay to Clarendon, 28 September 1855, TNA, ADM/116/857, No. 34.
144. *The Economist*, 14 October 1854.
145. Schroeder to Marcy, 1 March 1854, No. 119; 5 April 1854, No. 124, NARA, M45, Vol. 8, Roll 9.
146. Mason to Marcy, 22 March 1854, BFSP, Vol. 46, p. 829; NARA, M34, Vol. 36.
147. Marcy to Buchanan, 13 April 1854, BFSP, Vol. 46, p. 835.
148. Seymour to Marcy, 13 April 1854, No. 2, NARA, M35, Vol. 16.
149. Marcy to Stoeckl, 14 April 1854, NARA, M99, Roll 82, f53; Seymour to Marcy, 2 June 1854, No. 4, NARA, M35 Vol. 16.
150. Stoeckl to Marcy, 15 April 1854, NARA, M39, Vol. 4–5, Roll 3.
151. Marcy to Stoeckl, 14 April 1854, quoted in Dowty, *Limits of Isolation*, p. 78. Note that this letter is not the same as the one from the same day cited earlier. The quotation is taken verbatim from Dowty, and perfectly fits Marcy's style and intentions. However, I have been unable to locate the original in the file given by Alan Dowty (which is the same as the one cited in the earlier footnote).
152. Buchanan to Marcy, 7 April 1854, private, NARA, M30, Vol. 65, Roll 61.
153. Dowty, *Limits of Isolation*, p. 4.
154. Marcy to T. H. Seymour, 9 May 1854, BFSP, Vol. 46, p. 841.
155. Sartiges to Marcy, 28 April 1854, BFSP, Vol. 46, pp. 838–839. An identical British note was sent by Crampton on the 21st.
156. Marcy to Crampton, 28 April 1854, BFSP, Vol. 46, p. 839; an identical note was sent to the French: Marcy to Sartiges, 28 April 1854, M99, Roll 21.
157. Buchanan to Marcy, 19 May 1854, No. 33, NARA, M30, Vol. 66, Roll 62.

158. Drouyn de Lhuys to Sartiges, 8 June 1854, AGKK IV/2, p. 277, fn. 1.
159. Hatzfeld-Manteuffel, 30 October 1854, GStA Berlin, Hauptabteilung II, MdA I 2.4.1 Abt.I No. 7909 (Acta die Verhandlungen mit den Vereinigten Staaten von Nord-Amerika wegen des Abschlußes eines Neutralitäts-Vertrages betreffend (Acta)), f73.
160. Convention entre la Russie et les Etats-Unis d'Amerique relative au droit des neutres sur mer, signée a Washington, le 22 Juillet 1854, Martens NRG, Vol. 16, No. 78, p. 571; BFSP, Vol. 45, p. 125. Russia ratified the treaty on 31 October 1854.
161. By mid-September the treaty had still not reached the Russian capital; Seymour to Marcy, 15 September 1854, No. 8, NARA, M35, Vol. 16.
162. Marcy to Schleiden, 4 August 1854, NARA, M99, Vol. 57.
163. Marcy to Mason, 7 August 1854, No. 25, NARA, M77, Vol. 15 (France), Roll 55.
164. Marcy to Henry Bedinger, 8 September 1854, No. 7, NARA, M77, Vol. 14 (Denmark), Roll 50; Marcy to O'Sullivan, 8 September 1854, No. 4, NARA, M77, Vol. 14 (Portugal), Roll 134.
165. Marcy to Grabow, 4 August 1854, GStA Berlin, Acta, f3; Grabow to Manteuffel, 6 August 1854, *ibid.*, f1.
166. These arguments are set out by Manteuffel in a later letter to August von der Heydt, 9 February 1855, *ibid.*, f128.
167. Manteuffel to Bernstorff, 27 August 1854, *ibid.*, f10. Identical letters were sent to ministers in Paris and Vienna as well as Cabinet colleagues von der Heydt, Waldersee, Simon and to the Admiralty.
168. Hatzfeld to Manteuffel, 22 August 1854, *ibid.*, f12. The letter only arrived in Berlin on 14 September.
169. Hatzfeld to Manteuffel, 14 September 1854, *ibid.*, f22.
170. Arnim to Manteuffel, 13 September 1854, *ibid.*, f17.
171. Bernstorff to Manteuffel, 11 September 1854, *ibid.*, f18.
172. Note that any US administration making such an offer would be violating the 1818 Neutrality Act.
173. Von der Heydt-Manteuffel, 19 September 1854, GStA Berlin, Acta, f24.
174. Waldersee to Manteuffel, 16 October 1854, *ibid.*, f59.
175. Manteuffel to Gerolt, 29 September 1854, *ibid.*, f30.
176. Manteuffel to Bernstorff, 4 October 1854, *ibid.*, f47; the draft is dated 2 October 1854, *ibid.*, f46.
177. Circular by Manteuffel, 1 October 1854, *ibid.*, f45.
178. Particularly since Prussia was one of the few states that did not explicitly ban port entry to privateers in its neutrality declaration. See Declaration of 20 April 1854, printed in Soetbeer, *Actenstücke Vol. III*, p. 2.
179. *Preußische Correspondenz*, 4 October 1854, p. 1.
180. Königsmarck to Manteuffel, 5 October 1854, GStA Berlin, Acta, f51.
181. Drouyn de Lhuys to André, 1 February 1855, AGKK IV/2, No. 448, p. 823.
182. The letter sent to Manteuffel by Gerolt on 27 November, GStA Berlin, Acta, f99, states – based on information from Marcy – that the Hanseatic towns had replied in an evasive way, at the same time as the Dutch, which confirmed to Manteuffel that the information provided by the Hanseatic towns themselves that they had not received an invitation was wrong. See Kamptz to Manteuffel, 20 December 1854, f109.
183. Westphalen to Manteuffel, 9 October 1854, *ibid.*, f54.
184. Arnim to Manteuffel, 23 October 1854, *ibid.*, f70.

185. Schroeder to Marcy, 10 October 1854, No. 139; 9 November 1854, No. 140; 7 December 1854, No. 143, NARA, M45, Vol. 8, Roll 9.
186. Prussian Legation Copenhagen to Manteuffel, 8 October 1854, GStA Berlin, Acta, f52.
187. The Palmerston memorandum was written on 2 September 1854, AGKK III/3, No. 575, p. 861; Victoria to Clarendon, 3 September 1854, AGKK III/3, No. 576, p. 863.
188. Marcy to Robert Dale Owen, 8 September 1854, No. 8; 29 November 1854, No. 10, NARA, M77, Vol. 14, Roll 170.
189. Traité de commerce et de navigation entre les Etats-Unis d'Amerique et le royaume des Deux-Siciles, signé à Naples, le 1 Octobre 1855, Martens NRG, Vol. 16, No. 70, p. 521.
190. Owen to Marcy, 7 September 1855, printed in Miller, David Hunter: *Treaties and other International Acts of the USA, Vol.VI*, Washington 1942, p. 264.
191. Manteuffel to Bernstorff, 18 December 1854, GStA Berlin, Acta, f105.
192. *Morning Post*, 10 October 1854.
193. Bernstorff to Manteuffel, 10 October 1854, GStA Berlin, Acta, f61.
194. Gerolt to Manteuffel, 27 November 1854, *ibid*. f99.
195. I have been unable to find such requests, but the Ministry of the Interior recommended their use to break the Danish blockade, and forwarded a memorandum on the legal and practical issues of privateering against Denmark to the (unimpressed) Foreign Ministry, Ministry of the Interior to Schleinitz, 20 March 1850, Bundesarchiv Lichterfelde, R 901/86565, Neutralität No. 5 (März 1850–1913 betr. Kaperbriefe).
196. Marcy to Gadsden, 9 September 1854, No. 34; 31 November 1854, No. 40, NARA, M77, Vol. 17, Roll 113.
197. Marcy to David L. Gregg, 18 October 1854, No. 10, NARA, M77, Vol. 2, Roll 99.
198. *New York Times*, 7 November 1854, p. 1; reprinted in *The Economist*, 25 November 1854.
199. William Gray, 'American Diplomacy in Venezuela 1835–1865', *Hispanic American Historical Review*, Vol. 20, No. 4 (November 1940), pp. 551–574, p. 569.
200. Excerpts of the speech were first published in Britain in the *Daily News* of 18 December 1854, a full version was printed in the *Morning Chronicle* one day later.
201. The paper was reprinted and discussed in, among others, the *Daily News*, 16 January 1855.
202. *The Times*, 19 December 1854, p. 6. See also *Manchester Examiner and Times*, 20 December 1854.
203. Bernstorff to Manteuffel, 10 February 1855, GStA Berlin, Acta, f137.
204. Gerolt to Manteuffel, 9 January 1855, *ibid.*, f123.
205. Declaration of Accession of 26 March 1855, printed in Miller, *Treaties*, p. 121.
206. Declaration of Accession of 9 June 1855, *ibid.*, p. 139.
207. Convention Regarding the Rights of Neutrals at Sea, signed by United States and Peru on 22 July 1856, printed in Miller, *Treaties*, p. 413. For the differences secured by Peru in comparison with the original treaty with Russia, see Clay to Marcy, 26 July 1856, *ibid.*, p. 420. The treaty with Bolivia was only concluded on 13 May 1858, *ibid*, p. 733.
208. Convention entre les États-Unis d'Amerique et le royaume des Deux-Siciles, relative au droit des neutres sur mer, signée à Naples, le 13 Janvier 1855, Martens NRG, Vol. 15, No. 77, p. 569, ratified by Naples on 14 July 1855; Marcy to Owen, 10 March 1855, No. 13, NARA, M77, Vol. 14, Roll 170.

209. La Cour to Drouyn de Lhuys, 10 November 1854, AGKK IV/2, No. 307, p. 597.
210. The pleased French Foreign Minister sent the news about the Portuguese decision directly to Naples, Drouyn de Lhuys to La Cour, 24 March 1855, AGKK IV/3, No. 39, p. 136.
211. The content of the circular and the reaction to it are described by French Foreign Minister Drouyn de Lhyus to the Prussian Minister, Hatzfeld; the circular was not sent to Berlin because the French knew that negotiations were already under way. Hatzfeld to Manteuffel, 4 April 1855, GStA Berlin, Acta, f158; Walewski to Thouvenel, 6 March 1855, AGKK IV/3, p. 136, fn. 6: 'il a vraiment perdu la tête'.
212. Marcy to August Belmont, 6 December 1854, No. 2, NARA, M77, Roll 123 (Netherlands).
213. Marcy to O'Sullivan, 12 May 1855, No. 7, NARA, M77, Vol. 14, Roll 134.
214. Gerolt to Manteuffel, 9 January 1855, GStA Berlin, Acta, f123.
215. Buchanan to Marcy, 19 January 1855, No. 57, NARA, M30 Vol. 66, Roll 62.
216. Hatzfeld to Manteuffel, 4 April 1855, GStA Berlin, Acta, f158.
217. Gerolt to Manteuffel, 11 December 1855, *ibid.*, f117.
218. Von der Heydt to Manteuffel, 19 February 1855, *ibid.*, f136.
219. Manteuffel to Gerolt, 28 February 1855, *ibid.*, f139.
220. Admiralty to Manteuffel, 17 March 1855, *ibid.*, f149.
221. Schroeder to Marcy, 9 November 1854, No. 140, NARA, M45, Vol. 8, Roll 9.
222. Canitz to Manteuffel, 24 November 1854, GStA Berlin, Acta, f78.
223. Seibels to Belgian Foreign Ministry (Copy), 23 April 1855, *ibid.*, f164; Creptowitsch to Belgian Foreign Ministry (Copy), 19 May 1855, *ibid.*, f166.
224. Clarendon to Palmerston, 6 April 1856, printed in Malkin, *Inner History*, p. 26.
225. Arnim to Manteuffel, 18 January 1854, GStA Berlin, Acta, f126.

3 'Catching Brother Jonathan in the Trap which He Laid for Us' – The Genesis of the Declaration of Paris

1. Mason to Marcy, 31 October 1855, No. 85, NARA, M34, Vol. 37, Roll 40.
2. Mason to Marcy, 15 November 1855, private, *ibid.*
3. Palmerston to Clarendon, 24 September 1855, quoted in Kenneth Bourne, 'Lord Palmerston's "Ginger-beer" Triumph, 1 July 1856', in Kenneth Bourne and D. C. Watt (eds.), *Studies in International History*, London 1967, pp. 145–171, p. 154.
4. Buchanan to Marcy, 30 October 1855, No. 98, NARA, M30, Vol. 68, Roll 64.
5. Clarendon to Buchanan, 16 November 1855; Buchanan to Clarendon, 16 November 1855, quoted in Bourne, *Ginger Beer Triumph*, p. 158.
6. Wood to Admiral Lyons, 1 October 1855, *ibid.*, p. 155.
7. Mason to Marcy, 15 November 1855, private, NARA, M34, Vol. 37, Roll 40.
8. See his pamphlet, *L'Alliance Anglaise*, Paris 1838, or his obituary in *Moniteur Universel*, 4 October 1868.
9. Marcy to Buchanan, 25 June 1855, No. 96, NARA, M77, Vol. 16, Roll 75.
10. Buchanan to Clarendon, 30 August 1855; Buchanan to Marcy, 31 August 1855, NARA M30, Vol. 68, Roll 64.
11. Clarendon to Cowley, 2 November 1855, No. 1273, TNA, FO/27/1059.
12. Memorandum on a Draft of Despatch from Lord Clarendon to Mr. Crampton at Washington, 10 September 1854, printed in Bourne, *Ginger Beer Triumph*, p. 149f.
13. Cowley to Clarendon, 25 November 1855, quoted in Anderson, *Further Light*, p. 384.

14. Note confidentielle pour le Ministre d'affaires étrangères, 17 November 1855, Vincennes, CC⁴1251.
15. Mason to Marcy, 3 December 1855, No.91, NARA, M34, Vol. 37, Roll 40.
16. Clarendon to Cowley, 23 November 1855, No. 1354, TNA, FO/27/1059.
17. Walewski to Mason, 22 December 1855, AMAE, Affaires diverses politiques, Etats-Unis, Box 6, No. 43 (droit maritime), f8.
18. Mason to Marcy, 15 January 1856, No. 110, NARA, M34, Vol. 38, Roll 41.
19. Marcy to Mason, 7 February 1856, No. 77, NARA, M77, Vol. 15, Roll 55.
20. Mason to Marcy, 28 February 1856, No. 120, NARA, M34, Vol. 38, Roll 41.
21. Buchanan to Marcy, 22 January 1856, No. 114, NARA, M30, Vol. 68, Roll 64.
22. Clarendon to Crampton, 20 March 1856, AGKK III/4, No. 555, p. 902.
23. Palmerston to Panmure, 30 March 1856, *ibid.*, No. 595, p. 947. Queen Victoria would have preferred to see an entire division moved; as well as a permanent settlement of German mercenaries in Canada, Victoria to Palmerston, 31 March 1856, *ibid.*, No. 597, p. 948.
24. Clarendon to Cowley, 4 and 6 June 1856, printed in Bourne, *Ginger Beer Triumph*, p. 165f.
25. Dallas to Marcy, 6 June 1856, quoted in Dowty, *Limits of Isolation*, p. 214.
26. *The Times*, 5 February 1856, p. 10.
27. *The Times*, 15 February 1856, p. 6.
28. *Leeds Mercury*, 23 February 1856.
29. Clarendon to Granville, 12 March 1856, AGKK III/4, No. 529, p. 868.
30. Palmerston to Victoria, 30 March 1856, *ibid.*, No. 588, p. 942.
31. Walewski to Moustier, 29 February 1856, AGKK IV/3, No. 409, p. 781.
32. Walewski to Moustier, 10 March 1856, *ibid.*, No. 419, p. 794. In his first letter home, Manteuffel reported that Walewski had taken the English by surprise, who were very upset because of his arrival, Manteuffel to Balan, 29 March 1856, AGKK II/2, No. 438, p. 869.
33. William E. Echard, *Napoleon III and the Concert of Europe*, London 1983, pp. 63–72.
34. Protocol No. 22, Martens NRG, Vol. 15, pp. 753–764.
35. Baumgart, *Friede von Paris*, p. 221.
36. This is the date given on the first draft that Walewski sent to London, now in TNA, FO/27/1171. The identical earliest draft in the archive of the French Foreign Ministry is undated, AMAE, Memoires et documents, France, Vol. 2117, 'Congrès de Paris, 1856: Pièces diverses', No. 35, f96.
37. 'L'Angleterre et la déclaration de Paris du 16 Avril 1856', undated, *ibid.*, No. 37.
38. Clarendon to Palmerston, 4 April 1856, AGKK III/4, No. 608, p. 963.
39. Palmerston to Clarendon, 5 April 1856, *ibid.*, No. 609, p. 964.
40. Palmerston to Victoria, 5 April 1856; Victoria to Palmerston, 6 April 1856, quoted in Malkin, *Inner History*, p. 30.
41. Clarendon to Palmerston, 6 April 1856, printed in *ibid.*, p. 26.
42. Wood had welcomed a convention against privateering but was concerned about a possible evasion by the USA, Wood to Clarendon, 7 April 1856, Bodleian, Mss.Clar.Dep.c48, f510.
43. Cabinet Minutes respecting the Declaration of Paris of 1856, TNA, FO/881/5104.
44. Palmerston to Clarendon, 8 April 1856, BL, Add.48580, f70/138.
45. The protocol says 'Liberté des consciences' instead of the correct 'Liberté des cultes', see Martens NRG, Vol. 15, p. 757.
46. *Ibid.*, p. 760: 'Il ajoute que l'Angleterre est disposée à y renoncer définitivement, pourvu que la course soit également abolie pour toujours'.

47. Buol to Werner, 8 April 1856, AGKK I/3, No. 337, p. 584.
48. Protocol of the Cabinet meeting of 9/04/1856, *ibid.*, No. 338, p. 585.
49. Protocol of the Cabinet meeting of 9 April 1856, *ibid.*, No. 338, p. 585.
50. Clarendon to Walewski, 11 April 1856, available online at the site of the Walewski family archive at http://www.digi-archives.org/fonds/facw/static/walewski.html under the signature 'CHFCAW-1-ACW-COR-056-24'.
51. AMAE, Memoires et documents, France, Vol. 2117, 'Congrès de Paris, 1856: Pièces diverses', No. 35, f96.
52. Palmerston to Clarendon, 12 April 1856, BL Add.48580, f80/162.
53. Palmerston to Clarendon, 13 April 1856, printed in Malkin, *Inner History*, pp. 34–35.
54. Protocol No. 23, 14 April 1856, Martens NRG, Vol. 15, pp. 765–768.
55. See the final draft in AMAE, Memoires et documents, France, Vol. 2117, 'Congrès de Paris, 1856: Pièces diverses', No. 34, f93.
56. Clarendon to Palmerston, 14 April 1856; Clarendon to Victoria, 14 April 1856, quoted in Malkin, *Inner History*, p. 36.
57. Palmerston to Clarendon, 15 April 1856, BL, Add.48580, f84/170. The sentence in question refers to the possibility 'that the uncertainty of the law and of the duties in such a matter gives rise to differences of opinion between neutrals and belligerents which may occasion serious difficulties, and even conflicts', and remained in the signed document.
58. Printed in Martens NRG, Vol. 15, p. 791; and in the annex of the session protocol on pp. 767–768.
59. Hamilton, *Anglo-French Seapower*, p. 180. The same claim is made by Anderson, *Further Light*, p. 384.
60. Protocol No. 24, 16 April 1856, Martens, NRG, Vol. 15, pp. 768–769.
61. Clarendon to Palmerston, 17 April 1856, No. 115, TNA, FO/27/1169, f181–185; Bodleian, Mss.Clar.Dep.c56, f249.
62. House of Lords, 22 May 1856, Vol. 142, Col. 511, 522.
63. *Ibid.*, 486, 509, 536.
64. *Ibid.*, 529.
65. *Ibid.*, 488.
66. *Ibid.*, 514.
67. *Ibid.*, pp. 495–498.
68. House of Lords, 22 May 1856, Vol. 142, Col. 501. Although navies were rapidly switching to steamers, most merchant vessels were still sailing craft. See Charles K. Harley, 'The Shift from Sailing Ships to Steamships, 1850–1890: A Study in Technical Change and its Diffusion', in Donald N. McCloskey (ed.), *Essays on a Mature Economy: Britain after 1840*, Princeton 1971, pp. 215–234, 216.
69. *Ibid.*, 544.
70. Hobson, *Imperialism at Sea*, p. 66.
71. Nadelmann, *Global Prohibition Regimes*, pp. 479–526.
72. *La Presse*, 19 June 1856, p. 1.
73. *Economist*, 30 August 1856.

4 'That Moral League of Nations Against the United States' – The Declaration of Paris and the Marcy Amendment

1. Dowty, *Limits of Isolation*, p. 234.
2. Semmel, *Liberalism and Naval Strategy*, pp. 71–72.

3. Hamilton, *Anglo-French Seapower*, pp. 181–182.
4. Mason to Marcy, 5 April 1856, No. 133, NARA, M34, Vol. 38, Roll 41.
5. *New York Times*, 13 May 1856, p. 1.
6. Dallas to Senator G.W. Jones, 20 August 1856, quoted in Dowty, *Limits of Isolation*, p. 230.
7. Mason to Marcy, 25 April 1856, No. 140, NARA, M34, Vol. 38, Roll 41. Mason also made the proposal in a written form, claiming that it was 'a suggestion of the President', Mason to Walewski, 26 April 1856, AMAE, Affaires diverses politiques, Etats-Unis, Box 6, No. 43, f12.
8. Dallas to Marcy, 1 May 1856, No. 8, NARA, M30, Vol. 69, Roll 65.
9. Sartiges to Walewski, 5 May 1856, AGKK IV/3, No. 445, p. 836.
10. Walewski to Persigny, 5 May 1856, AMAE, Corr. Politique Angleterre, Vol. 704, f287.
11. Walewski to Persigny, 13 May 1856, *ibid.*, f296.
12. Persigny to Walewski, 14 May 1856, *ibid.*, f307. Walewski agreed, Walewski to Persigny, 21 May 1856, *ibid.* Vol.705, f20.
13. See his letter to the Minister in the Netherlands: Clarendon to Abercromby, 26 May 1856, TNA, FO/83/487, No. 48.
14. Clarendon to Bligh, 3 June 1856, *ibid.*, No. 20.
15. A translated version of the Prussian circular of 26 May 1856 can be found in *ibid.*
16. Belmont to Marcy, 29 May 1856, No. 86, NARA M42, Vol. 17, Roll T-21.
17. See Robert Sampson, *John L. O'Sullivan and His Times*, Kent, Ohio 2003.
18. O'Sullivan to Marcy, 2 May 1856, No. 29; 30 May 1856, No. 31; 2 June 1856, No. 32; 4 June 1856, No. 33, NARA, M43, Vol. 17, Roll 16.
19. O'Sullivan to Marcy, 8 June 1856, No. 34, *ibid.*
20. O'Sullivan to Soulé, 12 June 1856, *ibid.*
21. O'Sullivan to Marcy, 13 June 1856, No. 35, *ibid.*
22. O'Sullivan to Marcy, 28 June 1856, No. 36, *ibid.*
23. See, for example, the despatch to Peru, Marcy to Clay, 14 July 1856, printed in Miller, *Treaties*, p. 422.
24. Marcy to Belmont, 14 July 1856, RSC, M77, Roll 123. See also Marcy to O'Sullivan, 14 July 1856, No. 16, NARA, M77, Vol. 14, Roll 134.
25. Marcy to Sartiges et al., 28 July 1856, NARA, M99, Roll 21; BFSP, Vol. 55, p. 589.
26. Lumley to Clarendon, 18 August 1856, TNA, FO/412/5, No. 7, p. 11.
27. Lumley to Clarendon, 5 August 1856, TNA, FO/412/5, No. 6, p. 11.
28. O'Sullivan to Soulé, 19 June 1856, NARA, M43, Vol. 17, Roll 16.
29. O'Sullivan to Marcy, 7 July 1856, No. 37; O'Sullivan to Soulé, 4 July, 8 July 1856, *ibid.*
30. Howard to Clarendon, 8 June 1856; 18 June 1856; 27 June 1856, TNA, FO/83/487, p. 41, 59, 77.
31. Clarendon to Howard, 26 June 1856, *ibid.*, No. 85, p. 63.
32. O'Sullivan to Marcy, 7 July 1856, No. 37, NARA, M43, Vol.17, Roll 16.
33. This was correct. See the Portuguese Declaration of Accession, 28 July 1856, Enclosure A to O'Sullivan to Marcy, 8 August, No. 40, *ibid.*
34. O'Sullivan to Marcy, 18 July 1856, No. 38, *ibid.*
35. O'Sullivan to Marcy, 20 July 1856, No. 39, *ibid.*
36. Marcy to O'Sullivan, 22 July 1856, No. 18, NARA, M77, Roll 134, Vol. 14; O'Sullivan to Marcy, 18 August 1856, No. 40, NARA, M43, Vol. 17, Roll 16.
37. O'Sullivan to Marcy, 8 September 1856, No. 44, *ibid.*

38. Henry Bedinger to Marcy, 6 September 1856, Schule to Bedinger, 10 September 1856, NARA, M41, Vol. 5, Roll 7.
39. Schroeder to Marcy, 26 September 1856, No. 172, NARA, M45, Vol. 8, Roll 9.
40. Belmont to Marcy, 2 September 1856, No. 95, NARA, M42, Vol. 17, Roll T-21.
41. See, for example, the despatch to Mexico, Marcy to John Forsyth, 29 August 1856, No. 5, NARA, M77, Vol. 17, Roll 113; or to Peru, Marcy to Clay, 29 August 1856, printed in Miller, *Treaties*, p.423, or Nicaragua, Wheeler to Ferrer, 26 September 1856, *ibid.*, p. 145.
42. Ferrer to Wheeler, 29 September 1856, *ibid.*, p. 146.
43. Charles Eames to Marcy, 23 December 1856, No. 28, NARA, M79, Vol. 10, Roll 11.
44. Wyllie to Gregg, 8 April 1857, printed in Miller, *Treaties*, p. 133. The late reply was caused by internal turmoil and an illness of the Foreign Minister.
45. Gregg to Marcy, 23 June 1857, *ibid.*, p. 134.
46. Belmont to Marcy, 30 September 1856, private, NARA, M42, Vol. 17, Roll T-21.
47. Dallas to Marcy, 6 May 1856, quoted in Dowty, *Limits*, p. 231.
48. Gorchakov to Stoeckl, 22 June 1856, cited in Frank A. Golder, 'Russian-American Relations During the Crimean War', *American Historical Review*, Vol. 31, No. 3 (April 1926), pp. 462–476, p. 475.
49. Seymour to Marcy, 16 September 1856, No. 85; 28 November 1856, No. 93, NARA, M35, Vol. 17.
50. Marcy to Mason, 4 October 1856, No. 94, NARA, M77, Vol. 15, Roll 55.
51. Mason to Marcy, 1 September 1856, No. 162, NARA, M34, Vol. 39, Roll 42.
52. *The Times*, 20 August 1856, p. 8; *Liverpool Mercury*, 20 August 1856; *Freeman's Journal and Daily Commercial Advertiser*, 20 August 1856.
53. *New York Times*, 4 September 1856, p. 4. With most continental papers in favour, the British press was almost evenly split. See Francis R. Stark, *The Abolition of Privateering and the Declaration of Paris*, New York 1897, p. 150 for a discussion.
54. *The Times*, 21 August 1856, p. 6, reprinted, for example, in *Glasgow Herald*, 22 August 1856, and *Freeman's Journal and Daily Commercial Advertiser*, 22 August 1856. This article convinced Richard Cobden that the 'great revolution' in maritime law would succeed. See Cobden to Henry Richard, 21 August 1856, CLP (BL Add.43658 f125–31).
55. *Liverpool Mercury*, 22 August 1856; *The Era*, 24 August 1856; *Aberdeen Journal*, 27 August 1856; *Morning Chronicle*, 2 September 1856; *Manchester Guardian* (reprinted in the *Glasgow Herald*, 27 August 1856).
56. *Leeds Mercury*, 21 August 1856; *Belfast News-Letter*, 23 August 1856.
57. *Reynold's Newspaper*, 24 August 1856; *Daily News*, 27 August 1856.
58. Reprinted in *Glasgow Herald*, 27 August 1856.
59. *Glasgow Herald*, 10 September 1856.
60. Cowley to Clarendon, 4 October 1856, No. 1204, TNA, FO/412/5, No. 9, p. 16.
61. Observations of the Queen's Advocate on the Answer of the United States' Government respecting Maritime Law (by J. D. Harding), 27 September 1856, *ibid.*, No. 8, p. 13.
62. Palmerston to Clarendon, 4 October 1856, Bodleian, Mss.Clar.Dep.c50, f127; Clarendon to Cowley, 7 October 1856, No. 1201, TNA, FO/412/5, No. 10, p. 17.
63. Ferdinand Hamelin to Walewski, 11 September 1856, AMAE, Affaires diverses politiques, Box 6, No. 43, f22.
64. Walewski to Minister of Finance and Minister of Commerce, 14 October 1856, *ibid.*, f25.

65. Foreign Ministry memorandum (probably written by LeClerq, Walewski's delegate to the 'working group'), October 1856, *ibid.*, f31–37.
66. Cowley to Clarendon, 27 October 1856, No. 1319, TNA, FO/412/5, No. 11, p. 17.
67. Opinion by Dr. Lushington, 31 October 1856, TNA, FO/412/5, No. 12, pp. 17–21.
68. Mason to Marcy, 21 October 1856, No. 172, NARA, M34, Vol. 39, Roll 42.
69. O'Sullivan to Marcy, 28 September 1856, No. 45, NARA, M43, Vol. 17, Roll 16.
70. Marcy to O'Sullivan, 25 October 1856, No. 20, NARA, M77, Vol. 14, Roll 134.
71. Mason to Marcy, 27 October 1856, No. 174; Mason to Marcy, 3 November 1856, No. 175, NARA, M34, Vol. 39, Roll 42.
72. Walewski to Persigny, 8 December 1856, AMAE, Affaires diverses politiques, Box 6, No. 43, f39; Mason to Marcy, 7 November 1856, No. 177; Mason to Marcy, 17 November 1856, No. 179, NARA, M34, Vol. 39, Roll 42.
73. Lumley to Clarendon, 9 November 1856, No. 101, TNA, FO/412/5, No. 14, p. 22; Stoeckl to Marcy, 28 November 1856, printed in *The Times*, 30 December 1856, p. 8, and in Ludwig Karl Aegidi/Alfred Klauhold, *Frei Schiff unter Feindes Flagge*, Hamburg 1866, p. 20.
74. Marcy to Mason, 8 December 1856, No. 95, M77, Vol. 15, Roll 55.
75. The speech was given on 7 November, *The Times*, 8 November 1856.
76. *Aberdeen Journal*, 12 November 1856.
77. Note that Cobden's letter was not a reaction to Palmerston: he had decided in October that he would write a letter to persuade the Manchester Chamber of Commerce to submit a motion to the government. See Cobden to W. S. Lindsay, 12 October 1856, CLP (CP290, f128).
78. Cobden to Thomas Bexley, President of the Manchester Chamber of Commerce, 8 November 1856, printed in *The Times*, 24 November 1856, p. 7; *Daily News*, 22 November 1856; *Manchester Times*, 22 November 1856; *Morning Chronicle*, 24 November 1856; *Leeds Mercury*, 25 November 1856; *Glasgow Herald*, 28 November 1856; *Hull Packet and East Riding Times*, 28 November 1856; *Newcastle Courant*, 28 November 1856.
79. *Liverpool Mercury*, 28 November 1856.
80. While avoiding making use of his name, Cobden had ensured that the *Morning Star* strongly endorsed the idea and rejected the anti-American tone of the *Saturday Review*. See *Morning Star*, 22, 24, 28 August 1856.
81. *The Standard*, reprinted in *Belfast News-Letter*, 28 November 1856.
82. *The Times*, 25 November 1856, p. 8.
83. *Aberdeen Journal*, 3 December 1856.
84. Franklin Pierce lost the confidence of his Democratic Party after his first term and was not renominated, but replaced by James Buchanan. His term ended on 4 March 1857.
85. State of the Union Address, 2 December 1856, printed in Aegidi/Klauhold, *Frei Schiff*, p. 21.
86. Cowley to Clarendon, 1 December 1856, TNA, FO/412/5, No. 15, p. 23.
87. Walewski to Persigny, 8 December 1856, AMAE, Affaires diverses politiques, Box 6, No. 43, f39.
88. Letter of 8 December 1856, printed in *The Times*, 11 December 1856, p. 5; Cobden to John Bright, 20 December 1856, CLP (BL Add.43650 f240–242).
89. Lumley to Clarendon, 14 December 1856, TNA, FO/412/5, No. 20, p. 26.
90. *The European*, 13 December 1856, p. 72.
91. Rumpff to Smidt, 6 January 1857, StAB, 2-R.11 dd, bound volume 'Declaration of Paris 1856'.

92. Dallas to Marcy, 9 January 1857, No. 37, NARA, M30, Vol. 70, Roll 66.
93. Marcy to Dallas, 31 January 1857, No. 48, NARA, M77, Vol. 17, Roll 76.
94. Dallas to Marcy, 28 February 1857, No. 44, NARA, M30, Vol. 70, Roll 66.
95. Mason to Marcy, 3 March 1857, No. 206, NARA, M34, Vol. 40, Roll 43.
96. Mason to Walewski, 2 March 1857, AMAE, Affaires diverses politiques, Etats-Unis, Box 6, No. 43, f45; Dallas to Clarendon, 24 February 1857, BFSP, Vol. 55, p. 599.
97. Cobden to Lindsay, 24 August 1856, CLP (CP290, f31–32); 16 January 1857, CLP (CP290, f129–130); 4 February 1857, CLP (CP290, f131).
98. House of Commons, 9 March 1857, Vol. 144, Col. 2083–2086.
99. House of Commons, 9 March 1857, Vol. 144, Col. 2087–2088, 2094.
100. Dallas to Marcy, 19 March 1857, No. 47, NARA, M30, Vol. 70, Roll 66.
101. Mason to Marcy, 18 March 1857, No. 212, NARA, M34, Vol. 40, Roll 43.
102. Cass to Dallas, 3 April 1857, No. 60, NARA, M77, Vol. 17, Roll 76; Dallas to Clarendon, 25 April 1857, BFSP, Vol. 55, p. 602.
103. Rücker to Smidt, 27 May 1857, StAB, 2-R.11 dd, bound volume 'Declaration of Paris 1856', referring to information given to him by Dallas.
104. *The Times*, 25 April 1857, p. 9.
105. *Chicago Daily Tribune*, 5 August 1857, p. 2; the article referred to is the one discussed below, *The Times*, 16 July 1857, p. 8.
106. Piggott, *Declaration of Paris*, pp. 148–149; Stockton, *The Declaration of Paris*, p. 364.
107. Malkin, *Inner History*, p. 41.
108. Lambert, *Great Britain and Maritime Law*, p. 16.
109. Minute by the Earl of Clarendon, undated (late March 1857?), TNA, FO/412/5, No. 23, p. 29.
110. Dallas to Marcy, 8 December 1856, quoted in Dowty, *Limits*, p. 231.
111. Dallas to Marcy, 12 December 1856, *ibid.*, p. 233.
112. Marcy to Dallas, 4 January 1857, printed in Aegidi/Klauhold, *Frei Schiff*, p. 23.
113. Dallas to Marcy, 19 December 1856, No. 34, NARA, M30, Vol. 70, Roll 66.
114. Marcy to Dallas, 4 August 1856, private, Library of Congress, Marcy Papers, Vol. 71.
115. Alexandre Walewski, *Rapport a L'Empereur sur la Publication des notes officielles portant accession a la declaration du congrès de paris du 16 avril 1856, relative au droit maritime on temps du guerre*, Paris 1858.
116. Piggott, *Declaration of Paris*, p. 138.
117. Charles Eames to Guterriez, 20 November 1856; Eames to Marcy, 23 December 1856, No. 28, NARA, M79, Vol. 10, Roll 11.
118. Howden to Clarendon, 23 May 1856, TNA, FO/83/487, No. 162.
119. Howden to Clarendon, 7 June 1856, *ibid.*, No. 198, pp. 39–40.
120. A. C. Dodge to Pastor Diaz, 8 August 1856, NARA, M31, Vol. 40, Roll 39.
121. Nicomedes Pastor Diaz to Dodge, 2 September 1856, NARA, M31, Vol. 40, Roll 39; Dodge to Marcy, 11 October 1856, *ibid.*
122. Bolivia, Venezuela, Guiana, Paraguay and Mexico remained aloof, but, with the exception of the latter, trade with Europe was comparatively small.
123. Petition of Citizens of Leeds on Illegal Abandonment of Rights at Paris Presented to the House of Commons on 30 June 1857, *The Times*, 1 July 1857, p. 6.
124. Cobden to Lindsay, 14 May, 1857, CLP (CP290, f131–132); 23 June 1857, CLP (CP290, f133–135). Quotation taken from Cobden to Lindsay, 4 July 1857, CLP (CP290, f138–139).

125. House of Commons, 14 July 1857, Vol. 146, Col. 1487–1492.
126. *The Times*, 16 July 1857, p. 8.
127. House of Commons, 14 July 1857, Vol. 146, Col. 1488.
128. Palmerston to Clarendon, 27 September 1856, Bodleian, Mss.Clar.Dep.c50, f108.
129. Palmerston to Clarendon, 26 December 1856, *ibid.*, f496.

5   'The United States Have a Vote in Framing the Maritime Law of this Age' – The Cass Memorandum and Bremen's Campaign for the Marcy Amendment

1. The campaign is largely forgotten, but note a first scholarly reference in Rolf Hobson, 'Prussia, Germany and Maritime Law from Armed Neutrality to Unlimited Submarine Warfare 1780–1917', in Rolf Hobson and Tom Kristiansen (eds.), *Navies in Northern Waters, 1721–2000*, London 2004, pp. 97–116, p. 102. For a more detailed account based on archival sources, see Jan Martin Lemnitzer, 'A Few Burghers in a Little Hanseatic Town – Die Bremer Seerechtskampagne von 1859', *Bremisches Jahrbuch*, Vol. 83 (2004), pp. 85–109.
2. Malmesbury to J. Hodson, 20 May 1859, Parliamentary Papers, *Correspondence Relating to Affairs of Italy February–June 1859*, No. 42, p. 62, 1859–2 (2527) XXXII.443.
3. *Morning Chronicle*, 26 May 1859.
4. Cass to Mason, 16 June 1859, No. 188, NARA, M77, Vol. 15, Roll 55.
5. Instructions to naval commanders, 23 June 1859, Vincennes, CC⁴1251 (confusingly, inside a folder titled 'Documents on the war of 1877'). The states mentioned are Buenos Ayres (which had seceded from the treaty party Argentina in 1853), Costa Rica, Spain, the USA, the Sandwich Islands (Hawaii), Mexico, Nicaragua, Paraguay and Venezuela. Confusingly, New Granada (modern Colombia) and Uruguay are also listed, although both states had joined the declaration in 1856. The Sardinian proclamation of 20 May 1859 refers to the Declaration of Paris but does not mention a restriction to signatories, *The Times*, 24 May 1859, p. 7.
6. Cass to Mason, 27 June 1859, No. 190, NARA, M77, Vol. 15, Roll 55.
7. Cass to John W. Morgan, 26 September 1859, No. 10, NARA, M77, Vol. 17, Roll 76.
8. Quotation from instruction to Portugal, Cass to Joseph R. Chandler, 16 November 1859, No. 10, NARA, M77, Vol. 14, Roll 170; see also Cass to John W. Morgan, 16 November 1859, No. 13, NARA, M77, Vol. 17, Roll 76; Cass to Henry Murphy, 30 June 1859, RSC, M77. Roll 123.
9. *Leeds Mercury*, 17 May 1859.
10. *The Times*, 20 June 1859, p. 7.
11. *Caledonian Mercury*, 20 May 1859. Three weeks later, more than 40 Austrian vessels had been taken, *Daily News*, 10 June 1859.
12. Instructions to naval commanders, 23 June 1859, Vincennes, CC⁴1251.
13. *Daily News*, 11 May 1859; *Morning Chronicle*, 16 May 1859; *Liverpool Mercury*, 31 May 1859.
14. *Glasgow Herald*, 31 May 1859.
15. Parliamentary Papers, *Correspondence with United States Government Respecting Right of Visit of American Vessels by British Cruisers*, 1857–1858 (2446) XXXIX.365.

16. Derby to Victoria, 11 May 1859, cited in Gabriele Metzler, *Grossbritannien, Weltmacht in Europa: Handelspolitik im Wandel des europäischen Staatensystems 1856 bis 1871*, Berlin 1997, p. 100. The proclamation of 13 May is printed in *The Times*, 14 May 1859, p. 10.
17. *The Times*, 17 May 1859, p. 5.
18. *Liverpool Mercury*, 24 May 1859.
19. Hammond to John Glover, 18 May 1859, printed in *The Times*, 20 May 1859, p. 7.
20. *The Times*, 30 May 1859, p. 10; 31 May 1859, p. 7.
21. See the reprinted articles in *The Times*, 15 June 1859, p. 10; and *Glasgow Herald*, 11 July 1859.
22. *Liverpool Mercury*, 11 July 1859.
23. *New York Herald*, 8 July 1859, reprinted in *Morning Chronicle*, 22 July 1859.
24. Cass to Dallas, 29 May 1859, No. 185, NARA II, M77, Roll 76, Vol. 17.
25. Cass to John W. Morgan, 26 September 1859, No. 10, NARA, M77, Vol.17, Roll 76; Cass to R. W. Calhoun, 31 December 1859, No. 8, NARA, M77, Vol. 15, Roll 55.
26. Schleiden to Cass, 2 April 1857, printed in Aegidi and Klauhold, *Frei Schiff*, p. 24. Schleiden to Smidt, 24 April 1857, StAB, 2-R.11 (*Schiffahrt zur See*) dd. (*Seerecht in Kriegszeiten, 1795–1870*), bound volume 'Die Pariser Erklärung von 1856'.
27. Schleiden to Smidt, 23 June 1857, StAB, *ibid.*
28. Geffcken to Smidt, 4 August 1859, StAB, 2-R.11dd, bound volume 'Die Seerechtskampagne von 1859'.
29. Rumours that Dallas might soon accede to the Declaration of Paris in London circulated at the time, *New York Times*, 15 August 1859, p. 1.
30. Rücker to Smidt, 3 August 1859, StAB, 2-R.11dd, bound volume 'Die Seerechtskampagne von 1859'.
31. *Bremer Handelsblatt*, 29 October 1859.
32. Hermann Henrich Meier (1808–98) had been a member of the first national assembly in 1849 (Casino party) and later became a national-liberal member of the Reichstag (1867–71, 1878–87). See Heinrich Best/Wilhelm Wege, *Biographisches Handbuch der Abgeordneten der Frankfurter Nationalversammlung 1848–49*, Düsseldorf 1996, p. 234.
33. Andreas Schulz, *Vormundschaft und Protektion   Eliten und Bürger in Bremen 1750–1880*, Munich 2002, p. 48; Herbert Schwarzwälder, *Geschichte der Freien Hansestadt Bremen*, Vol. II, Bremen 1995, pp. 237–239.
34. Cass to Mason, 24 May 1859, No. 185, NARA, M77, Vol. 15, Roll 55.
35. Schulz, *Vormundschaft und Protektion*, p. 476.
36. *Bremer Handelsblatt*, 2 December 1859.
37. *Weserzeitung*, 8 December 1859.
38. The resolution of 2 December 1859 is printed in English in Aegidi/Klauhold, *Frei Schiff*, No. XVI, p. 58.
39. Chamber of Commerce session protocol, 18 November 1859, ABCC, SX3 'Seerecht in Kriegszeiten' Vol. 1, No. 11.
40. Lewis Ricardo responded by urging John Russell to change the British position, Lewis Ricardo to Rücker, 27 December 1859, SAB, 2-R.11dd, bound volume 'Die Seerechtskampagne von 1859'.
41. Duckwitz to the Syndicus of the chamber of commerce, 17 November 1859, ABCC, S X 3 'Seerecht in Kriegszeiten', Vol. 1, No. 1.
42. See, for example, Isaac Willen to Cass, 13 December 1859, No. 64, NARA, T-184, Roll 10.

43. Examples of articles in France include *Le Nord – Journal International*, 9 December 1859, *Le Salut Public – Journal de Lyon*, 20 December 1859, *Le Sémaphore de Marseille*, 21 December 1859. Austria: *Triester Zeitung*, 6 December 1859. Germany: *National-Zeitung*, 16 December 1859, *Neue Hannoversche Zeitung*, 14 December 1859.

44. *Birmingham Daily Post, Liverpol Mercury, Hull Packet and East Riding Times*, all 9 December 1859; *Leeds Mercury*, 13 December 1859.

45. The *Weserzeitung*, 10 December 1859, criticised the resolution and urged concentrating on what was achievable; see also *Morning Chronicle*, 16 December 1859.

46. *Bremer Handelsblatt*, 10 December 1859; the letters to the campaigners (describing the efforts taken elsewhere) can be found in ABCC, SX3 'Seerecht in Kriegszeiten'.

47. Marseille Chamber of Commerce to Ministry of Trade, 30 December 1859, printed in Aegidi/Klauhold, *Frei Schiff*, p. 79; Bordeaux Chamber of Commerce to the President of the Bremen Chamber of Commerce, 30 December 1859, ABCC, S X 3 'Seerecht in Kriegszeiten', Vol. 1, No. 23.

48. Merchants of St. John's (New-Brunswick) to Russell, 2 January 1860, Aegidi/Klauhold, *Frei Schiff*, p. 74–75; ABCC, S X 3 'Seerecht in Kriegszeiten', Vol. 1, No. 35.

49. *The Economist*, 17 December 1859; see also *Daily News*, 17 December 1859 and 18 December 1859, *Manchester Guardian*, 12 December 1859, *Morning Post*, 27 December 1859, *Hull Advertiser*, 17 December 1859.

50. *The Times*, 10 December 1859, p. 6. For the *Weserzeitung*, 13 December 1859, this article was actually a sign of weakness: 'He who has steel arrows in his quiver will hardly throw rotten eggs.'

51. See the letter by 'John Campbell', *The Times*, 17 December 1859, p. 5; Rücker was also behind the *Daily News'* attack on *The Times*, Rücker to Smidt, 12 December 1859, SAB, 2-R.11dd, bound volume 'Die Seerechtskampagne von 1859'.

52. *The Times*, 17 December 1859, p. 6.

53. *Manchester Weekly Times and Examiner*, 14 January 1860. See Art. 3 of the Treaty of Zurich of 10 November 1859, Parliamentary Papers, *Correspondence Relating to Affairs of Italy (from Signature of Preliminaries of Villafranca to Postponement of Congress)*, 1860 (2609) LXVIII.1, Inclosure in No. 226, p. 231.

54. *The Times*, 14 January 1860, p. 8.

55. *Report of a Special Committee of the Chamber of Commerce of the State of New York*, 10 February 1860, *On Maritime Intercourse in Time of War*, New York 1860; *Chicago Press and Tribune*, 10 February 1860, p. 4.

56. Their correspondence can be found in the files of Bremen's Washington legation, StAB, 4.48–17.4.

57. The senator responsible for foreign affairs, Johann Heinrich Smidt, saw no chance of success after his enquiries in London and Washington, Bremen Senate to the Committee for Maritime Law, 9 December 1859, printed in Aegidi and Klauhold, *Frei Schiff*, p. 61. Smidt (1806–78) officially became Senate Commissioner for Foreign Affairs only in 1874, but attended to the day-to-day operations for Arnold Duckwitz (1802–81), who simultaneously served as President of the Senate. See Tobias C. Bringmann, *Handbuch der Diplomatie 1815–1963*, Munich 2001, p. 58.

58. Klaus Peter Schröder, *Das Alte Reich und seine Städte*, Munich 1991; pp. 90–91; Hans Wiedemann, *Die Außenpolitik Bremens im Zeitalter der Französischen Revolution 1794–1803*, Breme n 1960, pp. 153–161.

59. See §27 of the *Reichsdeputationshauptschluss* of 25 February 1803, printed in Ernst Rudolf Huber, *Dokumente zur deutschen Verfassungsgeschichte, Vol.1*, Stuttgart 1978, No. 1, pp. 1–28.

60. See §41 of the Final Act of the Minister conferences of Vienna of 15 May 1820, *ibid.*, No. 31, pp. 91–100.

61. *Bremer Handelsblatt*, 2 July 1859. See also Carl Wilhelm Asher, *German Resolutions and British Policy: Observations on the Past, Present and Future of International Law*, Hamburg 1860, p. 3. Note that Bremen's military strength was negligible: it had no navy and its army was miniscule, even by the standards of the German Confederation's 10th Army Corps, exclusively composed of small and ministates. In 1859, Bremen's contribution to this corps amounted to 672 men and 4 horses. See Jürgen Angelow, *Von Wien nach Königgrätz – Die Sicherheitspolitik des Deutschen Bundes im europäischen Gleichgewicht (1815–1866)*, Munich 1996, Annex 6, pp. 326–329.

62. *Liverpool Mercury*, 11 May 1859.

63. Memorandum by Dr Geffcken, 15 November 1859, printed in Aegidi and Klauhold, *Frei Schiff*, pp. 53ff. See also Geffcken to Smidt, 4 August 1859, StAB, 2-R.11dd, bound volume 'Die Seerechtskampagne von 1859'; Geffcken to Smidt, 4 November 1859, StAB, *ibid.* At the time, it was generally expected that a congress would meet soon, settling Italian affairs and discussing other matters as well, Joseph Wright to Cass, 9 November 1859, No. 102, NARA, M44, Roll 9.

64. 'Eine Aufgabe für den Congress', *Preußische Jahrbücher*, Vol. 4, No. 6 (1859), p. 612. The article was published anonymously but a copy of it in the StAB files bears the handwritten annotation 'Minister-Resident Geffcken', SAB, 2-R.11 dd, bound volume 'Die Seerechtskampagne von 1859'.

65. Geffcken to Smidt, 5 November 1859, *ibid.*

66. Geffcken to Smidt, 29 November 1859, *ibid.*

67. Wright to Cass, 30 November 1859, No. 105, NARA, M44, Roll 9.

68. Wright to Cass, 7 December 1859, No. 106, *ibid.*

69. Wright to Cass, 14 December 1859, No. 107, *ibid.* See also Hodges to Duckwitz, 30 December 1859, printed in Aegidi and Klauhold, *Frei Schiff*, p. 85.

70. Geffcken to Golstein, 31 December 1859, *ibid.*, pp. 86–87.

71. Geffcken to Smidt, 4 January 1860, ABCC, SX 3 'Seerecht in Kriegszeiten', Vol. 1, No.30 (copy).

72. Geffcken to Smidt, 6 January 1860, ABCC, *ibid.*, Vol. 1, No. 31 (copy). His interview with the Belgian King is described in Geffcken to Smidt, 8 January 1860, ABCC, *ibid.*, Vol. 1 No. 32a (copy).

73. Chevalier was an important adviser to Napoleon III and is best known for drafting the 1860 free trade agreement between France and Britain, together with Richard Cobden and John Bright. For the most recent scholarship, see Michael Drolet, 'Industry, Class and Society: A Historiographic Reinterpretation of Michel Chevalier', *English Historical Review*, Vol. 123, No. 504 (October 2008), pp. 1229–1271.

74. Geffcken to Smidt, 10 January 1860, ABCC, SX 3 'Seerecht in Kriegszeiten', Vol. 1, No. 32b (copy).

75. Circular of 11 January 1860, printed in Aegidi and Klauhold, *Frei Schiff*, pp. 87ff.

76. Senate of Hamburg to Straténus, 27 January 1860; Senate of Lübeck to Straténus, 31 January 1860, *ibid.*, pp. 90–91.

77. Merck to Smidt, 25 December 1856, SAB 2-R.11dd, bound volume 'Die Pariser Erklärung von 1856'.
78. Platen Hallermund to Straténus, 28 January 1860; Blixen Finecke to Du Bois, 7 February 1860, printed in Aegidi and Klauhold, *Frei Schiff*, pp. 90–93.
79. *Triester Zeitung*, 7 November 1859, p. 1.
80. Central-Seebehörde to Ministry of Trade, 4 October 1859, HHStA Vienna, Aussenministerium, allgemeine Registratur, F36, No. 5.
81. Ministry of Trade to Foreign Ministry, 31 October 1859, *ibid.*, f146.
82. Bruck to Rechberg, 18 November 1859, *ibid.*
83. Foreign Ministry memorandum, 20 November 1859, *ibid.*
84. Rechberg to Thun, undated copy (late November 1859?), *ibid.*
85. Cass to John W. Morgan, 26 September 1859, No. 10, NARA, M77, Vol. 17, Roll 76.
86. Rechberg to Metternich, undated copy (late November 1859?), HHStA Vienna, Aussenministerium, allgemeine Registratur, F36, No. 5.
87. Bruck to Rechberg, 4 December 1859, *ibid.*
88. Rechberg to Bruck, 9 December 1859, *ibid.*
89. Cass to R. W. Calhoun, 31 December 1859, No. 8, NARA, M77, Vol. 15, Roll 55. This order was repeated for the new Minister sent to Paris, Cass to Charles J. Faulkner, 20 January 1860, No. 2, *ibid.*
90. Smidt to Schleiden, 10 December 1859, StAB, 2-R.11dd, bound volume 'Die Seerechtskampagne von 1859'.
91. Buchanan to Perit, 31 March 1860, printed in *The Times*, 21 April 1860, p. 12.
92. Wright to Cass, 29 February 1860, No. 118, NARA, M44, Roll 9.
93. Pourtalès to Schleinitz, 31 December 1859, APP, Vol. 1, No. 559, p. 845. See also William E. Echard, *Napoleon III. and the Concert of Europe*, London 1983, pp. 115–123, and Edith Saurer, 'Der Kongreß findet nicht statt. Der Kongreßplan von 1859', *Römische Historische Mitteilungen*, Vol. 11 (1969), pp. 110–126.
94. Bernstorff to Prince Regent, 22 December 1859, APP, Vol. 1, No. 555, p. 841.
95. Rücker to Smidt, 10 December 1859, StAB, 2-R.11dd, bound volume 'Die Seerechtskampagne von 1859'.
96. Brück to Rechberg, 20 January 1860, HHStA Vienna, Aussenministerium, allgemeine Registratur, F36, No. 5.
97. Rechberg to Brück, 7 February 1860, *ibid.*
98. Brück to Rechberg, 31 March 1860, *ibid.*
99. Geffcken to Smidt, 4 January 1860, ABCC, SX 3 'Seerecht in Kriegszeiten', Vol. 1, No. 30 (copy).
100. See, for example, *Daily News*, 18 December 1856, which described the Congress of Paris as a waste of time but praised its labours on maritime law: 'This is, indeed, a worthy subject for the deliberations of a great Areopagitic Council of the Nations!' The term was often used regarding the expected congress to settle the Italian question, *Daily News*, 22 March 1859, 11 November 1859; *Morning Chronicle*, 31 March 1859; *Lloyd's Weekly Newspaper*, 24 April 1859; *Belfast News-Letter*, 18 August 1859; *Liverpool Mercury*, 2 December 1859; *Leeds Mercury*, 3 December 1859; *Invalide Russe*, reprinted in *Daily News*, 8 November 1859; *Independente* (Italy), reprinted in *Daily News*, 14 November 1859.

101. Romanian nationalists employed the term when they appealed to the congress to allow the union of the Danubian Principalities, *Daily News*, 18 December 1857.
102. In 1818, Gentz had referred to the European congress as the 'European areopagus'. See Eckhart Conze, 'Wer von Europa spricht, hat Unrecht: Aufstieg und Verfall des vertragsrechtlichen Multilateralismus im europäischen Staatensystem des 19. Jahrhunderts', *Historisches Jahrbuch*, Vol. 121 (2001), pp. 214–241, p. 231.
103. Geffcken to Smidt, 5 November 1859, SAB, 2-R.11dd, bound volume 'Die Seerechtskampagne von 1859'.
104. Oertzen to Crull, 18 January 1860, printed in Aegidi and Klauhold, *Frei Schiff*, p. 89.
105. O'Sullivan to Marcy, 18 October 1856, No. 47, NARA, M43, Vol. 17.
106. *Lloyd's Weekly Newspaper*, 13 November 1859; *Liverpool Mercury*, 1 December 1859. While the *Derby Mercury*, 22 August 1859, explicitly describes it as a continental concept, French Foreign Minister Thouvenel favoured referring to the congress in this way. See *Morning Chronicle*, 21 June 1860.
107. See Lars Maischak, *German Merchants in the Nineteenth-Century Atlantic*, Cambridge 2013. Maischak employs this and other arguments to question the category of 'Hanseatic liberalism' coined by Andreas Schulz.
108. Most of this money was spent on printing and mailing the resolution, cf. the final bill of the campaign, enclosed in ABCC, SX3, No. 12.
109. Rücker to Senate, 24 February 1860, StAB, 2-R.11dd, bound volume 'Die Seerechtskampagne von 1859'. Cobden sent a letter to the campaigners promising that he would do all in his power to enforce the adoption of the principle, Cobden to Fritze, 22 March 1860, ABCC, SX 3, No.43.
110. Cobden to Lindsay, 1 March 1860, CLP (CP290, f305–307).
111. Lindsay to Russell, 14 October 1859, Parliamentary Papers, *Letter from Mr. Lindsay to Lord J. Russell on Belligerent Rights in reference to Merchant Shipping*, 1860 (2649) LXVIII.643, No. 1, p. 1.
112. Hammond to Lindsay, 19 October 1859, *ibid.*, No. 2, p. 6.
113. *Morning Chronicle*, 7 April 1860.
114. *The Times*, 5 April 1860, p. 8.
115. *The Times*, 19 April 1860, p. 10.
116. Cobden to Lindsay, 26 April 1860, CLP (CP290, f.141–142).
117. See Report by the Select Committee on Merchant Shipping, 7 August 1860, Parliamentary Papers, *Select Committee on State of Merchant Shipping. Report, Proceedings, Minutes of Evidence, Appendix, Index*, 1860 (530) XIII.1, p. xiv. Naturally, Lindsay's increasing prominence in maritime matters alerted the attention of Bremen's campaigners, who caught up with him in Washington. See Lindsay to Schleiden, 17 November 1860, StAB, 4.48–17.4.
118. Cobden to Bright, 29 December 1859, CLP (BL Add.43651 f48–55).
119. Cobden to Gladstone, 5 January 1860, CLP (BL Add.44135).
120. See Article 11 of the treaty, Parliamentary Papers, *Treaty of Commerce between Her Majesty and the Emperor of the French. Signed at Paris, 23 January 1860* (2607) LXVIII.467. In shipping circles, it was perceived as confirmation that Britain would not treat coal as contraband. See the Merchant Shipping Report cited above, p. 258.
121. House of Lords, 16 February 1860, Vol. 156, Col. 1106–1130.

122. House of Commons, 17 February 1860, Vol. 156, Col. 1270ff.
123. Cobden to Bright, 18 February 1860, CLP (BL, Add.43651, f93–96); Cobden to Gladstone, 25 February 1860, CLP (BL Add.44135).
124. House of Commons, 20 February 1859, Vol. 156, Col. 1362–1427, 1378.
125. Order in Council, 7 March 1860, Parliamentary Papers, *Correspondence Respecting Affairs in China, 1859–60*, 1861 (2754) LXVI.1, Inclosure 3 in No. 28, p. 56; *The Times*, 27 June 1860, p. 12.
126. Instructions to naval commanders, 23 June 1859, Art. 12, Vincennes, CC⁴1251; *Liverpool Mercury*, 3 June 1859.
127. *Daily News*, 11 May 1859.
128. Wright to Cass, 7 March 1860, No. 119, NARA, M44, Roll 9.
129. *Morning Post*, 27 December 1859.
130. Cobden to Lindsay, undated (May 1860), CLP (CP290 f113–114).

6 The Declaration of Paris and the American Civil War

1. Even an essay published in 2007 by a well-known expert on the history of the Civil War blockade avoids the thorny questions of maritime law that were involved. See David G. Surdam, 'The Union Navy's Blockade Reconsidered', in Bruce Elleman and S. C. M. Paine (eds.), *Naval Blockades and Seapower – Strategies and Counterstrategies, 1805–2005*, New York 2006, pp. 61–70.
2. Frank J. Merli, *The Alabama, British Neutrality and the American Civil War*, Bloomington 2004, p. 19.
3. *Chicago Tribune*, 21 January 1861, p. 2.
4. *Chicago Tribune*, 25 February 1861, p. 2. The *New York Times*, 18 April 1861, p. 4, echoed that call after the issue of letters of marque had been announced.
5. *New York Times*, 20 April 1861, p. 2.
6. *New York Times*, 28 April 1861, p. 4.
7. *New York Times*, 20 April 1861, p.4.
8. The declaration of 19 April 1861 is printed in Roy P. Basler, (ed.), *The Collected Works of Abraham Lincoln, Volume IV*, New Brunswick, NJ, 1953, p. 338–339.
9. *Bristol Mercury*, 4 May 1861.
10. Gideon Welles to Flag Officer Stringham, 1 May 1861, NARA, RG 59 (State Department), Entry No. 966 (letters sent by Gideon Welles regarding blockade in 1861): 'a lawful maritime blockade requires the actual presence of an adequate force stationed at the entrance of the port'.
11. Gideon Welles, *Report of the Secretary of the Navy to the President, 1 December 1862*, printed in *New York Journal of Commerce*, 2 December 1862, p. 1.
12. *Liverpool Mercury*, 4 May 1861.
13. France later confirmed that in that case it would have fought the Confederate privateers, Thouvenel to Dayton, 7 September 1861, FRUS, p. 252.
14. Seward to Charles Francis Adams et al., 24 April 1861, FRUS, p. 34. The instruction was also sent to Denmark and Belgium, in the latter case because the local minister was also the acting envoy to France in the absence of a minister in Paris.
15. *The Times*, 31 May 1861. The article was immediately sent to Seward by a concerned Adams, Adams to Seward, 31 May 1861, FRUS, p. 96.
16. Dallas to Seward, 2 May 1861, FRUS, p. 84.

17. *New York Times*, 18 April 1861, p. 4.
18. House of Commons, 2 May 1861, Vol. 162, Col. 1378–1379.
19. House of Commons, 6 May 1861, Vol. 162, Col. 1565–1567. The decision was communicated to Washington on the same day, Russell to Lyons, 6 May 1861, TNA, FO/414/15, No. 2, p. 2.
20. Harding to Russell, 16 May 1861, TNA, FO/412/6, No. 102, p. 95.
21. Adams to Seward, 14 June 1861, FRUS, p. 103.
22. House of Lords, 10 May 1861, Vol. 162, Col. 1832–1833.
23. Proclamation of Neutrality in the Contest between United States and Confederate States, 13 May 1861, BFSP, Vol. 51, p. 165.
24. House of Lords, 16 May 1861, Vol. 162, Col. 2077–2080; 2080–2081.
25. The undated memorandum is copied as an enclosure to Lyons to Russell, 13 June 1861, No. 279, TNA, FO/5/766.
26. Russell to Cowley, 6 May 1861, TNA, FO/414/15, No. 1, p. 1.
27. Russell to Cowley, 11 May 1861, *ibid.*, No. 3, p. 3.
28. Cowley to Russell, 13 May 1861, *ibid.*, No. 6, p. 4.
29. Russell to Lyons, 18 May 1861, *ibid.*, No. 10, p. 5; FRUS, p. 149.
30. Thouvenel to Mercier, 11 May 1861, copied as an enclosure to Lyons to Russell, 13 June 1861, No. 279, TNA, FO/5/766.
31. Russell to Lyons, 18 May 1861, TNA, FO/414/15, No. 11, p. 8.
32. Adams to Seward, 21 May 1861, FRUS, p. 90; Russell to Lyons, 21 May 1861, TNA, FO/414/15, No. 13, p. 10.
33. Lyons to Russell, 4 June 1861, *ibid.*, No. 14, p. 10.
34. Lyons to Russell, 6 June 1861, cited in Lynn Marshall Case and Warren F. Spencer, *The United States and France: Civil War Diplomacy*, Philadelphia 1970, p. 86.
35. Seward to Dayton, 17 June 1861, FRUS, p. 224; Seward to Dayton, 22 June 1861, FRUS, p. 229; Lyons to Russell, 17 June 1861, printed in Piggott, *Declaration of Paris*, p. 420.
36. Lyons to Russell, 17 June 1861, cited in Case and Spencer, *Civil War Diplomacy*, pp. 88–89.
37. Sanford to Dayton, 28 May 1861, cited in *ibid.*, p. 91.
38. Dayton to Seward, 30 May 1861, FRUS, p. 216; Dayton to Thouvenel, 31 May 1861, FRUS, p. 223.
39. Russell to Lyons, 21 June 1861, TNA, FO/414/15, No. 15, p. 11.
40. Rechberg to Wickenberg, 23 August 1861, HHStA Vienna, Aussenministerium, allgemeine Registratur, F36, No. 5.
41. Lyons to Russell, 12 July 1861, TNA, FO/414/15, No. 33, p. 26.
42. Russell to Lyons, 26 June 1861, *ibid.*, No. 17, p. 15.
43. Dayton to Seward, 12 June 1861, FRUS, p. 223.
44. Dayton to Seward, 7 June 1861, FRUS, p. 220.
45. Law Officers to Russell, 1 June 1861, TNA, FO/412/6, No. 111, p. 102.
46. House of Commons, 3 June 1861, Vol.163, Col. 471–472. The French Declaration of 10 June 1861 is printed in *Moniteur Universel*, 11 June 1861, p. 1.
47. Lyons to Russell, 17 June 1861, No. 283, TNA, FO/5/766.
48. Declaration of 17 June 1861, printed in *Gaceta de Madrid*, 19 June 1861, p. 1.
49. Netherlands: James Pike to Seward, 16 June 1861, FRUS, p. 353, Italy: Marsh to Seward, 6 July 1861, *ibid.* p. 323; Bremen: Seward to Schleiden, 30 July 1861, NARA, M99, Roll 57.
50. *New York Times*, 12 June 1861; *New York Herald*, 16 June 1861.

51. Seward to Dayton, 1 July 1861, cited in Case and Spencer, *Civil War Diplomacy*, p. 98. On the same day, he reminded Adams in London that a quick accession without the Marcy amendment was what he desired. See Seward to Adams, 1 July 1861, FRUS, p. 111.
52. Dayton to Seward, 12 June 1861, FRUS, p. 223; Dayton to Seward, 5 July 1861, FRUS, p. 234.
53. Seward to Sanford, 8 July 1861, FRUS, p. 61.
54. Adams to Seward, 19 July 1861, FRUS, p. 114: Adams to Russell, 11 July 1861, FRUS, p. 115; Adams to Seward, 12 July 1861, FRUS, p. 113.
55. Case and Spencer, *Civil War Diplomacy*, p. 95.
56. The first draft in English is actually dated '13 May', making it very probable that the French were informed earlier than Case claims.
57. Russell to Cowley, 17 July 1861, cited in Case and Spencer, *Civil War Diplomacy*, p. 96.
58. Russell to Adams, 18 July 1861, TNA, FO/414/15, No. 28, p. 22.
59. Dayton to Seward, 22 July 1861, cited in Case and Spencer, *Civil War Diplomacy*, pp. 98–99.
60. Dayton to Seward, 30 July 7. 1861, FRUS, p. 237.
61. Russell to Adams, 31 July 1861, FRUS, p. 126.
62. Adams to Seward, 2 August 1861, FRUS, p. 124.
63. Dayton to Adams, 5 August 1861, FRUS, p. 248.
64. Cowley to Russell, 8 August 1861, TNA, FO/414/15, No. 39, p. 28.
65. Cowley to Russell, 12 August 1861, TNA, FO/414/15, No. 40, p. 29; Cowley to Russell, 14 August 1861, *ibid.*, No. 41, p. 29.
66. Cowley to Russell, 20 August 1861, *ibid.*, No. 48, p. 32.
67. Norman B. Ferris, *Desperate Diplomacy, William H. Seward's Foreign Policy, 1861*, Knoxville, TS 1976, p. 84.
68. Case/Spencer, *Civil War Diplomacy*, p. 79, Brian Jenkins, *Britain and the War for the Union, Vol. 1*, Montreal 1974, p. 41.
69. Seward to Dayton, 6 July 1861, FRUS, p. 231.
70. Seward to Schleiden, 29 May 1861, NARA, M99, Roll 57; StAB, 4.48–17.4; cf. Schleiden to Seward, 30 May 1861, *ibid.*
71. Schleiden to the Senate Commission for Foreign Affairs, 3 June 1861, printed in Aegidi/Klauhold, *Frei Schiff*, p. 105f.
72. Schleiden to Seward, 17 July 1861, StAB, 4.48–17.4.
73. Seward to Schleiden, 18 July 1861, *ibid.* Seward to Schleiden, 17 July 1861, NARA, M99, Roll 57.
74. Schleiden to Seward, 18 July 1861, *ibid.* Schleiden to the Senate Commission for Foreign Affairs, 19 July 1861, printed in Aegidi/Klauhold, *Frei Schiff*, p. 109f.
75. Lyons to Russell, 25 July 1861, TNA, FO/414/15, No. 38, p. 28.
76. Lyons to Russell, 8 July 1861, *ibid.*, No. 31, p. 25.
77. Seward to Dayton, 26 July 1861, FRUS, p. 235.
78. Seward to Adams, 17 August 1861, FRUS, p. 128.
79. Seward to Adams, 21 July 1861, FRUS, p. 117.
80. Seward to Adams, 7 September 1861, FRUS, p. 141; Lyons to Russell, 20 September 1861, BFSP, Vol.55, p. 587. The last suspension was sent to Italy, Seward to Marsh, 22 November 1861, FRUS, p. 327.
81. Cowley to Russell, 24 September 1861, BFSP, Vol. 55, p. 587. Lyons to Russell, 6 December 1861, *ibid.*, p. 588.

82. Mercier to Thouvenel, 9 September 1861, AMAE, Affaires diverses politiques, Etats-Unis, Box 6 (droit maritime), No. 44.
83. Napier to Russell, 26 August 1861, No. 269; 27 August 1861, No. 277, TNA, FO/65/578.
84. Lyons to Russell, 17 June 1861, TNA, FO/414/15, No. 19, p. 16.
85. Wright to Seward, 15 May 1861, FRUS, p. 39; Schleinitz to Gerolt, 13 June 1861, printed in Aegidi/Klauhold, *Frei Schiff*, p. 102; Jones to Seward, 20 July 1861, FRUS, p. 188. Rechberg to Hülsemann, 1 July 1861, FRUS, p. 190.
86. Law Officers to Russell, 25 June 1861, TNA, FO 412/6, No. 142, p. 132.
87. *New York Herald*, 15 June 1861.
88. A printed copy of the act is enclosed to Lyons to Russell, 19 July 1861, TNA, FO/5/768, No. 357.
89. Lyons to Russell. 20 July 1861, TNA, FO/5/768, No. 363. The despatch includes the excerpts from the French and British instructions.
90. Welles to Lincoln, 5 August 1861, available at *Abraham Lincoln Papers at the Library of Congress*, Manuscript Division, American Memory Project, http://memory.loc.gov/ammem/alhtml/malhome.html
91. Seward to Hülsemann, 22 August 1861, HHStA Vienna, Aussenministerium, allgemeine Registratur, F36, No. 7.
92. Apponyi to Rechberg, 15 August 1861, *ibid.*, No. 5. See also Russell to Bloomfield, 31 July 1861, *ibid.*
93. Robert Bunch to Russell, 15 December 1860, printed in *American Historical Review*, Vol. 18, No. 4 (July 1913), pp. 783–787, p. 784.
94. See Frank Lawrence Owsley, *King Cotton Diplomacy: Foreign Relations of the Confederate States of America*, Chicago 1959; James McPherson, *The Battle Cry of Freedom: The Civil War Era*, New York 1988, p. 383.
95. Bunch to Lyons, 16 August 1861, BFSP, Vol. 55, p. 581.
96. Cowley to Russell, 9 May 1861, TNA, FO/414/15, No. 4, p. 3.
97. Lyons to Russell, 8 June 1861, *ibid.*, No. 16, p. 12; Lyons to Russell, 13 June 1861, *ibid.*, No. 18, p. 15.
98. Russell to Lyons, 12 July 1861, *ibid.*, No. 24, p. 20.
99. Lyons to Russell, 12 July 1861, *ibid.*, No. 27, p. 22.
100. Lyons to Bunch, 5 July 1861, *ibid.*, Enclosure 1 to No. 30, p. 23.
101. Memorandum by William Henry Trescott, 17 August 1861, printed in: 'The Confederacy and the Declaration of Paris', *American Historical Review*, Vol. 23, No. 4 (July 1918), pp. 826–835.
102. The resolution is printed in BFSP, Vol. 55, p. 584.
103. Bunch to Lyons, 16 August 1861, TNA, FO/414/15, Enclosure 1 to No. 58, p. 39.
104. Adams to Russell, 3 September 1861, FRUS, p. 150, Seward to Adams, 17 August 1861, FRUS, p. 130.
105. BFSP, Vol. 55, p. 584. The application form for letters of marque is printed on p. 586.
106. Overall, letters of marque were given to at least 52 captains, but the Confederate records are incomplete. See Spencer Tucker, *Blue and Gray Navies – The Civil War Afloat*, Annapolis, MD 2006, p. 74, and William Robinson, *The Confederate Privateers*, New Haven 1928, p. 231.
107. Tucker, *Blue and Gray Navies*, p. 73.
108. Statement of Thomas J. More, master of the *Dixie*, 6 August 1861, TNA, FO/414/20, Enclosure to No. 62, p. 73.

109. Commander H. D. Hickley to Rear-Admiral Milne, 8 July 1861, *ibid.*, Enclosure 2 to No. 35, p. 33.
110. *New York Herald*, 10 August 1861, reprinted in Thomas Scharf, *The Confederate States Navy, Vol. I*, New York 1887, p. 93.
111. US Bureau of the Census, *Historical Statistics of the United States – Colonial Times to 1957*, Washington 1960, p. 445.
112. Stuart L. Bernath, *Squall across the Atlantic: American Civil War Prize Cases and Diplomacy*, Berkeley 1970, p. 5.
113. Brian Mitchell, *European Historical Statistics, 1750–1975*, London 1980, p. 646. There is no evidence of a significant rise in registered tonnage in any European merchant navy.
114. US Bureau of the Census, *Historical Statistics of the United States*, p. 445.
115. Lyons to Russell, 4 June 1861, printed in Piggott, *Declaration*, p. 419.
116. Robinson, *Confederate Privateers*, p. 139.
117. Jefferson Davis to Lincoln, 6 July 1861, printed in Robinson, *Confederate Privateers*, pp. 133–134.
118. House of Lords, 16 May 1861, Vol. 162, Col.2081–2086.
119. Lyons to Russell, 8 July 1861, TNA, FO/414/15, No. 31, p. 25.
120. Robinson, *Confederate Privateers*, p. 148ff.
121. *Chicago Tribune*, 15 June 1861, p. 4.
122. Bunch to Lyons, 16 August 1861, BFSP, Vol. 55, p. 581.
123. James S. Pike to Seward, 12 June 1861, FRUS, p. 350.
124. Bradford Wood to Seward, 19 July 1861, FRUS, p. 313. This was even before Seward asked the Danes for particular vigilance to prevent a rumoured Confederate privateering project in the Cattegat, Seward to Bradford Wood, 7 August 1861, NARA, M77, Vol. 14, Roll 50.
125. Instruction to naval commanders by Rear-Admiral Alexander Milne, 30 May 1861, TNA, FO/414/20, Enclosure 2 to No. 11, p. 13.
126. Harding to Russell, 13 June 1861, TNA, FO/412/6, No. 126, p. 118.
127. Hammond to the Secretary to the Admiralty, 14 June 1861, TNA, FO/414/20, No. 16, p. 16.
128. Lyons to Russell, 18 July 1861, No. 350, TNA, FO/5/768.
129. Robinson, *Confederate Privateers*, p. 40.
130. *Ibid.*, p. 123.
131. *Ibid.*, pp. 155–158, 165–167.
132. Spencer Tucker, *A Short History of the Civil War at Sea*, Wilmington 2002, p. 112.
133. Adams to Seward, 27 March 1863, FRUS 1863 Vol. 1, p. 180.
134. Baron Van Zuylen to Pike, 17 September 1861, FRUS, p. 368.
135. Seward to Adams, 11 November 1861, FRUS, p. 176. Adams to Russell, 30 September 1861, FRUS, p. 161; Seward to Adams, 29 October 1861, FRUS, p. 167. Seward to Tassara, 15 July 1861, FRUS, p. 267.
136. Baudin to Thouvenel, 6 January 1862, AMAE, Affaires diverses politiques, Etats-Unis, Box 6 (droit maritime), No. 45, f3.
137. Sanford to Seward, 2 July 1861, FRUS, p. 58.
138. Schleiden to the Senate Committee for Foreign Affairs, 22 July 1861, printed in Aegidi/Klauhold, *Frei Schiff*, p. 110f.
139. *New York Times*, 17 December 1862, p. 2.
140. *New York Times*, 19 December 1862, p. 4; 6 January 1863, p. 2; *The Times*, 1 January 1863, p. 10.
141. *New York Times*, 21 January 1863, p. 8.

142. *New York Times*, 18 February 1863, p. 1, 4, 8; see also *The Times*, 4 March 1863, p. 12.
143. *New York Times*, 19 February 1863, p. 4; 24 February 1863, p. 4; 28 February 1863, p. 4.
144. *New York Times*, 22 February 1863, p. 3. Bierwirth had been a close ally of Bremen Minister Schleiden in promoting the campaign for the Marcy Amendment in 1860.
145. *New York Times*, 3 March 1863, p. 8.
146. *The Times*, 5 March 1863, p. 9; this interpretation was discussed on the front page of the *New York Times*, 21 March 1863.
147. Seward to Adams, 19 February 1863, FRUS 1863 Vol. 1, p. 135. A similar despatch was sent to Dayton: Seward to Dayton, 20 February 1863, FRUS 1863 Vol. 2, p. 713.
148. Memorandum of 31 March 1861, AMAE, Affaires diverses politiques, Etats-Unis, Box 6 (droit maritime), No. 45, f49ff.
149. Cowley to Russell, 4 April 1863, cited in James P. Baxter, 'Some British Opinions as to Neutral Rights, 1861 to 1865', *American Journal of International Law*, Vol. 23, No. 3 (July 1929), pp. 517–537, p. 537.
150. Seward to Adams, 9 March 1863, FRUS 1863 Vol. 1, p. 163.
151. *The Diary of Gideon Welles, Vol. 1*, Boston 1911, p. 246/247 (entry of 10 March 1863).
152. Sumner to Lincoln, 18 March 1863, available at *Abraham Lincoln Papers at the Library of Congress*, Manuscript Division, American Memory Project, http://memory.loc.gov/ammem/alhtml/malhome.html
153. *New York Times*, 24 March 1863, p. 4. The aggressive tone of this editorial was not overlooked in Britain, *The Times*, 7 April 1863, p. 9.
154. *New York Times*, 27 March 1863, p. 4; *New York Times*, 28 March 1863, p. 4.
155. Seward to Adams, 24 March 1863, FRUS 1863 Vol. 1, p. 178; *New York Times*, 3 April 1863, p. 4; Welles to Seward, 31 March 1863, printed in Welles, *Diary Vol. 1*, pp. 252–256.
156. Dayton to Seward, 9 April 1863, FRUS 1863 Vol. 2, p. 724.
157. *Times*, 16 April 1863, p. 14; 20 April 1863, p. 12, referring to US news of 7 April.
158. Seward to Adams, 7 April 1863, FRUS 1863 Vol. 1, p. 231; Seward to Dayton, 7 April 1863, FRUS 1863 Vol. 2, p. 723.
159. Adams to Seward, 27 March 1863, FRUS 1863 Vol. 1, p. 180.
160. Seward to Adams, 13 April 1863, *ibid.*, p. 245.
161. David Herbert Donald, *Charles Sumner, Vol. II*, New York 1996, pp. 108–111. The interpretation by Seward's biographer, who claims it was intended to fight blockade runners, is not supported by any evidence. See John M. Taylor, *William Henry Seward – Lincoln's Right Hand*, New York 1991, p. 215.
162. Adams to Seward, 7 April 1863, FRUS 1863 Vol. 1, p. 228.
163. *The Times*, 1 May 1863, p. 9.
164. James Baxter III, 'The British Government and Neutral Rights, 1861–1865', *American Historical Review*, Vol. 34 (October 1928), pp. 9–29; Bernath, *Squall across the Atlantic*, p. 12. Spencer Tucker argues that this was inspired by Britain's 'historic practice' of demanding respect for paper blockades. See *Blue and Gray Navies*, p. 71. Both Howard Jones and Amanda Foreman have recently argued that Britain ignored reports of the blockade's ineffectiveness to secure an advantage in case 'Great Britain might find herself in the similar position of mounting a feeble blockade', Amanda Foreman, *A World On Fire*, London 2011, p. 211;

Howard Jones, *Blue and Gray Diplomacy: A History of Union and Confederate Foreign Relations*, Chapel Hill, NC, 2010, p. 56.

165. An address to the British Public and all sympathizers in Europe, from the London Confederate States Aid Organization, undated (late 1862), FRUS 1863 Vol. 1, p. 22.
166. Lyons to Russell, 20 May 1861, TNA, FO/414/20, No. 3, p. 3.
167. House of Lords, 16 May 1861, Vol. 162, Col. 2081–2083.
168. Instruction to naval commanders by Rear-Admiral Alexander Milne, 30 May 1861, TNA, FO/414/20, Enclosure 2 to No. 11, p. 13.
169. Bunch to Lyons, 17 May 1861, *ibid.*, Enclosure 1 to No. 3, p. 4.
170. William Mure to Russell, 18 June 1861, *ibid.*, No. 30, p. 29.
171. Commander H. D. Hickley to Milne, 29 July 1861, *ibid.*, Enclosure 2 to No. 49, p. 55.
172. Commodore Dunlop to Secretary to the Admiralty, 29 August 1861, *ibid.*, No. 53, p. 57.
173. Bunch to Russell, 25 July 1861, *ibid.*, No. 59, p. 65; Fullarton to Russell, 12 August 1861, *ibid.*, No. 63, p. 73.
174. Captain Fabre to Mercier, 2 September 1861, *ibid.*, Enclosure to No. 69, p. 85.
175. Bunch to Russell, 20 August 1861, *ibid.*, No. 68, p. 84.
176. Russell to Lyons, 8 June 1861, *ibid.*, No. 7, p. 8.
177. Milne to Secretary to the Admiralty, 14 October 1861, *ibid.*, Enclosure 1 to No. 93, p. 110; Bunch to Lyons, 5 November 1861, *ibid.*, Enclosure 3 to No. 107, p. 135.
178. Russell to Lyons, 6 November 1861, *ibid.*, No. 97, p. 118.
179. Harding to Russell, 20 October 1861, *ibid.*, No. 277, p. 260.
180. Russell to Lyons, 8 November 1861, *ibid.*, No. 99, p. 118.
181. Cridland to Russell, 7 October 1861, *ibid.*, No. 104, p. 121.
182. Fullarton to Russell, 11 October 1861, *ibid.*, No. 105, p. 132.
183. Russell to Lyons, 15 February 1862, *ibid.*, No. 124, p. 149.
184. Seward to Adams, 17 February 1862, FRUS 1862, p. 36. Seward to Adams, 6 March 1862, *ibid.*, p. 42.
185. *The Times*, 10 February 1862, p. 6.
186. House of Commons, 7 March 1862, Vol. 165, Col. 1158–1230; House of Lords, 10 March 1862, Vol. 165, Col. 1237–1243.
187. House of Commons, 18 July 1862, Vol. 168, Col. 511–578.
188. Howard Jones, *Blue and Gray Diplomacy*, p. 165.
189. *Ibid.*, p. 254.
190. Memorandum of 11 March 1863, AMAE, Affaires diverses politiques, Etats-Unis, Box 6 (droit maritime), No. 45, f37ff.
191. Brian Jenkins, *Britain and the War for the Union, Vol. 2*, Montreal 1980, pp. 15–17.
192. House of Commons, 30 June 1863, Vol. 171, Col. 1778.
193. Bernath, *Squall across the Atlantic*, p. 11.
194. Jones, *Blue and Gray Diplomacy*, p. 161; James McPherson, *War on the Waters: The Union and Confederate Navies*, Chapel Hill NC, 2012, p. 49.
195. David G. Surdam, *Northern Naval Superiority and the Economics of the American Civil War*, Columbia, SC 2001, pp. 4–6.
196. See Stephen Neff, *Justice in Blue and Gray*, London 2010, p. 175.
197. James Baxter III, 'The British Government and Neutral Rights, 1861–1865', *American Historical Review*, Vol. 34 (October 1928), pp. 9–29.
198. Bernath, *Squall across the Atlantic*, p. 163.

199. James McPherson, *Battle Cry of Freedom*, p. 386; *War on the Waters*, p. 128.
200. Kenneth Bourne, 'British Preparations for War with the North, 1861–1862', *English Historical Review*, Vol. 76 (1961), pp. 600–632.
201. James McPherson, *Battle Cry of Freedom*, pp. 390–391.
202. Thouvenel to Mercier, 3 December 1861, printed in Case and Spencer, *Civil War Diplomacy*, pp. 202–204.
203. Adams to Seward, 10 January 1862, cited in *ibid.*, p. 206.
204. Moniteur Universel, 6 December 1861, cited in *ibid.*, p. 242.
205. *Journal de St. Pétersburg*, 11 January 1862.
206. Dayton to Seward, 27 January 1862, FRUS 1862, p. 310.
207. House of Lords, 6 February 1862, Vol. 165, Col. 42.
208. Law Officers to Russell, 15 January 1862, TNA, FO/412/7, No. 6, p. 5; Russell to Lyons, 23 January 1862, FRUS 1862, p. 249.
209. See Neff, *Justice in Blue and Gray*, p. 191.
210. Adams to Seward, 7 March 1862, FRUS 1862, pp. 44–45. Adams to Seward, 13 November 1862, FRUS 1863 Vol. 1, pp. 4–5.
211. Welles to William McKean, 25 November 1861, cited in Bernath, *Squall across the Atlantic*, p. 53.
212. Seward to Lyons, 8 March 1862, cited in *ibid.*, pp. 37–38.
213. Hammond to Admiralty, 25 March 1862, TNA, FO/97/42; William G. Romaine to Milne, 28 March, 6 April 1862, TNA, ADM/128/58.
214. The judgement is printed as Enclosure 3 to Stuart to Russell, 19 August 1862, Parliamentary Papers, *Correspondence Respecting Seizure of British Schooner Will-o'-Wisp by United States Ship Montgomery, at Matamoros, June 3 1862*, 1863 (3195), LXXII.513, No. 8, p. 10. Stuart was charge d'affaires at the British mission in Washington during Lyons' trip to Europe in summer 1862.
215. Russell to Stuart, 2 October 1862, *ibid.*, No. 12, p. 13.
216. Bernath, *Squall across the Atlantic*, pp. 39, 53.
217. Stuart to Russell, 8 August 1862, TNA, PRO/30/60/10.
218. Welles to Naval Commanders, 18 August 1862, printed in Welles, *Diary Vol. 1*, pp. 79–80.
219. Lyons to Seward, 24 November 1862, FRUS 1863 Vol. 1, p. 464.
220. Thomas J. Boynton to Seward, 6 January 1863, FRUS 1863 Vol. 1, p. 497.
221. Grazebrook made his offer on 20 May 1861. See Robinson, *Confederate Privateers*, p. 239.
222. House of Lords, 23 April 1863, Vol. 170, Col. 554–560.
223. *Ibid.*, Col. 560–566, 566.
224. *Ibid.*, Col. 571.
225. Hammond to Grazebrook, 24 April 1863, printed in *Liverpool Mercury*, 5 May 1863, Lyons to Seward, 29 April 1863, FRUS 1863 Vol. 1, p. 580.
226. Grazebrook's letter, dated 26 November 1862, was first leaked to the *Liverpool Mercury*, 30 April 1863, and reprinted, for example, in the *Caledonian Mercury*, 1 May 1863 and the *Daily News*, 5 May 1863.
227. The judgment of 25 May 1863 is reprinted in *Leeds Mercury*, 26 June 1863.
228. House of Lords, 18 May 1863, Vol. 170, Col. 1818–1826.
229. *Ibid.*, Col. 1826–1833, 1831.
230. House of Commons, 19 May 1863, Vol. 170, Col. 1987–1988.
231. Welles to Seward, 5 March 1864, enclosed in Seward to Lyons, 9 March 1864, FRUS 1864 Vol. 2, pp. 547–548.
232. Law Officers to Russell, 26 April 1864, TNA, FO/83/2221.
233. House of Lords, 18 May 1863, Vol. 170, Col. 1834.

234. An example of such a list, here including *Springbok* and *Peterhoff*, is F. H. Morse to Adams, 24 December 1862, FRUS 1863 Vol. 1, p. 51.
235. Milne to Stuart, 2 August 1862, printed as Enclosure 1 to Stuart to Russell, 8 August 1862, Parliamentary Papers, *Correspondence Respecting Instructions Given to Naval Officers of the United States in Regard to Neutral Vessels and Mails*, 1863 (3127), LXXII.447, No. 1, p. 1; Glen N. Wiche (ed.), *Dispatches from Bermuda: The Civil War Letters of Charles Maxwell Allen, United States Consul at Bermuda, 1861–1888*, Kent OH, 2008, *passim*.
236. House of Commons, 23 April 1863, Vol. 170, Col. 578.
237. Note that Russell was not afraid of a war with the USA should Britain be forced into one. See Russell to GC Lewis, 24 March 1863, TNA, PRO/30/22/31, f89.
238. *The Bermuda* – 70 U.S. 514 (1865), also available online at http://supreme. justia.com/cases/federal/us/70/514/case.html; *The Springbok* – 72 U.S. 1 (1866), also available online at http://supreme.justia.com/cases/federal/us/72/1/case. html#F2; *The Peterhoff* – 72 U.S. 28 (1866), also available online at http:// supreme.justia.com/cases/federal/us/72/28/case.html
239. See Bernath, *Squall across the Atlantic*, p. 66.
240. McPherson, *War on the Waters*, p. 128.
241. See Art. 22 (5), *Declaration Concerning the Laws of Naval War, 26 February 1909*, 208 Consol. T. S. 338 (1909). In Art. 24 (1) the declaration even allows food to be treated as contraband, something that the US prize courts never dared to do.
242. See Art. 31, 32, 34.
243. House of Commons, 17 March 1862, Vol. 165, Col. 1599–1703.
244. *Chicago Tribune*, 4 April 1862, p. 3.
245. *New York Times*, 2 April 1862, p. 4; 7 April 1862, p. 2.
246. Seward to Dayton, 8 April 1862, FRUS 1862, p. 329; Seward to Bradford Wood, 8 April 1862, NARA M77, Vol. 14, Roll 50.
247. *The Times*, 20 March 1862, p. 7.
248. Reprinted in *The Times*, 7 February 1862, p. 9. See also Laurent-Basile Hautefeuille, *Quelques Questions de Droit International Maritime: à propos de la Guerre d'Amérique*, Leipzig 1861; *ibid.*, *Nécessité d'une Loi Maritime pour regler les rapports des Neutres et des Belligerants*, Paris 1862.
249. *The Times*, 12 March 1863, p. 10.
250. Cobden to Henry Ashworth (Manchester Chamber of Commerce), 10 April 1862, printed in *The Times*, 18 April 1862, p. 10.
251. House of Lords, 6 February 1862, Vol. 165, Col. 35–36 (Derby), 41–42 (Granville).
252. House of Lords, 10 February 1862, Vol. 165, Col. 113–115.
253. House of Commons, 17 March 1862, Vol. 165, Col. 1699.
254. Adams to Seward, 20 March 1862, FRUS 1862, p. 50.
255. Gerolt to Bismarck, 30 December 1865, Bundesarchiv Lichterfelde, R 901/ 33573, f10.

7   'Announcing Our Withdrawal from the Declaration' – The Declaration of Paris and the Franco-German War of 1870

1. See Charles Iain Hamilton, *Anglo-French Naval Rivalry 1840–1870*, Oxford 1993.
2. Fiume Chamber of Commerce to Ministry of Trade, 5 March 1864; Börsen-Deputation of Trieste to Ministry of Trade, 1 April 1864, HHStA Vienna, Außenministerium, allgemeine Registratur, F36 (Schiffswesen), No. 7.

3. Ministry of Trade to Ministry of the Navy, 16 April 1864; Ministry of the Navy to Johann Bernhard von Rechberg, 21 April 1864, *ibid.*
4. Foreign Ministry memorandum, 25 April 1864, *ibid.*
5. Menshagen to Rechberg, 1 December 1864, *ibid.*
6. *Journal de Genève*, 28 December 1864.
7. Russell to Bonar, 13 February 1865, HHStA Vienna, Außenministerium, allgemeine Registratur, F36 (Schiffswesen), No. 7 (Copy).
8. Ministry of the Navy to Mensdorff-Pouilly, 26 April 1865, *ibid.*
9. Menshagen to Mensdorff-Pouilly, 20 December 1864, *ibid.*
10. See the Austrian decree of 13 May 1866, GStA Berlin, Vol. 2.4.1 Abt.I Haupt.II, MdAII, No.5568 'Blockade von Seehäfen, 1864–70', f38.
11. Decree of 19 May 1866, *ibid.*, f18.
12. Roon to Bismarck, 20 June 1866, *ibid.*, f57. Bismarck commented 'Lieber nicht' in a marginal.
13. Bismarck to Roon, 21 June 1866, *ibid.*, f58; Roon to Bismarck, 22 June 1866, Bundesarchiv Lichterfelde, R/901/33573, 'Das Seerecht der Neutralen, Januar 1866 bis Dezember 1872', f70.
14. Phillipsborn to Bismarck, 17 May 1866, *ibid.*, f15.
15. *New York Times*, 20 June 1866, p. 4. The Austrian decree had been published on 7 June 1866, p. 4.
16. Seward to Johannes Rösing, 18 August 1866, NARA, M99, Roll 57.
17. *The Times*, 25 May 1866, p. 5.
18. *The Times*, 23 May 1866, p. 9.
19. House of Commons, 31 May 1866, Vol. 183, Col. 1551–1552.
20. *The Times*, 23 June 1866, p. 9.
21. Fiume Chamber of Commerce to Ministry of Trade, 22 November 1866, HHStA Vienna, Aussenministerium, allgemeine Registratur, F36 (Schiffswesen), No. 8. They also demanded a precise definition of contraband and a prohibition of naval blockades of undefended ports, and many petitions from, for example, Trieste, Spalato, Bagusa, Vienna and Brünn supported all three points. See *ibid.*
22. Wüllerstorf-Urbair to Beust, 27 February 1867, *ibid.*
23. Roon to Bismarck, 21 May 1867, Bundesarchiv Lichterfelde, R/901/33573, f120.
24. Elders of the merchants of Danzig to Bismarck, 22 May 1867, *ibid.*, f122–129.
25. Bismarck to Roon, 30 May 1867, *ibid.*, f130, Bismarck to Gerolt, 30 May 1867, *ibid.*, f131.
26. Gerolt to Bismarck, 9 July 1867, *ibid.*, f146.
27. Bismarck to Roon, 27 July 1867, *ibid.*, f148.
28. Documents on the Italian initiative can be found in the same file. See in particular Bismarck's circular of 22 August 1867, f158. Half hearted Prussian requests for diplomatic assistance of the Italian campaign did not have any impact. See Werther to Beust, 26 August 1867, HHStA Vienna, Aussenministerium, allgemeine Registratur, F36 (Schiffswesen), No. 8.
29. Decree of 18 July 1870, printed in *Königlich Preußischer Staatsanzeiger*, 19 July 1870.
30. Fish to Gerolt, 22 July 1870, FRUS 1870, No. 172, pp. 217–218.
31. *Chicago Tribune*, 20 July 1870, p. 1.
32. Gerolt to Fish, 25 July 1870, Parliamentary Papers, *Further Correspondence respecting War between France and Prussia: 1870–71*, 1871 (C.244) LXXI.1, Enclosure 2 in No. 10, p. 10.
33. Granville to Bernstorff, 21 October 1870, printed in *ibid.*, No. 219, p. 161.

34. *Leeds Mercury*, 12 July 1870.
35. Berthemy to Fish, 3 August 1870, FRUS 1870, No. 100, p. 135.
36. Circular of 17 July 1870, AMAE, CP Prusse, Vol. 379, f284.
37. Michael Howard, *The Franco-Prussian War: The German Invasion of France, 1870–1871*, London 1961, p. 74; Geoffrey Wawro, *The Franco-Prussian War: The German Conquest of France in 1870–1871*, Cambridge 2003, p. 189.
38. Wawro, *Conquest*, p. 190, Howard, *Invasion*, p. 75.
39. British newspapers expected an announcement of the blockade shortly after hostilities had begun, *Belfast News-Letter*, 20 July 1870.
40. Bancroft to Fish, 1 September 1870, FRUS 1870, No. 157, pp. 204–205. The USA had only sent one warship to monitor the conflict, which was in the North Sea, *London Times*, 16 August 1870, p. 10.
41. Cited in Dora Neill Raymond, *British Policy and Opinion during the Franco-Prussian War*, New York, London 1921, p. 123.
42. House of Commons, 25 July 1870, Vol. 203, Col. 877.
43. The premium varied between 15,000 and 50,000 Thaler, depending on the size of the sunken vessel; see *Provinzial-Correspondenz*, Vol. 10 No. 26, 26 June 1872, the Royal Prussian Decree relative to the Creation of a Volunteer Naval Force of 24 July 1870 is printed in BFSP, Vol. 61, pp. 692–693. See also Sir Travers Twiss, *Belligerent Right on the High Seas, since the Declaration of Paris (1856)*, London 1884, p. 12.
44. The protest dated 20 August 1870 is printed in BFSP, Vol. 61, pp. 693–694.
45. Granville to Marquis de Lavalette, 24 August 1870, BFSP, Vol. 61, p. 694. Granville also sent a despatch to the North German government to remind it of its duties under the declaration, Granville to Loftus, 24 August 1870, *ibid.*, p. 695.
46. *Chicago Tribune*, 19 July 1870, p. 3.
47. Wawro, *Conquest*, p. 191.
48. Loftus to Granville, 30 July 1870, Parliamentary Papers, *Further Correspondence Respecting War between France and Prussia*, 1870 (C.210) LXX.115, No. 83, p. 72.
49. Granville to Loftus, 3 August 1870, BFSP, Vol. 60, p. 973. This stance was supported by the *Pall Mall Gazette*, 1 August 1870, and *The Times*, 8 October 1870, p. 6.
50. Bernstorff to Granville, 1 September 1870, Parliamentary Papers, *Further Correspondence Respecting War between France and Prussia: 1870–71*, 1871 (C.244) LXXI.1, No. 61, p. 38.
51. Granville to Bernstorff, 15 September 1870, *ibid.*, No. 132, p. 77.
52. *The Times*, 21 September 1870, p. 10.
53. *Leeds Mercury*, 7 September 1870; *The Times*, 20 September 1870, p. 8.
54. Bancroft to Fish, 22 September 1870, No. 137, NARA, M44, Vol. 17, Roll 16. This assessment was confirmed by Commander Breese of the USS *Plymouth* after he returned from his cruise of the Baltic, Bancroft to Fish, 13 October 1870, No. 150, *ibid.*
55. Bancroft to Fish, 22 August 1870, No. 125, NARA, M44, Vol. 17, Roll 16; *Leeds Mercury*, 8 September 1870.
56. Bancroft to Fish, 15 September 1870, telegram, NARA, M44, Vol. 17, Roll 16.
57. Wawro, *Conquest*, p. 192.
58. *Provinzial-Correspondenz*, Vol. 8, No. 38, 21 September 1870; *Times*, 21 September 1870, p. 10.
59. *Glasgow Herald*, 15 September 1870; Bancroft to Fish, 16 September 1870, FRUS 1870, No. 161, p. 207.

60. *The Times*, 19 September 1870, p. 7; 26 September 1870, p. 7.
61. *The Times*, 24 September 1870, p. 12.
62. *Pall Mall Gazette*, 30 August 1870; *The Times*, 5 September 1870, p. 7.
63. *The Times*, 2 August 1870, p.8: *Birmingham Daily Post*, 4 August 1870.
64. *The Times*, 5 September 1870, p. 6.
65. *The Times*, 17 September 1870, p. 11.
66. *Freeman's Journal and Daily Commercial Advertiser*, 22 August 1870.
67. *The Times*, 25 August 1870, p. 5.
68. Granville to Bernstorff, 15 September 1870, Parliamentary Papers, *Further Correspondence Respecting War between France and Prussia: 1870–71*, 1871 (C.244) LXXI.1, No. 132, p. 77.
69. Contemporaries were well aware that the French naval campaign would be a global one, see *The Times*, 20 July 1870, p. 9.
70. Klöbe to Bismarck, 16 August 1870, Bundesarchiv Lichterfelde, R/901/33621; Wagner to Auswärtiges Amt, 25 August 1870, *ibid*.
71. Haupt to Bismarck, 23 October 1870, *ibid.*; *Diario official do imperio do Brasil*, No. 238, 16 October 1870. p. 1.
72. *Diario official do imperio do Brasil*, No. 241, 20 October 1870, p. 3.
73. Haupt to Bismarck, 6 October 1870, Bundesarchiv Lichterfelde, R/901/33621.
74. Ritter von Tusswald to Beust, 27 August 1870, HHStA Vienna, Aussenministerium, allgemeine Registratur, F36 (Schiffswesen), No. 9.
75. Ministry of Justice to Beust, 8 November 1870, *ibid*.
76. Neutrality declaration of 22 August 1870, FRUS 1870, No. 1, p. 45.
77. *The Times*, 12 October 1870, p. 4. The excerpt from the article of the *New York Tribune* is printed on the same page.
78. Fish to Washburne, 4 October 1870, FRUS 1870, No. 37, p. 70–71. This despatch was later cited by Republicans in Congress to contrast the more relaxed approach towards Britain in 1915, as an example of how to deal properly with belligerent vessels cruising off the US coast. See *New York Times*, 19 January 1915.
79. Proclamation regulating the conduct of vessels of war of either belligerent in the waters within the territorial jurisdiction of the USA, 8 October 1870, FRUS 1870, No. 2, pp. 48–49.
80. Bancroft to Fish, 13 October 1870, No. 150, NARA, M44, Vol. 17, Roll 16.
81. On 21 June 1870, 22 Europeans had been killed, among them the French Consul.
82. Granville to Loftus, 21 October 1870, Enclosure to Bancroft to Fish, 3 November 1870, No. 158, NARA, M44, Vol. 17, Roll 16.
83. Bancroft to Fish, 2 November 1870, No. 157; Thiele to Granville, 2 November 1870, Enclosure to Bancroft to Fish, 3 November 1870, No. 158, *ibid*.
84. Bancroft to Fish, 16 November 1870, No. 162, NARA, M44, Vol. 18, Roll 17.
85. Bancroft to Fish, 19 December 1870, No. 172; Washburne to Bancroft, 9 December 1870, *ibid*.
86. Favre to Washburne, 5 December 1870, *ibid*.
87. The declaration published in Japan in August 1870 is printed as an annex of the despatch by De Long to Fish, 10 October 1870, FRUS 1870, No. 131, pp. 188–189.
88. Medhurst to Wade, 25 January 1871, Parliamentary Papers, *Correspondence Respecting Capture of Vessels, Sophie Rickmers and Robert Rickmers, in China Seas*, 1871 (C.131) LXXI.347, Inclosure 1 in No. 6, p. 8.
89. Rehfues to Bismarck, 13 August 1866, Bundesarchiv Lichterfelde, R/901/33573, f105.
90. Rehfues to Bismarck, 27 December 1870, Bundesarchiv Lichterfelde, R/901/33623.
91. Bismarck to Fabrice, 10 April 1871, *ibid*.

92. *Norddeutsche Zeitung*, 30 September 1870.
93. Bismarck to Government of National Defence, 9 October 1870, Bundesarchiv Lichterfelde, R/901/33621.
94. Chaudordy (on authorisation of the Foreign Minister) to Bismarck, 28 October 1870, *ibid*.
95. Bismarck to Government of National Defence, 16 November 1870, *ibid*.
96. Wilke to Bismarck, 25 October 1870, Bundesarchiv Lichterfelde, R/901/33621. The despatch includes a *Daily News* article of the same day.
97. Declaration of Pilot William Donness of Leith, 5 November 1870, *ibid*.
98. Bernstorff to Granville, 8 November 1870, *ibid*. The German complaint was widely reported – for example, in the *Belfast Newsletter* and the *Glasgow Herald*, 12 November 1870.
99. Bernstorff to Bismarck, 14 November 1870, *ibid*.
100. Circular by Bismarck, 23 November 1870, *ibid*. See also Bismarck to Schweinitz, 22 November 1870, HHStA Vienna, Aussenministerium, allgemeine Registratur, F36 (Schiffswesen), No. 9.
101. The report by Commander Chevalier, dated 31 October, as well as the letter to the Navy Minister of the same day can be found in Vincennes, FF^{2}239.
102. The order is an undated marginal written on the letter of the maritime prefect cited previously.
103. Consul General Wilke had sent a report by the Consul in Newcastle about alleged burnings by the *Hortense* (renamed *Kleber*), Wilke to Bismarck, 29 October 1870, Bundesarchiv Lichterfelde, R/901/33621.
104. Note dated 3 December 1870, *ibid*., R/901/33622.
105. This suspicion was correct: the Aviso *Jerome Napoleon* had been renamed after the revolutionary general Louis Charles Antoine Desaix. See the *Preston Guardian*, 1 October 1870.
106. Hormoz to Favre, 28 December 1870, Vincennes FF^{2}235.
107. Hormoz to Navy Minister Fourichon, 28 December 1870, *ibid*.
108. Jonathan Steinberg, *Bismarck – A Life*, Oxford 2011, pp. 298–301; Howard, *Invasion*, p. 353f; Wawro, *Conquest*, p. 280.
109. Bismarck to Favre (via Washburne), 29 December 1870, Vincennes, CC^{4}1251 (confusingly, inside a folder titled 'Documents on the war of 1877').
110. Circular by Bismarck, 9 January 1871, Parliamentary Papers, *Further Correspondence Respecting War between France and Prussia: 1870–71*, 1871 (C.244) LXXI.1, No. 326, p. 252; printed in *Daily News* and *Times*, 16 January 1871, p. 9.
111. *New York Times*, 14 January 1871, p. 1.
112. Reichsgesetzblatt, Vol. 1, No. 4 (1871), p. 8. The decree was published in Britain shortly afterwards, *The Times*, 8 February 1871, p. 6.
113. Bernstorff to Bismarck, 23 November 1870, Bundesarchiv Lichterfelde, R/901/33621.
114. Granville to Bernstorff, 6 December 1870, Bundesarchiv Lichterfelde, R/901/33622.
115. Bismarck to Bernstorff, 22 December 1870, *ibid*.
116. Bernstorff to Bismarck, 6 January 1871, *ibid*.
117. See his letter to the Prussian Minister in Denmark, 11 April 1864, complaining about the lack of stationary vessels at port entrances, particularly at Swinemünde, GStA Berlin, Vol 2.4.1 Abt. I Haupt. II, MdA. II, No. 5568 'Blockade von Seehäfen, 1864–70', f4.

118. Excerpt of Bernstorff's report of 19 June 1864, printed in APP, Vol. 5, p. 246, fn. 1.
119. Bernstorff to Bismarck, 22 June 1864, *ibid.*, No. 167, p. 244; 23 June 1864, No. 169, p. 246.
120. Bismarck to Bernstorff, 24 June 1864; 28 June 1864; Bernstorff to Bismarck, 25 June 1864, *ibid.*, pp. 247–248, fn. 4.
121. Bismarck to Bernstorff, 12 January 1871, Bundesarchiv Lichterfelde, R/901/33622.
122. Bernstorff to Granville, 13 January 1871, *ibid.*
123. Granville to Bernstorff, 3 February 1871, *ibid.*
124. Bernstorff to Bismarck, 11 February 1871, *ibid.*
125. Granville to Bernstorff, 21 February 1871; Bernstorff to Bismarck, 25 February 1871, *ibid.*
126. Bismarck to Bernstorff, 20 February 1871, *ibid.* The correspondence was printed in the *Norddeutsche Zeitung*, 14 March 1871. It was also used in a strongly anti-British pamphlet. See Julius Hopf, *Die Wegnahme der "Frei" in britischem Gewässer*, Gotha 1871.
127. House of Commons, 17 February 1871, Vol. 204, Col. 387–396, 396–408, 447–455.
128. Treaty of Washington, 8 May 1871, Martens NRG, Vol. 20, p. 698.
129. Handwritten note dated 22 August 1872, on a protocol dated 18 August 1872, Bundesarchiv Lichterfelde, R/901/33573, f250.
130. For the Dutch proposal see *The Times*, 6 March 1871, p. 5. Among the many German pamphlets that demanded utilising the victory in this way was Heinrich Tecklenborg, *Die Freiheit des Meeres – Verbesserungsvorschläge zum Staatsvertrage über das Seerecht in Kriegszeiten geschlossen am 16. April 1856 zu Paris*, Bremen 1870, which the author (the president of the German Nautical Association) sent directly to Bismarck, 10 October 1870, Bundesarchiv Lichterfelde, R/901/33573, f186. Cf. the petition by the association, Tecklenborg to Bismarck, 11 March 1871, f215.
131. *Pall Mall Gazette*, 1 February 1871.
132. *New York Times*, 17 November 1870, p. 4; 3 December 1870, p. 4.
133. *The Times*, 15 December 1870, p. 9.
134. House of Commons, 21 April 1871, Vol. 205, Col. 1469–1478; 1479–1483; 1497.
135. *Ibid.*, 1487–1489; 1499.
136. *Pall Mall Gazette*, 22 April 1871; *New York Times*, 22 April 1871, p. 1.
137. *The Times*, 22 April 1871, p. 9. This stance was supported by the *Liverpool Mercury*, 24 April 1871.
138. *Pall Mall Gazette*, 14 March 1871.
139. House of Lords, 19 June 1871, Vol. 207, Col. 197ff.
140. *Ibid.*, 203–205.
141. *Ibid.*, 205–206.
142. *Chicago Tribune*, 20 June 1871, p. 1; *New York Times*, 20 June 1871, p. 1.
143. *The Times*, 20 June 1871, p. 9.

Conclusion: The Rise and Fall of the Declaration of Paris

1. Piggott, *Declaration of Paris*; Anderson, *Liberal State at War*.
2. See most recently Andrew Lambert, 'The Royal Navy and the Defence of Empire, 1856–1919', in Greg Kennedy (ed.), *Imperial Defence: The Old World Order 1856–1956*, London 2008, pp. 111–132.
3. Declaration of 28 March 1854, BFSP, Vol. 46, p. 36.

4. Clarendon to Cowley, 13 March 1854, AGKK III/2, No. 155, pp. 280–282.
5. Clarendon to Cowley, 2 November 1855, TNA, FO/27/1059.
6. Note confidentielle pour le Ministre d'affaires étrangères, 17 November 1855, Vincennes, CC⁴1251.
7. 'L'Angleterre et la déclaration de Paris du 16 Avril 1856', undated memorandum, AMAE, Memoires et documents, France, Vol. 2117, 'Congrès de Paris, 1856: Pièces diverses', f37.
8. Palmerston to Clarendon, 5 April 1856, AGKK III/4, No. 609, p. 964; Cabinet Minutes respecting the Declaration of Paris of 1856, TNA, FO/881/5104.
9. Congress protocol of 8 April 1856, Martens NRG, Vol. 15, p. 757.
10. Cass to Mason, 27 June 1859, No. 190, NARA, M77, Vol. 15, Roll 55.
11. Andrew Lambert, 'Great Britain and Maritime Law from the Declaration of Paris to the Era of Total War', in Rolf Hobson and Tom Kristiansen (eds.), *Navies in Northern Waters 1721–2000*, London 2004, pp. 11–40, pp. 14–16.
12. John Louis O'Sullivan to Marcy, 20 July 1856, No. 39, NARA, M43, Vol. 17.
13. Ethan A. Nadelmann, 'Global Prohibition Regimes: The Evolution of Norms in International Society', *International Organization*, Vol. 44, No. 4 (Autumn 1990), pp. 479–526. For a similar contemporary view, see *La Presse*, 19 June 1856, p. 1.
14. Bernstorff to Bismarck, 22 June 1864, APP, Vol. 5, No. 167, p. 244; 23 June 1864, No. 169, p. 246.
15. Protocol No. 24, 16 April 1856, Martens NRG, Vol. 15, pp. 768–769. Those criticising the regime included liberals such as Richard Cobden, as well as many Conservatives.
16. Lyons to Russell. 20 July 1861, TNA, FO/5/768, No. 363.
17. The USA had attempted to join but withdrew its application after it had become clear that Britain and France were unwilling to treat the Southern privateers as pirates.
18. McPherson, *Battle Cry of Freedom*, p. 386; Bernath, *Squall across the Atlantic*, p. 12.
19. House of Lords, 18 May 1863, Vol. 170, Col. 1826–1833, 1831.
20. Menshagen to Mensdorff-Pouilly, 20 December 1864, HHStA Vienna, Außenministerium, allgemeine Registratur, F36 (Schiffswesen), No. 7.
21. See the Austrian decree of 13 May 1866 and the Prussian decree of 19 May, GStA Berlin, Vol. 2.4.1 Abt. I, Haupt. II, MdA. II, No. 5568 'Blockade von Seehäfen, 1864–70', f18, 38.
22. Treaty of Commerce and Navigation of 26 February 1871, Art. XII, printed in Freeman Snow, *Treaties and Topics in American Diplomacy*, Boston 1894, p. 127.
23. Berthemy to Fish, 3 August 1870, FRUS 1870, No. 100, p. 135.
24. Granville to Marquis de Lavalette, 24 August 1870, BFSP, Vol. 61, p. 694. The Royal Prussian Decree relative to the Creation of a Volunteer Naval Force of 24 July 1870 is printed in BFSP, Vol. 61, pp. 692–693.
25. See the report by the *Desaix's* commander, dated 31 October, Vincennes FF²239.
26. Bismarck to Favre, 29 December 1870, Vincennes, CC⁴1251 (confusingly, inside a folder titled 'Documents on the war of 1877').
27. Bismarck to Bernstorff, 22 December 1870; Bernstorff to Bismarck, 6 January 1871, Bundesarchiv Lichterfelde, R/901/33622.
28. Handwritten note dated 22 August 1872, on a protocol dated 18 August 1872, Bundesarchiv Lichterfelde, R/901/33573, f250.
29. For this reason this book takes a different stance from Maartje Abbenhuis, who describes Bismarck's attitude as one of general disrespect for neutral rights and international law. See her recent article 'A Most Useful Tool for Diplomacy and

Statecraft: Neutrality and Europe in the "Long" Nineteenth Century, 1815–1914'
International History Review, Vol. 35, No. 1 (2013), pp. 1–22, pp. 11–12.

30. Reuß to Bülow, 21 November 1877, Bundesarchiv Lichterfelde, R/901/33628, f53.
31. Wickham Hoffman to William Evarts, 24 April 1878, No. 30, NARA, M35, Vol. 33.
32. See Matthew McCarthy's recent study, *Privateering, Piracy & British Policy in Spanish America, 1810–1830*, Woodbridge 2013.
33. Chilean Declaration of 26 September 1865, attached to a despatch from the French legation in Santiago to Drouyn de Lhuys, 9 October 1865, No. 67, AMAE, Correspondence Politique Chili Vol. 17.
34. William F. Sater, *Andean Tragedy: Fighting the War of the Pacific, 1879–1884*, Lincoln, NE 2007, p. 102/3.
35. Granville to Bernstorff, 15 September 1870, Parliamentary Papers, *Further Correspondence Respecting War between France and Prussia: 1870–71*, 1871 (C.244) LXXI.1, No. 132, p. 77: 'But if this principle were admitted, where is it to stop?'.
36. See the circular by French Foreign Minister Ferry, 20 February 1885, printed in: Ministère des Affaires Etrangères, *Documentes diplomatiques: Affaires du Chine*, Paris 1885, No. 14, p. 17.
37. Granville to Waddington, 27 February 1885, *ibid.*, No. 21, p. 30; Hochschild to D'Aunay, 4 March 1885, No. 25, p. 36; Rosenörn-Lehn to de Croy, 16 March 1885, No. 29, p. 43.
38. Arne Roksund, *The Jeune École: Strategy of the Weak*, Leiden 2007.
39. Sakuye Takahashi, *Cases on International Law During the China-Japanese War*, Cambridge 1899.
40. Nicholas Lambert, *Planning Armageddon: British Economic Warfare and the First World War*, Cambridge MA 2012, p. 84, 113.
41. The excellent article by Christopher Martin clarifies Fisher's real views and influence, 'The Declaration of London: A Matter of Operational Capability', *Historical Research*, Vol. 82, No. 218 (November 2009), pp. 731–755.
42. The idea was strongly rejected, Memorandum by Cecil Hurst (Foreign Office Legal Adviser), 16 February 1912, and Minute by Sir Eyre Crowe, 10 March 1912, printed in George Peabody Gooch and Harold Temperley, *British Documents on the Origins of the War, 1898–1914, Vol. VIII*, London 1932, No. 320, p. 391, No. 321, p. 392.
43. See Lambert, *Planning Armageddon;* but also Offer, *First World War.*
44. John Coogan, *The End of Neutrality: The United States, Britain, and Maritime Rights, 1899–1915*, Ithaca 1981.
45. See the correspondence in TNA, ADM/167/54, f262f.
46. Stephen Wertheim, 'The League That Wasn't: American Designs for a Legalist-Sanctionist League of Nations and the Intellectual Origins of International Organization, 1914–1920', *Diplomatic History*, Vol. 35, No. 5 (2011), pp. 797–836.
47. Leonard V. Smith, 'The Wilsonian Challenge to International Law', *The Journal of the History of International Law*, Vol. 13 (2011), pp. 179–208.
48. Article X says:

The Members of the League undertake to respect and preserve as against external aggression the territorial integrity and existing political independence of all Members of the League. In case of any such aggression or in case of any threat or danger of such aggression the Council shall advise upon the means by which this obligation shall be fulfilled.

Bibliography

a. Archives

Archive du Ministère des Affaires Étrangères, Quai d'Orsay (now relocated to La Courneuve), Paris, France [AMAE]
Archive of the Bremen Chamber of Commerce, Germany [ABCC]
Bodleian Library, Oxford [Bodleian]
British Library, London [BL]
Bundesarchiv Berlin-Lichterfelde, Germany [Bundesarchiv Lichterfelde]
Centre Historique de la Défense Vincennes, Archives Centrales de la Marine, Paris, France [Vincennes]
Geheimes Staatsarchiv Preußischer Kulturbesitz, Berlin-Dahlem, Germany [GStA Berlin]
Haus- Hof- und Staatsarchiv Vienna, Austria [HHStA Vienna]
Library of Congress, Washington DC, USA [LoC]
National Archive and Record Administration II, College Park, Maryland, USA [NARA]
Roosevelt Study Centre (microfilm archive), Middelburg, Netherlands [RSC]
State Archive Bremen, Germany [StAB]
The National Archives, Kew Garden, London [TNA]

b. Databases

19th Century British Library Newspapers (Gale Databases)
Abraham Lincoln Papers at the Library of Congress, Manuscript Division, American Memory Project, http://memory.loc.gov/ammem/alhtml/malhome.html
Historical Newspapers (New York Times, Chicago Tribune) (Proquest Databases)
House of Commons Parliamentary Papers (Proquest Databases)
The Economist Historical Archive 1843–2003 (Gale Databases)
The Times Digital Archive 1785–1985 (Gale Databases)

c. Source Collections

Aegidi, Ludwig Karl and Klauhold, Alfred, *Frei Schiff unter Feindes Flagge*, Hamburg 1866
Akten zur Geschichte des Krimkriegs [AGKK], Series I-V, edited by Winfried Baumgart, Munich 1979ff

I.   *Österreichische Akten zur Geschichte des Krimkriegs, Vol. 3*, edited by Winfried Baumgart, Munich 1979
II. *Preußische Akten zur Geschichte des Krimkriegs, Vol. 1*, edited by Winfried Baumgart and Ana Maria Schop Soler, Munich 1991; *Vol. 2*, edited by Winfried Baumgart, Wolfgang Elz and Werner Zürrer, Munich 1990
III. *Englische Akten zur Geschichte des Krimkriegs, Vol. 1*, edited by Winfried Baumgart, Munich 2005; *Vol. 2*, edited by Winfried Baumgart, Munich 2006; *Vol. 3*, edited by Winfried Baumgart and Martin Senner, Munich 1994; *Vol. 4*, edited by Winfried Baumgart and Wolfgang Elz, Munich 1988

IV. *Französische Akten zur Geschichte des Krimkriegs, Vol. 1*, edited by Winfried Baumgart, Munich 2003; *Vol. 2*, edited by Martin Senner, Munich 1999; *Vol. 3*, edited by Martin Senner, Munich 2001

Basler, Roy P. (ed.), *The Collected Works of Abraham Lincoln, Volume IV*, New Brunswick, NJ 1953

British and Foreign State Papers [BFSP], Compiled by the Librarian and Keeper of the Papers, Foreign Office, London 1801–

Die Auswärtige Politik Preußens 1858–1871 [APP], edited by the Historische Reichskommission, 11 Bände, Oldenburg 1933ff

Georg Friedrich von Martens *Nouveau Recueil General de Traites* [Martens NRG], edited by G. F. V. Martens, Ch. de Martens, F. Saalfeld and F. Murhard, Göttingen 1839–74, 10 Volumes

Gooch, George Peabody and Temperley, Harold, *British Documents on the Origins of the War, 1898–1914, Vol. VIII*, London 1932

Hansard's Parliamentary Debates, Third Series, Commencing with the Accession of William IV. Comprising the Period from October 26, 1830, to August 5, 1891 [House of Commons or House of Lords], London 1831–91, 356 Volumes

Marx, Karl and Engels, Friedrich, *Werke*, Vol. 15.4 [MEW], Berlin 1961

Ministère des Affaires Etrangères, *Documentes diplomatiques: Affaires du Chine*, Paris 1885

Papers Relating to the Foreign Relations of the United States, with the Annual Message of the President, [FRUS means Vol. 1 (1861), all other volumes are indicated by year], Volume 1 (1861)–

Soetbeer, Adolph (ed.), *Sammlung officieller Actenstücke in Bezug auf Schiffahrt und Handel in Kriegszeiten, Vol. III*, Hamburg 1854

'The Confederacy and the Declaration of Paris', *American Historical Review*, Vol. 23, No. 4 (July 1918), pp. 826–835

Tracy, Nicholas (ed.), *Sea Power and the Control of Trade: Belligerent Rights from the Russian War to the Beira Patrol, 1854–1970*, Aldershot 2005

Walewski, Alexandre, *Rapport a L'Empereur sur la Publication des notes officielles portant accession a la declaration du congrès de paris du 16 avril 1856, relative au droit maritime on temps du guerre*, Paris 1858

Welles, Edgar Thadeus, *The Diary of Gideon Welles, Vol. 1*, Boston 1911

d. Pre-1914 Pamphlets, Books and Articles

Asher, Carl Wilhelm, *German Resolutions and British Policy: Observations on the Past, Present and Future of International Law*, Hamburg 1860

Danson, John Towne, 'Our Commerce with Russia, in Peace and War', *Journal of the Statistical Society of London*, Vol. 17, No. 3 (September 1854), pp. 193–218

Drouyn de Lhuys, Edouard, 'Les Neutres Pendant la Guerre d'Orient', *Revue Maritime et Coloniale*, Vol. 23 (1868), pp. 658–668

Hautefeuille, Laurent-Basile, *Nécessité d'une Loi Maritime pour regler les rapports des Neutres et des Belligerants*, Paris 1862

Hautefeuille, Laurent-Basile, *Quelques Questions de Droit International Maritime: à propos de la Guerre d'Amérique*, Leipzig 1861

Hopf, Julius, *Die Wegnahme der "Frei" in britischem Gewässer*, Gotha 1871

Jomini, Antoine-Henri, *Diplomatic Study of the Crimean War, Volume II*, London 1882

Napier, Charles, *The History of the Baltic Campaign of 1854*, London 1857

Scharf, Thomas, *The Confederate States Navy, Vol. I*, New York 1887
Stark, Francis Raymond, *The Abolition of Privateering and the Declaration of Paris*, New York 1897
Takahashi, Sakuye, *Cases on International Law During the China-Japanese War*, Cambridge 1899
Tecklenborg, Heinrich, *Die Freiheit des Meeres –Verbesserungsvorschläge zum Staatsvertrage über das Seerecht in Kriegszeiten geschlossen am 16. April 1856 zu Paris*, Bremen 1870
Twiss, Sir Travers, *Belligerent Right on the High Seas, since the Declaration of Paris (1856)*, London 1884
Walewski, Alexandre, *L'Alliance Anglaise*, Paris 1838

e. Books

Anderson, Olive, *A Liberal State at War: English Politics and Economics During the Crimean War*, London 1967
Angelow, Jürgen, *Von Wien nach Königgrätz – Die Sicherheitspolitik des Deutschen Bundes im europäischen Gleichgewicht 1815–1866*, Munich 1996
Baumgart, Winfried, *Der Friede von Paris 1856. Studien zum Verhältnis von Kriegführung, Politik und Friedensbewahrung*, Munich 1972
Baumgart, Winfried, *The Crimean War 1853–1856*, London 1999
Bernath, Stuart L., *Squall across the Atlantic: American Civil War Prize Cases and Diplomacy*, Berkeley 1970
Best, Heinrich and Wege, Wilhelm, *Biographisches Handbuch der Abgeordneten der Frankfurter Nationalversammlung 1848–49*, Düsseldorf 1996
Bringmann, Tobias C., *Handbuch der Diplomatie 1815–1963*, Munich 2001
Bruce, Antony and Cogar, William, *An Encyclopedia of Naval Warfare*, Chicago and London 1998
Case, Lynn Marshall and Spencer, Warren F., *The United States and France: Civil War Diplomacy*, Philadelphia 1970
Chesney, Kellow, *The Crimean War Reader*, London 1960
Conacher, James B., *Britain and the Crimea, 1855–56: Problems of War and Peace*, Basingstoke 1987
Coogan, John W, *The End of Neutrality: The United States, Britain and Maritime Rights 1899–1915*, Ithaca 1981
Curtiss, John Shelton, *Russia's Crimean War*, Durham NC 1979
Donald, David Herbert, *Charles Sumner, Vol. II*, New York 1996
Dowty, Alan, *The Limits of American Isolation: The United States and the Crimean War*, New York 1971
Echard, William E., *Napoleon III and the Concert of Europe*, London 1983
Ferris, Norman B., *Desperate Diplomacy, William H. Seward's Foreign Policy, 1861*, Knoxville, TS 1976
Foreman, Amanda, *A World on Fire*, London 2011
Gillespie, Alexander, *A History of the Laws of War* (3 volumes), Oxford 2011
Hamilton, Charles Iain, *Anglo-French Naval Rivalry 1840–1870*, Oxford 1993
Hobson, Rolf, *Imperialism at Sea: Naval Strategic Thought, the Ideology of Sea Power, and the Tirpitz Plan, 1875–1914*, Boston 2002
Howard, Michael, *The Franco-Prussian War: The German Invasion of France, 1870–1871*, London 1961

Huber, Ernst Rudolf, *Dokumente zur deutschen Verfassungsgeschichte*, Vol. 1, Stuttgart 1978

Jenkins, Brian, *Britain and the War for the Union*, Vol. 1, Montreal 1974

Jenkins, Brian, *Britain and the War for the Union*, Vol. 2, Montreal 1980 (only the first volume is currently cited)

Jones, Howard, *Blue and Gray Diplomacy: A History of Union and Confederate Foreign Relations*, Chapel Hill, NC 2010

Kennedy, Paul, *The Rise and Fall of British Naval Mastery*, London 1976

Koskeniemi, Martti, *The Gentle Civilizer of Nations: The Rise and Fall of International Law 1870–1960*, Cambridge 2004

Lambert, Andrew, *Crimean War – British Grand Strategy, 1853–1856*, Manchester 1990

Lambert, Nicholas, *Planning Armageddon: British Economic Warfare and the First World War*, Cambridge, MA 2012

Maischak, Lars, *German Merchants in the Nineteenth-Century Atlantic*, Cambridge 2013

McCarthy, Matthew, *Privateering, Piracy & British Policy in Spanish America, 1810–1830*, Woodbridge 2013

McPherson, James, *The Battle Cry of Freedom: The Civil War Era*, New York 1988

McPherson, James, *War on the Waters: The Union and Confederate Navies*, Chapel Hill, NC 2012

Merli, Frank J., *The Alabama, British Neutrality and the American Civil War*, Bloomington 2004

Metzler, Gabriele, *Grossbritannien, Weltmacht in Europa: Handelspolitik im Wandel des europäischen Staatensystems 1856 bis 1871*, Berlin 1997

Miller, David Hunter, *Treaties and other International Acts of the USA*, Vol. VI, Washington 1942

Mitchell, Brian, *European Historical Statistics 1750–1975 (Second revised edition)*, New York 1980

Neff, Stephen, *War and the Law of Nations: A General History*, Cambridge 2005

Neff, Stephen, *Justice in Blue and Gray*, London 2010

O'Connell, Mary Ellen, *The Power and Purpose of International Law*, Oxford 2008

Offer, Avner, *The First World War: An Agrarian Interpretation*, Oxford 1989

Owsley, Frank Lawrence, *King Cotton Diplomacy: Foreign Relations of the Confederate States of America*, Chicago 1959

Piggott, Sir Francis, *The Declaration of Paris 1856. A Study, Documented*, London 1919

Pitt, M. R., 'Great Britain and Belligerent Maritime Rights from the Declaration of Paris, 1856, to the Declaration of London, 1909', PhD thesis (London School of Economics) 1964

Raymond, Dora Neill, *British Policy and Opinion during the Franco Prussian War*, New York and London 1921

Roberts, Adam and Guelff, Richard (eds.), *Documents on the Laws of War*, Oxford 2000

Robinson, William, *The Confederate Privateers*, New Haven 1928

Roksund, Arne, *The Jeune École: Strategy of the Weak*, Leiden 2007

Ronzitti, Natalino (ed.), *The Law of Naval Warfare: A Collection of Agreements and Documents with Commentaries*, Dordrecht, Boston and London 1988

Sampson, Robert, *John L. O'Sullivan and His Times*, Kent, Ohio 2003

Sater, William F., *Andean Tragedy: Fighting the War of the Pacific, 1879–1884*, Lincoln, NE 2007

Saul, Norman E., *Distant Friends – The United States and Russia, 1763–1867*, Lawrence, KS 1991

Schröder, Klaus Peter, *Das Alte Reich und seine Städte*, Munich 1991

Schulz, Andreas, *Vormundschaft und Protektion – Eliten und Bürger in Bremen 1750–1880*, Munich 2002

Schwarzwälder, Herbert, *Geschichte der Freien Hansestadt Bremen, Vol. II*, Bremen 1995

Seaton, Albert, *The Crimean War – A Russian Chronicle*, London 1977

Semmel, Bernard, *Liberalism and Naval Strategy – Ideology, Interest and Seapower during the Pax Britannica*, London 1986

Snow, Freeman, *Treaties and Topics in American Diplomacy*, Boston 1894

Steinberg, Jonathan, *Bismarck – A Life*, Oxford 2011

Surdam, David G., *Northern Naval Superiority and the Economics of the American Civil War*, Columbia, SC 2001

Taylor, John M., *William Henry Seward – Lincoln's Right Hand*, New York 1991

Tucker, Spencer, *A Short History of the Civil War at Sea*, Wilmington 2002

Tucker, Spencer, *Blue and Gray Navies–The Civil War Afloat*, Annapolis, MD 2006

US Bureau of the Census, *Historical statistics of the United States – Colonial Times to 1957*, Washington 1960

Wawro, Geoffrey, *The Franco-Prussian War: The German Conquest of France in 1870–1871*, Cambridge 2003

Wiche, Glen N. (ed.), *Dispatches from Bermuda: The Civil War Letters of Charles Maxwell Allen, United States Consul at Bermuda, 1861–1888*, Kent, OH 2008

Wiedemann, Hans, *Die Außenpolitik Bremens im Zeitalter der Französischen Revolution 1794–1803*, Bremen 1960

f. Articles

Abbenhuis, Maartje, 'A Most Useful Tool for Diplomacy and Statecraft: Neutrality and Europe in the "long" Nineteenth Century, 1815–1914', *International History Review*, Vol. 35 No. 1 (2013), pp. 1–22

Anderson, Gary and Gifford Jr., Adam, 'Privateering and the Private Production of Naval Power', *Cato Journal*, Vol. 11 (Spring and Summer 1991), pp. 99–122

Anderson, Olive, 'Some Further Light on the Inner History of the Declaration of Paris', *Law Quarterly Review*, Vol. 76 (1960), pp. 379–385

Baxter III, James, 'Some British Opinions as to Neutral Rights, 1861–1865', *American Journal of International Law*, Vol. 23, No. 3 (July 1929), pp. 517–537

Baxter III, James, 'The British Government and Neutral Rights, 1861–1865', *American Historical Review*, Vol. 34 (October 1928), pp. 9–29

Becker-Lorca, Arnulf, 'Universal International Law: Nineteenth Century Histories of Imposition and Appropriation', *Harvard International Law Journal*, Vol. 50, No. 2 (Summer 2010), pp. 475–552

Bourne, Kenneth, 'British Preparations for War with the North, 1861–2', *English Historical Review*, Vol. 76 (1961), pp. 600–632

Bourne, Kenneth, 'Lord Palmerston's "Ginger-beer" Triumph, 1 July 1856', in Bourne, Kenneth and Watt, D. C. (eds.), *Studies in International History*, London 1967, pp. 145–171

Bowden, Brett, 'The Colonial Origins of International Law. European Expansion and the Classical Standard of Civilization', *The Journal of the History of International Law*, Vol. 7, No. 1 (2005), pp. 1–24

Conze, Eckhart, 'Wer von Europa spricht, hat Unrecht: Aufstieg und Verfall des vertragsrechtlichen Multilateralismus im europäischen Staatensystem des 19. Jahrhunderts', *Historisches Jahrbuch*, Vol. 121 (2001), pp. 214–241

Drolet, Michael, 'Industry, Class and Society: A Historiographic Reinterpretation of Michel Chevalier', *English Historical Review*, Vol. 123, No. 504 (October 2008), pp. 1229–1271

Focarelli, Carlo, 'Review of O'Connel: The Power and Purpose of International Law', *European Journal of International Law*, Vol. 20 (2009), pp. 957–961, p. 957

Golder, Frank A., 'Russian-American Relations During the Crimean War', *American Historical Review*, Vol. 31, No. 3 (April 1926), pp. 462–476

Gough, Barry M., 'The Crimean War in the Pacific: British Strategy and Naval Operations', *Military Affairs*, Vol. 37, No. 4 (1973), pp. 130–136

Gray, William, 'American Diplomacy in Venezuela 1835–1865', *Hispanic American Historical Review*, Vol. 20, No. 4 (November 1940), pp. 551–574

Hamilton, Charles Iain, 'Anglo-French Seapower and the Declaration of Paris', *International History Review*, Vol. 4, No. 2 (May 1982), pp. 166–190

Hamilton, Charles Iain, 'Sir James Graham, the Baltic Campaign and War-Planning at the Admiralty in 1854', *Historical Journal*, Vol. 19, No. 1 (March 1976), pp. 89–112

Harley, Charles K., 'The Shift from Sailing Ships to Steamships, 1850–1890: A Study in Technical Change and its Diffusion', in Donald N. McCloskey (ed.), *Essays on a Mature Economy: Britain after 1840*, Princeton 1971, pp. 215–234

Henderson, Gavin B., 'Problems of Neutrality, 1854: Documents from the Hamburg Staatsarchiv', *Journal of Modern History*, Vol. 10, No. 2 (June 1938), pp. 232–241

Hobson, Rolf, 'Prussia, Germany and Maritime Law from Armed Neutrality to Unlimited Submarine Warfare 1780–1917', in Hobson, Rolf and Kristiansen, Tom (eds.), *Navies in Northern Waters, 1721–2000*, London 2004, pp. 97–116

Janis, M. W., 'Jeremy Bentham and the Fashioning of "International Law" ', *American Journal of International Law*, Vol. 78, No. 2 (April 1984), pp. 405–418

Lambert, Andrew, 'Great Britain and Maritime Law from the Declaration of Paris to the Era of Total War', in Rolf Hobson and Tom Kristiansen (eds.), *Navies in Northern Waters: 1721–2000*, London 2004, pp. 11–40

Lambert, Andrew, 'The Crimean War Blockade, 1854–1856', in Elleman, Bruce and Paine, S. C. M. (eds.), *Naval Blockades and Seapower – Strategies and Counter-Strategies, 1805–2005*, Abingdon 2005, pp. 46–61

Lambert, Andrew, 'The Royal Navy and the Defence of Empire,1856–1919', in Kennedy, Greg (ed.), *Imperial Defence: The Old World Order 1856–1956*, London 2008, pp. 111–132

Lemnitzer, Jan Martin, 'A few burghers in a little Hanseatic town – Die Bremer Seerechtskampagne von 1859', *Bremisches Jahrbuch*, Vol. 83 (2004), pp. 85–109

Malkin, William, 'The Inner History of the Declaration of Paris', *British Yearbook of International Law*, Vol. 8 (1927), pp. 1–44

Martin, Christopher, 'The Declaration of London. A Matter of Operational Capability', *Historical Research*, Vol. 82, No. 218 (November 2009), pp. 731–755

Nadelmann, Ethan A., 'Global Prohibition Regimes: The Evolution of Norms in International Society', *International Organization*, Vol. 44, No. 4 (Autumn 1990), pp. 479–526

O'Connor, Damian, 'Privateers, Cruisers and Colliers: The Limits of International Maritime Law in the Nineteenth Century', *RUSI Journal*, Vol. 150, No. 1 (February 2005), pp. 70–75

O'Malley, Pat, 'The Discipline of Violence: State, Capital and the Regulation of Naval Warfare', *Sociology*, Vol. 22, No. 2 (May 1988), pp. 253–270

Parillo, Nicholas, 'The De-Privatization of American Warfare: How the U. S. Government Used, Regulated, and Ultimately Abandoned Privateering in the Nineteenth

Century', *Yale Journal of Law & The Humanities*, Vol. 19, No. 1 (Winter 2007), pp. 1–95

Saurer, Edith, 'Der Kongreß findet nicht statt. Der Kongreßplan von 1859', *Römische Historische Mitteilungen*, Vol. 11 (1969), pp. 110–126

Scheuner, Ulrich, 'Privateering', in Bernhardt, Rudolf (ed.), *Encyclopedia of Public International Law, Vol 3*, Amsterdam and New York 1997, pp. 1120–1122

Smith, Leonard V., 'The Wilsonian Challenge to International Law', *The Journal of the History of International Law*, Vol. 13 (2011), pp. 179–208

Spencer, Warren F., 'The Mason Memorandum and the Diplomatic Origins of the Declaration of Paris', in Barker, Nancy and Brown Jr., Marvin (eds.), *Diplomacy in an Age of Nationalism: Essays in Honor of Lynn Marshall Case*, The Hague 1971, pp. 44–66

Stockton, Charles H., 'The Declaration of Paris', *American Journal of International Law*, Vol. 14, No. 3 (July 1920), pp. 356–368

Surdam, David G., 'The Union Navy's Blockade Reconsidered', in Bruce Elleman and S. C. M. Paine (eds.), *Naval Blockades and Seapower – Strategies and Counterstrategies, 1805–2005*, New York 2006, pp. 61–70

Tabarrok, Alexander, 'The Rise, Fall, and Rise Again of Privateers', *The Independent Review*, Vol. 11, No. 4 (Spring 2007), pp. 565–577

Wertheim, Stephen, 'The League That Wasn't: American Designs for a Legalist-Sanctionist League of Nations and the Intellectual Origins of International Organization, 1914–1920', *Diplomatic History*, Vol. 35, No. 5 (2011), pp. 797–836

Index

Note: Letter 't' following locators refers to tables.

Aberdeen Journal, 88
abolition of privateering, 12, 14, 20, 48, 52, 55, 70, 75–6, 80, 92, 100, 121, 125, 175–6, 184, 187
abolition regime against privateering, 73
Adams, Charles Francis, 121, 122, 124, 125, 130, 134, 136, 138, 141, 144, 145, 153
Alabama, 14, 133, 135, 137, 153, 157, 169–70
Alexander II, Tsar, 34
Alexandria, seizure of, 138
alliance
anti-British, 45
global, 61, 182
American Civil War, 115–16, 118, 139, 150–1, 160, 171, 179–80, 192
diplomacy of, 139
American privateers, 12, 23, 36, 59, 74, 78, 80, 83, 85, 87
American War of Independence in 1776, 120
anarchy, 6–7, 196
Anderson, Olive, 12, 24, 36
Anglo-American relations, 61, 119
Anglo-French alliance, 17, 45, 57–8, 60–1, 82–3, 112, 175, 189
Anglo-French deliberations, 21
Anglo-Prussian conflict, 55
Anglo-Russian crisis, 184
Anglo-US collaboration, 143
Anglo-US crisis, 58, 134
anti-Americanism, 61, 95
anti-slave trade campaign, 39
Appleton, John, 100
areopagus, European council as, 102, 107, 109–10, 191
armed neutrality, 10–11, 17, 24, 43–5, 50, 72, 74, 118, 139, 174, 189
confederacy of, 52
formal, 50

principles of, 44
triumph of, 176
arms smuggling, 33, 36, 51
Arpino, Don Guiseppe, 50
Asquith, Herbert Henry, 1st Earl of Oxford and, 150
Aube, Hyacinthe Laurent Théophile, 186
Austria (Austrian)
Central Authority for Maritime Trade, 107
merchant vessels, 155
ordinance, 98
port of Trieste, 181
privateer, 113
property, 107
Prussian alliance treaty, 34
Prussian trade, 155
Prussian war, 154–7
Sardinian dispute, 96, 177
trade, 107, 156
troops, 105
vessels, 98
auxiliary cruisers, 159, 182, 187

Baltic blockade, 28
Bancroft, George, 160
bankruptcy, 34, 101, 161
ban on privateering, bilateral, 21, 49
barbarism, 40, 48, 116, 124, 164
privateering as relic of, 40, 116, 124
Baumgart, Winfried, 62
Bentham, Jeremy, 2
Bermuda, 136, 141, 145, 148–9
Bernath, Stuart, 143–4
Bernstorff, Count Albrecht von, 33, 48, 51, 53, 165, 167–9
Berthemy, Jules de, 162
Bierwirth, Leopold, 104, 135
bilateral agreement, 183
bilateral treaties, 21, 23, 44, 68, 87, 170, 192

Bismarck, Prince Otto von, 16, 154–5, 157, 163–9, 178, 182–3, 189–90
blockade
  abolition of, 91–2, 151
  allied, 38
  cruiser, 63, 142–3, 160, 188
  formal, 51, 143
  illegal, 29, 195
  ineffective, 69, 117, 152, 158, 160, 168
  interpretation of, 90
  lawful, 119–20, 127
  principle of, 91
Bloomfield, John Arthur Douglas, 33, 51
Bluhme, Christian, 50
Bolivian privateering, 185
Bordeaux Chamber of Commerce, 39
Bremen–New York steamer line, 101
Bremer Handelsblatt, 101, 103, 105
Bright, John, 12, 20, 151
Bristol Mercury, 117
Britain (British)
  acceptance of Marcy Amendment, 111, 153
  ancient maritime rights, 12
  ancient principles, 73
  approach to maritime law, 27, 67
  blockade, 139–43; to receive strategic goods, 36; rights of neutrals, 139
  campaign to ban privateering as piracy, 43, 174
  commitment to creating new universal law, 67
  conflict with neutrals, 70
  duplicity, 13, 143
  free ships, free goods principle, 41, 45, 145
  idea of creating unanimous state practice, 44
  import from Russia, 27t
  interpretation of neutrality, 169
  letters of marque, 36–43
  maritime commerce, 111, 177
  maritime dominance, 20
  maritime rights, 56, 71
  maritime strength, 60
  merchant shipping, 131
  merchant vessels, 48, 85, 136
  military prestige, 60
  national security, 103
  naval supremacy, 154

neutrality, 136, 165, 167, 172
neutral rights, 143–50; compromised on, 36; continuous voyage doctrine, 143, 146, 148, 150; dual use goods, 148; permanent acceptance, 48
obligations under the Declaration of Paris, 112
package deal, idea of, 57
ship-owners, 111
shipping, 112–13, 159, 183
smugglers, 144
supremacy on the oceans, 48, 73, 179
territorial waters, 165
traders, 35, 140, 147
traditional maritime law, 68
treaty with Russia, 44
treaty with USA, 49, 51
violations of US neutrality, 60
Buchanan, James, 20–1, 23, 28, 40–2, 46, 54, 58–60, 90–1, 95–6, 104, 108, 113
Bunch, Robert, 129–32, 139–40
Burck, Karl Ludwig von, 107

Campbell, John, 132
Cardwell, Edward, 32
Caribbean Sea, 116
Cass, Lewis, 15, 91, 95–7, 101, 107, 177
Cass Memorandum, 15, 96, 99–100, 112–13, 177, 185
Catherine II, Tsarina, 10
Cavendish-Bentinck, George Augustus Frederick, 94, 112, 170
Chambers of Commerce as lobbyists, 102–4
Chevalier, Michel, 106
Chicago Tribune, 91, 116, 151, 159
Chinese Empire, 178
China's war with France in 1885, 185
Chinese ports, 163
Christianity, 41
Clarendon, George William Frederick Villiers, 4th Earl of, 11–12, 13, 18, 19–20, 22–4, 28, 31, 33–5, 40–3, 46, 48, 50, 53–4, 56, 58–72, 78, 81, 85, 88, 89, 91, 92, 95, 168–9, 174, 177, 185
Clavin, Patricia, 194
coal and contraband, 111–14
coal shipments, 98–9

coastal trade, 20–1, 140–1
Cobden, Richard, 12, 26, 87–8, 90, 93–4,
  102, 111–14, 151–2, 181
Cobden–Chevalier treaty, 15, 112
Colchester, Charles Abbott 2nd Baron, 31
Collier, Robert, 30
colonialism, 9–10
colonial possessions, 45
colonial settlers, 111
colonial trade, 20
commerce and navigation treaty, 22,
  47, 134
Committee for Trade of the Privy
  Council, 31
community-based enforcement, 7–8, 10
Congress of Berne, 3
Congress of Paris, 8, 60, 62–70, 85–6,
  110, 118, 158, 176, 192
  after-congress, 62
  Congress protocols, 79, 179
  end to privateering, 63–4
  last session, 69
  reform of maritime law, 62
Congress of Vienna, 65, 105, 176
continental war, 154, 170, 181
continuous voyage doctrine, 143, 146,
  148–50, 180
contraband, 15, 28, 47, 80, 92, 98–100,
  106, 111–13, 144, 159, 185
  abolition of, 92
  category, 150
  conditional, 28
  definition of, 13, 108, 159, 177, 185
  trade, 32–3, 136
Coogan, John, 189
Cornewall Lewis, George, 90
cotton imports from the United States,
  85, 117, 129, 135, 141–2, 145, 180
counter-insurgency tactics, 164
Cowley, Henry Wellesley, 1st Earl (known
  as The Lord Cowley between 1847
  and 1857), 21–2, 48, 59, 70, 88,
  125, 127
Cox, Samuel, 151–2
Crimean War, 1, 3, 8, 10–12, 14–15, 17,
  24, 26, 27, 36, 38, 44, 56–60, 70, 84,
  85, 86, 90, 96, 98, 120, 123, 145,
  161, 174, 175, 178, 183, 185
  British approach, 27
  end of the, 53

impact on naval side, 36
Maritime Law, 26
neutral rights, 12, 15, 20, 25, 34, 36,
  38, 40, 41, 46, 47–8, 50, 52, 56,
  58, 60, 64–5, 70, 96–7, 120, 174,
  178, 183
Prussia's activities, 161
Cruising blockades, 63, 142–3, 160, 188
Cushing, Caleb, 77
customary law, 3, 9, 15, 23–4, 44, 58, 67,
  69, 97, 100, 136, 142, 175–6, 191
  instantaneous, 3
  permanent, 15
  undisputed, 175
Customs Act, 127

Daily News, 29, 39
Dallas, George, 60–1, 76, 89, 91–2, 100
Danish fleet, 11
Danish interest, 50
Danish neutrality, 146
Danish-Prussian-Austrian conflict, 155
Danubian principalities, 110
Davis, Jefferson, 116, 129–33
declaration of 28 March 1854, 11, 22–4,
  45, 57
Declaration of Paris
  American Civil War, 150–3
  Bismarck's challenge, 164–72
  Confederate privateers, 126
  conservative campaign against, 95
  crucial innovation, 191
  new annex to the declaration,
    Walewski's proposal of, 86
  non-accession of US, 127
  original signatories, 86, 117
  as a package deal, 70, 175
  permanent reform of, 156
  principles of, 180
  protection for commerce in
    wartime, 170
  punishment for non-adherence, 78
  regime of, 115, 154, 163, 170, 195
  signatories vs. non-signatories, 99
  swift demise, 193
  undermine the success of, 81, 92
  unintended consequences, 155
  US accession, 121, 124–5
  violation of, 158
  Walewski's idea, 86–7, 91

Derby, Edward George Geoffrey
    Smith-Stanley, 14th Earl of, 71, 98,
    132, 139, 141
Desaix, 165–7, 182
diplomacy, 4, 94, 115, 139, 154
    private, 143
Disraeli, Benjamin, 152, 171
Dixie, 131
Dolphin, 146–7
Donald, David Herbert, 138
Dowty, Alan, 75
Drouyn de Lhuys, Edouard, 18–24, 33,
    46, 48, 54, 137
dual use goods, 28, 148
Duckwitz, Arnold, 102
Ducos, Theodore, 18–20, 22, 23
Dutch-Bremish declaration, 107, 181

economic liberalism, 110
economic warfare, 9, 30, 188
The Economist, 26, 30–1, 40, 74, 103
Edinburgh Review, 26
effective blockade
    definition of, 139, 192
    principle of, 79, 121, 130, 178
Ellenborough, Edward Law, 1ˢᵗ Earl
    of, 119
end of privateering, 129–34
enemy
    coast, 63, 141
    cruisers, 43
    destination, 148
    dispatches, 144
    goods, 11, 17–19
    government, 157
    merchant vessel, 177
    trade, 85, 156
    vessels, 11, 46, 182
English Channel, 113, 158
English textile industry, 129
The European, 89, 132
European civilization, 37
European diplomats, 82, 129
European hierarchy, 154
European law of nations, 2, 9–10, 176
European neutrals, 47, 127, 129,
    133, 142
European political system, 82
European powers, 9, 54, 57, 60, 66, 74,
    89, 128, 163, 176, 180

Ferdinand II, King of the Two Sicilies,
    50, 53
First Hague Peace Conference, 10, 187
First World War, 1, 8, 10–1, 159, 193–5
Fish, Hamilton, 162
Fisher, Sir John, 186, 188
Fiume Chamber of Commerce, 155
Florida, 133, 136
Foreign Enlistment Act, 119
Fort Sumter, 116
Fourichon, Maurice, 165–6
France (French)
    blockade, 160
    close blockades, 69
    coalfields, 112
    coaling station, 159
    commerce, 43
    dependence on British coal, 113
    franc-tireur guerrilla units, 164
    global war on German trade, 161–4
    influence on Britain, 57
    interests, 26, 60
    maritime law, 97
    merchant vessels, 161, 189
    naval ambitions, 158, 161
    navy, 161
    privateers, 64
    prize court procedure, 167, 169
    proposal for a multilateral treaty, 57
    Russian rapprochement, 83
    stance on maritime law, 45
    supportive of Marcy Amendment, 107
    suspension of traditional practices, 65
    traditional stance on neutral rights, 45
    US treaty of 1778, 21
    war against China, 185–6
    war with Germany, 16, 154, 163–4,
        170, 182, 192
    way of blockade, 157–61
Franklin, Benjamin, 51
Franz Joseph I, Emperor, 66
Frederick II, King of Prussia, 47
free-floating mines, 187
free ships, free goods principle, 11,
    17–18, 20, 23–4, 27, 31, 39, 41, 44,
    46, 54, 67, 71, 97, 105, 145, 174–5
Frei, 165, 167, 169
Friedrich Wilhelm IV, King of Prussia,
    33–4
Fritze, Alexander, 101

Gadsden, James, 52
Geffcken, Heinrich, 100, 105
General Postal Union, 3
Geneva Convention, 3
Gentz, Friedrich von, 109
German Confederation, 55, 78, 104–5,
    156, 164, 181
German Nautical Association, 170
Germany (German)
    armies, 166
    counter-insurgency tactics, 164
    customs union, 33
    diplomats fighting for neutral rights,
    161–2
    intervention in Sardinian-Austrian
    conflict in 1859, 97
    liberalism, 101
    logistics, 165
    trade, 163, 189
Gerolt, Friedrich von, 49, 51, 55, 126,
    153, 157
Gillespie, Alexander, 4
Glasgow Herald, 84
global abolition regime, 73, 178
global ban on privateering, 39
global community, 176
global economic crisis, 98
global governance, 74, 191
globalisation, first wave of, 7, 191
global opinion poll, 3
global shipping, safety of, 41, 102
Graham, Sir James, 12, 18, 20, 24, 30,
    38–40, 42
Granville, George Leveson-Gower, 2nd
    Earl Granville, 31, 65, 119–20,
    158–9, 163, 165, 167–9, 171,
    182, 185
Grazebrook, William Joshua, 146–7, 149
Great Depression, 195
Greek War of Independence, 118
Grey, Henry George Grey, 3rd Earl, 31, 73
Grey, Edward 1st Viscount Grey of
    Fallodon, 150
Gulf of Mexico, 116, 131, 140, 145, 147
Gwin, William, 38

Hague Peace Conference
    First Hague Peace Conference, 10, 187
    Second Hague Peace Conference, 10,
    14, 75, 177, 187

Hamelin, 161
Hamelin, Ferdinand-Alphonse, 59–60, 85
Hamilton, Charles Iain, 69, 75
Hanseatic merchants, 29, 158
Harding, John D., 18, 29, 84, 118
Hatzfeld, Count Maximilian Friedrich
    von, 33, 47
Herbert, Auberon, 169
Hermann, 101, 162
Hertha, 162–3
Hobson, Rolf, 73
Horsfall, Thomas, 19, 39, 151
Hudson Bay Company, 38
Hull Packet, 29

immunity of private trade, 153, 183
imperialism, 5, 186, 189
international civil society, 96
International Committee of the Red
    Cross, 3
International Criminal Court, 6–7
international law
    body of, 4, 196
    codified, 196
    compared to House Rules, 2, 6, 192–3
    creation of, 4, 6, 71
    customary, 3, 130, 176
    enforcement of, 192
    expansion of, 4
    grave violation of, 165
    history of, 4, 6, 120
    legitimacy of, 5
    norms of, 5, 45, 68, 109
    origins of, 7
    power of, 194, 196
    principle of, 157, 181
    purpose of, 4
    universalisation of, 9–10
    universal reform of, 67
international merchants, 8
international rivers, 65
International Telegraph Union, 3
international tribunal, 99

Jenkins, Brian, 125
Jeune Ecole, 186
Jones, Howard, 143
Journal de Genève, 155
Journal de St. Pétersbourg, 144
Journal du Havre, 43

Kamehameha III, King of Hawaii, 43, 55
Kennedy, Paul, 12

Labiche, Jean-Baptiste, 74
Labouchere, Henry, 64
Labuan, 145, 147
Lambert, Andrew, 13, 29, 34, 91
Lambert, Nicholas, 188
La Presse, 23
Law of nations, 2–3, 34, 66–9, 84,
    97, 109, 116–17, 119–20,
    128, 139
laws of war, 1, 7, 66, 164, 185–6, 188
League of Armed Neutrality, 11
League of Nations, 194–5
League to Enforce Peace, 194
Leeds Mercury, 61, 98
letters of marque, 14–15, 20–1, 36–42,
    48–9, 51–2, 55–7, 59–61, 65–6, 74,
    81, 93, 115–16, 118–21, 124,
    129–30, 133, 135–8, 167–8, 178–80,
    184–5, 187
liberal ideology, 11–13, 24, 173
liberalism, 12, 19
A Liberal State at War, 12
Lindsay, William Shaw, 90, 111
Liverpool Chamber of Commerce, 39
Liverpool Mercury, 117
London Post, 84
London Standard, 87
Lumley, Savile, 81
Lushington, Stephen, 85
Lyons, Richard Bickerton Pemell Lyons,
    1st Viscount, 121–4, 126, 128–32,
    136, 139–41, 146–7

Mahan, Alfred Thayer, 186
Malkin, William, 12, 91
Malmesbury, James Howard Harris, 3rd
    Earl of, 152, 171–2
Manassas, 133
Manchester Chamber of Commerce,
    61, 103–4
Manchester liberalism, 5
Manteuffel, Otto von, 33–4, 47–9, 51,
    55, 66
Marcy, William, 15, 44, 75, 176, 181
Marcy Amendment
    abolition of right of blockade, 89
    Anglo-French alliance, 83

assessing the implications, 94
Bremen campaign for, 100–10
international recognition of, 157
negotiations on the, 95
official rejection by Russell, 125
pressure on the Europeans to
    accept, 122
prime opportunity to secure, 126
protection of, 90
Russian support, 107
success of, 107
maritime balance of power, 48, 50, 73,
    80, 174, 179, 183
maritime equilibrium, 152
maritime law
    British approach, 27
    declaration on, 65, 76
    France stance, 45
    global code, 70
    reform of, 55, 59, 62, 102, 105, 107,
        153, 155, 181
    revolution in, 173
maritime nations, 31, 51, 55, 73, 110
    neutral, 10
    small, 106
maritime powers, 22, 31, 42, 45, 52,
    64–5, 72, 74, 80, 125, 127,
    138–9, 152
    major, 49
    minor, 48
    secondary, 181
    smaller, 17, 106
    superior, 51
maritime rights, 12, 24, 31, 56, 71, 79,
    94, 107, 112, 135
    ancient, 112
    neutral, 24, 79
maritime supremacy, 94, 171
maritime trade, 9, 107
maritime trading towns, 103
maritime war, 24, 59, 167, 187
Marx, Karl, 10
Mason, John, 21, 44, 47, 57, 76, 97
McPherson, James, 143–4, 149
Medusa, 163
Meier, Hermann Henrich, 101, 111
Melchers, Carl, 101
mercantilist principles, 20

merchant navy, 80, 94, 107, 164,
    173, 181
  neutral, 36
  statistics, 36
merchant vessels, 41, 43, 77, 107, 131,
    165, 184, 187, 190
  burned, 165
  sink, 190
Mercier, Edouard Henri, 121–2, 127–9
Merck, Carl Herrman, 106
Merli, Frank, 115
Mexican-American War, 39
Milner Gibson, Thomas, 19, 103
Mitchell, Thomas Alexander, 23
Molesworth, Sir William, 23
Monmouth, 140
Morning Chronicle, 30, 111
Morning Post, 51, 113
most-favoured-nation status, 50
multilateral law-making treaty, 3, 68, 86,
    176, 178, 192, 196
multilateral negotiations, 5, 70

Napier, Sir Charles, 90, 94
Naples, most-favoured-nation status
    from US, 50
Napoleonic Wars, 9, 36, 43, 63–4, 69,
    128, 139, 190, 193
Napoleon III, 19, 23, 62, 85–6, 92, 95,
    112, 135, 142–3, 158, 162, 166, 175,
    182, 192
National Intelligencer, 37
National War Committee, 135
natural law, principles of, 2
naval blockade, 26, 160–1
naval commanders, 33, 163, 188, 193
naval discipline, 159, 182
naval historians, 13, 173
naval steamers, 113
naval superiority, 38, 49, 94
naval warfare, 8, 85, 87, 98, 111
navigation treaty, 21–2, 47, 134
Neff, Stephen, 4
Nesselrode, Count Karl Robert, 38
Neufchatel crisis, 110
neutral destination, 147–8
neutrality, 34, 42, 97–9, 112, 115, 119,
    162–3, 169, 188, 195
  agreement, 38
  benevolent, 159

declaration, 43, 163
  for the Free Cities, 105
  laws of, 115–16, 127, 161, 180, 195
  permanent, 105, 181
neutral nations, 23, 28, 37, 39, 50, 134,
    145, 190
neutral ports, 14, 36, 43, 143, 145, 147,
    149, 160–2, 179–80, 188
neutral powers, 17, 31, 72, 141, 168, 170
neutral privileges, 97
neutral property, immunity of, 17
neutral rights, 8, 12, 21–2, 34, 36, 38, 46,
    48, 64, 73, 130, 179, 189, 193
  Anglo-US conflict, 114
  anti-British concept, 179
  anti-British stance on, 38
  confrontation over, 28
  convention on, 76
  liberal, 36, 44, 47, 77, 104, 120,
    179, 183
  US efforts to attain recognition, 43–4
neutral shipping, 73, 179–80
neutral stopover, 145, 150
neutral trade, 12, 19–20, 28, 85, 150,
    174, 179–80, 184–5, 187, 190, 192
neutral vessels, 9, 11, 17, 27, 59, 63, 93,
    144, 148, 151–2, 155, 180, 185
neutral waters, 146, 165
New York Chamber of Commerce,
    42, 108
New York Herald, 99, 124, 131
New York Journal of Commerce, 89
New York Stock Exchange, 116
New York Times, 37, 40, 52, 76, 84, 116,
    118, 124, 135, 137, 151, 156, 170
New York Tribune, 162
Nicolas I, Tsar, 44
Norddeutsche Zeitung, 164
Northern privateering, 134–8

Opdyke, George, 135
opinio juris, 3, 176, 191
Orion, 146
O'Sullivan, John Louis, 54, 78–82, 86,
    110, 177
Ottoman Empire, 8–11, 77, 183–4
ownership principle, 11

Pacific Mail Steamship Company, 116
Pall Mall Gazette, 170

Palmer, Roundell, 1st Earl of
    Selborne, 142
Palmerston, Henry John Temple,
    3rd Viscount, 11–2, 50, 58–60,
    62–5, 67–9, 75, 84–5, 87, 89–1,
    93–5, 103, 142, 144, 147, 150–1,
    175, 177
Panmure, Fox Maule-Ramsey, 11th Earl
    of Dalhouse (known as Lord
    Panmure between 1852 and
    1860), 64
Paris Peace Congress, 89, 107, 175, 190
Parrilo, Nicholas, 14
patriotism, 105, 158
peacekeeping, invention of, 195
Peace of Paris, 3
Peterhoff, 147, 149–50
Phillimore, John George, 23, 90
Phillimore, Sir Robert Joseph, 24
Phoenix, 131
Pierce, Franklin, 45, 51–3, 58, 60, 76–9,
    88–9, 116, 177
Piggott, Sir Francis, 11, 91
Pioneer, 133
Planning Armageddon, 188
port access, 14–15, 17, 43, 78, 83, 129,
    133–4, 184
positivism, 2
power politics, 3, 24, 83, 191
Preußische Provinzial-Correspondenz,
    49, 158
Price, David, 37
prisoners of war, 132, 137, 164
private diplomacy, 143
privateering as legalised piracy, 39, 42–3,
    48–9, 53, 66, 74, 133–4
privateering bill, 138
privateering controversy, 159
privateering heydays, 139
privateering obsolete, 134
Privy Council, 31
prize courts, 119, 133, 148, 165, 187
    new international, 187
    proceedings, 146, 163
    traditional, 99
prize regulations, 24
protocol 24, 77–82, 86, 158
Prussian-Austrian War (1866), 154

Quai d'Orsay, 75, 86

ratification procedures, 87, 191
Red Cross, 3
Revue de Droit International Public, 4
Ricardo, Lewis, 102
rights of neutrals, 1–2, 8, 52, 66, 73, 96,
    121, 129, 139, 179, 190
Roebuck, John Arthur, 142, 149
Roosevelt, Theodore, 194
Root, Elihu, 194
Royal Navy, 11, 13, 17–18, 24, 27, 38, 41,
    44, 50, 73, 84–5, 88, 93, 111, 118,
    140, 158, 173, 175, 179
Rücker, Alfred, 100
rule of 1756, 20–4
Rumpff, Vincent, 21
Russell, John, 1st Earl Russell, 18, 20,
    89–91, 94–5, 103, 111, 118
Russia (Russian)
    arms smuggling, 32–3
    capability to wage war, 35
    coastal trade, 20
    coastal waters, 30
    coastline, 18, 59
    commerce, 18
    consulates, 38
    diplomats, 55
    economy, 32, 35
    1855 campaign, 35
    export trade, 28
    export value, 35t
    imports, 30, 32, 35
    import value, 35t
    Japanese war, 187
    maritime rules, 32
    merchant navy, 32, 59
    national bankruptcy, 34
    privateering, 38, 43, 174
    privateer steamers, 58
    reroute of imports through Prussia, 32
    state-owned trade company in
        Alaska, 21
    supportive of the Marcy
        Amendment, 107
    trade, 30–1, 35
    treasury, 35
    treaty with Britain, 44
    Turkish war, 184

sailing ships, 43, 73
Sandwich Islands, 9

Saturday Review, 84
Savannah, 131–2, 140–1
Schleiden, Rudolf, 100
Schleinitz, Count Alexander Gustav
   Adolf von, 105–6
Scottish herring industry, 160
Second Hague Peace Conference, 10, 14,
   75, 177, 187
Second World War, 195–6
Security Council, 195
Seewehr, 158–9, 167, 182, 184
Semmel, Bernard, 12, 75
Seward, William, 117, 121–8, 132, 134,
   136, 138, 140, 141, 143, 146, 147,
   151, 157
Seymour, Thomas Hart, 28–9
ship-owners, 73, 87, 90, 131, 149, 155,
   158, 179
shipping tonnage, 131
Sino-Japanese war, 186
slavery, abolished, 39
slave trade, 39, 64–5, 67–8, 175
smugglers, 148–9
smuggling, 143, 146–7
social Darwinism, 5, 186, 195
Southern mercantile marine, 140
Southern privateering, 122–3
Southern privateers, 15, 118, 121, 124–6,
   132, 134, 136
sovereignty, 10, 60, 194
   national, 128
   territorial, 58
Spanish-American war, 187
Springbok, 147, 149
Stanley of Alderley, Edward John Stanley,
   2nd Baron, 32, 65
Statistical Society (becoming the Royal
   Statistical Society in 1887), 53
steamers, 9, 21, 26, 29, 37, 43, 101, 158
   ironclad, 133
   passenger, 190
   transatlantic, 170
Stockton, Charles, 12
Stoeckl, Eduard, 38, 44
submarine warfare, 183
Sumner, Charles, 127, 135–6
suppression of privateering, 36–43, 178
   attempt to ban privateering, 43
   concessions towards neutrals, 38

Dano-Swedish declaration of
   neutrality, 42
end of Napoleonic Wars, 36
Netherlands' declaration, 42
permanent guard to watch Stanley
   Harbour, 37
treaty to ban privateering, 40, 179
US efforts to extinguish
   privateering, 42

Taft, William H., 194
territorial sovereignty, 58
territorial waters, 162, 169
textile industry, 31, 117
Thouvenel, Edouard Antoine de, 120–3,
   125, 127–9, 144
The Times, 19, 23, 30–1, 37–8, 40, 53, 61,
   84, 88–9, 91, 94, 98–9, 103–4, 111,
   118, 136, 138, 141, 152, 156, 170–1
Tirpitz, Alfred von, 186
Trent, 115, 134, 144–5, 149, 151, 180
Trent crisis, 145
Trescott, William, 129
tributaries, 178

ultimate destination theory, 145
USA
   accession, 77, 117, 121, 124–5
   bankruptcy, 189
   blockade squadrons, 139
   bombardment of Greytown, 59
   complaints about interference with
      neutral trade, 150
   Declaration of Paris, 76
   diplomacy, 91, 162
   in favour of the Marcy
      Amendment, 104
   letters of marque, 120
   merchant vessels, 38, 131
   Naval Academy, 12
   neutrality, 162
   non-accession, 127
   position on maritime law, 97, 177
   position on privateering, 51
   privateering, 24, 36, 59, 61
   prize courts, 128, 148
   proposal, 57–62
   Russian treaty, 50–3, 56
   shipping business, 135
   trade, 91

USA – *continued*
  treaty campaign, 43–56; Anglo-French
    alliance, 45; Anglo-Prussian
    conflict, 55; colonial possessions,
    45; commerce and navigation
    treaty of 1828, 47; during the
    Crimean War, 86; freedom to
    trade as in full peace, 47; free
    ships, free goods principle, 46;
    reason for the failure, 56
  vulgar-minded bullies, 59

Versailles conference, 190
Victoria, Queen of the United Kingdom,
  23, 37, 50, 64
von der Heydt, August, 48, 55, 103

Waldersee, Count Friedrich Gustav
  von, 49
Walewski, Alexandre Florian Joseph,
  Count Colonna-Walewski, 18, 19,
22, 23, 53, 56–60, 62, 63, 65, 67, 69,
  70, 76, 77, 83, 84–92, 175–6
Walker, William, 61
Webb, James Watson, 37, 40
Welles, Gideon, 117, 128, 136, 145
Weserzeitung, 102
Westphalian Congress, 65, 175
Wilkes, Charles, 144
Will o' the Wisp, 145
Wilson, James, 27, 30–1, 135
Wood, Sir Charles, 58, 65
Wright, Joseph, 105
Wüllerstorf-Urbair, Bernhard von, 156

Zavala, Juan de, 1st Marquis of Sierra
  Bullones, 93
zero-sum game, 195
Zollverein, 33
van Zuylen van Nijevelt, Julius Philipp
  Jacob Adriaan, 106

Printed and bound by CPI Group (UK) Ltd, Croydon, CR0 4YY